————— *A Journal Briefing* —————

Whitewater
Volume III

—————————— *A Journal Briefing* ——————————

Whitewater
Volume III

From the Editorial Pages of
The Wall Street Journal.

Edited by Robert L. Bartley
with Micah Morrison & Melanie Kirkpatrick
and the Editorial Page staff

DOWJONES

Library of Congress Catalog Card Numbers:
94-79762

ISBN 1-881944-06-9

Printed in the United States of America

The Wall Street Journal.
Dow Jones & Company, Inc.
200 Liberty Street
New York, N.Y. 10281

Introduction

Whatever reservations you may have about Bill Clinton's Presidency, you have to admire him on a sheer animal level. From a dysfunctional family to a Rhodes scholarship. From a draft-resisting son of the '60s to the first member of his generation into the Oval Office. From defeat after his first term as governor to watching his Democratic Party foes collapse in the race for the Presidential nomination. From using state troopers to arrange sexual liaisons to a CBS appearance defended by his accomplished and formidable wife. From third in the polls behind George Bush and Ross Perot, through a saxophone solo on the Arsenio Hall show and a resounding comeback to win the Presidency with 43% of the vote. Like a modern Caesar, he came, he saw, he conquered.

So too in 1996, Bill Clinton confounded those of us who saw 43% as a ceiling, who thought that no one would vote for him a second time who hadn't voted for him the first time. Under the tutelage of pollster and strategist Dick Morris, the President remade his image, replacing health care reform with welfare reform, however grudgingly signed. Even the election of a Republican Congress in 1994 proved a boon to the President. On Election Day the bond markets bottomed out, sparking a financial and economic rally for which the President took credit in his re-election campaign. Since Franklin Delano Roosevelt, the first Democratic President to win two full terms is William Jefferson Clinton.

President Clinton succeeded in charming his way to 49% of the vote through a rain of scandal, doubts and controversy that now continues into a third volume under the general rubric of "Whitewater." Some issues were merely venal—whether the Clintons correctly accounted for the original Whitewater investment in tax returns filed from the Oval Office— "a can of worms," the late Vincent Foster wrote in the months before his death. Some were burgeoning scandals, notably the revelations of solicitation of illegal foreign campaign contributions that hit in the last month of the campaign. Mr. Clinton managed to shake this off in his re-election campaign—perhaps his most remarkable accomplishment as President.

Mr. Clinton's critics complain that the press went easy on Whitewater. Certainly the mainstream media, especially the television news powerful with mass audiences, did not provide the consistency of coverage recorded in this volume. Let alone was there a Walter Cronkite counting down days since hostages were taken in Iran. Yet media "spin" is a complex issue, and at the very least the Republicans bear some responsibility as well. In retrospect, Bob Dole's main chance as Republican nominee was to seize "the character issue" on day one and hammer at it into November. This he was loath to do—from decency, from fear of retaliation, from doubts that a "negative campaign" would work. By Election Day, voters knew just enough of scandal to provide a sort of inoculation against the thought that character really might matter after all.

The public, however, is not entirely devoid of judgment. In 1997 pollsters found that when asked what Bill Clinton would be remembered for in 25 years, respondents said "negative personal qualities" and "the Whitewater controversy." In a confirming poll, they voted by more than 2 to 1 that he'll be remembered for "controversies over his personal life and financial dealings" rather than "his accomplishments as president." Despite this assessment of both his character and his accomplishments, his job approval rating stood at nearly 60%.

History will also provide time to render a judgment on whether character and performance can be so easily divorced. In one television interview, James McDougal opined, "I think the Clintons really are sort of like tornadoes moving through people's lives, that I'm just one of the people left in the wake of their passing by, their—, but I have no whining or complaining to do, because I have lots of company." While Mr. McDougal was obviously entirely capable of hitting rocks on his own, he has a point about the company. Others left in the Clinton wake include Susan McDougal and loanmaster David Hale. The Rose Law Firm generally and specifically—partners Webster Hubbell, Vincent Foster and William Kennedy. Failed nominees such as Kimba Wood, Zoë Baird, Lani Guinier. As upstanding a Wall Street figure as Roger Altman, a series of White House counsels including Bernard Nussbaum and Judge Abner Mikva. Independent Counsel targets Henry Cisneros, Mike Espy and the late Ron Brown and his entourage.

So too Mr. Clinton seems to be taking a toll of American institutions. The phrase "Lincoln bedroom" will never carry the same connotation. Trade missions with American executives will scarcely be seen as a high calling. From the President's success, politicians of all stripes seem to be learning to avoid principle in favor of polls by Dick Morris clones. American foreign policy is clouded by campaign solicitations on both sides of the Taiwan Strait. The American military, caught between the reputation of the Commander-in-Chief and the demands of the First Lady, is wracked by the issue of gender. The CIA is also tarnished, and the FBI, and the institution of Independent Counsel is under siege.

In particular, the Department of Justice is staggering. In the early days of the administration, Philip Heymann left after asking White House Counsel Bernard Nussbaum, "Bernie, are you hiding something?" Webster Hubbell, now a confessed felon, was strongman at Justice when it reached the unprecedented decision to summarily replace all sitting U.S. Attorneys. As the second Clinton Administration opened, Attorney General Janet Reno's job was widely reported to be in jeopardy. Shortly later, she was almost alone, with most other high-level Justice positions vacant. She declined to appoint an independent counsel on the campaign-finance scandal; while this decision initially seemed defensible, it was called increasingly into question. When Justice opposed immunity for Buddhist monks before Senator Fred Thompson's committee, was it becoming an instrument of a coverup?

As President Clinton benefited from a Republican Congress, so he benefits from public cynicism toward all politicians. Indeed, "everyone does it" and "...cast the first stone" are principal themes of the remarkably successful Clinton defense. Yet it is one thing to agree with Bismarck that men should not know how laws and sausages are made, but it has to be another to conclude with Cole Porter that anything goes. Maintaining an ability to make distinctions is the mark of a healthy political elite, and a sturdy self-governing society. Bill Clinton is not the only force, or even the first President, eroding that capacity in our society, but he is currently the one on point.

President Clinton has won his second term, and beyond any reasonable doubt will serve it out. Yet far from moot, further investigation of "Whitewater" and its cousins is indispensable. The work of Independent Counsel Kenneth Starr, of Congressional investigators such as Senator Thompson, of skeptical journalists needs to proceed. We—the public and its future political leadership—do need to understand what has transpired. The current climate of hypocrisy toward our political leadership is anything but healthy. We need an accounting, some judgment of history, to begin to restore our faith in our political leadership and in our society.

ROBERT L. BARTLEY
Editor
The Wall Street Journal
July 8, 1997

TABLE OF CONTENTS

the architect of President Clinton's move to the right and "family values" campaign, disgraced himself in a toe-sucking episode with a Washington prostitute. This too did no harm to the President's poll numbers.

In September, the President stoked the fires of a simmering controversy when he refused to rule out a pardon for Ms. McDougal, telling PBS's Jim Lehrer that it was "obvious" that Independent Counsel Kenneth Starr was out to get the Clintons. In an earlier interview with CNN, Mr. Clinton had condemned "the abuse of the special-counsel law," setting the stage for increasingly bitter battles with Mr. Starr.

"In a second term," the Journal asked as Election Day drew near, "would President Clinton fire Mr. Starr, or pardon Susan McDougal, or generally use his Presidential powers to frustrate the law, or pardon his wife if indicted? In the coming election, it seems to us, the country ought to know what kind of Constitutional crisis it may be buying."

REVIEW & OUTLOOK

Clinton, McDougal and the IRS

When James McDougal appears for sentencing today on his Whitewater conviction, we'll get some hints at the value of his reported cooperation with Independent Counsel Kenneth Starr. His credibility as a witness is utterly tattered, of course, but that scarcely means his story is of no interest.

In particular, Mr. McDougal is likely to be telling prosecutors he figures that if he hadn't let the President and First Lady out of Whitewater, they would owe him about $50,000. At least, that's what he told Lloyd Grove of The Washington Post last April, for a Style Section story about his attending the President's videotaped testimony at the White House. And in turn, as John D. Hartigan details nearby [page 6], that

Bill Clinton

account raises serious issues about the accuracy and even honesty of the tax return the Clintons filed from the White House in 1993.

The Whitewater tax issue has been an ongoing one. House Banking Chairman Jim Leach charged a year ago, in a report endorsed by former IRS Commissioner Donald Alexander, that the Clintons underpaid the IRS by $13,272. The White House countered with a report by two former IRS Commissioners, Sheldon S. Cohen and Jerome Kurtz, and a third tax expert, John Nolan. They concluded that the House Banking report was wrong on most counts, but that the Clintons did owe an additional $2,910.

This admission was shoved out into last Memorial Day weekend. It was the third time the Clintons had admitted mistakes on their taxes, and brought total payments of back taxes and interest to $22,880—though the White House has stressed that most of the payments were voluntary because the statute of limitations has expired. Subsequently, the Senate Whitewater Committee majority report said the Clintons may still be understating their Whitewater-related income by $33,771, though a definitive resolution is not possible because many documents are missing.

The most intriguing tax issue concerns the agreement in which Mr. McDougal released the Clintons from any obligations relating to Whitewater. The agreement was brokered by Jim Blair, the Tyson Foods attorney who also helped with Mrs. Clinton's $100,000 commodity profits, and drafted by the late Vincent Foster. Mr. McDougal paid the Clintons $1,000, provided by Mr. Blair, and released them from any other Whitewater obligations. That is, he forgave them an obligation of about $50,000, or more precisely $58,000. What is the tax status of this transaction?

The Leach report asserted that it was $58,000 in income to the Clintons; the three-man White House team said that Whitewater was a corporation rather than a partnership, and shareholders were not liable for its debts. Mr. Clinton's obligation, though, would arise from an oral contract with Mr. McDougal to split any profit or expense 50-50. Arkansas case law provides precedent for enforcing such contracts, and the President has said in written interrogatories that he indeed considered himself obligated to put up half the money going into the venture. Necessarily so, since he's denied that from the first Whitewater was a sweetheart deal—as in fact it ultimately proved to be when Mr. McDougal assumed the obligations.

But if the Clintons had such an obligation, Mr. McDougal's forgiveness of it would constitute income. They should have reported this on their tax returns, then partially offset it by claiming a capital loss on the venture, ending up paying extra taxes of perhaps $15,000. But showing $58,000 in income from Mr. McDougal would have validated the Whitewater story from the onset. And in the end, the Clintons reported as income $1,000 for the McDougal-Blair payment, ignoring both the forgiveness of debt and the issue of capital losses.

We know, too, that the issue of how to report this transaction was deeply bothersome to Mr. Foster, who prepared the Clinton tax return three months before his suicide. His handwritten notes, pried out of the White House in July 1995, speak of a "can of worms you shouldn't open," and more specifically, "More importantly, would result in an audit of proof of basis." That is, an attempt to claim a capital loss would lead to an IRS audit of the entire Whitewater mess. So no capital gains basis was reported for the $1,000.

By now Whitewater has become a sprawling issue, embracing the Travel Office firings and the White House security passes. But the little land fling in the Ozarks itself lives on right into the Oval Office—in such particulars as whether the Administration tried to short-circuit investigations, and whether the First Couple leveled with the IRS.

Editorial Feature

More Clinton Tax Woes

By JOHN D. HARTIGAN

Lawyers involved in the continuing Whitewater investigations have said that James McDougal, convicted felon and former business partner of President Clinton, is cooperating with federal officials for a reduced sentence—scheduled to be announced today. Perhaps then Mr. McDougal may shed some light on a particularly disturbing new addition to the Clintons' long list of personal tax delinquencies.

James McDougal

According to the latest White House tally, President Clinton and his wife have now admitted that they shortchanged the U.S. Treasury on at least five of the federal income tax returns that they filed during his tenure as governor of Arkansas. Among other things, they understated their capital gains by $1,673, failed to report a $6,498 commodity trading profit, and took a total of $5,133 in improper deductions for interest payments that were actually made by other taxpayers.

But there's another tax violation that the Clintons have yet to acknowledge, and it's not only much more recent, but also much more flagrant. Specifically, the first Form 1040 they sent to the Internal Revenue Service after arriving in the White House failed to disclose a taxable $58,000 economic benefit that they received as the result of a 1992 agreement that released them from a Whitewater-related debt that they owed Mr. McDougal.

Without going beyond what's already in the public domain, the documents pointing to that violation include Whitewater accounting records, documents found in the files of the late Vincent Foster, and the president's written answers to a detailed set of interrogatories submitted to him by Pillsbury, Madison & Sutro, the law firm hired to investigate Whitewater by the Resolution Trust Corp. Taking all of these records into account, here is what is now known about how the Clintons came to owe the McDougals $58,000, how they got released from the obligation, why they wanted to keep this a secret, and what they did to cover it up.

To begin with, the president's answers to Pillsbury's interrogatories reveal that he and his wife made a serious blunder when they originally set up their 50-50 Whitewater venture with Mr. and Mrs. McDougal in mid-1978. Instead of putting a fixed dollar ceiling on the amount they would have to contribute to the venture if it couldn't generate enough cash to meet its needs, the Clintons agreed that they and the McDougals would each contribute half of whatever extra cash the venture might require, and that "any inequalities ultimately would be evened out from revenues of the venture or when the venture was sold."

As it turned out, the venture was never able to pay all of its bills, and the periodic cash infusions that were required to keep it afloat eventually reached a total of about $200,000. But instead of contributing their agreed-upon 50% share of that $200,000, the Clintons only came up with $42,000. As a result, the McDougals had to make up the difference by boosting their own overall cash contribution to $158,000 (i.e., the $100,000 they were obligated to provide themselves plus an additional $58,000 advanced on behalf of the Clintons).

Under Arkansas contract law, this placed the Clintons under a binding obligation to reimburse the McDougals for that $58,000 advance in accordance with their 1978 agreement, which provided that any inequalities between the two couples' respective contributions to their venture would eventually be evened up. But the way things actually worked out, the Clintons never had to pay any part of that $58,000 debt to the McDougals because a resourceful friend named Jim Blair came up with a clever way to get them off the hook.

Recognizing that Mr. McDougal might be interested in taking over sole ownership of Whitewater Development Co., Mr. Blair not only persuaded Mr. McDougal to purchase the Clintons' worthless WDC shares for $1,000, but also persuaded him to sign a Dec. 22, 1992 indemnity agreement releasing the Clintons from "any and all liability arising from . . . any . . . agreement related to or for the benefit of the Company."

In a single stroke, this canceled the Clintons' $58,000 debt without their having to pay the McDougals a nickel. But, by the same token, it also obligated the Clintons to include the $58,000 they saved in the total annual income reported on their 1992 federal income tax return. The reason for this is that getting excused from paying a business debt is the economic equivalent of receiving the same amount in cash, and, consequently, Section 61(a)(12) of the Internal Revenue Code requires any debtors so excused to treat that amount as taxable income.

Regrettably, however, that's not what the Clintons did. Knowing that their 1992 return would have to be released to the public, and fearful that the president would be pilloried by the press if the return revealed that he had received a five-figure financial favor from Mr. McDougal, the Clintons kept the $58,000 debt cancellation to themselves. They made out the return as if the only Whitewater income they received during 1992 was the $1,000 that Mr. McDougal paid them for their Whitewater Development shares.

What's more, the Clintons have kept up that pretense ever since, most notably when the president replied to Whitewater questions at a March 24, 1994, press conference by claiming, "I paid my debts," and "I do not believe we owe any back taxes." Indeed, just last May a hand-picked group of Clinton tax advisers issued a report suggesting that the $58,000 advanced by Mr. McDougal was really a corporate loan to WDC for which the Clintons had no responsibility, rather than a personal loan to the Clintons that they were legally obligated to repay under the terms of their 50-50 Whitewater contribution agreement.

But now that Mr. McDougal's telltale indemnity agreement has surfaced, the president may have to pay a very heavy price for all that obfuscation. If willful tax evasion is proved, that would be a felony. Under federal law, any public official convicted of that felony is subject to fine, imprisonment and removal from office.

And with good reason. To quote a recent Justice Department

press release announcing a successful tax fraud prosecution against a prominent Massachusetts legislator (Charles Flaherty, the former state House speaker): "Truthful compliance with the tax laws is a basic duty of all citizens. This is especially important when the taxpayer is a public official. Scheming to beat the IRS cheats every honest taxpayer."

Mr. Hartigan is a former general counsel of Salomon Inc.

Letters to the Editor

Whitewater Tax Liabilities

I write to correct certain fundamental errors in the Aug. 19 editorial-page article "More Clinton Tax Woes" by John D. Hartigan.

Mr. Hartigan asserts that the Clintons were legally obligated in 1992 to reimburse the McDougals for allegedly disproportionate capital contributions made by the McDougals to Whitewater Development Co. Inc. From that false premise, he alleges that the cancellation of this obligation—which he incorrectly pegs at $58,000—led to taxable income to the Clintons.

This is tendentious nonsense. There was, of course, no such legal obligation, and there is no tax liability, as the following facts establish.

In the interrogatories on which Mr. Hartigan relies, the Clintons were asked by the Resolution Trust Corp. about their "agreements (written or oral), expectations or understandings" about Whitewater project finances "as of August 1978"—the month in which the property was bought and almost a year before Whitewater Development Co. was incorporated. In response to that question, the Clintons stated that they "anticipated" that the two couples "would make equal contributions and that any inequalities ultimately would be evened out from revenues of the venture or when the venture was sold."

Thereafter, in June 1979, the couples reorganized their relationship, with significant tax consequences that Mr. Hartigan blithely ignores. The Clintons and McDougals transferred the Whitewater land, subject to the existing mortgage, into a newly formed corporation known as Whitewater Development Co. Inc., and they assumed the rights and obligations of shareholders. At the time of the reorganization, the Clintons and McDougals had each contributed the same amount of money to the venture and were equally obligated on all the property's outstanding indebtedness.

With these facts in mind, the flaws in the Hartigan argument are obvious.

First, the Clintons described to the RTC the arrangement they "anticipated" at the start of their partnership. They never suggested there was any legally binding agreement to contribute one-half the cash the McDougals (who ran the company) might decide to spend, and there was none. Arkansas contract law, to which Mr. Hartigan makes reference, does not support any different conclusion.

Second, and most important, even if there had been such a formal agreement initially, it was superseded when the relationship between the parties changed the following year and the rules applicable to corporations came into effect. Once a corporation was formed, the Clintons became shareholders and their liability was accordingly limited. And, since the Clintons and McDougals were equal contributors to the venture at this time, the termination of the prior arrangement would have been without tax consequences even under Mr. Hartigan's flawed analysis.

Since Whitewater was a corporation as of 1979, the contributions of the McDougals became contributions to the corporation, not to a partnership or joint venture with the Clintons. If the McDougals advanced funds to the corporation, their claim for repayment, if any, was solely against the corporation. A panel of experts (two former Internal Revenue Service commissioners and a former deputy assistant secretary for tax policy at the Treasury Department) recently reviewed the Clintons' taxes and emphasized an elementary and obvious point: "Corporations and shareholders are separate legal entities, and shareholders are not liable for the debts of their corporation. One of the most fundamental principles of the corporate/shareholder relationship is the limited liability of the shareholders." Indeed, it is for this very reason that this distinguished panel rejected any suggestion that the 1992 transaction (on which Mr. Hartigan focuses) was of any significant tax consequence to the Clintons:

"At the time of the stock sale by Mr. and Mrs. Clinton to Jim Mc-

Dougal, all of the WDC-related debt on which Mr. and Mrs. Clinton were personally liable had been repaid. Although WDC may have had a negative net worth of $117,394, this had no tax significance for Mr. and Mrs. Clinton as shareholders, because they were not entitled to deduct any portion of this loss and they did not realize any taxable gain on the disposition of their stock for federal income tax purposes (beyond the $1,000, which they reported in its entirety)."

Finally, even assuming (1) that the McDougals effectively "loaned" X amount to the Clintons, which the Clintons then invested in the corporation, and (2) that when the Clintons transferred their stock to Mr. McDougal in 1992 they "received" X amount by having their debt forgiven, the transaction would still be without tax effect. In that case, the Clintons would have an increased basis in their stock of X amount—the amount that went into the corporation on their behalf—and the transaction would be a wash: the transfer of stock with a basis of at least X amount in exchange for release of a purported X amount debt. Mr. Hartigan perversely fails to follow through on the logic of his own assumptions. If the Clintons owed the McDougals X amount, it is only because of contributions made to the corporation on their behalf, in which case the basis of their stock would be increased by a like amount. In short, even if Mr. Hartigan were right, he's still wrong.

DAVID E. KENDALL

Washington

(Mr. Kendall, of Williams & Connolly, is a personal lawyer for President and Mrs. Clinton.)

* * *

SEPTEMBER 6, 1996

Clinton Tax Argument: Double Nonsense

In regard to the Sept. 4 Letter to the Editor from David Kendall, President and Mrs. Clinton's personal attorney, in response to my Aug. 19 editorial-page article "More Clinton Tax Woes": Mr. Kendall challenges my contention that his clients deliberately shortchanged the IRS by failing to report a 1992 indemnity agreement that released them from their obligation to reimburse James

McDougal for contributing $58,000 to Whitewater Development Corp. (WDC) on their behalf.

Mr. Kendall concedes that the Clintons agreed to reimburse Mr. McDougal for such contributions when they initiated their Whitewater venture back in 1978, but claims that this Clinton commitment was automatically terminated when the venture was incorporated in 1979. That claim made, he then goes on to argue that, no matter how much money Mr. McDougal may have contributed to WDC for the Clintons, they didn't have any legal obligation to reimburse him, and, consequently, Mr. McDougal's 1992 release was a meaningless gesture with no economic value that the Clintons would have had to treat as taxable income.

Nonsense and double nonsense. Mr. and Mrs. Clinton have both given sworn written testimony that their original agreement with Mr. McDougal "did not change over time," and the courts of Arkansas have consistently held that incorporation of a business venture in no way excuses the venturers from carrying out their obligations under a venture-financing agreement that they entered into prior to incorporation. To cite two venerable Arkansas precedents, see *Bank of Des Arc v. Moody*, 110 Ark. 39 (1913) and *Engles v. Shaffer*, 143 Ark. 31 (1920).

The upshot is that the release that the Clintons obtained from Mr. McDougal in 1992 was anything but valueless. On the contrary, it constituted a clearly taxable $58,000 financial subsidy that the Clintons should have reported as ordinary income on line 22 of the first page of their 1992 return. Had they done so, they would have had to pay the IRS a tax of $17,980 on the subsidy less a $4,574 credit against their 1992 capital gain tax liability. Thus, the net effect of their concealment of the subsidy was to understate the amount they owed the IRS by $13,406. Other taxpayers have gone to prison for less.

JOHN D. HARTIGAN

Rye, N.Y.

REVIEW & OUTLOOK

Privileged First Lady

Last Thursday afternoon, with the nation awaiting Bob Dole's acceptance speech in San Diego, the Clinton Administration coughed up 2,000 pages of documents on the Travel Office scandal sought by Rep. William Clinger's House Oversight Committee. For months the White House refused to turn over the documents under the claim of executive privilege, but relented in the face of contempt of Congress charges that would result in embarrassing court hearings and a possible jail sentence for White House Counsel Jack Quinn.

The documents reveal a number of things. First, they provide extensive evidence confirming the David Watkins memo that Hillary Clinton was deeply involved in the Travel Office firings—in contradiction to her own official claims. Second, that the White House claims of executive privilege on these documents were utterly bogus. And third, as Chairman Clinger says, the White House has mounted an elaborate effort to conceal what happened with the Travel Office, and for that matter a long list of other Administration scandals.

Indeed, the documents indicate that Mrs. Clinton and Hollywood pal Harry Thomason discussed plans to fire the Travel Office staff even *before* the inauguration. This comes from the notes of Natalie Williams, an attorney specifically hired by the White House to sort through the First Lady's involvement. Her notes of a conversation with Mr. Thomason's attorney, Amy Sabrin, say that after the election Mr. Thomason spoke with Mrs. Clinton and pressed his view that the Travel Office workers "should be replaced" because of "disloyalty."

In other words, Travel Office Director Billy Dale, who had worked for every President since John F. Kennedy, was deemed disloyal and targeted for dismissal even before the Clintons left Little Rock. Mr. Thomason, of course, owned part of an air charter business that was interested in taking over the $12 million-a-year White House travel operation. Miss Williams went on to write that Mr. Thomason "Remembers telling DW should be replaced & that FL shares his view." DW is David Watkins and FL is the First Lady.

Six days before the Travel Office firings, also, Mrs. Clinton twice brought up Travel Office issues in meetings on health care she had with Vincent Foster, the late White House Deputy Counsel, according to Miss Williams's notes. And during a later meeting with White House aides David Watkins and Patsy Thomasson, Mr. Foster "discussed general observation that HRC generally appeared less than satisfied with timeliness of decision-making, i.e. closure" on the Travel Office. "This entry could be used to suggest that the first lady's dissatisfaction with 'timeliness of decision-making' spurred the hasty actions of Watkins and others" in firing the Travel Office workers," Miss Williams wrote.

Hillary Clinton

In the weeks before his suicide, finally, Mr. Foster told Clinton friend James Lyons that the President and the First Lady "might require outside counsel to advise them on the Travel Office matter." Miss Williams argued that this probably only reflected his frustration over media coverage of the incident, but added, "For those predisposed, Foster's concern about the need for outside counsel to represent the First Family in the Travel Office matter might suggest they were somehow implicated in the affair."

George Stephanopoulos, with his usual brazenness, told Tim Russert Sunday that there was "nothing new" in the documents, and "the question is: Did she order any action? And she did not." In fact, in written responses to interrogatories to Mrs. Clinton from the General Accounting Office, W. Neil Eggleston, then White House associate counsel, said that "she had no role in the decision to terminate the employees." What the new documents describe sure sounds like a role to us, and we daresay, it probably would to a jury as well.

In this most ironic of elections, it is the incumbent who is a mystery, the candidate who asks voters to take a flier. My colleagues on the front page of this newspaper gamely argued this week that Mr. Clinton will be something called a "moderate" in a second term, which may even be right. But how can they tell?

It's impossible to tell from Mr. Clinton's re-election campaign, which combines uplifting rhetoric about the future with the hoariest demagoguery defending the entitlement past. It blends grand conservative talk about values with modest liberal proposals to regulate business.

Mr. Clinton wants to balance the budget but preserve Medicare as we know it, a contradiction larger than anything he claims Mr. Dole is presenting on taxes. The president says the "era of big government is over," but his miniature new ideas are more government in salami slices designed gradually to restore the credibility of bigger government. He wants voters to believe it's all true.

Bill Clinton

It's also impossible to divine anything from this week's Democratic convention, which was driven not by ideas but by emotions. (Republicans indulged in a similar New Age encounter session in San Diego, but least they had a platform as backbone.) One emotion is fear of Newt Gingrich. The other is a bathos so blatant that even Al Gore, a usually decorous man, exploited his own sister's death at tearful length to appear sensitive enough to his boss's antismoking crusade. But the theme "Democrats care" is hardly a guide to governing.

"We're a party in transition," admits one presidential adviser, "but we don't know what we're transitioning to. For the last two years the baling wire has been Newt."

In Clinton II, Democrats would tug at the lame-duck president like he's soft taffy. Already the president is promising liberals he'll "fix" the welfare bill he's still taking credit for signing. But liberals want to fix it with a nationwide public jobs program. New Democrats would prefer to establish a network to put welfare recipients in private jobs. This president might want to do both, but there won't be any money for either.

Republicans may have their own splits on discrete issues such as abortion and immigration. But Democrats can't agree even on the core 21st-century question of whether the welfare-entitlement state is sustainable in a global economy.

Which means that Mr. Clinton's real direction may depend less on him than on who controls Congress. If Republicans keep their majority, Mr. Clinton would probably keep triangulating. But if Democrats come back, he'd bend to the liberals who will retake committee chairs. Jesse Jackson and Mario Cuomo have advertised their own support for Mr. Clinton as just such a raw political calculation.

Mr. Clinton would also have to bend to the AFL-CIO, which would call in the $35 million in chips it has placed on this election. This would matter when the probable second-term recession struck, an event that would sorely test the president's first-term fealty to the bond market. His temptation would be to blame Fed Chairman Alan Greenspan, or to break his balanced-budget pledge, or both.

But the biggest imponderable of all is something Mr. Clinton can do very little about—Kenneth Starr. The independent counsel's career prosecutors will follow evidence wherever it leads, even into Hillary Rodham Clinton's village. A consultant like Dick Morris can resign, if at the price of more doubts about the kind of company this president likes to keep, from Arkansas to the Beltway. But how would Mr. Clinton handle an indicted first lady? Ideology aside, a vote to re-elect Bill Clinton is a gamble that scandal won't overwhelm his ability to govern.

Democrats advertised last night's acceptance speech as the outline for Mr. Clinton's second term, but previous speeches have rarely been guides to how this president has behaved. He is a political improvisationist, making it up as he goes along. Cast by friend or foe, a vote for a second Clinton term requires a suspension of disbelief.

Review & Outlook

The November Stall

ABC Interviewer: Did Mr. Clinton know about your loan?

Susan McDougal: That's probably something that my attorney would not want me to talk about. I hate that, guys! I hate that! Come here and talk to me! God, I hate this Diane! Sorry!

Diane Sawyer: Did he?

Mrs. McDougal's brother [?]: That's a perfect answer.

Susan McDougal: Jeez, I hate that, though!

Brother [?]: That's the only answer you have.

Susan McDougal: That's the only answer I have.

—*Interview with Susan McDougal and her brother and fiancee on ABC News Primetime Live, Sept. 4, 1996.*

For also refusing to answer this question in the privacy of a grand jury chamber, Mrs. McDougal has been held in contempt of court and faces going to jail as early as Monday unless she changes her mind. The loan at issue is $300,000 from David Hale's Capital-Management Services, a small business investment company subsequently closed at taxpayer expense. Some $50,000 of it ended up in the account of Whitewater Development Co., owned jointly by Mrs. McDougal, her husband, Jim, and Bill and Hillary Clinton. Mr. Hale has confessed that the loan was fraudulent, and has charged that then-Governor Clinton asked him to make it. The President has denied he knew about the loan, for example in the videotaped testimony played at the trial in which the McDougals and former Arkansas governor Jim Guy Tucker were all convicted of various counts.

If Governor Clinton knew about the loan, he was party to a conspiracy to defraud the taxpayer. If President Clinton knew about the loan, he perjured himself in sworn testimony from the White House. Presumably Jim McDougal, now cooperating with Independent Counsel Kenneth Starr, is backing Mr. Hale's account rather than Mr. Clinton's. Mrs. McDougal refuses to give her version, or to answer yes or no to the question of whether the President's trial testimony was true. Unless she has reason to believe the President lied, of course, there is no point to the angst she now displays.

She cites advice of her counsel, who has cooked up a batch of legally preposterous arguments the only point of which can be to keep the matter on appeal until after the November election. Her counsel is an old Arkansas hand named Bobby McDaniel, who keeps saying things such as prosecutors don't care about Susan, they are out for Bill and Hillary. Who's he working for, we wonder? ABC reported that Mrs. McDougal's lawyers "are in regular contact" with the White House.

Jim McDougal's lawyer, Sam Heuer, another old Arkansas hand close to the Clintons, seems to have vanished now that his client has started cooperating. Who was paying him, we also wonder? It now develops that Alan Dershowitz, who runs a big-money law practice under cover of a professorship at Harvard, is also advising Mrs. McDougal. We think he had an obligation to disclose this to us, and to readers, when he wrote our Rule of Law column earlier this week about the evils of plea bargains.

Lately Mr. Clinton has been displaying an unaccustomed and probably calculated testiness when asked about the various Whitewater scandals. He keeps citing the big legal fees run up by aides, and lately has been promising to pay them somehow. Judicial Watch, a conservative watchdog, says this is an attempt to influence witnesses; Mr. Dershowitz's point was that prosecutors do the same thing. Fair enough, but prosecutors are required to tell juries about inducements for witnesses. We do not know who is paying the likes of Mr. McDaniel or Mr. Heuer; Craig Livingstone of White House security office infamy—represented by the top-rank criminal firm that used to include Deputy Attorney General

Jamie Gorelick—refuses to tell investigators who has contributed to his legal defense fund.

Then, too, in influencing witnesses, the President has a trump card. He can issue pardons, either via the usual Justice Department pardon process or at his own initiative. The White House has said no pardons are under consideration for Whitewater figures, but has refused to rule out the prospect. If the purpose of Mrs. McDougal's bizarre judicial and television performance seems mysterious, the answer is simple. It's the pardon, stupid.

* * *

The McDougal contempt citation is but one of the scandals rolling off the President's back since the start of the lachrymose Democratic convention. We read, for example, of an IRS investigation of Newt Gingrich's college course; we've not heard of an investigation of the controversy between John Hartigan and Clinton lawyer David Kendall over the President's personal tax return (see Letters today for the latest installment—page 12). Perhaps at one level the Dick

Susan McDougal

Morris revelations and resignation can be chalked up to the observation that this Administration did not invent sin. But at another level, Mr. Morris was the architect of Mr. Clinton's attempts to co-opt the family values issue; the manner of his fall turns over the doubling cube in the game of hypocrisy.

We were especially intrigued, too, by a little passage in the Star article on Mr. Morris, about his working secretly with the Saudi Arabian royal family on a fund for scholarships for Gulf War veterans. Another Clinton intimate, David Edwards, solicited the Saudis for contributions to a Middle Eastern studies center in Arkansas. It occurs to us that there may be a connection here to the mystery of all this legal-defense money.

Especially so given the adventures of Arief Wiriandinata, as revealed by the Knight-Ridder Washington bureau. Mr. Wiriandinata recently became one of the largest contributors to the Democratic Party; he and his wife ponied up $425,000 before departing to their native Indonesia. Mr. Wiriandinata, a 30-year-old landscape architect who lived in a modest townhouse, had the advantage of being able to contribute legally because he held a green card.

His wife was the daughter of the late Hashim Ning, a co-investor in Lippo Group, the big Indonesian conglomerate headed by Mochtar Riady. Lippo was once, in conjunction with Arkansas's Stephens family, part-owner of the Worthen Bank in Little Rock. Lippo has also been prominent as the chief client of Webster Hubbell just before, and presumably during and after, his sojourn in the federal penitentiary. Interrogators for the Senate Whitewater committee never succeeded in ascertaining how much Lippo paid Mr. Hubbell, or for what.

* * *

Another mid-convention revelation, barely noticed, was a White House memo saying that Mrs. Clinton ordered a delay in advising the President, let alone the appropriate law-enforcement authorities, about the discovery of the note by Vincent Foster discovered torn up after his death. The memo, by White House lawyer Miriam Nemetz, was among 2,000 pages of documents turned over to Congressman William Clinger's oversight committee under threat of a contempt citation. Ms. Nemetz reported that Mack McLarty, then White House Chief of Staff, told Presidential adviser David Gergen that "the first lady was very upset and believed the matter required further thought and the President should not yet be told."

White House spokesman Mark Fabiani said the memo was based on "fifth-hand" information. This is fair enough, but if it had been released when first subpoenaed instead of withheld under an entirely bogus claim of executive privilege, Congressional committees might have been able to ascertain the truth, exculpatory or otherwise, before the coming election.

* * *

Whatever its deficiencies in organizing a foreign policy, the Clinton White House has been consummately professional in constructing scandal defenses. This is clear enough in the nearby excerpts from a 12-page "task list" compiled by Associate White House Counsel Jane Sherburne. The document, another of the 2,000 pages for which executive privilege was brazenly claimed, was compiled in December 1994, just weeks after the GOP sweep of Congress. The Administration's checklist of its own myriad vulnerabilities missed few details. It promised, for example, to "monitor" Webster Hubbell's

Nolan/**)

    h. Cisneros (**)

    I. Brown (**)

    j. Hubbell (**)

    k. Ickes/union representation (**)

    l. Stephanopoulos/NationsBank (**)

    m. State Department—passport files (**)

    n. Archives—abuse of personnel system (**)

    o. Legal Defense Fund (Mills)

    p. Health Care Task Force (Neuwirth)

    q. White House operations (drugs, passes, Helicopters) (Mills/Nolan)

    r. Residence renovations (Neuwirth)

    s. Presidential immunity (Sloan)

    t. White House Arkansans (Thomasson, Nash, Rasco) (**)

    u. PIC surplus (Presidential Inaugural Committee)

    v. Improper electioneering (SBA) (**)

    w. GSA (Roger Johnson (**)

    x. Value partners (Neuwirth)

    y. Presidential campaign (FEC audit) (**)

    z. Commodities (Kendall/**)

    aa. Gubernatorial campaigns (Lindsey, Wright) - record keeping (Kendall/**)

    ab. Gubernatorial campaigns—MGSL (Madison Guaranty S&L) (Kendall/**)

    ac. Whitewater/MGSL (Kendall/**)

    ad other MGSL/McDougal Kendall/**)

    ae. Rose Law Firm (HRC work for MGSL; Frost Case, FSLIC representation) (Kendall/**)

    af. David Hale/Susan McDougal/SBA (Kendall/**)

    ag. Tucker (**)

    ah. Lasater (bond deals; cocaine; Roger Clinton) (**)

    ai. Use of loans to achieve legislative initiatives (**)

    aj. ADFA (political favors; Larry Nichols) (**)

    ak. Mena Airport (**)

    al. Troopers (**)

    am. Women (Kendall/Bennett/**)

Point 2 of the memo identifies "key Republican objectives," establishes basic research tasks, and outlines an "offensive structure" that includes "W&C" (the Williams & Connolly law firm, the Clintons' personal lawyers) and "surrogates" to speak on behalf of the Administration. Points 3-5 outline research and memos to be completed in matters related to Vincent Foster, the Madison Guaranty criminal referrals, and the Resolution Trust Corp. investigation of Madison.

* * *

6. White House/Treasury Contacts. . . .

c. Truthfulness of White House and other Administration witnesses (referral of testimony to Starr—Ickes, Stephanopoulos)

I. consult with lawyers

ii. identify areas of vulnerability

iii. research re perjury

iv. press response. . . .

7. Smaltz Investigation

a. Espy—ethics (Mills)

b. Beyond Espy ethics (Hatch Act, Tyson's)

i. determine charter, scope of inquiry

ii. determine press strategy

iii. identify congressional interest

iv. assemble public record

v. fact gathering. . . .

11. Hubbell

a. monitor cooperation

b. determine press strategy/develop talking points. . . .

21. Other Pre-Inaugural. . . .

b. Negative Associations

i. Jim Guy Tucker

ii. David Hale (SBA)

iii. Jim McDougal

iv. Dan Lasater (bond deals, cocaine, Roger Clinton)

Players and Institutions Mentioned in Sherburne Memo

BENNETT, Robert. Attorney in Paula Jones sexual harassment case.

BROWN, Ron. Former Commerce Secretary. Was under investigation by Independent Counsel Daniel Pearson. Killed in a plane crash in Croatia on April 3.

CERF, Christopher. Associate W.H. Counsel.

CISNERNOS, Henry. Housing Secretary. Under investigation by Independent Counsel David Barrett.

FROST: auditing firm involved with Madison S&L and Rose Law Firm.

FSLIC: Federal Savings and Loan Insurance Corp.

HALE, David. former Arkansas insider and key Whitewater witness.

HATCH ACT: Bars solicitation of campaign contributions from government employees.

HUBBELL, Webster. Former Associate Attorney General; jailed in the Whitewater probe.

ICKES, Harold. W.H. Deputy Chief of Staff.

JOHNSON, Roger. Administrator of the Government Services Administration.

KENDALL, David. Clintons' personal attorney.

LASATER, Dan. Convicted cocaine distributor and longtime Clinton friend.

LINDSEY, Bruce and WRIGHT, Betsey. Top Clinton aides from Arkansas.

McDOUGAL, Susan. convicted on multiple fraud counts in Whitewater trial along with husband **Jim Mc-Dougal** and

Arkansas **Gov. Jim Guy Tucker.**

MGSL: Madison Guaranty Savings & Loan.

MILLS, Cheryl. Associate W.H. Counsel.

NASH, Bob. Agriculture Department official.

NEMETZ, Miriam. Associate W.H. Counsel.

NOLAN, Beth. Associate W.H. Counsel.

RASCO, Carol. Domestic policy adviser.

SHERBURNE, Jane C. Associate W.H. Counsel.

SMALTZ, Donald. Appointed independent counsel to investigate then-Agriculture Secretary Mike Espy.

STEPHANOPOULOS, George. Senior White House aide. NationsBank provided him with home loan.

STEPHENS, Jay. Attorney hired by Resolution Trust Corp. to investigate civil claims against Madison Guaranty S&L.

NEUWIRTH, Stephen. Associate W.H. Counsel.

SLOAN, CLIFFORD. Associate W.H. Counsel.

THOMASSON, Patsy. Arkansas associate of cocaine distributor Dan Lasater and head of White House Office of Administration.

TUCKER, Jim Guy. Former Governor of Arkansas, convicted of multiple fraud counts in Whitewater prosecution.

TYSON'S: Arkansas Poultry giant Tyson Foods.

VALUE PARTNERS. Investment partnership of Hillary Clinton, Vincent Foster and Webster Hubbell.

REVIEW & OUTLOOK

The President's Protectors

Watching Susan McDougal's wide-eyed performances on national television, it might have been easy to forget that a jury of 12 Arkansans just convicted her of four felony counts related to defrauding the government of $300,000. This was somehow glossed over in the interest of attracting Larry King's next guest, as of course was the entirely separate charge by the Los Angeles district attorney that she ripped off conductor Zubin Mehta and his wife of at least $150,000 through forgery and the unauthorized use of credit cards.

Susan McDougal

We mention this to give some perspective to Ms. McDougal's play for sympathy, and possibly a Presidential pardon, in choosing jail for contempt rather than testify to the Whitewater grand jury in Little Rock. Her choice of jail and verbal assault on the prosecutors who'd just convicted her only serves the interest of President Bill Clinton, who's also profited from some stonewalling by Security Office problem Craig Livingstone.

Under Judge Susan Webber Wright's contempt ruling, Ms. McDougal must either testify to the grand jury or stay in jail until September 30, when in any event she will start serving her two-year fraud sentence. After that, she may well have to serve out at least some of the contempt time. Her California trial is slated to begin in Santa Monica later this year. While the other problems remain, she could resolve the contempt issue by testifying. If she believes Mr. Clinton did not know of the $300,000 fraudulent loan or the $50,000 of it that benefited the Whitewater Co., she need only say so. Instead she accuses Kenneth Starr of looking for something on the President, which of course is precisely what his charter as independent counsel says he is supposed to do.

For his part, Mr. Starr released a statement saying that Ms. McDougal and her attorney Bobby McDaniel were "brazenly trying to deceive the public. Ms. McDougal and Mr. McDaniel persist in misrepresenting the substance of a conversation with my staff during which Ms. McDougal was offered the opportunity to voluntarily provide complete and truthful information about matters within the jurisdiction of this office. Ms. McDougal and Mr.

Craig Livingstone

McDaniel were specifically told that under no circumstances would we recommend a specific sentence to the Court on her felony convictions or do anything to limit the Court's sentencing discretion; nor could we control the California State and Federal authorities who are investigating and prosecuting Ms. McDougal for embezzlement and tax evasion."

ABC reports that Ms. McDougal's lawyers "are in regular contact" with the White House. So, we would imagine, is Randall Turk, Craig Livingstone's attorney. Mr. Turk is high-priced talent from the same firm that once employed Deputy Attorney General Jamie Gorelick. Mr. Livingstone has been resisting requests to disclose the names of contributors to his legal defense fund and to appear before the House Government Reform and Oversight Committee.

But Mr. Livingstone may have had a change of heart recently. This week he will go before the Whitewater grand jury in Washington, and he has accepted service of a subpoena to talk to the House committee next week. Perhaps the strategy path chosen by Susan McDougal—to a jail cell for contempt of court, with time off to testify to Larry King—has caused Mr. Livingstone to rethink where his interests lie.

Review & Outlook

Will Anyone Believe?

The record may some day show that the character issue finally attached itself to Bill Clinton at a campaign stop in Rancho Cucamonga, where the White House press corps drenched Press Secretary Mike McCurry with withering skepticism over the President's health records (see excerpts of the exchange on page 34). Stunned, the White House shoved out more testimonials by doctors who have examined Mr. Clinton recently, and announced that he would be willing to be interviewed by Dr. Lawrence Altman of The New York Times.

Fine, but will anyone believe? E. Connie Mariano, the Navy doctor who serves as the President's personal physician, offered one sentence looking back from her own exam: "No history of hypertension, diabetes, tuberculosis, sexually transmitted disease, cancer, stroke or heart disease." In this Dr. Mariano is no doubt relying on what the patient told her. In interviewing the President, Dr. Altman would have to do the same, even while remembering how Paul Tsongas's doctors lied to him about lymphoma in 1992—and perhaps also how Bill Clinton lied that year about his draft history and relations with Gennifer Flowers.

There's little reason to believe Mr. Clinton is not physically up to his job, but his longstanding resistance to scrutiny suggests that something embarrassing lurks in his medical history—if not relating to sex perhaps to depression or even, like his brother, drugs. Our experience is that every time this White House runs a big stonewall, it conceals something worth knowing, then something behind that. On why it's hard to believe the President about his health, or for that

Editorial Feature

'Only a Few of Us Are Running for President'

Excerpts from an exchange on the President's health records between the White House press corps and Press Secretary Mike McCurry, on the road in California, Sept. 12, 1996. A related editorial appears nearby (Page 31).

Q: So there's nothing in any of these medical records that a normal person might consider embarrassing to the President?

Mr. McCurry: I wouldn't say that. . . . [A]ll of us undergo tests that I'm not sure that any of us would want to have spread out and printed on the front page of the newspaper.

Q: But only a few of us are running for President, Mike. . . .

Q: But, Mike, can you characterize a test that you think would be embarrassing? I mean, what sort of test result do you think would be embarrassing to release? I can't think of one. I'm asking you to —

Mr. McCurry: Well, I'm not going to do that and provide you the satisfaction. But just think for a minute.

Q: I don't get it—sorry.

Q: We can imagine a few, but what —

Mr. McCurry: I'll explain it to you later.

Q: Actually, a transmitted disease is —

Q: Yes. Does he have a sexually transmitted disease? I mean, what is —

Q: Jesus!

Mr. McCurry: Good God, do you really want to ask that question?

Q: No, I'm just asking what is embarrassing.

MR. McCURRY: If he had—we have an obligation to report on the President's medical condition. The President, we reported to you after his May 24th physical exam, is in excellent overall health. That's an astonishing question to have just been posed here at the White House.

Q: Well, you're raising the question there's something embarrassing. . . .

Q: The astonishing question, did you answer that, or say that it's inappropriate to be asked?

MR. McCURRY: I said that if there had been—if there was anything related to a disease or health condition the President had it would have been accurately and timely reported to you. . . .

Q: And there's nothing in the records that, if they were to be released, would be considered politically damaging to the President?

MR. McCURRY: The President's "records"—quote, unquote—were released in 1992 when he ran for office. Now, records—we released summaries of those records by the qualified physicians that attended to then Governor Clinton so that people could have an accurate profile of his health. And we have then annually provided, I think, more than ample information that brings people up to date upon conclusion of his annual exam.

Q: Mike, just to clarify then —

Q: Mike, you are saying the President does not now have and has not since he entered the White House, been treated for a sexually transmitted disease?

MR. McCURRY: Boy, I tell you, I'm astonished you're asking that question —

Q: I don't want to.

MR. McCURRY:—but it's obvious that he has not because that would have been reported at the time that he had his annual medical exam, or alternatively, we would have affirmatively provided you that information.

Q: So you're saying, Mike, again just to clarify, that if he had any type of disease it would have been in those reports?

MR. McCURRY: I'm saying that the White House has an obligation to affirmatively provide information on the President's medical condition. . . .

Q: You keep referring to tests. It seems that what you're saying is that he had tests for something that could come back positive it would have been embarrassing and you would have had to release the information that it was positive. So he's had these tests —

MR. MCCURRY: If any of the President's test results which we reported to you had been something abnormal there would have been, I think, among all of you a desire to have more information about that. But because the President's test results reflected, substantiated Dr. Mariano's statement that he was in excellent overall health, since they all fell within the normal parameters of a person his age with his health characteristics, to my knowledge, no one has raised the specific issue about any of those test results.

Q: Mike, you seem to be saying that even taking the test—let's say an HIV positive—taking a test for HIV, or some other sexually transmitted disease, just taking the test is in and of itself embarrassing.

MR. MCCURRY: Look, I'm trying to keep some level of dignity here. I'm talking about things like rectal exams, okay. Do you want to have all those things spread out there?

All right, enough's enough on this subject, I think. Do you guys—what's the time?

Q: We really have reached a new low.

MR. MCCURRY: You guys are really bored. It's hard to know that there is a campaign under way here.

Review & Outlook

Running Out the Clock

Someone coaching the White House on scandal control must have been a big fan of Dean Smith's old four-corner offense at North Carolina. You get a lead, then throw the ball around the perimeter, while the other team runs itself ragged as the clock runs down. As currently run by the White House, the game plan is to keep material out of the hands of the GOP's congressional investigating committees. If they can run this strategy for another 45 days, dodging even a subpoena, and President Clinton wins re-election, they'll then tell press interviewers that the voters have spoken on Bill Clinton's character—no story.

Last week, the White House responded in its fashion to a six-week-old subpoena for its draft copy of former FBI agent Gary Aldrich's book, "Inside the Clinton White House": It shipped the book over to the FBI for safekeeping. Recall that the White House had been given Mr. Aldrich's book early on by the FBI's eager-to-please Counsel Howard Shapiro. The White House then used its sneak preview copy to mount a campaign to bludgeon Mr. Aldrich and discredit the book.

Today, the FBI seems to have concluded that doing business with these folks carries dangers: The bureau promptly returned the original Aldrich text, saying it would be "inappropriate" to accept it in light of the subpoena for it. Stymied, the White House has finally turned the book over to Rep. William Clinger's House Oversight Committee. White House Counsel Jack Quinn says he's now concerned that there may be "public disclosure" of material Mr.

Aldrich deleted from his book at the FBI's request.

Pass the ball to Susan McDougal, the Whitewater convict. Ms. McDougal showed up on NBC's eager-to-please "Today" show to say she would remain in jail and continue to refuse to answer a grand jury's questions because prosecutors "are trying to ruin a Democratic president."

The Clinton bench isn't bad at playing slowdown, either. This week Democrats on Rep. Clinger's committee staged a walkout rather than vote on the committee's final report, which criticizes the White House for abusing the doctrine of executive privilege in its attempt to withhold documents and information about the abrupt Clinton firing of the career Travel Office staff. Also, the Clinton bench talks trash.

Rep. Henry Waxman declared: "I leave this committee with absolute disgust for it and its chairman." Rep. Paul Kanjorski denounced the GOP Congress and declared "like horses, we should take it out and shoot it." This sort of thing is expected from the Waxmans and Kanjorskis of the party, but how does a moderate Democrat such as Rep. Karen Thurman of Florida end up as an accomplice? Serious politicians ought to have a better reason than to claim they joined the walkout because not every Democrat was allowed to criticize the report in front of the TV cameras.

Karen Thurman

But even this committee's Democrats couldn't ignore the refusal of Craig Livingstone to show up for a scheduled deposition. Mr. Livingstone is the former bar bouncer turned White House personnel-security director who resigned after it came to light that he rummaged through some 900 confidential FBI files on Bush and Reagan Administration appointees.

Mr. Livingstone had agreed to appear this past Monday. He would also have been asked about new revelations that indicate he may have played a role in the alleged removal of documents from the late Vincent Foster's White House office. A memo reluctantly turned over by the White House notes that Mr. Livingstone arrived at his office at 7:15 a.m. on the morning after Vincent Foster's death, an hour earlier than Mr. Livingstone has testified he arrived. The timing discrepancy is crucial because Secret Service officer Bruce Abbott has testified that early that morning he saw Mr. Livingstone and another person walking away from the area of Mr. Foster's office with a box of documents.

Mr. Livingstone failed to show up for his deposition. His lawyer Randy Turk explained the absence by claiming that the committee was harassing his client. When Rep. Clinger sought to issue a subpoena to compel testimony, he was at first attacked by committee Democrats who said Mr. Livingstone "has been through enough." But even Democrats couldn't let Mr. Livingstone thumb his nose at Congress and so agreed to issue the subpoena and compel his appearance next Tuesday.

Craig Livingstone

It will be interesting to see if Mr. Livingstone shows up. If he does, there is also the matter of his refusal to comply with a two-month-old Congressional subpoena asking for the names of people who have contributed to the legal defense fund that is paying his hefty bills. Not to mention the question of who's paying Susan McDougal's legal fees. But don't hold your breath on any of this. The White House is passing and the clock is running.

Editorial Feature

Why Voters May Choose A Man They Don't Trust

It's the mystery of this political year: Most Americans say they don't trust President Clinton, but every opinion poll still shows him leading in his bid for a second term. Why doesn't presidential "character" seem to matter any more?

In trying to answer that question, theories abound. And some of those theories say as much about the state of our politics as anything

Potomac Watch

By Paul A. Gigot

the candidates are saying this year. So as therapy for puzzled (or depressed) readers, let's consider the explanations for why Americans may re-elect the most ethically challenged president since Richard Nixon:

• *Voters think all politicians are corrupt.* If no one in politics tells the truth, then Mr. Clinton is simply meeting industry standards.

To adapt a Pat Moynihan phrase, we have defined political deviancy down. Sherman Adams was run out of town for accepting a vicuna coat while White House chief of staff in the 1950s. Now a first lady can get a $100,000 commodities windfall with the help of a Tyson Foods big shot, and voters assume everyone does it. Republicans didn't help their claim to the high road by putting Sen. Al D'Amato in charge of the Whitewater probe. On the other hand, even the upright Rep. Bill Clinger's Travelgate revelations don't seem to dent cynical public opinion.

Something like this voter cynicism also seems to be afflicting Bob Dole's tax cut proposal: In the latest Journal/NBC poll, 36% of all voters say they expect their taxes to increase if Mr. Clinton wins. But if Mr. Dole wins, 33% expect their taxes to go up too, despite Mr. Dole's pledge to cut them by 15%. The poor Kansan is paying a price in credibility he doesn't deserve to pay for the tax betrayals of George Bush in 1990 and Bill Clinton in 1993.

● *Americans are as corrupt as their politicians.* It used to be that liberals blamed the voters for their political defeats, but this year the right is giving it a try. In his new book, "Slouching Towards Gomorrah," Robert Bork, our own Cato the Elder, suggests that Mr. Clinton is the epitome of America's self-indulgent, morally depraved, wanting-it-both-ways culture. (Keep the book away from depressed relatives.)

Bill Clinton

This fall-of-Rome analogy is always tempting, but it's hard to square with what the 1996 campaign says about the temper of our times. Arguments about the culture that Dan Quayle was ridiculed for making in 1992 are now staple Clinton campaign themes. And Dick Morris may be the spectacle who proves his own rule: As a consultant he understood his candidate must run as someone who deplores the personal behavior of people like Dick Morris.

With the help of a religious revival, Americans are returning personal responsibility to the center of our political conversation. Welfare reform passed, after all. Joycelyn Elders had to go, and Bill Clinton signed the Defense of Marriage Act. Bill Bennett is a bestseller. There are as many signs of revival as rot.

● *The diminished presidency.* Maybe voters just don't think the White House matters much anymore. Foreign policy counts for less after the Cold War, and presidential "character"—courage, constancy, honesty—is the stuff of an international crisis.

With Congress reasserting its domestic ascendency, a president has power mainly as a check on legislative excess. Mr. Clinton has shrewdly played on this notion by campaigning as a brake on the Gingrich Congress while embracing its general direction. His own second-term agenda is so small that almost no one has noticed—which is precisely his political intent. He doesn't want voters to think he wants government to do very much at all.

● *Ken Starr*. This is a logical carom shot suggested by Journal Editor Robert Bartley. By creating the office of independent counsel to vet ethics, we have taken ethics out of politics. So voters have come to believe that unless a counsel such as Mr. Starr indicts someone, there's no ethical problem.

Voters figure they can ignore the work of congressional committees as mere score-settling, while a president's attorney general is liberated from all investigating responsibility. By not completing his own probe before the election, Mr. Starr is thus serving as a shield for Mr. Clinton against real voter scrutiny.

The irony is that—here's the double carom—if Mr. Clinton wins, he'll quickly turn around and claim his election victory as a shield against Mr. Starr. He'll say voters knew everything about Whitewater and the rest when they gave him a second term, and that Mr. Starr just wants to overturn their wishes.

So go ahead, readers, pick your favorite theory. My own is that Mr. Clinton merely fulfills voters' low expectations for all politicians, although there is one other possibility: That character does still matter, and may yet work against Mr. Clinton by Nov. 5. Mr. Clinton's approval rating, at 55%, remains low for a president who has governed during what have been arguably the most placid four years of this century: No war, no riots, no recession.

A president who had earned the country's admiration would be doing better. In the next seven weeks, the Dole campaign will try to remind voters about the differences between Mr. Clinton's record and his rhetoric. Perhaps as voters confront the reality of four more years, they'll think again about re-electing a president they don't trust.

REVIEW & OUTLOOK

Pardon Me

In some extraordinary statements Monday, President Clinton stoked Susan McDougal's hopes of a Presidential pardon, and stepped up the White House campaign against Independent Counsel Kenneth Starr. Before the voters go to the polls in November, it seems to us, Mr. Clinton owes them a forthright explanation about what he would do about both of these issues in a second term.

Susan McDougal

Ms. McDougal, a felon convicted by a jury of Arkansans, has been refusing to tell a grand jury whether Mr. Clinton knew about illegal loans, and whether he told the truth in testimony in her trial. There being no legal basis for this refusal, Judge Susan Webber Wright has committed her for contempt, in advance of her prison sentence on Whitewater charges. If Ms. McDougal believes the President did not know and did tell the truth, she can purge the contempt by testifying to this effect.

Instead of taking this simple step, she and her attorney—old Arkansas hand Bobby McDaniel—have been attacking Mr. Starr. They say he wants her to make up evidence against the President, so they refuse to tell the truth. This non sequitur has been extensively and uncritically advertised by Larry King and Bryant Gumbel. It is now amplified by the President of the United States.

Especially since Ms. McDougal also has been dropping hints on a

Little Rock radio station that she may decide to testify after all, her position can be understood only as a ploy for a Presidential pardon. Pressed by Jim Lehrer's questioning (excerpts are printed on page 50), the President was careful not to rule out the possibility. Readers, and for that matter Ms. McDougal, may appreciate a briefing on how the pardon process works.

As Mr. Clinton notes, there is a "regular process" at the Justice Department, which considers about 300 cases submitted each year. Applicants fill out lengthy forms, submit character references and undergo an FBI background check. The Justice Department's pardon attorney reviews the case and passes it on to the Deputy Attorney General with suggestions, who passes it to the Attorney General with recommendations. The petition then goes to the White House, a process that can take years, which is probably not what Ms. McDougal and the others have in mind.

A President is not obligated to follow this process, however. By the power vested in him by Article Two of the Constitution, a President can simply order that pardons be granted. That's what President Bush did with his Christmas 1992 pardons of former Defense Secretary Caspar Weinberger and five other government officials for conduct related to the Iran-Contra affair. Mr. Bush correctly called Independent Counsel Lawrence Walsh's pursuit of the six "the criminalization of policy differences," and his pardons put an end to it.

President Bush pointedly did not pardon five other Iran-Contra figures—Thomas Clines, Richard Secord and three others—who had either pleaded guilty or been found guilty of felonies by a jury. The difference was clear, as Terry Eastland wrote for us at the time: "The six, all government officials at the time of their 'crimes' while the five were not, did not profit or seek to profit from their actions." This precedent would rule out a pardon for Ms. McDougal, obviously, and whatever the President's interest in stringing her along through the elections, he should tell her so.

The balance of the President's remarks are even more disturbing. He and his colleagues are obviously starting a campaign against Mr. Starr, as earlier they blocked Donald Smaltz's investigation of Don Tyson (see page 46). The President accuses Mr. Starr of trying to suborn lies, and coyly says it's "obvious" that Mr. Starr is out to get him and the First Lady. Earlier, in an August 25 interview on CNN, Mr. Clinton condemned "the abuse of the special-counsel law."

Now, Mr. Starr is an officer of the court, appointed pursuant to the application of Attorney General Janet Reno. His original mandate was to investigate violations of federal criminal law "relating in any way to James B. McDougal's, President William Jefferson Clinton's, or Mrs. Hillary Rodham Clinton's relationships with Madison Guaranty Savings and Loan, Whitewater Development Corporation, or Capital Management Services Inc." On subsequent application of the Attorney General, Mr. Starr's mandate has since been expanded twice, to cover the Travel Office firings and the apparent abuse of FBI files by the White House security office.

If the Administration thinks Mr. Starr is abusing the office, why does it keep sending him more work? Because it delays the latest scandal through the elections. And the President is now laying a basis for turning on Mr. Starr after the elections, preparing to claim that the voters have proclaimed everyone innocent. The special prosecutor law provides that the Attorney General can dismiss an independent counsel "for good cause," though presumably the meaning of this phrase ultimately would be determined by courts on appeal.

We've never been keen on the special counsel statute, but it was upheld 8-1 by the Supreme Court. Mr. Starr is doing his appointed duty, and his mandate specifies President Clinton as among those to be investigated. In a second term, would President Clinton fire Mr. Starr, or pardon Susan McDougal, or generally use his Presidential powers to frustrate the law, or pardon his wife if indicted? In the coming election, it seems to us, the country ought to know what kind of Constitutional crisis it may be buying.

REVIEW & OUTLOOK

The Smaltz Convictions

On another Whitewater front, a federal jury in Washington yesterday convicted California agribusiness giant Sun-Diamond Growers on eight counts of giving illegal gifts to former Agriculture Secretary Mike Espy. While the sums were relatively small—involving gifts of sports tickets, meals, transportation and gifts, including $2,400 worth of luggage—the convictions represent an important step forward for Independent Counsel Donald Smaltz's investigation, establishing the credibility of a probe that has come under withering attack by the Clinton Administration and its Arkansas allies.

Donald Smaltz

Last week, Mr. Smaltz indicted the chief lobbyist for Arkansas poultry giant Tyson Foods on charges of lying to federal investigators about gifts to Mr. Espy. And in a separate action Monday, Tyson Foods senior chairman Don Tyson settled an insider-trading suit brought by the Securities and Exchange Commission; without admitting guilt, Mr. Tyson agreed to pay a fine. The SEC had charged that Mr. Tyson passed inside information to a friend regarding Tyson's impending takeover of Arctic Alaska Fisheries Corp., which the friend converted into a $46,125 profit.

Mr. Smaltz certainly is familiar with Mr. Tyson. Shortly after his appointment as independent counsel, Mr. Smaltz went to Arkansas to explore Tyson links to Mr. Espy. According to a report in Time magazine, he turned up a former Tyson pilot who began talking about cash payments that he flew from Tyson headquarters in northwest Arkansas to Little Rock, allegedly for then-Governor Clinton. Shortly after the Time story, the Clinton Administration went on the offensive against Mr. Smaltz, and Tyson Foods cried foul, declaring the investigation "a politically motivated witch hunt."

Then in February 1995, when Mr. Smaltz went to Attorney General Reno to expand his probe into an area he wouldn't identify publicly, she turned him down. In early 1996, Mr. Smaltz sought a different expansion of his investigation, later revealed to involve Mr. Espy's chief of staff. This time he went straight to the U.S. Court of Appeals' special division. Ms. Reno's Justice Department opposed the expansion; the special division granted it.

The obvious question raised by the Smaltz investigation is, What's going on at Justice? The thought occurs to us that Mr. Smaltz was obstructed by Ms. Reno when he sought to investigate Mr. Tyson. Banned, in effect, from Arkansas, Mr. Smaltz turned to Tyson's chief Washington lobbyist in an attempt to get to the bottom of his corner of the Whitewater swamp. Mr. Smaltz hit solid ground yesterday with the Sun-Diamond convictions.

With the attacks on Mr. Starr now starting to resemble the tactics employed against Mr. Smaltz when he ventured into the Arkansas murk, it's time for some committee to start issuing subpoenas to the Justice Department and the independent counsels themselves. The first order of business should be to find out if the Clinton Administration is working through Justice to shut down these independent counsels.

Editorial Feature

Kenneth Starr's Mandate

Following are excerpts from the Aug. 5, 1994, order appointing Kenneth Starr as independent counsel to investigate Whitewater-related crimes. The order was approved by a panel consisting of U.S. Circuit Judge David B. Sentelle and Senior Circuit Judges John D. Butzner Jr. and Joseph T. Sneed. A related editorial appears nearby [page 43].

. . . ORDERED by the Court in accordance with the authority vested in it by 28 U.S.C. Sec. 593(b) that Kenneth W. Starr. . . be and he is hereby appointed Independent Counsel with full power, independent authority, and jurisdiction to investigate to the maximum extent authorized by the Independent Counsel Reauthorization Act of 1994 whether any individuals or entities have committed a violation of any federal criminal law, other than a Class B or C misdemeanor or infraction, relating in any way to James B. McDougal's, President William Jefferson Clinton's, or Mrs. Hillary Rodham Clinton's relationships with Madison

Kenneth Starr

Guaranty Savings & Loan Association, Whitewater Development Corporation, or Capital Management Services, Inc. . . .

The Independent Counsel shall have jurisdiction and authority to investigate any violation of 28 U.S.C. Sec. 1826, or any obstruction of the due administration of justice, or any material false testimony or statement in violation of federal criminal law, in connection with any investigation of the matters described above. . . .

The Court, having reviewed the motion of the Attorney General that Robert B. Fiske, Jr., be appointed as Independent Counsel, has determined that this would not be consistent with the purposes of the Act. This reflects no conclusion on the part of the Court that Fiske lacks either the actual independence or any other attribute necessary to the conclusion of the investigation. Rather, the Court reaches this conclusion because the Act contemplates an apparent as well as an actual independence on the part of the Counsel. As the Senate Report accompanying the 1982 enactments reflected, "[t]he intent of the special prosecutor provisions is not to impugn the integrity of the Attorney General or the Department of Justice. Throughout our system of justice, safeguards exist against actual or *perceived* conflicts of interest without reflecting adversely on the parties who are subject to conflicts." S. Rep. No. 496, 97th Cong., 2d sess. at 6 (1982) (emphasis added). Just so here. It is not our intent to impugn the integrity of the Attorney General's appointee, but rather to reflect the intent of the Act that the actor be protected against perceptions of conflict. As Fiske was appointed by the incumbent administration, the Court therefore deems it in the best interest of the appearance of independence contemplated by the Act that a person not affiliated with the incumbent administration be appointed. . . .

Editorial Feature

'Out to Get the Clintons?'

From an interview with President Clinton on PBS's "NewsHour With Jim Lehrer," Sept. 23, 1996:

MR. LEHRER: Susan McDougal told a federal judge in Little Rock the other day the reason she was refusing to testify before a grand jury is she believed Kenneth Starr, the independent counsel, "was out to get the Clintons," end quote. Do you agree with her?

PRESIDENT CLINTON: Well, I think the facts speak for themselves. And I think all we know about her—she said what she said, and her lawyer said that he felt they did not want her to tell the truth. They wanted her to say something bad about us, whether it was the truth or not. And if it was false, it would still be perfectly all right. And if she told the truth and it wasn't bad about us she simply would be punished for it. That's what her lawyer said.

MR. LEHRER: Do you believe him?

PRESIDENT CLINTON: I think that the facts speak for themselves. There's a lot of evidence to support that.

MR. LEHRER: But do you personally believe that's what this is all about, is to get you and Mrs. Clinton?

PRESIDENT CLINTON: Isn't it obvious?

MR. LEHRER: You obviously believe that, right?

PRESIDENT CLINTON: Isn't it obvious? I mean, you know, look at the D'Amato hearings. What do [the] D'Amato hearings reveal? Witness after witness after witness testifying that as governor, every time I was given a chance to do something unethical or ethical, I chose the ethical path.

Witness after witness after witness and they still—whenever a question was answered they'd go ask a bunch of new questions.

But the American people have figured that out. They'll get that. I'm not worried. I trust the people, and I think that's what we should be doing.

MR. LEHRER: If you're re-elected would you consider pardoning the McDougals, and Jim Guy Tucker [during] a second term?

PRESIDENT CLINTON: I've given no consideration to that. And you know, their cases are still on appeal. And I would—my position would be that their cases should be handled like others, they should go through—there's a regular process for that, and I have regular meetings on that, and I review those cases as they come up after there's an evaluation done by the Justice Department. And that's how I think it should be handled.

died this month.)

Some 20 years later, the case of Little Rock's soft criminal syndicate followed a radically different course. There U.S. Attorney Paula Casey was a former University of Arkansas law student of Bill Clinton. She was also a former Clinton campaign volunteer who had never litigated a significant case before a jury before Mr. Clinton nominated her to be the top U.S. prosecutor in their home state. (Her husband, Gilbert L. Glover, has served as staff chief counsel of the Arkansas Public Service Commission since 1988.)

In March 1992, just as Mr. Clinton began to take the lead in the Democratic presidential primaries, New York Times reporter Jeff Gerth produced a front-page story that threatened Mr. Clinton's drive for the nomination: Mr. Gerth spotlighted Bill and Hillary Clinton's Whitewater land-development partnership with Jim and Susan McDougal and then-Gov. Clinton's appointment of the state securities commissioner who gave Mr. McDougal's failing S&L favored treatment. Mr. Clinton, besieged by the press in Houston days before the Super Tuesday primaries, declared, "I know we lost over $25,000 on this deal. I never made a penny on it." Mr. Clinton's campaign staff rushed out an ostensibly independent report by a "forensic accounting firm" and Denver lawyer James Lyons, actually a longtime Clinton supporter, that claimed the Clintons in fact lost "approximately $68,900."

But investigators at the federal Resolution Trust Corporation could not forget the story. They uncovered dozens of questionable loan transactions involving seven Arkansas banks and 12 corporations doing business with Mr. McDougal's failed S&L; the principals included the Clintons and Gov. Tucker. And investigators nagged the Justice Department to open criminal investigations. But in the election year, the Bush administration was reluctant to appear to be using the Justice Department to attack an opponent.

In the meantime the federal Small Business Administration began to suspect improprieties at the Small Business Investment Corporation, an SBA-chartered lending company owned by Judge David Hale, a crony of Mr. McDougal and Mr. Clinton. The SBA asked Little Rock's interim U.S. attorney to investigate. By the time Ms. Casey was appointed, bureaucrats were beginning to see connections between the Hale and McDougal investigations. But before it got started, the investigation into Arkansas's soft criminal syndicate was already hopelessly bungled by Ms. Casey's refusal to strike a bargain with Mr. Hale.

On July 20, 1993, Vincent Foster, a longtime friend of Bill Clinton and a Little Rock law partner of Hillary Rodham Clinton, was working in his office as deputy White House counsel. He was charged with extricating the Clintons from their Whitewater partnership with the McDougals. That morning he got phone calls from his old Little Rock law firm and from Mr. Lyons, the Denver lawyer who had papered over the Whitewater story.

At 1:35 p.m. in Little Rock, a U.S. magistrate signed an FBI search warrant for the seizure of Judge David Hale's SBIC files, including those on his $300,000 loan to Susan McDougal to "clean up some members of the political family," as Jim McDougal had explained it. Four hours later, Foster left the White House and, according to police reports,

Vincent Foster

drove eight miles to an isolated Civil War fort in Virginia, sat down beside a cannon, put his 1913 Colt Army revolver to his head and pulled the trigger.

His suicide shocked the public and inflamed media interest. With Justice Department attorneys and investigators hammering at the White House for access to Foster's office and papers, the next day the FBI raided David Hale's Little Rock office. Mr. Hale's lawyer, Randy Coleman, began the familiar dance of attorneys representing implicated figures, sending signals prosecutors are normally obliged to explore. He told Ms. Casey that Mr. Hale could offer information on a list of relevant people and transactions, and even volunteered to let the FBI tape conversations with Mr. Hale's co-conspirators. "If you indict Hale, these opportunities will be lost," Mr. Coleman warned.

He got no response. Instead, Mr. Hale was publicly indicted—forever closing this most promising possibility of penetrating the Arkansas syndicate.

Independent Counsel Kenneth Starr convicted several of Mr. Hale's co-conspirators, including Stephen Smith, Mr. Clinton's former chief of staff in Little Rock, as well as the McDougals and Mr. Tucker. As a co-conspirator, Mr. Hale could have taped them all. He also could have taped Bruce R. Lindsay, a top White

House aide who had directed Mr. Clinton's 1990 gubernatorial campaign finances.

If Ms. Casey had displayed the integrity and ingenuity that George Beall had—if she had determined to administer justice without fear or favor—the collection of scandals known as Whitewater would be playing out much differently today. So would the Clinton administration, and, needless to say, so would the 1996 presidential election.

Mr. Methvin is a Washington-based contributing editor of The Reader's Digest.

REVIEW & OUTLOOK

Asides

Where Is Mari Anderson?

The Senate Judiciary Committee issued a subpoena last week for Mari Anderson, a former assistant to former White House security chief Craig Livingstone. Chairman Orrin Hatch said that the subpoena has not been served because Ms. Anderson "has, in effect, gone into hiding." The Committee wants to talk to her about Mr. Livingstone's claim that she neglected to make six months of entries in a log of who examined sensitive FBI files. The log ends at the bottom of a page with March 29, 1994, and resumes at the top of a page the next Sept. 21, when someone else took over. Rose Mary Woods, who took the blame for the famous 18½-minute gap in the Watergate tapes, was maybe just a piker.

Editorial Feature

Clinton's Campaign Against Ken Starr

Bill Clinton is running for re-election by doing some negative campaigning against Whitewater Independent Counsel Kenneth Starr. The point of this effort, on display last week in an interview on PBS with Jim Lehrer, would appear to be to intimidate Mr. Starr into deciding against an indictment of Hillary Rodham Clinton before Election Day. Whether Mr. Clinton succeeds in this or not, he is positioning himself to pardon Mrs. Clinton.

Mrs. Clinton's potential legal problems are obvious. In addition to her documented role in the sham real estate deal known as Castle Grande, she has made various representations and actions that could amount to false statements and obstruction of justice. The independent counsel law requires the investigation of these matters.

Rule of Law

By Terry Eastland

But before any indictment is made, a fair-minded prosecutor must weigh such considerations as provability (a matter that goes to the quality of witnesses and evidence) and jury appeal. Because Mrs. Clinton would be a high-profile defendant, her trial could well become another media circus, like O.J. Simpson's, in which the evidence against a defendant counts for very little even with a jury. Any decision about indicting her before Nov. 5 also encompasses the presumably constraining consideration, noted publicly by Mr. Starr, of how an indictment close to the election might unfairly affect it.

Mr. Clinton's campaign against Mr. Starr charges prosecutorial misconduct that impugns his personal character and reputation and previews the nastier and more intense campaign the counsel can expect if Mrs. Clinton is indicted. At the very least it would seem that Mr. Clinton wants Mr. Starr to hold off on an indictment until after the election, for he remembers well the political uses of a pre-election indictment. On Oct. 30, 1992, Lawrence Walsh's reindictment of Caspar Weinberger in connection with Iran-Contra included documents appearing to implicate President Bush. Candidate Clinton quickly seized on this "October Surprise," declaring that Mr. Bush "has not been telling the truth" about his role in Iran-Contra—or anything else.

Mr. Clinton's public attacks against Mr. Starr constitute a judgment that words are better weapons, for now, than the powers of office. An ordinary prosecutor accused of pursuing someone for political or vindictive reasons—it's "obvious" that Mr. Starr is out to get him and his wife, Mr. Clinton told Mr. Lehrer—would be investigated by the Justice Department. Such a prosecutor could be disciplined and even removed.

Ken Starr

In fact, the statute that governs Mr. Starr's work provides for his removal by the attorney general for "good cause." Taking this step would require the attorney general to make a well-documented case that could survive judicial scrutiny. (Under the law, a removed counsel may challenge the action in the federal courts.) In addition, the removal would have to satisfy a Congress and a public that still remember President Nixon's firing of Watergate special prosecutor Archibald Cox, which led to the passage of the original independent counsel law. Of course, the judges who appointed the fired counsel likely would name a new one, so the investigation would continue.

There are no signs that Attorney General Janet Reno is preparing to fire Mr. Starr. A White House spokesman says Mr. Clinton's complaint has not been passed to the Justice Department and a Justice spokesman says no such complaint has been received. More to the point, the president's charges are too vague to provide a basis for removal. Asked to spell out details of what Mr.

REVIEW & OUTLOOK

Character Questions

In a better world, the Presidential debate Sunday would plumb the great issues of our time: economic growth, the post-Cold War world, education, families and the like. In today's world such questions are a rather empty exercise, as public lassitude about the campaign indicates. After all, when we hear answers, we are forced to ask: Why should we believe? Do their positions have anything to do with how they would behave when elected?

Bill Clinton

The real issue of the day, that is to say, is manifestly an issue of character. This is not a matter of one aberrant personality. Lyndon Johnson was hounded from office over something called the "credibility gap," and Richard Nixon resigned not because of the Watergate break-in but because of the lies in its aftermath. George Bush was cashiered essentially for breaking his "read my lips" pledge. Political positions of candidates everywhere are driven by mindless polls and focus groups, not by any serious thought, let alone attempts at leadership. The trend is as deep as it is worrisome to the future of democracy.

With that having been said, Bill Clinton represents a new nadir. Putting aside personal peccadilloes and possible petty crimes, here is an incumbent President who presents himself as the opposite of what he was four years ago. "The era of big government is over," the architect of national health care tells us. Under the tutelage of the now scandalized Dick Morris, he has remolded himself in the image of the 1994 Congressional elections—in his acceptance speech even taking credit for point one of the GOP Contract, applying to Congress the laws that apply to others. But what will he actually do in a second term? The same thing he has done all his career, which is to please the last person who talks to him.

And why not; it has worked for him through Hope, Hot Springs, Oxford, Little Rock and Washington. His undeniable personal charm has always prevailed, whether with alcoholic stepfathers, draft boards, Gennifer and Hillary, Susan McDougal and voters in a hopeless-looking 1992 election. The polls now show him charming his way to re-election, ironically helped by the financial-market boom triggered by the 1994

STATE OF ARKANSAS
Executive Department

PROCLAMATION

TO ALL WHOM THESE PRESENTS SHALL COME ... GREETINGS:

WHEREAS, Danny Ray Lasater was convicted in the United States District Court for the Eastern District of Arkansas, Pulaski County, Arkansas, on December 18, 1986, of the crime of Knowingly and Intentionally Conspiring to Possess with the Intent to Distribute, and to Distribute Cocaine and sentenced to 30 months and $50,000 fine; and

WHEREAS, the State Board of Paroles and Community Rehabilitation has recommended that a conditional restoration of State rights, including the right to own and possess firearms, be granted;

NOW THEREFORE, I, BILL CLINTON, by virtue of the power and authority vested in me as Governor of the State of Arkansas, do hereby conditionally restore all rights, privileges and immunities enjoyed prior to conviction, including the right to own and possess firearms; provided, however, that no such restoration is effective until a federal removal of disabilities has been granted.

IN TESTIMONY WHEREOF, I hereunto set my hand and caused to be affixed hereto the Great Seal of State in the Governor's Office, Little Rock, Arkansas this 13th day of November, 1990.

BILL CLINTON
GOVERNOR

W. J. (BILL) McCUEN
SECRETARY OF STATE

Republican victory and now perking into the real economy. And after November, why should he not expect to charm his way past Paula Jones, Kenneth Starr, Travelgate, the FBI files and hassles over Presidential pardons for various factotums and perhaps his wife?

He may very well get away with it, but only at the cost of demeaning his office and further cheapening our politics. At least Johnson, Nixon and Bush were held to account for the loss of credibility. Are we as a nation now going to conclude merely that all politicians are rogues, that there's no point in trying to distinguish shades of gray? Are we going to give up on politics, sending a message to future politicians that character is irrelevant?

* * *

In Sunday's debates, Mr. Clinton will turn his charm on the television audience, while Bob Dole has the task of persuading people that not all politicians are hopeless, that he might actually carry out promises such as cutting tax rates 15%. But what can they say, or what can moderator Jim Lehrer ask, that might actually shed light on character? Mr. Dole, are you really less dishonest than your opponent; Mr. Clinton, in a second term, will you promise to be a good boy? As it happens, two illuminating issues are now in the news: full disclosure and the pardon power.

The Clintons have a long history of stonewalling on release of information. They initially released their tax returns after 1980, for example, and later we found that the 1979 return had some $100,000 in commodity profits. The Rose Law Firm billing records were under subpoena for two years before turning up in the White House family quarters; their discovery led to the recent FDIC report implicating Mrs. Clinton in the Castle Grande scam.

Now the stonewall has been erected around two reports on the failure of the Administration's drug policy, a Defense Department letter and a joint letter from FBI Director Louis Freeh and DEA head Thomas Constantine. The Freeh letter, according to Newsweek, complained of a lack of "any true leadership." The White House refuses to share these letters with the Congress, transparently to conceal politically damaging truths, but ostensibly on grounds of executive privilege, dubious for official memos. Why hide the truth?

* * *

With Susan McDougal going to jail in pursuit of a pardon on her Whitewater conviction in Arkansas, the Administration's mantra is that no consideration is being given to the issue. Since this leaves all options open for the future, perhaps history may be instructive. Mr. Clinton has issued 53 Presidential pardons, the fewest of any President of this century. The Washington Times has established that one of the lucky few is Jack Pakis, a former Hot Springs bookie.

Mr. Pakis was convicted in 1972 in an FBI sting designed to clean up the Arkansas gambling capital, and is now about to turn 76. Perhaps his pardon is unobjectionable, but it is also true that he happens to be a longtime betting buddy of Virginia Kelley, the President's late mother, whose autobiography celebrated the Hot Springs gambling culture. Mr. Pakis's son Michael is also a close friend of Presidential brother Roger.

Last Saturday, also, Senator Paul Coverdell took the Senate floor to ask that the White House "clarify" the Presidential pardons or offers of pardons to drug dealers. The Congressional Record includes his list of names: David Christopher Billmaier, Carl Bruce Jones, Candace Deon Leverenz, Susan Lauranne Prather, Patricia Anne Chapin, Jackie A. Trautman, Johnny Palacios—sentenced in various districts for crimes involving distribution of marijuana, amphetamines, LSD, cocaine and other controlled substances. As of yesterday, the Senator says, "We have been unable to obtain a statement as to the rationale for the pardons."

All of which recalls the notorious gubernatorial pardon of cocaine convict Dan Lasater, Roger's sometime employer, another friend of Mrs. Kelley, a contributor to Clinton political campaigns and recipient of bond contracts from Mr. Clinton's state administration. This document, reproduced alongside, is decidedly curious. Mr. Lasater was convicted in federal court, but pardoned by a state governor, pending "a federal removal of disabilities."

On its face, that is, this is a meaningless document. Its evident purpose is to give Mr. Lasater some bragging rights, as Mr. Lasater has for years said he was convicted of "social distribution" of cocaine, though the law draws no distinction between selling cocaine and giving it away for various favors. Earlier this year, incidentally, an Arkansas judge sentenced Bill McCuen, who countersigned the Lasater "pardon," to 17 years in prison for accepting bribes and a kickback. Not so incidentally, Patsy Thomasson, who ran Mr. Lasater's business while he was in jail, remains in the Clinton White House, though relieved of former duties such as overseeing the drug testing programs for White House personnel.

*   *   *

Based on this history, pick your pardon question. Or make it broader: Mr. President, you've recently accused Independent Counsel Kenneth Starr in effect of trying to suborn perjury. If you think that, why don't you exercise your right to fire him for cause? If not, will you apologize?

These questions, and many related ones, will not go away even if Mr. Clinton is re-elected. Better they should be addressed during the campaign than after. While direct light may be elusive, in watching the debate we should be asking ourselves whether faulty character will once again give us a second term paralyzed by Constitutional crisis.

Editorial Feature

Another Agent Speaks Out

By MICAH MORRISON

THE SHENANDOAH VALLEY, Va.—For more than two years, Congress has been trying to get straight answers from the White House on drug-related issues. After Rep. Frank Wolf (R., Va.) com-

Dennis Sculimbrene

plained in March 1994 that more than 100 White House staffers had failed to get final security clearances and permanent passes, the White House set up its own drug-testing program. This June, news emerged from congressional oversight hearings that the man in charge of issuing passes, White House personnel security chief Craig Livingstone, had his own FBI clearance held up because of past drug use. Today "there are still many unanswered questions about the White House drug-testing program," says Ned Lynch, a spokesman for the House Civil Service Subcommittee, chaired by Rep. John Mica (R., Fla.), which has been probing White House compliance with the Drug-Free Federal Workplace order. "Evidence presented in recent testimony about the drug experiences of White House employees continues to give us great concern," Mr. Lynch adds.

None of this comes as a surprise to retired FBI Special Agent Dennis Sculimbrene, who was the senior agent at the FBI's liaison office in the White House from 1986 to April 1996. His job was to

Justice Department with embezzling funds.

Top White House officials had begun inquiring about the Travel Office staff, their lifestyles and political affiliations, "only a few weeks into the administration," Mr. Sculimbrene says. The officials were then-Deputy White House Counsel William Kennedy, then-Director of Administration Patsy Thomasson and presidential aide Jeff Eller. "I told them I thought Billy Dale was an upright, honest guy and that there was no trouble there," Mr. Sculimbrene recalled. "Those firings were strictly a fabrication."

During the FBI investigation of Mr. Dale, Mr. Sculimbrene says, he made his opinion known to an FBI supervisor. But despite Mr. Sculimbrene's familiarity with the case and the players, he was never interviewed by the FBI. "No one ever came to see me about the case," he says.

Within the FBI, tensions began to mount over the impending trial. "Around August of 1995, I had a shouting match with the supervising agent on the Dale case, David Bowie," Mr. Sculimbrene says. "Bowie told me Dale would have pled guilty long ago 'if it weren't for those rich Republicans giving him money.' I told him that was a wrongheaded remark and that I should have been interviewed for the investigation. Bowie told me I had nothing relevant to say, and then threatened me with an [FBI] Office of Professional Responsibility investigation. We were really going at it."

Shortly after that encounter, Mr. Sculimbrene says, he was told by the FBI that he had to take a random drug test. "I'd never had one before, and I'd never heard of anyone in my age group having to take a drug test—I was 51 at the time. I thought that was quite a coincidence after my argument with Bowie."

In what Mr. Sculimbrene describes as another "coincidence," the possibility of a prestigious job lofted his way shortly before his testimony at the Dale trial. The incident raises questions about the nature and timing of an offer that could be construed as an attempt to buy his silence. Mr. Sculimbrene says that he was approached by a mid-level member of the presidential personnel office from Arkansas and encouraged to apply for a job as inspector general at the Department of Veterans' Affairs. "The official told me he had talked to Patsy [Thomasson] about the offer," Mr. Sculimbrene says. Ms. Thomasson, a Clinton intimate and former associate of Arkansas cocaine convict Dan Lasater, ran the personnel office. "After I testified at the Dale trial," Mr. Sculimbrene recalls, "I ran into the official again. He told me the job was out of the question, now that I had testified."

Mr. Sculimbrene had been subpoenaed as a defense witness at the Dale trial; he testified in October 1995. On Nov. 16, after deliberating less than two hours, a jury acquitted Mr. Dale of all charges. But Mr. Sculimbrene's troubles were just beginning.

In February 1996, he was notified that the FBI's Office of Professional Responsibility was investigating him for alleged misuse of a government parking pass. "I thought it was some sort of sick joke," Mr. Sculimbrene says. Within a few weeks, he was interviewed by OPR investigators and presented with a new notice of more serious charges: An anonymous letter had been received charging him with making racist comments, speaking to the media and "time and attendance fraud." Mr. Sculimbrene says the FBI rank and file is demoralized by the FBI leadership and its misuse of such OPR investigations. "The OPR process causes terrible injury and is a burning issue for agents," Mr. Sculimbrene says. "It's being used as a personal management tool to control agents. Sometimes a case can hang over an agent for years, causing terrible stress."

Gary Aldrich

Mr. Sculimbrene eventually was cleared in the OPR probe. But behind the scenes, a dramatic clash was shaping up, one that eventually would lead to Mr. Sculimbrene's resignation. In January, Mr. Sculimbrene's former partner, Gary Aldrich, had submitted the manuscript of his book to the FBI for review. The FBI general counsel, Howard Shapiro, promptly shipped a copy to the White House, it was revealed at House oversight hearings this summer. Mr. Sculimbrene says that he was also notified to expect a visit from Mr. Shapiro, who in the end sent two agents to question him about Mr. Aldrich and the FBI's White House liaison office. "In January, I imagine right after learning of the manuscript, Director [Louis] Freeh ordered the liaison office shut down immediately. Cooler heads prevailed at the time, but not for long, as it turned out."

Mr. Sculimbrene says that before the agents visited him at Mr. Shapiro's direction, "I had no idea that Gary was writing a book about the White House. But after reading it, I can tell you it is largely true." A scathing critique of White House mores, "Unlimited Access: An FBI Agent Inside the Clinton White House," became No. 1 on the bestseller lists and created a firestorm when it was published in June. It also probably spelled the end of Mr. Sculimbrene at the FBI.

In April, he was relieved of his responsibilities at the White House. His White House pass was revoked in May, his work assignments were taken away, and he was ordered to undergo a fitness-for-duty exam, prior to reassignment to street duty. Mr. Sculimbrene filed an administrative complaint with the FBI alleging he had been denied "reasonable accommodation" for his disability in his job transfer and new duty assignments. It later emerged in congressional oversight hearings that at the same time, Mr. Livingstone, still at the White House, had ordered *Mr. Sculimbrene's* FBI background file, saying it was required for a reinvestigation of the agent.

In July, after the Aldrich book appeared and Mr. Sculimbrene testified before House and Senate committee investigators, FBI Counsel Shapiro sent two agents to Mr. Sculimbrene's home to question him about notes he had taken in a 1993 interview with then-White House Counsel Bernard Nussbaum that suggested that Mr. Livingstone—suddenly famous in the wake of Filegate revelations—had been hired at Hillary Clinton's urging. "I viewed that visit as highly improper," Mr. Sculimbrene says. "Mr. Shapiro should have been taking no action in the matter, as it had been turned over to the independent counsel."

In late July, expecting to resume duties after medical exams, Mr. Sculimbrene says he was "stunned" to learn he had been ordered to go to Chicago for a psychiatric examination. "This seemed to confirm all I had learned from White House sources about ongoing efforts to discredit me," he says. In August, Mr. Sculimbrene quit the FBI. A few weeks later, the FBI liaison office at the White House was shut down. Agents conducting background investigations now work out of an FBI field office in Washington.

"That's a damn shame," Mr. Sculimbrene says. "The public is not well served by such a move. It's one thing to remove me; it's another to shut down the whole office."

Mr. Morrison is a Journal editorial page writer.

An Emerging Nation

"Who Is Mochtar Riady?" a Journal editorial asked as early as March 1996 (see Volume II). In the last month of the presidential campaign, the Indonesian billionaire and his Lippo Group became household words. A entirely new front of controversy erupted—Indogate, or the controversy over illegal foreign campaign contributions.

In a page-one story on October 8, 1996, Wall Street Journal reporters Glenn Simpson and Jill Abramson detailed the funneling of campaign cash from various entities—many of them foreign and legally barred from making political contributions—to the Clinton campaign. The Simpson-Abramson story traced the web of Arkansas insiders linked to Lippo interests.

The original Journal editorial had explored the long association of Mr. Riady, his son James and the Lippo Group with various Arkansans, in particular former Associate Attorney General Webster Hubbell, who resigned from the Justice Department in 1994. While negotiating a plea bargain with the Whitewater independent counsel, Mr. Hubbell received a fee—later reported to be about $100,000—from the Lippo Group for undisclosed services. In his plea bargain with Mr. Starr, Mr. Hubbell admitted to mail fraud and tax evasion and agreed to cooperate in exchange for a recommendation for a reduced sentence. Yet when the time for sentencing came, Mr. Starr showed what he thought of Mr. Hubbell's cooperation; there was no recommendation for leniency.

The suspicion of Hubbell "hush money" proved to be only the tip of the Lippo iceberg. At the center of the rapidly growing controversy was a former high-ranking Lippo employee named John Huang, who left Lippo to join the Commerce Department in 1994. In January 1996, Mr. Huang moved to the Democratic National Committee as vice chairman of the finance committee, where he raised millions for the Clintons.

"Most Asian businessmen, working there and in the U.S., strive to perform honestly and ethically," the Journal noted as the new scandal grew. "But the Riady and Lippo stories that have appeared this week suggest very strongly that some of the least attractive mores of Asian commercial transactions are now being imported into the American political system via dummied up contributions to a Presidential campaign."

While election skirmishes and Indogate dominated the news, the Journal continued to track other developments as well, including strange gaps in the White House logs showing who was looking at sensitive FBI files. In Washington, House Oversight Committee Chairman William Clinger closed the books on his investigation into the Travel Office and FBI files affairs with a blistering report on White House conduct and a recommendation that seven Clinton aides be investigated for possible perjury or obstruction of justice. In an exclusive prison interview with Journal writer Micah Morrison, Arkansas insider David Hale predicted that Hillary Clinton would be indicted on multiple obstruction and perjury counts related to Whitewater.

REVIEW & OUTLOOK

Who Is Mochtar Riady--II?

With just 27 days remaining in the election, people in politics now have to come to terms with the financial relationship between Bill Clinton and the billionaire Riady family, which is to say between the corruption-prone provinces of Arkansas and Indonesia. The relationship was the subject of a front-page article Tuesday in this paper by Glenn R. Simpson and Jill Abramson, a follow-up story yesterday and a column Monday by William Safire in the New York Times. We might add that the first "Who Is Mochtar Riady?" appeared here March 1.

Before getting into the details of the Clinton-Mochtar connection, we would like to make a few general points. Just in the past week, yet another story ran in a major newspaper about how "Whitewater" was so complex and sprawling that few people "cared" and so none of the cloudy ethical water that's poured through the White House sluice gates since January 1993 matters. But given the stakes, there comes a point at which refusing to incorporate these events into the November decision—pro or con—approaches irresponsibility. At a minimum, it somehow seems to us it matters whether America or Indonesia sets the tone for the world's commercial and political practices.

The Tuesday account by Mr. Simpson and Ms. Abramson of the Journal was about how Asian commercial interests contributed millions of dollars to the Clinton re-election effort. And central to this campaign funding effort has been the Lippo Group of Indonesia that is controlled by Mochtar Riady. Now, the story made quite clear that these contributions do not obviously violate U.S. campaign finance laws against direct foreign contributions; they exploit loopholes. Yet we should take deep pause at the manner of their solicitation, the role of U.S. Commerce Secretary Ron Brown, the extended family of Arkansas cronies who swim as pilot fish around both Messrs. Clinton and Riady, and the commercial benefits coincidentally realized by Lippo.

Lippo is a huge Asian conglomerate; Mr. Riady is one of the handful of entrepreneurs who've become billionaires under Indonesia's Suharto regime. Lippo's Little Rock connections date back to 1984; during the years of the Clinton governorship it entered into a partnership with Arkansas financier Jackson Stephens; Lippo put $16 million into the stock of Worthen Bank and made James Riady, Mochtar's son, a bank director.

Mochtar Riady

The Riadys have since sold out of Worthen, as later did the Stephens family. But Lippo retains an Arkansas presence, not least through Joe Giroir, former managing partner of the Rose Law Firm. He acts as a rainmaker for Lippo, and himself. The Journal story reported: "One of Mr. Giroir's biggest successes to date has been a $1 billion deal between Entergy, which is based in New Orleans, and Lippo to build a power plant in China. The transaction was heavily promoted by the late Commerce Secretary Brown on a 1994 trade trip to China."

Mr. Brown's Commerce Department was also home to John Huang, now vice chairman of the DNC finance committee and funnel for virtually all those millions in Asian contributions. To pursue investments with U.S. companies, the Lippo group also hired a former roommate of Bill Clinton's, Paul Berry, who worked through the Arkansas International Development Corp. set up by Mr. Giroir. And Lippo was also generous with Webster Hubbell, paying him for unspecified legal work on his trip from the Justice Department to federal prison. The amount was never revealed in Mr. Hubbell's depositions, but was reported by Mr.

Safire as $250,000.

The Indonesian connection also appeared in the recent Tucker-McDougal trial as well. One of the first witnesses was Dwight Harlan, whom the prosecution flew back from Indonesia, where he works for a Giroir entity. Mr. Harlan testified that Tucker had made him the figurehead president of the Castle Sewer & Water utility, one of the central scams in Mr. Starr's successful case against Tucker and the McDougals. Mr. Harlan identified mortgages, checks and deeds from Castle transactions.

Another interesting name suddenly surfacing is Melinda Yee, who raised funds for the Democrats in 1992, joined Mr. Brown at Commerce, and is described by a former Administration official as having "a very close relationship with James Riady," the son. Ms. Yee set up a luncheon during a Clinton visit to Indonesia in 1994 for some

James Riady

Indonesian businessmen at James Riady's home with Commerce officials Jeffrey Garten and David Rothkopf. Currently, Ms. Yee is employed by Mayor Willie Brown in San Francisco, where the realities are at least made manifest without apology: She handles *both* fund raising and Asian trade matters.

Needless to say, a resume such as Ms. Yee's attracts our attention these days, so we looked further. Reading the Associated Press, Washington Post and Washington Times, we discover Melinda Yee in the middle of the criminal investigation of Ron Brown before his death. The Brown independent counsel was looking into allegations that a Tulsa gas company, Dynamic Energy, put Mr. Brown's son Michael on its board and provided a $60,000 Washington golf membership. And in early 1994 (the year Ms. Yee was setting up Riady-Clintonite lunches in Indonesia), Dynamic put her mother Helen on its board too. The AP sued successfully for release of court documents in the lawsuit involving Dynamic principals, and the documents allege that the company hired Michael Brown "to gain influence with the Department of Commerce."

In Lippo's Hong Kong boardroom hangs a portrait of Mochtar Riady with Bill and Hillary. The Journal's Tuesday story reported the unveiling of a Clinton bust just last year at the National Gallery, given in honor of Mochtar Riady. Among the attendees: Lippo rainmaker and former Rose partner Joe Giroir. White House aides kept Mr. Clinton away from the event to avoid an explicit Riady connection. On his visit to Indonesia, however, the President did attend a reception with Mr. Riady, allowing him "face time" to parade his relationship with the President of the United States before his fellow Indonesian influentials.

*　*　*

Throughout the entire history of all these stories about the political behavior of Bill Clinton and his circle, the establishment consensus has been that nothing will suffice as proof short of Abscam-type videotapes. But proof of what? Our central point, since the earliest editorials, has never been about proving crimes in court but about standards of political conduct, about "Arkansas mores" imported into the national government. Most Asian businessmen, working there and in the U.S., strive to perform honestly and ethically. But the Riady and Lippo stories that have appeared this week suggest very strongly that some of the least attractive mores of Asian commercial transactions are now being imported into the American political system via dummied-up political contributions to a Presidential campaign.

So sure, David Kendall and Mark Fabiani can no doubt explain in detail why any cash flowing out of Asia and into the Clinton coffers is all perfectly legal. Maybe, but this a campaign that is truly "building a bridge," and the question is whether the American political system is about to cross over it and into the swamp on the other side.

Editorial Feature

Who'll Look Out for the Little Guy?

By Ted Van Dyk

I first cast a vote for a Democratic presidential candidate in 1940 when, at age six, I was lifted by my father in a voting booth in the

Bellingham, Wash., high school library to cast his vote for him. My dad, an unschooled and unskilled immigrant sawmill worker, worshipped Franklin Roosevelt as a leader "for the little guy." A few years later I was passing out campaign literature for President Truman. Since I turned 21 I have cast my vote for every Democratic presidential nominee and have worked for or advised most of them.

Bob Dole

I fully expect to vote Democratic again in 2000, particularly if my party's candidate is Al Gore or one of several other leaders I respect for their integrity and seriousness. But this Nov. 5 I will vote for Bob Dole. I think he can be trusted to look after the well being of all Americans—including "the little guy"—while President Clinton, regrettably, cannot. In voting for Mr. Dole I will be supporting the best interests of my country and the traditions of my party.

I have known Bill Clinton since I was policy director of the McGovern campaign, which he served as a Texas coordinator. He was introduced to the campaign by his Oxford classmate Rick Stearns, a studious and able man who is now a federal judge in

against Mr. Dole. He has frightened senior citizens into believing that Mr. Dole and Republicans would take away benefits earned over a lifetime, when in fact the benefits would increase in real terms even under the GOP plan. By resting his campaign on this lie, Mr. Clinton has diminished the possibility of solving the problem next year should he be re-elected.

The president says he is protecting "Medicare, Medicaid, education and the environment." In fact, by evading the need for entitlement reform, he is endangering the entitlement programs and gutting the resources available for education, the environment and everything else in the budget.

Mr. Dole, in contrast with Mr. Clinton, embodies his generation's belief that political leadership entails recognizing the country's problems, dealing with them truthfully and attempting to rally Americans behind their solution. The Dole generation—and particularly Democrats of that generation—believed in an agenda-driven politics, not a politics-driven agenda.

That sort of approach is precisely what the country needs. If the presidency continues to be occupied by a politician who is driven by expediency and self-interest and holds the truth in a high disregard, our national character and our capacity to govern ourselves will continue shamefully to deteriorate.

Mr. Dole's former Senate colleagues know him as an honorable, serious, patriotic man who keeps his word and as a champion of the underdog. Like Hubert Humphrey, George McGovern, the Kennedys and others, Mr. Dole has fought the powerful on behalf of the powerless. In the privacy of their voting booths, I suspect a majority of present and former Democratic senators will cast their votes for Mr. Dole on Nov. 5. As I cast my vote, I will have very much in mind my father, who lifted me in the voting booth in 1940. He worked a lifetime with his hands, had little, asked for nothing and loved America. In voting for Bob Dole I will vote for "the little guy"—for the poor, minorities and ordinary people who deserve leadership worthy of them

Mr. Van Dyk has been active in Democratic national politics for 35 years. He advised Paul Tsongas in 1992.

REVIEW & OUTLOOK

The Six-Month Gap

One of the most explosive revelations in the Watergate scandal came when it was learned that a mysterious 18½-minute gap had appeared in a tape of President Nixon's first White House meeting on the break-in at Democratic headquarters. Presidential secretary Rose Mary Woods claimed she had accidentally caused the erasure, but Nixon's Watergate counsel Fred Buzhardt quickly admitted he could see no way the gap was accidental and that Ms. Woods "has no defense."

It has now been learned by the Senate Judiciary Committee that there is a six-month gap in the log showing who in the Clinton White House checked out sensitive FBI files from then security chief Craig Livingstone's office. Mr. Livingstone claims the log apparently wasn't kept for those months, but his assistant, Mari Anderson, has given a deposition to the Judiciary Committee in which she maintains that she indeed kept the log from March to September 1994 and that the pages are missing (excerpts appear on page 86). The question raised by the missing logs is, who wanted to see the 900 confidential background files of former Reagan and Bush staffers that the White House improperly obtained from the FBI? But no logs, no answer—no problem.

When Senate Judiciary Chairman Orrin Hatch scheduled a televised hearing for last Thursday to hear Ms. Anderson's testimony, the White House had Democratic Senators threaten to block Senate adjournment unless the hearing was delayed until after the election.

With Senators eager to leave town and campaign, Chairman Hatch threw in the towel and instead released Ms. Anderson's deposition.

Mari Anderson, who worked in the White House until September 1994, is no disgruntled former employee. She says she worked well with Mr. Livingstone. But she rejects Mr. Livingstone's contention that she suffered from "burnout" and may not have kept the logs current. "There are pages that are not there," she says.

Ms. Anderson also contradicted Mr. Livingstone's claim that the collection of the 900 files was "a bureaucratic snafu" created by an outdated Secret Service list that his office used to order background files. Ms. Anderson told investigators that "everyone in the office knew" that they were obtaining FBI files on "people who were no longer working there." She herself pointed out to Mr. Livingstone that the list included such names as former Secretary of State James Baker and Bush press secretary Marlin Fitzwater. She struck out their names with a black magic marker, and was surprised to learn that background files on both men were later obtained by Anthony Marceca, Mr. Livingstone's investigator.

Craig Livingstone

Another background file given to the White House by the FBI was that of Billy Dale, the fired director of the White House Travel Office. Ms. Anderson reveals that an attempt to get the files of Mr. Dale and other Travel Office employees was made at the time of their firings. She recalls hearing Mr. Livingstone discuss the files with someone on the phone and then asking to have them brought to him. The files had been shipped out of the White House, but Mr. Marceca requested Mr. Dale's file seven months later. A few months after that, Mr. Dale was indicted for embezzling Travel Office funds. A jury acquitted him in two hours.

White House spokesman Mark Fabiani dismisses Ms. Anderson's testimony by repeating his mantra that "there is absolutely no evidence that these files were used improperly." Well, until Ms. Anderson's deposition, it was also the White House's contention that there was no evidence the files were *obtained* improperly on purpose. Given Mr. Livingstone's record of playing partisan hardball and that the roguish Mr. Marceca has admitted misusing material from his own FBI file, we have doubts that the dossiers on GOP appointees stayed unread and unused during their entire 30-month stay at the White House.

The Media Research Center reports that the three major networks have done a total of one story on Ms. Anderson or the six-month gap. But they have aired 11 stories on Newt Gingrich's ethics matters since Sept. 26. Dan Thomasson, vice president for news at Scripps Howard Newspapers, wrote this week that there is "a direct parallel" between the FBI file scandal and Richard Nixon's enemies list. "The shenanigans of 24 years ago were wrong and the press was right to challenge them," he says. "The scandalous behavior of the Clintons is no exception. Hiding behind executive privilege and persisting in a steady stream of shameless and obvious fabrications should bring down the wrath of us all."

Any White House is expected to be meticulous about its official record-keeping. It's one thing for this White House to lose such sensitive logs, not care and refuse to find them. But why should the rest of us accept this?

Q: Okay.

A: But I do remember that the files were discussed, and Craig was talking on the phone, and he asked—I can't remember if it was me or Lisa. I believe it was me, to go and pull these files, and I gave them to Craig. That's all I remember.

Q: So you don't know who he was talking to on the telephone?

A: I have no recollection of who he was talking to on the phone. . .

* * *

Q: Do you know why individuals such as James Baker or Marlin Fitzwater's files would have been actually ordered from the FBI?

Q: First of all, do you have an understanding of whether—while you were there at the office, do you have an understanding whether James Baker's file was requested?

> *"Everybody in the office knew that we had gotten background investigations of people who were no longer working there."*

A: Not to my knowledge. I never saw it.

Q: Well, in fact, it was, and it seemed a little bit odd that Mr. Marceca would not have recognized those two individuals as examples.

A: Two?

Q: James Baker and Marlin Fitzwater.

A: Oh. Was Marlin Fitzwater's requested?

Q: Yes.

A: Oh.

Q: Do you have any explanation for why Mr. Marceca after having gone through a check of who appeared to be turned and—

A: I cannot speak for Tony. I don't know why. . . .

Q: Do you recall if James Baker and Marlin Fitzwater that you saw and marked out?

A: Yes; I have a specific memory of marking out James Baker and Marlin Fitzwater, because there was a big joke that those were the only two names that I could remember. And I went through and did the same thing with the Bushes and the Quayles, and we then handed the list over to Tony and said okay, go through it, and if there are any more names that you'd recognize that are Bush appointees, let's go ahead and mark them and then, make another request of Secret

Service to take these people off the lists. And then, after we do that, we will request one later.

*　*　*

Q: So what happened then?

A: We got a new list.

Q: Did you review that new list to see if those names were on it?

A: I didn't pick that one up. That list, I don't think I picked up. I don't remember going back and reviewing it.

Q: Do you have any knowledge if, indeed, the names that you just mentioned—Fitzwater, Baker, the Quayles, the Bushes—were not on this, we'll call it the third Secret Service list that was requested?

A: I believe that there was some mention that they were not on the list any more.

Q: Mention by whom?

A: Either Craig or Tony; I'm not 100—I can't remember. But it was someone in the office mentioned well, at least they're not on this list. And I just went on assuming that the list had been cleaned up to the best of our ability. . . .

Q: Okay, what significance did you attach to the fact that the people that you had requested FBI background files on were actually no longer with the White House?

A: From my understanding, I really didn't attach that big a deal to them, because I didn't, one, know who these people were. I just assumed that a majority of them were just people who had maybe stayed over a day, a month or what not, and then, they had departed the White House after saying okay, hi, new personnel; this is the way it's been done; okay, now that I've trained you, bye. And so I just— . . .

Q: Now, when you learned that somebody had left, what would happen to their FBI background file that was, I guess, currently in Room 84?

A: It was currently contained in the vault, and what we had said was that—pardon me; or what I should say we had established was that we created a drawer that all people who had been—

Q: When you say we, who was aware at that point?

A: The office, just the office in general. Everybody in the office knew that we had gotten background investigations of people who were no longer working there. And in some cases, we didn't know when they left. And in some cases, it was not very clear as to when

Hale's offered plea bargain. The new Independent Counsel Kenneth Starr then takes Mr. Hale's testimony and obtains convictions of the governor of Arkansas and the business partners of the President and Mrs. Clinton.

It's about hastening to appoint an Arkansas crony named Webster Hubbell to the Justice Department's "number three" job, where he back-channels to the Oval Office, forcing the Attorney General to assert publicly that she is in full charge of her department. The subpoenaed Rose Firm billing records lie quietly in the associate attorney general's home.

Article II section three is about this Justice Department's senior tier telling the Tyson Independent Counsel Donald Smaltz that he may not expand his inquiry; on presentation, three federal judges tell the counsel that he may expand. He convicts Sun-Diamond Growers of wrongfully influencing the Agriculture Secretary.

It's about this Justice Department stomping Billy Dale. After the White House fires the Travel Office so that it can hire crony Harry Thomason's replacement workers, Justice brings a federal prosecution of Billy Dale, which a jury throws out in two hours. Travelgate is case history for Article II, section three.

So is the Arthur Coia story. Arthur Coia, the head of the laborers union, somehow got the Justice Department's effort to throw him out transformed into a decree to let *him* clean up his union's Mafia ties, even as Mr. Coia hobnobs with the fellow in charge of faithfully executing the nation's laws. Meanwhile the Coia union makes a $1.1 million campaign contribution from the union to the Democrats in 1994 and gets the First Lady to address its Florida convention.

Sometime soon we may get a short commentary on Article II, section three from federal Judge Royce Lamberth. It fell to Judge Lamberth to experience one of the earliest legal stonewalls when the White House refused to divulge the names of Mrs. Clinton's health care task force, offering reasons that Judge Lamberth ultimately called "preposterous."

Judge Stanley Sporkin, while recently dismissing as premature a congressional lawsuit to overturn the Administration's refusal to comply with the ballistic missile act it just signed into law, said in his opinion that the court "will not condone the executive branch defying the explicit laws enacted by Congress."

In the space below we discuss the Lippo affair, which hasn't yet reached, like all else on the vulgar C-word list, the status of "nobody cares." The affair's central character in the U.S. is John Huang, who in the early 1990s was working in Los Angeles for Lippo, whose L.A. bank ran into money laundering problems with the FDIC. In July 1994 Lippo sent Mr. Huang to work in Ron Brown's Commerce Department and that December the FDIC settled with the Lippo bank, which got to admit no wrongdoing. The records are sealed.

And, yes, Article II, section three is about the proper use of the Presidential pardon, about the miraculous apparition of Hillary's subpoenaed billing records, about high Treasury appointees providing "heads-up" briefings to the White House on possible federal criminal referrals involving Whitewater.

At the risk of eliciting censure from the gentlemen and gentleladies now keeping campaign standards strong and high in our politics, we wish to ask: Has Bill Clinton taken care that the laws of this country are faithfully executed? And if he and his milieu are given a second term, will the law apply equally to all? If asked about any or all of these incidents, we imagine the President would have something to say. But pardon us for suggesting that any responsible person should think to ask; it might get too close to the matter of character.

REVIEW & OUTLOOK

The Indonesian Connection

The Clinton Presidency has been marked by amazing revelations, such as $100,000 commodity profits and subpoenaed billing records showing up in the White House family quarters. The latest stunner is that the fellow the President has out soliciting all Asia for political contributions left a Los Angeles bank under the cloud of violations of the Bank Secrecy Act, the centerpiece of the regulatory effort against using banks to launder drug money.

John Huang

This of course does not necessarily mean that John Huang or Lippo Bank were actually involved in drugs or other illicit transactions. The bank's attorney, Gordon M. Bava, has said, "Those allegations are totally, completely false." He said, "The bank was never accused of or involved in any money-laundering activities. Nor were any of its officers, directors or employees. If there were that kind of allegation made, it would most likely have been based on deficiencies in record-keeping—that is, filing reports with the Treasury Department." He says, however, that he is forbidden by law to discuss the details of the cease-and-desist agreement under which the bank agreed to follow the Bank Secrecy Act.

The agreement specified compliance with regulations to keep track of large cash transactions as well as bank checks, cashiers' checks, money orders and travelers checks. The bank also agreed to report to regulators any "known or suspected criminal activity." Cease and desist means there had been violations, prior to its signature of agreement in December 1994. Since Mr. Huang left as head of Lippo in the U.S. and vice chairman of the bank in July, it's safe to assume the violations took place on his watch. Congressional investigators ought to inquire, indeed, whether his exit got a little shove from the FDIC.

While at it, investigators ought to ask a few more questions, like, who owns this bank anyway? It's listed as an "affiliate" of the Lippo Group, an Indonesian conglomerate owned by billionaire Mochtar Riady. But after the Bank of Credit & Commerce International scandal, foreign-owned banks are supervised by the Federal Reserve, though somehow Lippo is supervised by the FDIC. The FDIC also disciplined the bank for "hazardous lending" in 1990. There is also the issue of how the bank got a charter in the first place.

In any event, after leaving Lippo, Mr. Huang was hired by Ron Brown at the Commerce Department, and went from there to fundraising tasks at the Democratic National Committee. In one case, the DNC returned a $250,000 check from a Korean company after it was revealed by the Los Angeles Times as an illegal payment by a foreign entity. Mr. Huang was also responsible for the $450,000 in contributions from Arief Wiriadinata and his wife; the DNC says this is kosher because Mr. Wiriadinata holds a green card, and his wife is the daughter of a wealthy Lippo executive who recently died. In all, Mr. Huang has raised $4 million to $5 million.

Lippo also paid well for the legal advice of Webster Hubbell, who received fees, at best report $250,000, after his disgrace at the Justice Department and before starting his jail term. Craig Livingstone, the disgraced former White House Security chief, has refused to reveal contributors to his legal defense fund, despite the obvious question of whether it consists of "offshore" money.

The issue with Mr. Huang's overseas fund-raising is the same issue he faced with the Bank Secrecy Act. We make banks report on large cash transactions so that the money can be traced, because we know that large sums are moving around the world illicitly, from drug traffic in particular. We should be careful about foreign political money for precisely the same reason. Whose money is this, really? It's somehow typical of this Administration that the seriousness of the question goes unrecognized.

REVIEW & OUTLOOK

Just Say So What

"Let me remind you that my family has suffered from drug abuse. I know what it's like to see somebody you love nearly lose their lives. And I hate drugs, Senator." So, in the first debate, President Clinton poured out his heart as he raged on against drugs. In fact, Bill Clinton's retreat in the drug war is among the worst transgressions for which his Administration should be called to account.

We'll review the policy record in a moment. But first consider just what we've learned in recent weeks about the Clinton Administration's attitudes toward drugs:

• Former FBI agent Gary Aldrich writes a best-seller in which he details how the White House sloughed off FBI concerns that senior members of the White House staff might still be using drugs. The thrust of his observations is confirmed by his FBI partner Dennis Sculimbrene.

• Hiding behind claims of executive privilege, the White House refuses to release a 1995 memo from the heads of the FBI and the DEA slamming his drug policy.

• Senator Paul Coverdell takes to the Senate floor to name seven drug dealers who have received pardons or offers of pardons from President Clinton.

• John Huang, in charge of collecting Asian contributions for the Democratic campaign, once headed a Los Angeles bank that fell under the eye of the enforcers of the Bank Secrecy Act, one of whose main aims is to keep drug-money launderers from using U.S. banks.

As for pure policy, the Administration's catalog of sins is astonishing in scope. Within weeks of taking office, the White House slashed the staff of the Drug Czar's office to 25 from 147. Soon thereafter, the Drug Enforcement Agency lost 227 agents. Other law-enforcement agencies—Customs, Coast Guard, FBI, Defense—also lost staff and resources. The Surgeon-General talked up legalization while the President himself kept quiet on the subject of drugs. Representative

Barry McCaffrey

Charles Rangel went so far as to say on CNN in 1994: "I've been in Congress over two decades and I've never, never, never found any Administration that's been so silent on this great challenge to the American people." Congressman Rangel is talking about what we'd call the moral failure of the President's drug policy, which by now is well known.

Thanks to a GAO report out this spring, we've also learned more in recent months about the Administration's policy on interdiction— seizing or otherwise disrupting drug shipments before they reach our borders. Virtually all cocaine and heroin and 75% of marijuana is imported. While we can't realistically hope to shut the doors against all illegal drugs, experience from the 1980s and early '90s proves we can keep out enough to drive up the price, which is an important factor in reducing demand.

Yet in 1993, the Administration announced a "controlled shift" away from interdiction. For example, as commander of the Southern Command, General Barry McCaffrey, now the President's tough-talking Drug Czar, downgraded drug interdiction to his number three priority from number one. The Caribbean, under jurisdiction of the neighboring Atlantic Command, suffered a particularly sharp cutback. According to the GAO, funding for interdiction there has fallen by more than 40% on Mr. Clinton's watch. Surveillance is way back; today there are far fewer ships in the region, far fewer flyovers and far fewer radar stations.

As a result, there are also far more drug dealers.

Ever alert to an opening into their main market, the drug kingpins have found one in Puerto Rico. A shipment of cocaine typically is air-

special White House counsel; William Kennedy, a former White House lawyer and law partner of Hillary Clinton's; and security operatives Craig Livingstone and Anthony Marceca. Mrs. Clinton was not named in the letter to Mr. Starr, but Rep. Clinger's committee concluded she played a major role in the Travel Office events despite her sworn denials. It found a series of White House aides became part of the effort to shield her from scrutiny. To wit:

• The House committee located the origins of the Travel Office firings in an extensive set of internal memos that showed the firings were instigated by Harry Thomason to take over the office and steer business to an aviation firm he co-owned. Mr. Thomason has denied any such intent.

• White House Counsel Bernard Nussbaum had possession of a notebook kept by the late Vincent Foster detailing the events leading up to the Travel Office firings, but withheld it from law enforcement officials for nearly a year. A Justice Department official called the White House's lack of cooperation and candor on the notebook "unprecedented."

In the FBI file scandal, a 1993 background report indicates Mr. Nussbaum told an FBI agent that Mrs. Clinton was responsible for hiring former bar bouncer Craig Livingstone as White House security chief. Mr. Nussbaum denies saying that, though his deputy Mr. Kennedy made the same statement to another FBI agent.

• The Oversight Committee concluded that in her position as a White House counsel, Jane Sherburne impeded numerous investigations of the Travel Office and FBI files. A memo she wrote directed that taxpayer-paid White House lawyers "monitor" the cooperation of convicted Justice Department official Webb Hubbell with prosecutors. On the FBI files, Ms. Sherburne was improperly told by the FBI that it had the memo quoting Mr. Nussbaum that Mrs. Clinton had sponsored Craig Livingstone. She promptly notified both White House officials and defense lawyers for Mr. Livingstone and others of the contents of a private FBI background file, according to the committee.

• Former chief of staff Mack McLarty told investigators he had only one meeting with Mrs. Clinton on the Travel Office firings. After his handwritten notes surfaced indicating there had been "HRC pressure" for the firings, he acknowledged a second meeting had taken place.

• William Kennedy has denied telling four FBI agents that the bureau should become involved in the Travel Office firings because "the highest levels" of the White House were interested. The committee notes that his denials "are in direct conflict with the testimony of the four FBI agents."

• Craig Livingstone and Anthony Marceca contradicted each other's testimony on how they came to order 900 sensitive FBI files on Republican appointees. Mari Anderson, Mr. Livingstone's chief assistant, has further testified that "everyone in the office knew that we had gotten background investigations of people who were no longer working there." Both Messrs. Livingstone and Marceca have claimed the files were ordered because of an "innocent bureaucratic snafu."

Some of this conduct may lead to grand jury indictments. More Congressional probes are inevitable, unless the Clinton campaign gets its November wish. The Boston Globe reported last week that a "senior strategist" for the Clinton campaign says it is "prepared to go all-out to recapture the House." If Democrats retake control, the strategist told the Globe, "It would put a stop to all those investigations." If nothing else bothers voters, they might ponder the prospect of blindfolded Democratic committee chairmen eschewing any Congressional oversight of a second Clinton term.

Editorial Feature

Hale Predicts Hillary Indictment

By MICAH MORRISON

TEXARKANA, Tex.—Susan McDougal, who is refusing to testify before a Whitewater grand jury, has been dominating the national media with jailhouse interviews from the Faulkner County jail, in Conway, Ark., some 200 miles northeast of the Federal Prison Camp here. She's appeared in widely circulated pictures being led off to jail in leg irons, has been repeatedly interviewed by Arkansas radio and television stations, was on National Public Radio and MSNBC-TV last week, and has done star turns on national television whacking softball questions from Larry King and Bryant Gumbel.

David Hale

No one has stopped off in Texarkana, though, to talk to David Hale, the prisoner the Arkansas jury believed when it convicted Ms. McDougal, her husband, Jim, and former Arkansas Gov. Jim Guy Tucker of 24 fraud and conspiracy charges for the looting of Madison Guaranty Savings & Loan and Mr. Hale's government-backed lending company, Capital Management Services. For his own confessed role in defrauding the government, Mr. Hale is serving 28 months in this federal prison.

Unlike Mr. Hale and her husband, Ms. McDougal never took the stand when she was convicted and sentenced to two years in prison.

Another judge tacked on up to 18 months for contempt when she refused to answer questions about whether, as Mr. Hale had testified, President Clinton knew of bogus Madison loans and whether he'd lied in his trial testimony. Since then, Ms. McDougal and her attorney, old Arkansas hand Bobby McDaniel, have taken to the airwaves in what is widely viewed as a campaign for a pardon. President Clinton has responded by pointedly refusing to rule out pardons for figures in the Whitewater affair.

In his first prison interview, Mr. Hale, looking tanned and surprisingly fit, offers some eye-popping views: "Hillary Clinton is going to be indicted after the election," he says. "It's a certainty." However, she immediately will be pardoned by her husband, Mr. Hale predicts, as will Mr. Tucker. But Susan McDougal is out of luck—the White House is stringing her along until after the election, with the help of Mr. McDaniel, Mr. Hale says, and will abandon her afterward.

Can Mr. Hale, a convicted felon at the heart of the Whitewater inquiry, be believed? Special counsels Robert Fiske and Kenneth Starr believed him, because his tale unfolded into a skein of confirming testimony. It squares, for example, with the testimony of Resolution Trust Corp. investigator Jean Lewis before congressional committees. On the basis of this evidence, an Arkansas grand jury indicted and an Arkansas trial jury convicted the state's governor and the president's former Whitewater partners. Mr. Hale has spent a lifetime navigating the murky terrain of Arkansas politics, and he knows the principals on both sides of the investigation.

Mr. Starr's office refuses comment on Mr. Hale's predictions, and of course prosecutors are bound to silence by federal rule 6(e) covering grand jury testimony. But in more than two years as a cooperating witness, inmate Hale spent literally hundreds of hours with federal investigators. He knows more about their evidence than anyone not bound to silence. Certainly his views on Mrs. Clinton are as relevant as Susan McDougal's vilification of Mr. Starr.

"I can tell you that Hillary is going to be indicted on 13 to 18 counts involving obstruction of justice, lying to federal investigators, and misleading federal regulators," Mr. Hale says. "I believe some of the charges will relate to obstruction at the White House."

In particular, he cites the Castle Grande land deal, in which Mr. McDougal's Madison Guaranty made nonrecourse loans to Seth Ward, a Madison insider, to inflate the thrift's net worth. Transactions for Castle Sewer & Water, part of the Castle Grande project, were included in the Whitewater trial. Ms. McDougal was not charged in the Castle Sewer flip; Mr. McDougal was acquitted on a Castle Sewer fraud count, but Mr. Tucker was convicted.

In statements to regulators, Mrs. Clinton has repeatedly sought to minimize the legal work she did on Castle Grande, resulting in numerous controversies since the Clintons moved into the White House. The missing billing documents found in the White House family quarters, for example, covered the Rose Law Firm's billings on the project. Last month, the Federal Deposit Insurance Corp. reported Mrs. Clinton had contacts with Mr. Ward and other Madison officials during the Castle Grande transactions, and that a document she drafted had been used by Madison "to deceive federal bank examiners."

As a cooperating witness, inmate Hale spent hundreds of hours with federal investigators, and knows more about their evidence than anyone not bound to silence.

"Hillary conspired with Seth Ward and Jim McDougal to mislead federal regulators on the deal," Mr. Hale charges. "I had several conversations with Hillary about Castle loans myself," says Mr. Hale. "One of the conversations was on the date we closed the loan to Castle Sewer & Water and Madison put $500,000 into Capital Management." Mr. Starr already has won several convictions and guilty pleas from figures in the Castle Grande deals, including Madison S&L appraiser Robert Palmer, and Mr. McDougal is now cooperating with the Whitewater probe. "Jim has very significant information to offer about these transactions," Mr. Hale says.

Mr. Hale firmly believes there will be no pre-election "October Surprise." That would "not be something in Kenneth Starr's character," he says. "The most important thing to Starr is the rule of law, and he has his eye on history. He knows that any indictments at the highest level would be represented as partisan politics. He wants to stand—or at least have a chance of standing—for the rule of law above politics. An indictment after the election will be met with a firestorm, for sure, and I believe the president will immediately pardon Hillary, declaring the whole thing partisan politics."

Mr. Hale says his cooperation agreement with Mr. Starr and

grand jury secrecy considerations bar him from discussing many aspects of the case. He will not elaborate on his conversations with Mrs. Clinton, for example. And despite his own testimony involving Mr. Clinton in the conspiracy surrounding the bogus loans, he will not predict an indictment of the president, though does say it's a "maybe." While Mr. Hale did not receive his hoped-for sentence reduction in exchange for his extensive cooperation, he is a big supporter of Mr. Starr. "A decision to indict the first lady, and maybe even bring charges against the president, would be viewed by history as a decision that shows we live under a government of laws, not men. It's on Starr's shoulders. I just hope he has the courage to continue."

This, of course, is the opposite of the view Ms. McDougal has been proclaiming. "Susan will never, ever get a pardon from Bill Clinton," Mr. Hale says. "Instead, if she talks, the Clintons will do what they are so very good at—they'll mount a campaign to discredit her." Mr. Hale further claims that her attorney, Mr. McDaniel, is merely keeping his client on ice until after the election. Mr. Hale claims that Ms. McDougal told an unidentified mutual friend that "she wanted to talk to the independent counsel, but couldn't because of the deal Bobby [McDaniel] had with the White House."

Outtakes from the Sept. 4 edition of ABC's "PrimeTime Live," a subject of litigation between Mr. Starr and ABC, appear to support Mr. Hale's claim of White House coordination with Mr. McDaniel. In excerpts released by a Little Rock judge, Ms. McDougal was asked whether she felt her lawyers "had a loyalty to the White House." Ms. McDougal said, "it would be hard to find any attorneys in Arkansas who don't, you know, feel some loyalty to the Clintons. It's a small state, and they're attorneys, and most attorneys do love the Clintons." She did not respond to a question on what "people in the White House say to your attorneys." Asked about reports she and Mr. Clinton had had an affair while he was governor, Ms. McDougal replied that "it's too personal for me right now to even begin to talk about things like that."

In his prison interview, Mr. Hale predicted a pardon not only for Mrs. Clinton but Mr. Tucker, who was convicted on two fraud counts in the Whitewater trial and faces three other charges in a separate tax fraud case brought by Mr. Starr. "Bill will either pardon [Mr. Tucker] or commute Jim Guy's sentence," Mr. Hale says, "using the excuse of poor health, because Jim Guy needs a new liver."

But the fix has been in since Oct. 6, 1993, when Gov. Tucker met privately with Mr. Clinton in the Oval Office, Mr. Hale says. "Days after I went public with my accusations against the Arkansas political elite, Jim Guy flew to Washington to have a private meeting with Bill. The excuse was state business about the Arkansas National Guard or something, but that's ridiculous." Again citing an unidentified mutual friend, Mr. Hale says, "Webb Hubbell and Clinton gave Jim Guy assurances that he would never spend a day in jail. And he never has."

Mr. Hale calls the Clintons "the Harry and Harriet Houdini of American politics. They are master escape artists." They will help Mr. Tucker because they have to, he says, but "Susan is a joke to them. They'll just string her along until after the election and if there's a problem later, then will come the campaign to discredit her as a person of low morals. They've already got her on national television saying what a wonderful person Bill is; what more do they need?"

Mr. Morrison is a Journal editorial page writer.

REVIEW & OUTLOOK

Asides

Where Is John Huang?

It's been two weeks since the scandal involving former Lippo Group executive John Huang's solicitation of foreign campaign cash broke, and Mr. Huang has yet to talk with reporters. If there's nothing to hide, why's he hiding? When pressed about it Sunday, Senator Chris Dodd, chairman of the Democratic National Committee, where Mr. Huang works, said his employee would meet with the media. "I'm certain that it will be done," he said on "Face the Nation." Once off camera, however, Mr. Dodd reneged. DNC Press Secretary Amy Tobe claimed Mr. Dodd had only said he would "take a look" at making Mr. Huang available. She says Mr. Dodd "has decided to stick with the DNC's longstanding policy that staff shouldn't talk to the press." Staff? This obvious stonewall only heightens suspicions about Mr. Huang's activities as a Commerce Department trade official. A current Commerce official told the Los Angeles Times yesterday that Mr. Huang was in a "perfect position to influence U.S.-Indonesia policy. He had all of the information, he had access to CIA information. He was in a position to influence the State Department." If President Clinton really wants all the facts on Mr. Huang's fund-raising on the table he should call the DNC and tell them not to keep him in protective seclusion until after the election.

John Huang

Editorial Feature

The White House Plays Politics With the IRS

By JOSEPH FARAH

When charitable organizations are targeted for Internal Revenue Service audits, the last thing their directors want to do is go public. IRS attention, after all, can frighten away those tax-deductible personal contributions and foundation grants that are the lifeline for a nonprofit. My organization, the Western Journalism Center, is currently being audited. But I'm going public, because the evidence suggests the White House is using the IRS as a political attack dog.

Just a month after Republicans won control of Congress in 1994, the Clinton White House drafted an action plan to deal with individuals and organizations raising questions about a series of administration scandals, from Travelgate to Whitewater. Associate Counsel Jane Sherburne wrote a memo naming names, outlining strategy and assigning staff to handle specific targets. The memo was made public only last month, when it was released to congressional investigators and excerpted on this page.

The Western Journalism Center was the only news organization targeted for action. We were singled out for supporting the investigative reporting of Christopher Ruddy, which has focused attention on questions and inconsistencies surrounding the death of White House Deputy Counsel Vincent Foster.

This July, just months after the IRS had given final approval to the center's tax-exempt status as a 501(c)3 educational organization, we were audited for the first time in our five-year history. When the examiner met with our accountant, it became clear the IRS was not concerned with our bookkeeping procedures or fund-raising techniques, but, rather, with our choice of investigative reporting projects.

When our accountant questioned the direction, extent and propriety of the probe, IRS Field Agent Thomas Cederquist blurted, "Look, this is a political case, and it's going to be decided at the national level."

Among the thousands of documents demanded of the center for that political decision are all those "related to the selection of Christopher Ruddy as an investigative reporter and how the topic was selected." The IRS also wants to know who served on the review committee to choose the Foster project, what kind of peer-review process was employed in his selection, what other projects were considered and why our advertisements don't present "opposing viewpoints."

Hazel O'Leary

Why do I assume a connection between the White House targeting of the Western Journalism Center in December 1994 and the IRS audit in 1996? For one thing, the Sherburne memo listed our organization as the "Western Center for Journalism." That is, indeed, our official legal name. But it's strange that the White House would use it. It appears nowhere in our ads, in our brochures, on our letterhead or in any of the dozens of news stories that have been written about us. It does appear in one place in Washington, D.C.—in our official filings with the Internal Revenue Service.

The IRS isn't the only federal agency harassing the Western Journalism Center. Days after The Wall Street Journal named several of our donors in a 1995 news story, one of them—the founder of a publicly traded international corporation heavily reliant on federal contracts—received a call from Energy Secretary Hazel O'Leary. He says Ms. O'Leary told him his company's government business would be in jeopardy if he continued to support the Western Journalism Center. The warning was effective: He has not donated any money since.

Given the history of government harassment of the center and its contributors, perhaps you can understand my reluctance to turn

Editorial Feature

They Always Believed In a Place Called Jakarkansas

Why, asks an alert reader, has "little or nothing been made of the Rose Law Firm's $3 million payment to the FSLIC to quiet investigation into that firm's involvement in FirstSouth, which failed Dec. 4, 1986?"

At the very least, the Rose connection to the biggest S&L boondoggle in Arkansas (costing taxpayers $600 million, compared to $60 million for Madison Guaranty) throws a light on financial doings in the state. And since Indonesians are the flavor of the month, it also

Business World

By Holman W. Jenkins Jr.

offers a timely look at their history of unpropitious investing with Jack Stephens, head of the Stephens financial conglomeration, who once claimed that "one of my greatest sales [was] to bring Mochtar to Arkansas."

He meant, of course, Mochtar Riady, the Lippo Group impresario at the center of the Democrats' contributions scandal, Webb Hubbell's employer of last resort, and the business partner of various Arkansans associated with the Clinton age in Little Rock.

Mr. Riady was a piker, though, compared to the Indonesian billionaire who got away: Liem Sioe Liong, a golfing buddy of President Suharto's whose family is said to account for 5% of the Indonesian economy. Mr. Riady started as a clerk in one of Mr. Liem's banks. Returning the favor, Mr. Riady invited his former boss to join him and Jack Stephens in taking control of Little Rock's Worthen Bank. But something about his representatives being called to a meeting with FSLIC lawyers later soured Mr. Liem on Arkansas, and he has since receded. Not before writing a $5 million check to FSLIC, though, to resolve the same mess that entangled Rose—a mess that one attorney for the feds now calls a "pyramid of legal genius."

For those who think Whitewater won't add up to anything unless all the spokes point back to Bill and Hillary Clinton, one lesson may

Mochtar Riady

be this: The Clintons were never more than a spoke on a wheel with its center elsewhere, but as the guardians of the public weal in Arkansas, they're as interesting for what they learned to spin with as for what they spun themselves.

Hillary Clinton's juggling of the roles of gubernatorial wife, lawyer and real estate investor, for instance, was but a faint echo of her boss's crosshatching of extracurricular pursuits. Along with heading up Rose, which was lead counsel to both Stephens and Worthen

bank, Joe Giroir found time to become quite a banker himself, acquiring four rural Arkansas institutions in the early 1980s, largely with money borrowed on a 10-year installment plan. He secured these loans with his just-purchased bank shares.

These acquisitions soon paid off when Gov. Clinton signed a banking reform law (largely drafted by Rose), and Mr. Giroir traded his empire to Worthen for a sizable chunk of Worthen stock. A few months earlier, the Stephenses and Riadys had scarfed up a controlling interest in the bank, and Mr. Giroir joined them on the board. As soon as was decent, he also sold half his stake to Balder Corp., owned by Andree Halim, son of Mr. Liem, Indonesia's plutocrat di tutti plutocrats.

Mr. Giroir says his Indonesian friends are "almost quixotic" in their attachment to Arkansas. That adjective certainly applies to their Worthen investment.

James Riady, Mochtar's 28-year-old son, was quietly named "president," even though Worthen already had a president. As a bank spokesman explained: "Riady was given the title partly so he could carry a little more weight while conducting international business." What the family mostly bought, though, was a lesson in partnering up with those who buy banks without using any money.

For a glorious moment, Mr. Giroir was worth $40 million on paper, but the bottom almost immediately fell out of Worthen's share price after the bank lost $52 million playing patty-cake with a New Jersey bond firm. Only a spontaneous injection of Stephens capital stopped federal regulators from seizing the institution.

The mess was considerable, and became even more so when First-South, which was financing Mr. Giroir, failed for unrelated reasons. In the investigations that followed, the dealings of the Worthen principals were discovered to be more zestfully incestuous than Americans normally think healthy, although the Riadys must have felt like they'd discovered a place called Jakarkansas.

• A Worthen internal report found one of the bank's major shareholders, Jack Stephens, hadn't "fully disclose[d] the entire transaction" between himself and Mr. Giroir. Mr. Giroir's purchase of the National Bank of Commerce of Pine Bluff was discovered to have been partly financed by Mr. Stephens, and an "oral agreement" gave Mr. Stephens 80% of the proceeds when the bank was resold to Worthen.

• The U.S. Comptroller of the Currency found a bundle of unlawful insider loans to the various principals. Interestingly, there was also an unsecured $5 million loan from Mr. Giroir's Fayetteville bank to Messrs. Riady and Stephens before the latter bought their stake in Worthen. One upshot of the feds' poking around was the end of Worthen's global ambitions, including the closing of its short-lived New York and L.A. offices. James Riady, who found other business to occupy him on the West Coast, was little seen in Little Rock anymore.

• With a secret payment of $3 million, Rose nixed a federal lawsuit over the FirstSouth fiasco. Mr. Giroir had not only been a major borrower and shareholder, but Rose provided a glowing opinion on the propriety of his dealings with the thrift. In the most interesting of these, FirstSouth pledged its own assets to secure a letter of credit for Mr. Giroir from a Dallas bank, while FirstSouth itself only got Mr. Giroir's and Balder's much-depreciated Worthen shares as security. (That's how the Liems ended up negotiating with the FSLIC for the return of their Worthen stock.) "Nobody at FirstSouth could explain what the deal was," recalls an FSLIC attorney.

Mr. Giroir was soon obliged to leave Rose, pushed out by the triumvirate of Webb Hubbell, Vince Foster and Mrs. Clinton. But it says something about Little Rock that he snagged most of the firm's prize clients, including the Stephens empire and Worthen, as he was heading out the door. As for the Riadys, they were bought out at a loss of $20 million or so by Jack Stephens. But no hard feelings: They put Mr. Hubbell on the payroll and are hip-deep in new ventures with Mr. Giroir. And for the price of a few campaign contributions, they came away with a U.S. president to flaunt around Asia in furtherance of their empire.

One outcome wasn't surprising: Alone among the original investors, the Stephens family hit the jackpot when Worthen was sold to Boatmen's Bancshares and Boatmen's was sold to NationsBank. In true Arkansas style, the Stephens' investment bank even supplied the "fairness opinion" for the NationsBank deal.

REVIEW & OUTLOOK

In Defense of Asians

The controversy swirling around Democratic contributions impresario John Huang is not really about Asians, or even foreign political contributions, or about the financing of election campaigns, which after all have to be financed somehow. What it's about is Arkansas.

We know that many good and God-fearing citizens of Arkansas take offense at this shorthand, and we have no intention of indicting them all. Yet our President emerged from a culture and milieu that certainly is prominent in this poor, plutocratic, one-party state. President Clinton's history is littered with John Huangs native and foreign. Consider the personages he and his wife have attracted over the years:

Red Bone and Jim Blair with their commodity trades. Jim and Susan McDougal with their S&L. Dan Lasater, cocaine convict and friend of the President, his brother and mother. Patsy Thomasson, Mr. Lasater's chief of staff and later White House administrative chief. Gennifer Flowers and others. Betsey Wright, bimbo patroller. The Rose Law Firm triumvirate: Vincent Foster, deceased; Webster Hubbell, jailed; and William Kennedy, out the back door of the White House, along with David Watkins. David Edwards, currency trader with Arab connections. Gov. Jim Guy Tucker, convicted. Judge Henry Woods, booted off the case by the appellate court. Surely this is a rich crop from a small state.

Moving to Washington, we find a proliferation of independent counsels. For the President and First Lady, of course. Also for Mike

Espy, resigned as Agriculture Secretary. For Commerce Secretary Ron Brown, an investigation cut short by his death. And for poor Henry Cisneros. We have John Dalton confirmed as Navy Secretary and Jamie Gorelick as Pentagon counsel and deputy attorney general without benefit of public hearings. We find Ira Magaziner getting the benefit of prosecutorial discretion on a perjury referral for lying about membership of the White House Health Care Task Force. We have Arthur Coia, hobnobbing with the First Couple while getting the opportunity to clean up his own crime-ridden union. We have Craig Livingstone and Anthony Marceca installed in the White House and traducing 900 FBI files. (Chuck Colson went to jail for one.)

Bill Clinton, obviously, exerts a powerful magnetism. In some way or another, he attracts corner-cutters. And repels many who care about their reputation, witness the non-so-quiet departure of Philip Heymann from Justice or Abner Mikva from the revolving-door White House counsel's office. Not to mention Billy Dale and other Travel Office employees hounded out of their jobs for Clinton cronies, and White House-FBI liaison Dennis Sculimbrene hounded out of his job for doing the right thing. Why should we be surprised that this magnetism has an international reach?

For that matter, Mr. Huang is himself an old Arkansas hand. Early in his career with the Lippo Group he ended up in Little Rock as an executive for the Worthen Bank. Mochtar Riady's Indonesian investment empire had landed there after trying to buy Bert Lance's First National Bank of Georgia, bringing along the even more powerful Salim group and forging a local partnership with Jackson Stephens's local financial powerhouse. When Lippo left Little Rock, Mr. Huang went along to Los Angeles to become vice chairman of Lippo Bank and president of Lippo Group USA. Mr. Huang's departure from the Los Angeles bank came before the FDIC cease-and-desist agreement extracted alongside [page 121], but after the examination to which it refers. Soon after he was toiling for Secretary Brown, and later raising money for the DNC. Should we be surprised that he ended up with checks that had to be returned, or staged fundraisers among Buddhist monks? (The one surprise is the central involvement of Vice President Al Gore in the Buddhist scam, and also in starting Craig Livingstone's career.)

Now, there are special concerns about foreign contributions. Business practices common in Indonesia are unacceptable here, and we think the world's markets will create more prosperity faster if our standards prevail. There is the particular problem of the potential for drug money. When we see Lippo paying a Webster Hubbell, it looks like hush money to undermine the U.S. legal system, and we wonder who else is receiving it. Mr. Livingstone perhaps? And foreign giants are not subject to the same scrutiny as big U.S. contributors such as Archer-Daniels-Midland, whose generosity bought it no exemption from price-fixing prosecutions.

That having been said, we don't think solutions are to be found in tighter and tighter restrictions on campaign funding, more laws of the sort already unenforceable. Nothing will work without some in-born sense of moral limits among our political leaders. And while there are no lily-white politicians, there are very considerable shades of gray, especially apparent this year. Yes, the Republicans raise money, too, some of it from foreign sources. But this year's crop of Republicans are not the ones caught laundering money by slipping envelopes of cash to Buddhist monks, nor does it display the colorful set of characters surrounding Bill Clinton in Arkansas and later.

The way to clean up politics is not to fiddle with the financing rules. The way to clean up politics is to elect more honest politicians.

Letters to the Editor

The Indictment Numbers Game

I was intrigued by the portion of your Oct. 23 editorial ("In Defense of Asians") that attacks the mores of the Clinton White House by counting the number of independent counsels appointed to investigate whether high Clinton administration officials violated the law. You counted up four independent counsels investigating three Clinton cabinet members and, you claim, the President and Mrs. Clinton.

Lloyd N. Cutler

If we are going to play the numbers game, the Reagan/Bush record is much worse. During their terms of office, at least nine independent counsels were appointed to investigate six cabinet members: Attorney General Meese (three times); Labor Secretary Donovan; Housing Secretary Pierce; and in the Iran-Contra investigation, not only Defense Secretary Weinberger (indicted, pardoned before trial), Attorney General Messe and Secretary of State Shultz, but according to Independent Counsel Walsh's report, President Reagan himself.

According to the Walsh Report, the subjects of the Iran-Contra investigation also included key White House aides such as National Security Adviser Poindexter (indicted, convicted, conviction reversed), his aide Col. North (indicted, convicted, conviction reversed), Chief of Staff Regan, and CIA Director (with cabinet status) Casey. Other independent counsel looked into the conduct of key White House aides Lyn Nofziger (indicted, convicted, conviction reversed), Michael Deaver (indicted, convicted), and an aide to Chief of Staff James Baker.

If we were to count by the number of actual indictments, instead of the number of independent counsel appointed, five Reagan/Bush cabinet members and key White House aides were indicted compared with none so far in the Clinton administration, unless you count the third-ranking officer of the Justice Department, Webster Hubbell, for private conduct occurring before he joined the administration.

Of course, none of these numbers proves anything except that the independent counsel law requires the attorney general of the day to seek the appointment of an independent counsel whenever he or she concludes, after 90 days of Department of Justice investigation without subpoena power, that "further investigation is warranted." This of course is a very low threshold, and should be corrected by amending the statute to require at least a finding of probable cause to believe that a crime has been committed.

Moreover, as I am sure The Wall Street Journal would agree, even indictments are mere accusations, and the person indicted is entitled to a presumption of innocence until convicted in a legally fair trial. To assume that an indictment carries a presumption of guilt is wholly unwarranted. And to assume a presumption of guilt from the mere fact that an independent counsel has been appointed is even less justifiable.

LLOYD N. CUTLER
White House Counsel

Washington

Editorial Feature

The FDIC and Lippo Bank

Recently, questions have been raised about contributions to the Democratic Party from individuals associated with the Lippo financial conglomerate, based in Indonesia. In December 1994, the Lippo Bank in Los Angeles received a cease-and-desist order from the Federal Deposit Insurance Corporation. Between the April 1994 FDIC examination and the December order, John Huang left his position as vice chairman of the Los Angeles bank to work at the U.S. Commerce Department, where he had access to sensitive U.S. trade strategy. According to yesterday's Wall Street Journal, Mr. Huang also "lobbied to relax the rules on foreign banks operating in the U.S." Mr. Huang left the Commerce Department late last year to become vice chairman of the Democratic National Committee. The FDIC's cease-and-desist order against Lippo Bank was terminated in March of this year. Excerpts of the 1994 order follow:

. . . The FDIC considered the matter and determined that it had reason to believe that the Bank [Lippo Bank] had engaged in unsafe or unsound banking practices and had committed violations of law and/or regulations. The FDIC, therefore, accepted the CONSENT AGREEMENT and issued the following:

ORDER TO CEASE AND DESIST

IT IS HEREBY ORDERED, that the Bank, its institution-affiliated parties, as that term is defined in section 3(u) of the Act, 12 U.S.C. Sec. 1813(u), and its successors and assigns cease and desist from operating in violations of the following laws, rules, and/or regulations:

(a) Section 326.8 of the Rules and Regulations of the Federal Deposit Insurance Corporation, 12 C.F.R. Sec. 326.8, as more fully described on pages 2 and 2-a of the FDIC's Compliance Report of Examination as of April 5, 1994; . . .

IT IS FURTHER ORDERED . . .

1. Within 30 days from the effective date of this ORDER, the bank shall designate a qualified full-time senior officer as a Bank Secrecy Act Officer, to assure Bank's internal controls are in compliance with the BSA. This individual will be provided with the necessary training, authority, and responsibility to effectively administer the Bank's BSA program. The Regional Manager of the FDIC's San Francisco Regional Office ("Regional Manager") shall be advised in writing of the same. . . .

4. Within 60 days from the effective date of this ORDER, the Bank shall provide a system for independently testing its policies, procedures, and practices for compliance with the Bank Secrecy Act and the Financial Recordkeeping regulations 31 C.F.R. Part 103. The independent testing is to be conducted on an annual basis in compliance with the procedures described in the FDIC Statement of Policy entitled "Guidelines for Monitoring Bank Secrecy Act Compliance." The independent testing should be conducted by qualified, trained and experienced third parties, such as independent public accountants or specialists in this subject matter, who are not, in any manner, affiliated with the Bank or any of the Bank's subsidiaries or affiliates. Written reports documenting the testing results and providing recommendations for improvement shall be presented to the Bank's audit committee. . . .

(ii) outline an on-going training program for appropriate Bank personnel;

(iii) set forth specific review procedures for monitoring compliance with applicable regulations;

(iv) ensure compliance with the recordkeeping and reporting requirements for currency transactions over $10,000 (31 C.F.R. 103.22);

(v) ensure compliance with the recordkeeping requirements for the purchase of Bank checks and drafts, cashier's checks, money orders and traveler's checks (31 C.F.R. Sec. 103.29); and

(vi) ensure the identification and timely, accurate and complete reporting, to law enforcement and supervisory authorities, of known or suspected criminal activity perpetrated against or involving the Bank's branches, consistent with all applicable federal and state laws, rules, regulations and guidelines. These requirements are in addition to the Bank's ongoing compliance program in all other areas.

6. Within 30 days from the effective date of this ORDER, the Bank shall correct all violations of law described on pages 2 through 2-a-7 of the FDIC's Compliance Report of Examination as of April 5, 1994, to the extent that correction is within the Bank's capability, and implement procedures to prevent their recurrence. The Bank's actions as required by this paragraph shall be satisfactory to the Regional Manager as determined at subsequent examinations and/or visitations. . . .

October 28, 1996

Letters to the Editor

LippoBank Denies Charges Against It

The Journal's characterization of LippoBank in its Oct. 11 article "FDIC Acted Against Lippo in Money-Laundering Case" and the impression left by the subsequent reprinting [page 121] of the FDIC's Cease and Desist Order—a routine compliance examination—are false, misleading and damaging to the bank. As those familiar with banking regulations are aware, the Bank Secrecy Act is a record-keeping statute, not a '"money-laundering" statute. The facts are:

The FDIC did not allege or find that LippoBank of California was involved in "money laundering" or any other criminal activity. In lifting its order against the bank in January of this year, the FDIC concluded that ". . . the Bank has implemented a comprehensive and effective Bank Secrecy Act program and has complied fully with the outstanding Cease and Desist Order."

Unlike the many large and well-respected financial institutions that have had substantial fines levied against them for deficiencies related to the Bank Secrecy Act, neither the FDIC nor the U.S. Treasury Department sought to levy fines against LippoBank. Nonetheless, the Journal has seen fit to single us out for pejorative treatment in order to support its theories regarding matters unrelated to the bank.

We have not been involved in any way with any campaign finance activities of one of the bank's former officers. To infer otherwise is totally false and misleading. Further, the bank has not been privy to any information regarding U.S. trade policy.

LippoBank—with more than 50% of its loans serving low-to-moderate income customers—is a safe and secure institution committed to close cooperation and compliance with all regulatory bodies

JAMES PER LEE
President
LippoBank

Los Angeles

The Campaign Heats Up

In the final weeks of the Presidential campaign, Bill Clinton maintained his lead in the polls despite an almost daily barrage of new developments in the campaign finance scandal. As the Journal put it less than a week before the election: With the political establishment poised to confer re-election on Messrs. Clinton and Gore, "we have learned that John Huang was involved in an apparently illegal $245,000 contribution from a Korean businessman, since returned; facilitated a relationship of mutual benefit between Bill Clinton and the Riadys of Indonesia; and set up a shady fund-raiser at a Buddhist temple, which the featured speaker, Vice President Al Gore, now calls a 'community outreach' event."

The Administration sought to delay questions as much as possible, and certainly through the election. As the candidates raced to Election Day, for example, Mr. Huang dodged both the media and a subpoena from U.S. District Judge Royce Lamberth. Jerome Zeifman, former chief counsel to the House Judiciary Committee during the Nixon impeachment inquiry, drew national attention when he wrote in the Journal that Indogate "has produced a cancer on the Clinton presidency painfully reminiscent of the cancer that brought down Nixon." And a Journal editorial, "The Jones Standard," spotlighted changing media attitudes toward the Paula Jones sexual harassment case, also pushed past the election with litigation the Supreme Court later rejected in a 9-0 decision.

Clinton fund-raiser recently in the news.

All these parties have been named in a lawsuit brought by the watchdog group Judicial Watch, which for more than two years has been seeking documents from the Ron Brown days at Commerce to determine if his famous global trade junkets were also used to pay back or shake out campaign contributions for the Clinton-Gore re-election effort. The department's lawyers and lawyers for the office of federal attorney Eric Holder, who has attributed his job to Mr. Brown's efforts, have been resisting the group's search for the documents.

Let us divert a moment. If the mention of Judge Lamberth's name in this context is familiar to some of our readers, it's because we've all been down this resistance road before. Back in 1993, Judge Lamberth was among the first to discover what the Clintonites learned in law school when he adjudicated the suit seeking the identity of the people on Hillary's famous Health Care Task Force.

The Administration's lawyers said it didn't have to tell anyone who was on the task force, that the secret group was somehow exempt from the law governing federal advisory committees. An appeals court remanded the case to Judge Lamberth, who had said the government "submitted meritless relevancy objections in almost all instances" and that at least one excuse was "preposterous." Judge Lamberth referred Health Czar Ira Magaziner for possible perjury, but Mr. Holder declined to prosecute. The judge's current docket includes his announced intention to impose sanctions and fines for misconduct on the White House. So now with the Brown documents case it's deja vu all over again.

The case rings a bell in a second way, the Clinton practice of cleansing the office of any politically sensitive official in the Administration who dies. After Vincent Foster's 1993 suicide, White House General Counsel Bernie Nussbaum kept the Secret Service outside Mr. Foster's office while he and others went through files. Two years later, Congressional investigators used subpoena power to obtain the Foster Travelgate diary held by Mr. Nussbaum. Other Congressional subpoenas have been flouted right up to the brink of contempt of Congress votes.

It is getting late in the campaign, and we look forward to this Sunday when presumably some 90% of the nation's editorial pages, interrupting their quest for better campaign finance laws, will publish their endorsements of Bill Clinton for re-election. No doubt there will be a lot of coughing and caveating about distasteful "character" problems and whatnot, but make no mistake: The bar is being lowered on standards for the Presidency and public office generally. Just Tuesday, Vice President Gore finally explained his speaking appearance at the infamous Buddhist temple fund-raiser that John Huang arranged. The Vice President said he thought it was a "community outreach" event.

So while the nation's pundits and editorialists bend a knee to this relentless Presidential sophistry, it falls to the judicial branch to ferret out the truth. For all the press self-congratulation over the Watergate scandal, after all, it was up to Judge John Sirica to break the case by threatening provisional 40-year sentences to the perpetrators of two-bit burglary.

Until Judge Lamberth stepped up to defend court procedures, it appeared that the Clinton campaign, spouting as Mr. McCurry did about a need to "prepare" for a federal investigation, would succeed in secreting away John Huang until after the election. Assuming that the U.S. marshals don't have to track Mr. Huang into the mountains, Judge Lamberth's subpoenas at least ensure that lawyers for Judicial Watch will get to ask him some questions for all the rest of us about Bill Clinton's ways with money. Welcome to Subpoenaville.

Editorial Feature

Why the Character Issue Doesn't Cut Against Clinton

Gary Bauer, the family-values conservative, thinks the press missed the story last week when a protester on a San Diego beach called a jogging President Clinton a "draft-dodging, yellow-bellied liar." She added, "I'm voting for you," Mr. Bauer cracks.

That's the way it seems to frustrated conservatives as Bob Dole's assaults on President Clinton's ethics falter; polls show the character issue simply doesn't resonate. This isn't a new phenomenon; 24 years ago Americans overwhelmingly re-elected Richard Nixon, who wasn't to be confused with St. Francis of Assisi.

Politics & People

By Albert R. Hunt

But the conservatives' effort to draw parallels to the aftermath of that election, and the threat of a Nixon impeachment, are unpersuasive. On Election Day 1972 only sketchy details of the Watergate break-in were starting to emerge; an independent counsel was more than six months away. Today there has been an independent counsel investigating President Clinton for two and a half years, as well as 74 days of hearings by four congressional committees on the various allegations.

A compelling case hasn't been made. In those few instances where the Clintons are vulnerable, the critics lack credibility. Newt Gingrich or Alfonse D'Amato complaining about ethical transgressions is like Louis Farrakhan decrying bigotry.

Certainly Bob Dole is a man of character. But he too lacks credibility when he lambastes the president for policy vacillations while embracing a huge tax cut that is at variance with his whole career, or when he launches into uncharacteristic immigration-bashing. And no one—literally no one—has benefited more from our campaign-financing system of legalized bribery than has the former senior senator from Kansas.

The Whitewater case centers on the type of penny-ante corruption endemic to most small states—cozy relationships between the regulators and the regulated. But the congressional hearings produced no evidence that the Clintons parlayed this into any financial windfall. Moreover the precedent of investigating what a president did years before assuming office is troubling.

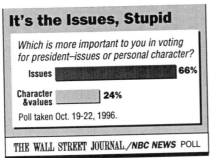

It's the Issues, Stupid

Which is more important to you in voting for president—issues or personal character?

Issues — 66%

Character & values — 24%

Poll taken Oct. 19-22, 1996.

THE WALL STREET JOURNAL./*NBC NEWS* POLL

The Clintons' conduct in the White House is another matter. But it's tough to make a case of obstruction on Whitewater since it's not clear what was obstructed. The firing of the White House Travel Office is dicier. Whether there was any illegality is dubious, but the way it was handled was appalling. And what in the world was Clinton crony Harry Thomason, who was at the center of this disgraceful performance, doing at the Democratic convention in Chicago?

More disturbing are all the unanswered questions about lower-level White House henchmen clandestinely accumulating the FBI files of prominent Republicans. In this presidential campaign, Mr. Clinton should be forced to offer a fuller explanation.

But this has gotten lost in the maze, not because of press inattention but because of the sloppiness of Mr. Clinton's critics. With Sen. D'Amato and the heavy-handed House Republican leadership scattering their shots, the landscape is littered with the wreckage of failed allegations, indistinguishable from the few relevant ones.

Also, the anti-Clinton cause hasn't been helped by independent counsel Kenneth Starr. Mr. Starr, a respected jurist, was named under tainted circumstances engineered by a judge who's a political lackey of Jesse Helms. Instead of then bending over backward to appear fair, Mr. Starr acted like a man bent on scoring political points to secure a future Supreme Court appointment. He continued to represent tobacco interests and spoke at Clinton-bashing Pat Robertson's Liberty University law school.

The one ethics charge that undeniably rings true centers on the latest campaign fund-raising scams. The catalyst was a Los Angeles Times expose that the Democratic National Committee received a $250,000 contribution from a South Korean firm, violating the prohibition against foreign entities contributing to U.S. politicians. This led to revelations about Democratic fund-raiser John Huang and nearly $1 million of contributions linked to his former employer, the Lippo Group of Indonesia.

Common Cause, which has pushed campaign finance reform for years, makes a forceful case that both 1996 presidential campaigns are blatantly breaking the law. That makes it tough for Republicans to play the Asian card here and convince voters that the Democrats engaged in some uniquely untoward activity.

The Democrats' performance in recent years on campaign financing *has* been disgraceful; the Republicans have been even worse. Both a 1992 measure sponsored by former Senate Majority Leader George Mitchell, vetoed by President Bush, and one proposed this year by Republican Sen. John McCain and thwarted by Bob Dole, among others, would have closed down many of the soft-money loopholes. These have enabled companies, unions and other special interests—like Lippo—to funnel some $200 million this year to the political parties as a cover to aid the presidential candidates. Separately, Bob Dole has for years been a legislative bag carrier for such big contributors as Archer-Daniels-Midland, Gallo Wine and the tobacco companies.

Fred Wertheimer, the former head of Common Cause, assails President Clinton's stonewalling of the Indonesian connection: "His silence is deafening." And he zeroes in on Sen. Dole's allegation that this amounts to laundering contributions to the Clinton campaign through the Democratic party: "What Dole is really admitting is that everybody has been lying all along. All this soft money is intended for the benefit of the presidential campaigns. In an effort to take advantage of the Indonesian contributions, he is admitting that both of them are engaged in a scam."

Mr. Wertheimer is nonplused by the Johnnys-come-lately who only a few months ago were saying what we need is more money in American campaigns, and who now profess shock at the Clinton money machine. "We absolutely don't want foreign interests influencing our policies," he says. "But we don't want anybody buying influence. The $2 million that Philip Morris spends for the very same purpose as Lippo is just as dangerous for American citizens."

The analogy to Nixon in 1973 is a pipe dream of partisans, many of whom believe that the Clinton presidency itself is somehow illegitimate. That's not to say the second Clinton term won't have more than its share of peril; there's cause for Clinton voters to be nervous. But Bob Dole and the critics have not credibly made a case to vote against the president on these grounds.

REVIEW & OUTLOOK

Trifling With the Courts--II

Yesterday in this space, we reported the manhunt for John Huang, the former Lippo Group executive and now notorious fund-raiser for the Democratic National Committee. Once again as we went to press last night, Mr. Huang was nowhere to be found. After holding court

John Huang

sessions today and threatening DNC officials with subpoenas, federal district Judge Royce Lamberth has given Mr. Huang's Beltway lawyer until 9:30 this morning to produce him.

Judge Lamberth approved the subpoena for Mr. Huang on Tuesday so that he would answer questions about connections between his DNC fund-raising and his former trade job at the Department of Commerce. When U.S. marshals arrived at the DNC on Tuesday afternoon to serve Mr. Huang, an Asian gentleman standing in the lobby ran away from them. DNC officials then told the marshals that they didn't know how to find Mr. Huang. Joe Sandler, the DNC's general counsel, said the only address he had for him was in California. When the marshals then went to his home address in suburban Washington as provided by the Commerce Department, they were told by a relative he doesn't live there. Later that day, Judge Lamberth's office asked Mr. Sandler to appear in court the next morning.

However, yesterday morning Mr. Sandler sent word during the hearing that he wasn't coming. After Judge Lamberth threatened to send a marshal to subpoena him, the DNC's lawyer suddenly showed up at the court and was asked by the judge whether he was going to "continue to play games about being served."

Mr. Sandler denied he was playing games and introduced John Keeney of Hogan & Hartson as Mr. Huang's lawyer. Mr. Keeney is also on the board of trustees of the DNC's Lawyers Council. Mr. Keeney asked Judge Lamberth to "limit the scope" of Mr. Huang's deposition. "There has been a huge politicization of this that is totally unwarranted," Mr. Keeney told Judge Lamberth. He then explained that he "had not been able to reach his client" about the subpoena. Mr. Huang's lawyer told Judge Lamberth yesterday that his client is not in Washington, D.C., but assured the court that Mr. Huang would return *late next week* and would answer a more narrow set of questions sometime after that. Mr. Keeney said he couldn't compel Mr. Huang to return to Washington, D.C.

"But, I can," Judge Lamberth interrupted him.

He then scheduled another hearing on Mr. Huang's compliance for this morning. Mr. Keeney quickly left the court-room and refused to answer questions from the two reporters present—from the Washington Times and this page. When asked if Mr. Huang had done anything illegal or unethical at the DNC, Mr. Sandler replied: "Not as far as we know."

Late yesterday afternoon, John Keeney faxed a letter to Larry Klayman of Judicial Watch, which had sought the subpoenas, saying he had contacted his client and "Mr. Huang has agreed

Royce Lamberth

that he will appear on any of the following days: Nov. 6, 7 or 8." The election is Nov. 5, and Judge Lamberth's schedule will have to adjust.

Meanwhile, Ira Sockowitz is hanging tough. Judge Lamberth on Tuesday approved a subpoena for Mr. Sockowitz, who was Ron Brown's special counsel at Commerce. The watchdog group Judicial Watch wants to ask him to answer questions about files that may have been taken from Mr. Brown's office and stored.

Mr. Sockowitz's lawyer faxed a letter yesterday to the district court requesting that the subpoena be modified "to extend the time for required response to and including Monday, Nov. 4."

And so just as the political establishment confers re-election on Messrs. Clinton and Gore, we have learned that John Huang was involved in an apparently illegal $245,000 contribution from a Korean businessman, since returned; facilitated a relationship of mutual benefit between Bill Clinton and the Riadys of Indonesia; and set up a shady fund-raiser at a Buddhist temple, which the featured speaker, Vice President Al Gore, now calls a "community outreach" event.

Meanwhile, the press secretary of the Clinton White House laughingly tells annoyed reporters Mr. Huang isn't available "because it takes time to talk to you." But this week, when an ongoing lawsuit seeking information into Ron Brown's trade junket operation results in a subpoena to force Mr. Huang's appearance, virtually the entire Washington press corps ignores the story, not even bothering to cover the appearance of DNC officials and Mr. Huang's Hogan & Hartson lawyer before a federal judge. (Though Brian Ross broadcast a good report on ABC News last night.)

So far, Bill Clinton's use of the executive branch of government to buffalo the others has been an extraordinary spectacle. Investigations by the legislative branch have been turned aside, its subpoenas flouted. The press, the fourth branch of government, has largely quit. Some 2,500 accredited Washington reporters have transferred their judgment and authority to the pollsters.

Now, however, in Judge Royce Lamberth, the Administration will attempt to buffalo the third branch. It may suit Mr. Clinton's purposes to stonewall the details of the Huang operation past Nov. 5, even at the risk of incurring obstruction of justice charges. But the larger game is setting the stand-off terms for the much larger constitutional struggle with the judiciary that will ensue should Mr. Clinton make it past November 5.

Editorial Feature

A Cancer on the Presidency

By JEROME M. ZEIFMAN

Sadly, as a life-long Democrat and chief counsel of the House Judiciary Committee at the time of the Nixon impeachment inquiry, I cannot in good conscience vote to re-elect Bill Clinton. Having  reached this decision, I am proud to be among those Democrats who have chosen principle over party. Defeating Mr. Clinton would help revive the traditional moral values of the Democratic Party—as they existed under Presidents Roosevelt, Truman, Kennedy, Johnson and Carter.

Having long championed traditional Democratic causes, I simply cannot accept Mr. Clinton's shameless election-year surge to the right as his chosen means of winning a second term.

Bill Clinton And like most if not all traditional Democrats, I have grave reservations about the Clintons' morality and ethics. In my view there is now probable cause to consider our president and first lady as felons, who are likely to be indicted after the Nov. 5 election.

The misdeeds of the Clinton administration have fallen into a pattern of deceit and corruption that now clearly justifies denying Mr. Clinton a second term in office. To date more than 30 high administration officials have been investigated, fired or forced to resign, and the White House has illegally obtained more than 900 confidential

FBI files. Four independent counsels have been appointed, three to investigate cabinet members and one to investigate the president himself.

The White House suppressed documents under subpoena. The Department of Justice, the FBI and the Treasury Department have been politicized and misused to prosecute or investigate innocent staffers of the White House Travel Office. The president's Health Care Task Force operated secretly in gross violation of federal disclosure laws, misled the federal courts and ignored conflict-of-interest laws.

The most recent scandal, involving former Commerce Department official and Democratic Party fund-raiser John Huang (who still has failed to answer a summons issued by District Judge Royce C. Lam-

---

This mixing of U.S. policy with partisan fund-raising has produced a cancer on the Clinton presidency painfully reminiscent of the cancer that brought down Nixon.

---

berth), is but another hauntingly familiar throwback to my days as an investigator of Watergate crimes and a wide variety of other forms of presidential misconduct. The 1972 Republican Committee to Re-Elect the President (CREEP) was involved in many shady operations that mixed legitimate government funding operations with the illegitimate refunneling of money through backdoor corporate contributions into CREEP coffers.

Now it appears that Mr. Huang, and his former associates from the Indonesian Lippo financial conglomerate, were unlawfully funneling contributions from foreign sources (that had both corporate and political interests in U.S. policy) into Democratic Party coffers. This mixing of U.S. policy with partisan fund-raising—not to mention the questionable background of some of the institutions and individuals given top clearance by the White House and the DNC—has produced a cancer on the Clinton presidency painfully reminiscent of the cancer that brought down Nixon.

I am particularly saddened that the Clintons now believe that their unethical and unlawful acts in the pursuit of power will be condoned by all but a few Democrats in the name of party unity. During the

Nixon impeachment inquiry it was my view that the core of Nixon's corruption was his belief that in politics his ends justified any means at all.

Ironically, it is now the Clinton administration that has given renewed intensity to the corrupt notion that immoral means can be legitimized in the pursuit of political ends. If Mr. Clinton is re-elected it will be testimony to his success in putting politics before principle. A second Clinton term would polarize the nation even more dangerously than did Richard Nixon's—this time with Republicans as the new defenders of integrity in government and Democrats as the defenders of a corrupt administration. If Mr. Clinton is defeated, Democrats may find a new strength—and long remember the folly of marching in lockstep in support of a corrupt president in the name of party unity.

Richard Nixon

By all accounts Robert Dole is a man of personal integrity. His principles are conservative, and I will continue to oppose them. Yet because I must remain true to my traditional Democratic moral values, I will vote for Mr. Dole.

Mr. Zeifman was chief counsel to the House Judiciary Committee at the time of the Nixon impeachment inquiry. He is author of "Without Honor: The Impeachment of President Nixon and the Crimes of Camelot" (Thunder's Mouth Press, 1996).

Editorial Feature

The Department of Political Favors

By JOHN H. FUND

It appears as if John Huang, the mysterious Democratic National Committee senior fund-raiser who scarfed up contributions from Indonesian gardeners to Buddhist nuns living under a vow of poverty, will finally have to answer someone's questions today. Having evaded the media and a subpoena for a week with the help of the DNC, Mr. Huang is finally scheduled to give a deposition this morning in a lawsuit that seeks to uncover links between campaign contributions and his actions as a Commerce Department trade official. Mr. Huang's deposition will be made public so a bit more of the iceberg of the Clinton campaign's foreign-contribution scandal may be glimpsed by voters before they cast ballots next week.

John Huang

The watchdog group Judicial Watch, which brought a Freedom of Information Act lawsuit for Commerce Department documents over two years ago, says the Clintonites have had good reason to aid Mr. Huang in his efforts to avoid U.S. marshals who have tried to serve him with a subpoena. Judicial Watch counsel Larry Klayman believes that Commerce Department-sponsored trade missions were used as a vehicle to raise money for the Democratic Party. "International trade policy has been perverted into a blatant vehicle for overseas and domestic fund-raising," he says. "John

Huang was at the center of those efforts." Mr. Klayman is a conservative, but Charles Lewis of the liberal Center for Public Integrity agrees with his concerns about Mr. Huang. After examining the documents Judicial Watch has so far pried out of Commerce, Mr. Lewis says they "support the notion that favorable treatment was given to friends of Ron Brown, Bill Clinton and the Democratic Party."

The Commerce Department has always had elements of a politicized favor factory, but the Clinton administration has pushed the envelope. A DNC brochure obtained by the Chicago Sun-Times offered "managing trustees," who gave $100,000 invitations "to participate in foreign trade missions." A former Democratic Party official says the DNC was not referring to Commerce missions, but he admits that "some people would misunderstand what was offered."

Judge Lamberth expressed irritation with Commerce officials: "The search was either inadequate or documents were destroyed. That's the only conclusion."

Melinda Moss, a former top fund-raiser for the DNC, became Commerce's director of business liaison in charge of selecting executives for foreign trade missions. Ms. Moss says the executives were selected "on merit," but she resisted responding to the FOIA request for files on the trip selection process. When Mr. Klayman of Judicial Watch contacted her to ask about the months-long delay on his request, she refused to turn over the documents. "She called me an ugly word, and later slammed down the phone and hung up on me," Mr. Klayman recalls.

The documents that have so far been reluctantly turned over to Mr. Klayman may explain why Ms. Moss and other Commerce officials don't want to release any more. A June 1994 memo from Chris Brown, business manager for Entergy Power Development Group, discusses a meeting with Commerce officials regarding "Entergy's China projects." Mr. Brown said that he met with Jude Kearney, a former Clinton staffer in Arkansas who then became a deputy assistant secretary at Commerce. They discussed an upcoming trade mission to China, Mr. Brown wrote, and Mr. Kearney "indicated the competitive nature of being selected to ride on the plane with the Secretary. Also indicat-

Keeney has filed motions asking that the deposition not be video-taped and that questions be restricted to Mr. Huang's time at Commerce. Late yesterday, Judge Lamberth ruled against Mr. Keeney's motions and gave Mr. Klayman wide latitude to ask questions of Mr. Huang and to make the answers public.

Corporate executives in Arkansas have long known of Bill Clinton's fondness for insider ties between government and business. One former Clinton supporter told me that "Clinton has a very pro-business policy. He favors one business at a time, starting with his friends." The real lesson of the Huang-Lippo scandal is not the need for campaign finance reform, but the need to abolish the Commerce Department. It is in danger of becoming a vehicle for a crony capitalism that allows both domestic and foreign companies with dubious agendas to cash in political chits.

Mr. Fund is a member of the Journal's editorial board.

REVIEW & OUTLOOK

The Jones Standard

One of Bill Clinton's notable accomplishments in the Presidential campaign is being overlooked: He's killed sexual harassment. What progress women have made in recent years by blowing the whistle on the most odious forms of sexual insult is being swept out to sea as lib-

Paula Jones

eral commentators explain away the Clinton character issue. Check out the commentary by male writers in Time magazine or on the Washington Post op-ed page: Voters now are "pragmatic" about political sex and have concluded that the President's private behavior is irrelevant. So that's the end of that.

Alas, Paula Corbin Jones of Arkansas is still on her way to the Supreme Court with her sexual harassment case against Bill Clinton. And in the just-published November issue of American

Lawyer magazine, liberal journalist Stuart Taylor Jr., formerly legal correspondent for the New York Times, tacks against the prevailing nobody-cares spin in a lengthy investigation of the Jones case. He attacks the double standard applied to Mrs. Jones and concludes that Mr. Clinton probably is guilty.

In "Her Case Against Clinton," Mr. Taylor writes in the magazine, based in New York City, that he first thought Mrs. Jones was "lying, at least about the more lurid details." Now, he says, "I'm not so sure of that." Mrs. Jones's evidence is "highly persuasive." And generally overlooked by the media, he adds, "has been the fact that the evidence supporting Paula Jones's allegations of predatory, if not depraved, behavior by Bill Clinton is far stronger than the evidence supporting Anita Hill's allegations of far less serious conduct by Clarence Thomas." Our own comparison of choice would be Bob Packwood.

After reviewing the case and interviewing some of the witnesses, Mr. Taylor concludes in a 13-page article that there is "clear and convincing proof" that on May 8, 1991, then-Governor Clinton sent a state trooper to bring Mrs. Jones, a 24-year-old state employee, to a hotel room where he was waiting. Six witnesses, Mr. Taylor writes, contribute "impressive evidence" corroborating Mrs. Jones's claim that in the room Governor Clinton made sexually gross and explicit overtures to her. All six witnesses say Mrs. Jones told them "contemporaneously about Clinton's unwelcome advances," Mr. Taylor writes. Perhaps most potentially damaging to the President's assertion that there is nothing to the complaint, Mrs. Jones asserts that there are "distinguishing characteristics" in Mr. Clinton's genital area.

The Clinton Whitewater strategy of deny, delay and smear has worked well in the Jones case. Robert Bennett, Mr. Clinton's attorney, has pursued a shrewd, though legally dubious, claim of Presidential immunity, bumping the case to the Supreme Court, which will hear it—early next year. This has served to delay all fact-finding past the November election, but is also one of many reasons for predictions of a second-term nightmare. Mr. Taylor writes that Mr. Bennett has more delaying tactics at the ready.

Robert Bennett

Mr. Bennett has functioned effectively—and in our view, reprehensibly—in orchestrating the media campaign to discredit Mrs. Jones, most famously referring to her charges as "tabloid trash." Mr. Taylor pronounces the "Clinton-Bennett defense strategy [a] success in the media as well as the courts. The president's surrogates and supporters have diverted attention from the most relevant evidence by orchestrating a media blitz depicting Jones as a promiscuous, flirtatious, gold-digging, fame-seeking slut, unworthy of belief."

This is a smear operation, and one issue raised by the Jones story is, why would the media serve as its transmission belt? Mr. Taylor writes: "Part of it is class bias against what one Washington bureau chief called 'some sleazy woman with big hair coming out of the trailer parks.'" But it is also that "the political orientations of most reporters, editors and producers are at work here."

Of particular interest here are the decisions to remain silent that were made by the most politically hyper feminists. Mr. Taylor writes that "not a single one of the feminist groups that clamored first for a hearing for Anita Hill, and then for Clarence Thomas's head, has lifted a finger on behalf of Paula Jones. . . . And most striking, in my view, is the hypocrisy (or ignorance) and class bias of feminists and liberals—who proclaimed during the Hill-Thomas uproar that 'women don't make these things up,' and that 'you just don't get it' if you presumed Thomas innocent until proven guilty—only to spurn Jones's allegations of much more serious (indeed, criminal) conduct as unworthy of belief and legally frivolous."

These folks should watch the roof; it could fall quickly. Bob Packwood succeeded in delaying publication of a story on his sexual harassment of women until after he won a narrow 52% to 48% victory in 1992. Mr. Packwood put off nosy Washington Post reporters in an effort to run out the clock. The story was finally published on Nov. 22, three weeks after the election. Mr. Packwood called a news conference on Dec. 10 and issued a formal apology. Oregon voters were outraged; they felt Mr. Packwood had deceived them before they voted and many then initiated an unsuccessful effort to invalidate the Senate election. Mr. Packwood's approval nose-dived, he became a pariah who rarely returned to the state, and his credibility as a legislative leader was destroyed. Finally he resigned.

We'll leave it to the Clinton character essayists to write in post-election exemptions to the sexual harassment laws based on party affiliation. But whatever the outcome next Tuesday, the question in the Jones case is the same one in all the other non-sexual complaints: Are the Clintons simply above the laws that govern all the rest of us?

Letters to the Editor

I'm Simply Defending My Client

Your Oct. 30 editorial "The Jones Standard" accuses me, as President Clinton's counsel in the Paula Jones case, of asserting a "legally dubious" claim of presidential immunity and undertaking a "reprehensible" media campaign to "smear" Ms. Jones. These assertions are without foundation.

Our legal position—that in all but the most exceptional cases, private civil damages claims against an incumbent president should be deferred until a president leaves office—is supported by some of the nation's foremost constitutional law experts of both liberal and conservative bent. It is the same position that has been taken by the solicitor general of the United States in amicus briefs filed to protect the institutional interests of the presidency and the United States in this case. And at least two judges of the United States Court of Appeals for the Eighth Circuit, including one appointed to the bench by a Republican president, agreed with the soundness of this position.

A legal position endorsed by these independent experts and jurists could hardly be called "dubious." The Supreme Court evidently considered this position sufficiently valid to grant review of this issue, something it does in only a tiny fraction of cases presented for its consideration.

Your editorial was also dead wrong when it charged that I have attempted to "orchestrate a media campaign" to "smear" Ms. Jones. I haven't orchestrated a thing, and I haven't "smeared" Ms. Jones; I have simply responded to her highly publicized allegations against my client.

Ms. Jones first aired these charges several months before the suit was filed, at a fund-raising media event sponsored by the president's partisan opponents. When this failed to get significant media attention, her lawyers began giving interviews stating that they were "mulling over" whether to file suit. They held another news conference on the courthouse steps the day the complaint was filed. It was in response to press inquiries generated by this media circus that I described the complaint, accurately, as "tabloid trash with a legal caption." After all, the complaint contained gratuitous, titillating allegations—as referenced in your editorial—that were wholly unnecessary to make out a legal claim.

Paula Jones

The Journal's editorial staff evidently believes that a lawyer should remain mute when a calculatingly sensational complaint is filed in court impugning the integrity of one's client. Justice Anthony Kennedy, however, has a different view. As he stated in the case of *Gentile v. Nevada*, "an attorney's duties do not begin inside the courtroom door"; they include taking "reasonable steps to defend a client's reputation . . . to demonstrate in the court of public opinion that a client does not deserve to be tried." Responding to Ms. Jones's complaint—far from being "reprehensible"—falls squarely within the scope of these duties.

Of course, I have no objection to your generous remarks about the effectiveness of my legal strategy—a compliment I suspect you did not intend.

ROBERT S. BENNETT

Washington

Editorial Feature

What If Nixon Had No Shame?

By BENJAMIN J. STEIN

What I keep thinking is, "What if RN had known what a president can get away with?"

Richard Nixon, for whom I worked as a speechwriter, had a historic record of accomplishment. He liquidated the last vestiges of racial segregation in the public schools of the deep South. He made equal opportunity the hallmark of his administration. He prepared the endgame of the Cold War by opening up relations with China and stalemating the U.S.S.R. In 1973, he stood up for Israel against Soviet threats and thus began the Mideast peace process by showing that Israel was there for keeps. He ended the Vietnam War in a way that would have left some semblance of dignity had he not been undercut by Congress after he left.

Nixon was driven from office and kept from finishing his work by public outcry and congressional fury over his cover-up efforts after the Watergate break-in. Yet Nixon's coverup was a ramshackle, paste-up, poorly conceived job at best. What if he had been as bold as Bill Clinton, as far-seeing and as thorough?

What if Nixon had fired all the federal prosecutors on the first day of his administration and replaced them with officials who were totally and uncompromisingly loyal to him? There would have been no hounding of the Watergate burglars by prosecutors to start the whole skein unraveling. What if Nixon had made sure that Watergate cases were steered by his prosecutors to judges friendly to him? No "Maximum John" Sirica terrorizing the defendants into confession.

Suppose Nixon had raised money from his pal Ferdinand Marcos or other foreign sources to pay off the Cubans, E. Howard Hunt or G. Gordon Liddy? Say, $1 million for each of the boys on Jan. 21, 1973, if they kept their mouths shut.

Then, most beautiful of all, suppose Nixon told everyone connected with Watergate, from the Cubans to H.R. Haldeman and John Ehrlichman, that they should stonewall permanently in front of investigating committees. "No matter what they do," he could have said, "on Jan. 21, I will pardon you. I'll start laying the groundwork by telling the world what a partisan Archibald Cox is—we have plenty of evidence on that—and then when I've won the election, you'll get your payoff."

Richard Nixon

There would have been no need for a "Saturday Night Massacre." Nixon would have served the same purpose by using the pardoning power. Oh, and of course, Nixon would have burned the tapes and simply said they were lost.

What if the Republicans in Congress were as 100% disciplined as the Democrats now, with a solid stonewall of defense for RN and no lawmaker like William Cohen or Howard Baker willing to act impartially? What if Nixon had told them, "Boys, if we stick together, we can get away with it. There's nothing there to stop us, except our own sense of shame."

The New York Times and the Washington Post would have roared. So would have Walter Cronkite. But after all, how many divisions has the media?

The reason Nixon could not do it is that he was filled with shame and turmoil. He really did feel tortured and divided about Watergate and his own role in the drama. He could not organize a successful defense partly because of his loyalty to the Constitution, partly because he did not know how far the scandal would reach, but (I am convinced) mostly because he was crippled by his own sense of embarrassment. It was this vestigial, old-fashioned, quaint sense of shame that paralyzed him, as Arthur Miller wrote at the time, and kept him from acting most effectively to save himself.

Bill Clinton is modern man. Narcissistic, shameless, devoted only to self-aggrandizement. Shame never enters into the calculus because, after all, what good would it do him? Shame would diminish the memory and speed of the Clinton Central Processing Unit. Shame is a virus that eventually could disable the entire machine. Without it, you can organize a defense that laughs at court orders, sneers at congressional requests, and treats the Constitution as window dressing. Without it, you get a Watergate/Whitewater defense that actually defends.

But once the sense of shame is gone, what boundaries are left to a nation's ruler? Once the sense of shame has gone and the bionic president has shown how weak the Constitution is without his voluntary submission, then where does he stop, if anywhere? Just for example, what if in 2000 he decides he does not want to leave?

Mr. Stein is an actor, lawyer and adjunct professor of securities law at Pepperdine Law School.

REVIEW & OUTLOOK

Clinton's Supporters

In the next day or so, it was announced yesterday, Bill Clinton is going to give a major speech in favor of, and outlining his proposals for, campaign finance reform. There surely are many metaphors we could compose around such an apparition taking place in the midst of this week's revelations about the amazing world of John Huang, but by now the Clinton Presidency is beyond comparison. After four non-stop years of this, Bill Clinton floats in a realm of the brazen never before witnessed in this country's political history. And the Democratic Party and its high-minded intellectual apparatus swallow it with scarcely a gulp.

Given the stakes at this particular juncture in electoral history, it's understandable that significant Democratic defections from this Presidency were never in the offing. Should Mr. Clinton lose, and the Republicans hold Congress, the Democratic Party likely would enter the wilderness for a generation. So perhaps we should be content with the few honorable exceptions drawing a line at scandal—long-time Democratic consultant Ted Van Dyk and former Watergate counsel Jerome Ziefman published on this page, and perhaps a few others. We have to note, however, that not one major figure in the Democratic Party, none, has separated himself or herself from the squalor of this Presidency. The party elders and liberal spokesmen in the press choose instead to lash themselves to the mast, at least through Nov. 5.

So we now have Senator Chris Dodd obliged to step forward and personally man the bilge pumps while the John Huang scandal pours forth in the final week of the campaign. Documents pried out of the Commerce Department this week show that Mr. Huang, described by party spokesmen as a mid-level nobody, had phone messages left for him at Commerce by an amazing array of key Clinton cronies: Hollywood pal Harry Thomason, who tried to capture the White House Travel office; Denver lawyer James Lyons, whose report drove the press off Whitewater during the '92 campaign; Arkansas-in-Asia rainmaker Mark Middleton; Mack McLarty; Bruce Lindsey and even Harold Ickes. Mr. Huang by his own account Tuesday met at the White House with the President "quite a few times . . . many times."

Again, we want to make a distinction between traditional politics and this Presidency. No one in politics would blanch at senior Democrats defending any one or two of the Clinton scandals and outrages as they arose. Politicians aren't holy men and stuff happens. But if you roll the tape back to Bill Clinton's entrance on the national political scene in the '92 campaigns, one sees the first signs in the bizarre equivocations of "didn't inhale" and the draft-board mumbo-jumbo. Something here was uniquely amiss.

Chris Dodd

He won. But what was foretold in those odd early episodes reappeared. The Travelgate episode and the ensuing White House stonewalling was passed off by defenders as "inexplicably ham-handed." Somehow the "inexplicable" continued unabated—the equivocal excuses, the ideological sellouts and buybacks, the stonewalling (I can't recollect, my memory is impaired, I lied to my diary), the flouted subpoenas from Congress and the courts, and the debauched procedures of the FBI, Secret Service and IRS ("honest bureaucratic mistakes")—with the campaign's final week now spent mocking the campaign reporting rules and defying a federal judge.

But for all those Democrats who served long before Bill Clinton arrived and rewrote the standards of acceptable political conduct, it is beyond so much as a bleat of comment.

"An unusually good liar," is how Democratic Senator Bob Kerrey, a former Presidential contender, described Bill Clinton months ago in an interview. Not now. From the Senate campaign committees, Sen. Kerrey tries to ride the Clinton coattails with Mediscare ads for his candidates. The new standards are internalized.

Paul Sarbanes

We think of Whitewater committee stalwart Senator Paul Sarbanes, a Maryland Democrat. Sen. Sarbanes defended it all, and most skillfully. Then in the end, he signed onto the new standards, allowing the public humiliation of witness Jean Lewis. Sen. Sarbanes knows more than most, and we would give a nickel for his private thoughts as he enters the voting booth Tuesday, or for that matter the thoughts of Bob Kerrey or Bill Bradley or Daniel Patrick Moynihan.

Robert Kerry

The painful imperative of ensuring Democratic viability for the future is, we repeat, understandable. The screaming silence is not. And the flaccid hand-wringing of editorial endorsements appearing now is marginally better than, but oddly reflective of, the flaccid tone set by this Presidency's first term.

Whatever the result next Tuesday, these same Democratic elites will be back in public the next day insistently making their always high-minded arguments for high-minded causes. But Bill Clinton is debauching them as well; after this performance, there will be little reason to take their professions any more seriously than his.

Editorial Feature

How to Get a Drug Dealer Into the White House

By JEFFREY LORD

Last week Ross Perot lambasted the White House for inviting twice-convicted felon Jorge "Gordito" Cabrera to the White House for a Christmas party with the Clintons. "I never thought I would live to see a major drug dealer give 20,000 bucks . . . and then be invited to the White House for a reception," Mr. Perot said. "Now keep in mind, you can't get into the White House unless the Secret Service clears you. This guy had been convicted—arrested twice in the '80s. It's in the computer."

Mr. Perot is right—as I know first-hand from my days as an associate political director in the Reagan White House. One Friday President Reagan was scheduled to deliver a policy statement in the East Room, and my job was to round up a live audience. For any modern-day White House aide a request of this nature is routine, like asking Jack Kemp to throw a football. I did what I had done dozens of times— reach for my handy list of Washington-area Reagan supporters and start calling. Apologizing for the short notice, I dutifully explained the need at hand and asked if the person I was calling could spare an hour or so to come to the White House.

An hour before the actual event, having secured a good number of Reagan supporters to glide into the White House to cheer on our leader's latest pronouncement, I had long since moved on to the next project. And then the Secret Service called.

Firmly, leaving no room for me to doubt that he meant it, the agent told me flatly that one of my invited guests would not be allowed in the presence of the president or on the White House grounds. Period. I was stunned. Having served in the White House for some time, I knew the rules: Invitees had to submit their names and Social Security numbers for a computer check by the Secret Service. In almost four years on the White House staff I had never been told that someone I suggested as a potential guest of the president failed to pass muster.

Until X. In the interest of privacy and courtesy, I shall refer to the person in question only as X. I hadn't invited X to the White House before, but I well knew of X and X's family—longtime, vigorous and extremely well known and influential supporters of Mr. Reagan. But, the agent explained, X had a history that had brought him in contact with the police. I understood that I had unwittingly put the president, the White House staff and myself in an embarrassing position. With an hour to go before the event, I was being told X would literally be refused entrance on appearing at the northwest gate.

As a political aide, I had two highly unappetizing alternatives. If this were a major event and the invitation were anything other than what it was—a quick round-up of presidential allies to fill chairs for TV—I would have to go to my boss, perform a mea culpa and face the music, hoping the ground had not been laid for a run of press stories embarrassing to a genuine Reagan supporter. The second option was equally unappetizing: Track down X on the spot and explain the unhappy truth and retract the invitation.

Someone else answered the phone at the X residence, and I explained my mission. X was just getting in the car to come to the White House. Retrieved, X got on the phone. Mortified, I explained what had happened. To my surprise the response was gracious, kind and most forgiving. X, of course, was familiar with the problem and was surprised to receive a call in the first place. Sensing my great discomfort at such a personal intrusion, X thanked me for the invitation and asked that regards be passed on to the president. End of incident.

X's offense, unlike Jorge Cabrera's, had nothing to do with drugs, but most assuredly X was in the Secret Service computer. Other than calling X to cancel, which I did, there was only one other option open—and Mr. Perot precisely put his finger on that option: "Every now and then the White House just overrules them and says let 'em in anyhow." Meaning my latter-day Clinton counterpart presumably went to his White House superior, who ordered the Secret Service to admit Mr. Cabrera.

For those in the press who want to know the inside questions to ask in a case like this, here they are:

- Who on the White House staff initially put Mr. Cabrera's name on a guest list and why?

- What was that person's connection to Mr. Cabrera?

- Did the Secret Service notify anyone on the White House staff that Mr. Cabrera had a criminal record?

- Did the Secret Service try to prevent Mr. Cabrera from getting clearance?

- If so, was the Secret Service overruled by a member of the White House staff, the president or a member of the first family?

- If the answer to the last question is yes, who made the decision and why?

This White House is famous for its excuses. No doubt it will have 20,000 of them for the admission of Mr. Cabrera.

Mr. Lord, a Washington writer, served as White House associate political director from 1985-88.

Four More Years

On November 5, 1996, Bill Clinton triumphed over GOP challenger Bob Dole and won a second term as President, the first Democrat to be elected to two full terms since Franklin Delano Roosevelt. The President received 49% of the popular vote, compared with 41% for Mr. Dole and 8% for Ross Perot. Voters kept Newt Gingrich's House of Representatives, the first time Republicans retained a House majority since 1928, though with reduced numbers. In the Senate, Republicans returned more conservative, Democrats more liberal. "What ultimately emerges here," the Journal wrote, "is a picture of an electorate that hasn't made up its mind, in contrast perhaps to the 1994 electorate that seemed decisive."

Attention soon shifted to the President's new cabinet, particularly the fate of Attorney General Janet Reno, as battles over Whitewater, Indogate and White House stonewalls continued. Eyes on both sides of the controversy focused on Independent Counsel Kenneth Starr, continuing his investigation of the re-elected President.

REVIEW & OUTLOOK

Longing for Reagan

Poor Bob Dole has been taking a terrible beating this campaign, not so much from his opponents or even a surly press as from his own troops. If he had to rely on soldiers like today's Republicans, he'd have been dead on a hillside in Italy some 50 years ago.

It's of course true that Bob Dole is not an inspiring or, whatever, eloquent figure. It's true that he carries a load of compromises of 36 years in the legislative process, and that this clouds or can be used to cloud any message he tries to deliver. It's true that one can imagine a campaign strategy, in particular starting to hammer at the character issue the minute the GOP primaries were decided, that in retrospect might have been clearer and more successful. Yet in any important endeavor like a political campaign there are always moments of doubts, and like all human beings any candidate will always have shortcomings.

Ronald Reagan

Consider for a moment Mr. Dole's opponent, and his party's ability to swallow doubts about *him*. Here we have a candidate who in the space of four years, not 36, has gone from a middle-class tax cut to a huge tax increase, from an enormous socialized medicine scheme to ending the welfare entitlement, from the promise of a balanced budget to the current posture of defending Medicare, Social Security, college loans and every other government outlay. Yet this collection of inconsistencies seems to bother almost no one, while Mr. Dole's quite specific tax promises are written off because he was once a deficit hawk.

Similarly, President Clinton can deliver a smooth speech. But having seen the same act on behalf of so many conflicting causes, who can any longer possibly believe? To take the ultimate test of Presidential eloquence, who could better rally the nation in time of war? In a real pinch, the nation we know would be much quicker to follow Bob Dole's earnest stumbling than Bill Clinton's eloquent slickness. Who, similarly, would you rather work for personally? For all of President Clinton's charm over the dinner table, his Administration has been a personal disaster for one after another of his personal associates.

Bob Dole

Yet for all this, the *Republicans* chafe at *their* candidate. Mr. Dole's aides air their differences and doubts in the public prints, while Mr. Clinton's aides line up to take bullets, risking perjury for him before Congressional Committees. Senator Alfonse D'Amato defers to Senator Paul Sarbanes. Rep. Jim Leach scarcely chairs the Banking Committee the way Henry Gonzalez did. Various conservative intellectuals and even the stalwart Governor Tommy Thompson throw in the towel before the votes are counted.

We've criticized Democrats for an excessive, blind loyalty, and think that their current posture may yet do them harm in the long run. Yet if Bill Clinton wins Tuesday as predicted, it will be because he knows how to fight, and so do his supporters. This is a spirit to be admired, and one Republicans, without reaching Gonzalez-like extremes, should emulate more than they recently have. If you go down fighting it at least shows belief in your principles; indeed sometimes a losing campaign lays the basis for later triumph, as Republicans who lived through the contrast between 1964 and 1980 seem to have forgotten.

Republicans intimidated by public opinion polls might also remember the more recent elections of Governors Christie Whitman, George Pataki and John Engler. Last-minute decisions and come-from-behind polls have become almost a fixture of our politics. Even now, whether a Clinton lead looks insurmountable depends on the methodology of the poll, as John Fund explains nearby [page 173]. The best reading of the tracking polls is that as the character issue registered with the public over the last week, a substantial number of Clinton voters moved into the undecided column. If they continue on into the Dole column, the race will be in an area where a little extra effort could be decisive. Even now, the GOP has reason to Huang in there.

Republican diffidence has many roots, perhaps even genetic ones. But clearly the GOP was spoiled by Ronald Reagan—blessed with extraordinary charm, plain-spoken eloquence and the uncanny ability to look past petty detail to project a vision for the country and the world. Of course Bob Dole is not Ronald Reagan, but who is? Mr. Dole remains a better candidate than all the guys he trounced in the primaries, or anyone realistically available to the GOP this year, especially given that campaign finance limits preclude a bid by members of a younger and arguably tougher generation of GOP Governors and Congressmen.

Bob Dole is a creature of Kansas, the war and the Senate. As politicians go, he has a remarkable record of keeping his word, and we have no doubt whatever that he would do his best to deliver a 15% tax cut with accompanying spending cuts and the rest of his economic program. While no more immune than any other politician from the influence of "special interests" among his constituents, he is appropriately cynical about them. For all the compromises of a long career, his every instinct is toward smaller government and an honorable role in the world.

Which is to say, he may not be Ronald Reagan, but is entirely suited to carrying on Mr. Reagan's vision. The Democrats had only one FDR this century, and Republicans are not likely to get anywhere unless they understand they are not likely to get a second Ronald Reagan.

Editorial Feature

Clinton Campaign Is in a Class All by Itself

The news that President Clinton plans to conclude his re-election drive with a speech pledging campaign-finance reform only makes sense. It perfectly captures the audacity that has made his campaign so astonishing to watch.

There has never been another campaign even close to Mr. Clinton's for brass. No presidential candidate has ever remade himself so thoroughly, booted scandals beyond Election Day so skillfully, or taken credit for things so shamelessly. This is political talent of the highest order. So let us hail true virtuosity when we see it, because it may be all downhill after next Tuesday.

Potomac Watch

By Paul A. Gigot

Mr. Clinton's campaign-finance gambit is remarkable only because it is so typically Clintonian. Today or tomorrow, the White House says, the president will vow to purge the evil of money from politics.

He will, presumably, avoid repeating his July praise in Los Angeles for the "aggressive efforts" of his "longtime friend" John Huang, the suspect fund-raiser we now know visited the White House 81 times since July 1995. The president may include a quick mea culpa for the Democratic Party's sins, even as he insists he's personally supported reform all along.

He will no doubt then chide Speaker Gingrich for failing to pass reform this year, and Bob Dole for opposing a bill "that was supported even by his friend and fellow Republican, John McCain." He will then denounce a "corrupt system" that breeds "cynicism." And he will do it all with a straight face, if not with his signature lip bite.

In a single stroke, Mr. Clinton will 1) appeal to Ross Perot supporters; 2) divert scrutiny from *Democratic* campaign violations by shifting the blame to everybody; 3) appease the media and Common Cause scolds who care less about current law-breaking than they do about passing ever more laws; and 4) paint the next Congress, probably Republican-led, into the corner of passing spending limits that will tend to help Democrats.

Bill Clinton

A lesser politician wouldn't dare try this, much less come close to pulling it off. But Mr. Clinton is our first presidential aspirant whose apotheosis occurs as a candidate, not in office. Campaigning is what defines his life. He is both candidate and political consultant wrapped into one. Those who described consultant Dick Morris as the White House Svengali were unfair to Mr. Clinton. The president and Mr. Morris share the same political essence.

How could anyone have expected an old-style pol like Bob Dole to keep up? Mr. Dole is burdened with an ironic self-knowledge that induces him to blurt out his own political calculation. He's too honest for his own good. For him a campaign is a desert to cross to become president, not the promised land itself.

So in California, Mr. Dole calls affirmative action and immigration "wedge issues." But Mr. Clinton replies with the nifty obfuscation, "mend it, don't end it." The Kansan takes weeks to persuade himself he can justify proposing a tax cut, then gets the sod kicked out of him by the media for flip-flopping. But Mr. Clinton can propose a tax cut in 1992, then renege, then propose it again before vetoing it, and now propose it again in 1996—and still win style points for being so politically nimble.

Now, with his campaign-finance speech, Mr. Clinton may perform his greatest feat of political audacity. We know he first proposed reform in 1992 as a club against George Bush, then barely mentioned it while Democrats ran Congress. We also know that even as he shook hands with Newt Gingrich on the subject his agents were shaking down fat cats around the globe.

As Bob Woodward describes it in "The Choice": "Clinton personally had been controlling tens of millions of dollars' worth of DNC advertising. This enabled him to exceed the spending limits and effectively rendered the DNC an adjunct to his own reelection effort. He was circumventing the rigorous post-Watergate reforms. . . ."

Now Mr. Clinton will distance himself from what those same DNC fund-raisers were doing. He will say that passing new "reform" laws is more important than abiding by the old ones. And his advisers now say he will propose, for Congress, the same kind of spending limits his own campaign has been evading for two years. How brilliantly cynical can you get?

All the more so because Mr. Clinton knows spending limits go down well with the media, whose own power would increase. Candidate spending limits also won't be opposed by his allies, especially unions, which the Supreme Court will always (and correctly) allow to spend as much as they want on political speech under the First Amendment. The main losers would be Republicans, who would have less money to spend to compete with unions and a usually hostile media.

A less daring politician, or one with a sense of shame, would keep quiet and ride out his lead through the election. But Mr. Clinton is so brazen, and so sure of his own virtue, that he thinks he can turn even his own scandals into his own political advantage. And why not? He always has before.

Editorial Feature

It'll Be Close

By JOHN H. FUND

Although he has been a clear favorite to win for a year, President Clinton has always thought this would end up being a close election. One reason is that he's been surprised before. The first time he sought a second term, in 1980, the final newspaper poll in Arkansas showed him with a double-digit lead. He ended up losing 52% to 48% to Frank White, an inarticulate banker who had switched parties only months before. In 1992, the final Gallup poll showed Mr. Clinton with a 49% to 37% lead over President Bush. His final victory margin was half that, 43% to 37%, with Ross Perot going up five percentage points in the last couple of days. Unusually for a challenger, Mr. Clinton didn't get the bulk of undecided voters in 1992.

Much the same thing may happen to Mr. Clinton again. Both the Reuters/Zogby tracking poll and a new survey by GOP pollster Linda DiVall show Mr. Clinton's support slipping to 43%. Bob Dole is holding at 33% in both polls, and Mr. Perot is rising. The CNN/Gallup tracking poll shows Mr. Clinton with an 11-point lead and Mr. Perot surging to 11%. Other polls still show a larger Clinton lead.

The possibility of last-minute shifts in voter preference has been enhanced this year by the lack of public interest in the election and a 40% decline in network coverage of the campaign. The old adage was that voters never started to pay attention to the election until the World Series was over. The series used to end in early October, but the New York Yankees only won last Saturday.

The proliferation of polls has had a real impact on the subdued nature of this campaign. In 1992, media outlets commissioned a total of 125 polls. This year, CNN alone has conducted some 200. The poll-driven nature of campaign coverage has tended to depress voter interest and freeze perceptions of the candidates, because voters are told again and again that the race is over.

Still, while all polls have shown Mr. Clinton ahead significantly, the variations have been as dramatic as 14 points for polls taken at the same time. The biggest explanation for this gap lies in how polls handle the "undecided" voter and how they predict who "likely" voters will be.

Voters like to tell pollsters they plan to fulfill their civic duty and vote. A September survey found that 73% of those phoned said they planned to vote. In reality, about a third of those won't show up on Tuesday. That means polls must focus on those who will make up the actual electorate by trying to ask people if they know when Election Day is, if they watched any of the debates, or if they have filled out their sample ballot. Even with those efforts, polls consistently underpredict Republican turnout by six to eight percentage points. Pollster John Zogby says that because polls tend to include many Democrats, especially blue-collar women, who often don't vote, "the results may be skewed toward the Democrats." Harold Ickes, the deputy White House chief of staff, says the White House is worried about what could be a near-record low turnout.

Mr. Ickes adds that "there's also lots of undecided voters out there." In fact, there are more than in most elections, and their ranks may have recently grown, not shrunk. Most pollsters deal with voters who say they "don't know" how they will vote by asking them whom they lean toward. Mr. Zogby says that kind of "hard pushing" creates very "soft" supporters, who can easily change their minds or not vote at all. Mr. Zogby waits until the final polls to push voters because of the danger of inaccuracies. Even so, his latest tracking polls show the number of undecided voters is *increasing*. His Oct. 23-25 tracking poll found 89% of voters expressing a preference for the top three candidates. Now just 84% are.

The biggest reason isn't a surge for Mr. Dole or Mr. Perot, but the movement of Clinton voters into the undecided column. That indicates the race will be closer. A week ago, Democratic pollster Mark Mellman predicted that two-thirds of undecided voters will end up opting for Mr. Dole. That's because if an incumbent president can't convince voters to support him by the final week, many of them are looking for an excuse—any excuse—not to vote for him. In 1992, the University of Michigan found that 8% of voters decided how they would cast their ballots on Election Day itself. This year could see even more last-minute electoral shoppers, which should help Mr. Dole.

Many pollsters also suspect there is a hidden anti-Clinton vote that will depress his numbers as in 1992. Mr. Clinton is what we might call a "high maintenance" candidate, one who doesn't have a large reservoir of good will with the electorate. A recent CNN/Gallup poll found that 47% of voters do not think he is honest and trustworthy, an indication that some will find it easy not to turn out for him. The media and much elite opinion has tended to discount the "character" issue, lumping together everything from Paula Jones to the FBI file scandal as topics not really worthy of concern. Alone with their thoughts in

---

A week ago, a Democratic pollster predicted that two-thirds of undecided voters will end up opting for Mr. Dole. If an incumbent can't convince voters by the final week, many are looking for an excuse not to vote for him.

---

the privacy of the voting booth, some soft Clinton supporters may not be able to ratify his presidency and could swing to Mr. Dole or one of several third-party candidates.

Another reason the election is likely to be close is that the improved prospects of GOP congressional candidates may create an unusual bottom-up effect in some states that will lift Mr. Dole's numbers slightly. Approval ratings for Congress are at a 10-year high, and about a third more voters are planning to vote for their House incumbent than were in 1994.

Perhaps the biggest obstacle in the way of a Clinton landslide is the underlying conservative mood of the country. After the 1994 election, Americans indicated by nearly 2 to 1 that they preferred a smaller government and lower taxes to a bigger government that provided more services. That number has budged only a little despite all the troubles of the Dole-Gingrich Congress, which is surely a major reason Mr. Clinton has chosen to co-opt as many conservative issues as he can, from welfare to school choice, and to propose only a grab-bag of modest government initiatives.

Mr. Clinton learned in 1994 that this is a center-right country, and he has brilliantly accommodated himself to that fact. Even so, enough voters question the sincerity of his latest moderate makeover that he is likely to become the first presidential candidate since Woodrow Wilson in 1916 to win a second successive election without a majority of the popular vote. Democratic presidential candidates simply have

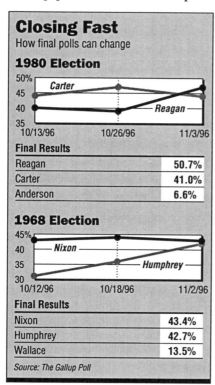

Closing Fast
How final polls can change

1980 Election

Final Results

Reagan	**50.7%**
Carter	**41.0%**
Anderson	**6.6%**

1968 Election

Final Results

Nixon	**43.4%**
Humphrey	**42.7%**
Wallace	**13.5%**

Source: The Gallup Poll

a hard time clearing the 50% hurdle: No Democrat since FDR has done so with the exceptions of Lyndon Johnson, who won a landslide against the hapless Barry Goldwater, and Jimmy Carter, who won 50.1% in the post-Watergate election of 1976. Just as in 1992, Mr. Clinton may wake up on Nov. 6 thanking Ross Perot for his margin of victory. Mr. Perot's 1992 supporters plumped for GOP candidates by over 70% in the 1994 midterm elections, and his voters are likely to give GOP congressional candidates a majority again this year.

President Clinton has maneuvered brilliantly in this campaign. But if he wins, not even his diehard partisans claim he will have much of a mandate. The country may well elect a Democrat who campaigned as easily the most conservative nominee of his party since the 1920s—yet probably will mete out no net losses to a Republican majority in Congress led by conservatives Trent Lott in the Senate and Newt Gingrich in the House. Such a result would represent a remarkable political comeback for the malleable Bill Clinton, but it would provide little evidence that the electorate has decided to rethink the message it sent in 1994.

Mr. Fund is a member of the Journal's editorial board.

REVIEW & OUTLOOK

Four More Years

I am the first president in history ever to have a special counsel involving activities that have nothing to do with my work as president, it all predated that, and that arose when there had not been a single, solitary serious assertion that I had done anything illegal. But I said, fine, we'll look into it if it makes everybody feel better and to have more confidence.

—News conference, March 3, 1995

1992

March: In a report arranged by the Clinton campaign, Denver lawyer James Lyons states the Clintons lost $68,000 on the Whitewater investment and clears them of improprieties. The issue fades from the campaign. July: Bill Clinton accepts the Democratic Party's Presidential nomination in New York. Aug. 31: Resolution Trust Corporation field officers complete criminal referral #C0004 on Madison Guaranty and forward it to Charles Banks, U.S. Attorney for the Eastern District of Arkansas.

1993

Jan. 20: Bill Clinton is sworn in as President of the United States.

March: Press clips about Whitewater are faxed from the office of Deputy Treasury Secretary Roger Altman to the office of White House Counsel Bernard Nussbaum. Mr. Altman also is serving as acting head of the Resolution Trust Corporation, an independent federal agency.

May: The White House fires seven employees of its Travel Office, The actions of Associate Counsel William Kennedy III, a former member of the Rose Law Firm, which included attempts to involve the FBI and the Internal Revenue Service in a criminal investigation of the Travel Office, are sharply criticized.

July: According to a White House chronology, Vincent Foster completes work on a blind trust for the Clintons. On July 20 the Little Rock FBI obtains a warrant to search the office of David Hale as part of its investigation into Capital Management Services. In Washington, Deputy White House Counsel Vincent Foster drives to Fort Marcy Park and commits suicide. According to testimony by a uniformed Secret Service officer, Mrs. Clinton's chief of staff Maggie Williams exits the counsel's suite that evening with an armful of folders; Ms. Williams denies the claim.

Bill Clinton

White House Counsel Bernard Nussbaum searches Mr. Foster's office, but denies access to Park Police and Justice Department investigators. In an angry phone call, Deputy Attorney General Philip Heymann asks, "Bernie, are you hiding something?" Documents, including Whitewater files, are removed. A torn-up note is found in Mr. Foster's briefcase.

September: Paula Casey, a longtime associate of the Clintons, turns down plea bargain attempts from David Hale's lawyer, who had offered to share information on the "banking and borrowing practices of some individuals in the elite political circles of the State of Arkansas." On Sept. 23 Mr. Hale is indicted for fraud.

On Sept. 29 Treasury General Counsel Jean Hanson warns Mr. Nussbaum that the RTC plans to issue criminal referrals asking the Justice Department to investigate Madison. The referrals are said to name the Clintons as witnesses to, and possible beneficiaries of, illegal actions. Mr. Nussbaum passes the information to Bruce Lindsey, a top White House aide. On Oct. 6 President Clinton meets with Arkansas Gov. Jim Guy Tucker at the White House.

November: In Little Rock, U.S. Attorney Casey recuses herself from the Madison case; in Kansas City, RTC investigator Jean Lewis is taken off the probe; in Seattle, President Clinton meets with Gov. Tucker in Seattle. December: The Washington Times reports that Whitewater files were removed from Mr. Foster's office. Surgeon General Joycelyn Elders announces support for drug legalization.

1994

January: Attorney General Reno appoints Robert Fiske as special counsel to investigate Whitewater; Deputy Attorney General Philip Heymann resigns. February: Mr. Altman meets with Mr. Nussbaum and other senior White House staff to give them a "heads-up" about Madison. March 5: White House Counsel Bernard Nussbaum resigns. March 14: Associate Attorney General Webster Hubbell resigns. March 18: Reports appear of Mrs. Clinton's 1970s commodities trades in which she turns a $1,000 deposit into $100,000 of profit trading through dealer Red Bone.

May: Former Little Rock resident Paula Corbin Jones files suit against President Clinton, charging he sexually harassed her while governor. June: Special Counsel Robert Fiske concludes that Mr. Foster's death was a suicide. July: Congressional hearings open. August: A three-judge panel removes Mr. Fiske and appoints Kenneth Starr as independent counsel.

Aug. 17: Deputy Treasury Secretary Roger Altman resigns. The next day, Treasury General Counsel Jean Hanson resigns. Sept. 12: Donald Smaltz is named independent counsel to investigate Agriculture Secretary Mike Espy. On Oct. 3, Secretary Espy resigns.

December: Former Associate Attorney General Webster Hubbell pleads guilty to two felonies in a scheme to defraud his former Rose Law Firm partners of $482,000.

1995

February: Arkansas banker Neal Ainley is indicted on five felony counts relating to Bill Clinton's 1990 gubernatorial campaign. He later pleads guilty to reduced charges and agrees to cooperate with the independent counsel. March: Whitewater real-estate broker Chris Wade pleads guilty to two felonies. May: David Barrett is appointed independent counsel to probe charges that Housing Secretary Henry Cisneros made false statements to the FBI.

June: Stephen Smith, a former aide to Gov. Bill Clinton, pleads guilty to misusing a Capital Management loan and agrees to cooperate with the independent counsel. July: Daniel Pearson is named independent counsel to probe business dealings of Commerce Secretary

REVIEW & OUTLOOK

Toward 2000

Analysts are calling this a "status quo election." The question is, what's the status quo?

This page has long believed in the inherent wisdom of the elec‐torate. A market, the collective result of many decisions by many minds, is "smarter" than any single participant. So too with elec‐tions. Financial analysts ask, What is the market telling us? Political analysts should ask, What are the voters telling us, in their collective wisdom? Sorting through the Tuesday election, from the top of the ticket down through the local initiatives, we must admit that a single message is hard to find.

President Clinton was re-elected to a second term, but with less than 50% of the vote. Voters retained Newt Gingrich's House of Rep‐resentatives, but with its GOP majority cut by about half. This is the first Democrat elected to two full terms since FDR, and the first time the Republicans have held a House majority since 1928. The stock market scanned this reality yesterday and rose 96 points. The unions' advertising barrage knocked off some House GOP freshmen, but the $35 million of workers' money that John Sweeney spent fell well short of Democratic control. Whither the AFL-CIO?

In the Senate, Republicans turned more conservative and Democ‐rats more liberal. Consider just one state, Kansas: Sam Brownback, a self-declared Reaganite, becomes the state's Senator, moving away from the centrist tenures of Bob Dole and Nancy Kassebaum. Massachusetts chose long-serving liberal Democrat Sen. John Kerrey over its moderate GOP governor, William Weld.

Meanwhile, any discernible message was delivered by a shrinking base: less than half of eligible voters went to the polls, the lowest turnout in 72 years. So what does it all mean?

You can argue that it was an incumbents' year, with a reasonable economy and a booming stock market, but in fact a fair number of incumbents were turned out as the Northeast went Democratic and the South Republican. No doubt we will hear about the year of the non-married woman. You can argue that voters want a smaller government, but want their entitlements too—is that wisdom?

You can argue that Bob Dole's failure was personal, but who would have been a better GOP candidate? By all accounts, virtually every national GOP figure, from Speaker Gingrich down, has spent the past year in the thrall of polls and focus groups. Maybe next time some candidate will try the novel idea of offering voters a personal belief system.

That said, it should be noted before he departs that Bob Dole, who in his career crossed many political rivers, chose to entrust his last voyage to the compass of conservative ideas born during the past 15 years. Yes, he lost, partly because he simply lacked the electronic smoothness required for the media age, and partly because of the Clinton co-options. But merely at the level of political calculation, Mr. Dole would not have chosen these ideas had he not sensed their power, as he articulated so well in his convention acceptance. At least he leaves that legacy very much intact for the younger, more conservative GOP generation emerging from this election.

The Republicans indeed have an agenda—whether a reformed tax system or more individual choice in medicine and education—but it's fair to say that its leaders haven't adequately explained to voters how their alternatives to the withering welfare state will mean a better society.

As for Mr. Clinton, it remains a form of genuine praise in this business to call someone a "political animal." He is surely that, surviving the setback of 1994 and ultimately prevailing against his opposition, even as he crosses the victory line bleeding from a hundred wounds. He now enters a short period of transition and reflection, with the news wires yesterday reporting resignations imminent from Secretaries Christopher, Perry and perhaps Kantor. There is a crucial and even symbolic decision to be made about the future of the Attorney General.

We will continue to hold this—or any—President accountable for his conduct of office. But we remain open on the eve of the second term to the possibility that this Presidency and the Republican Congress will find reason to address in good faith the start of construction on that famous bridge. Medicare, so debauched during the campaign, would be an appropriate test of the seriousness of purpose on both sides. After the Morris-inspired adeptness of the campaign, Mr. Clinton needs to tether his Presidency, lest it drift dangerously alone.

What ultimately emerges here is a picture of an electorate that hasn't made up its mind, in contrast perhaps to the 1994 electorate that seemed decisive. Yet the 1994 results still cast a long shadow, with GOP control of Congress confirmed and President Clinton trying to co-opt his opponents' agenda with such issues as a balanced budget, welfare reform and school uniforms, while all the time of course branding them as extremists. Ultimately, we suspect, voters sense they are at a turning point. But just now they're wondering what's around the next political corner.

That lack of political clarity should hold a warning for both the Democrats and Republicans. Perhaps the electorate did play its cards close to the chest in 1996. But for better or worse, Tuesday's election produced the cast of characters who will carry the country's fortunes toward the year 2000. We suspect that as America's voters cross the threshold of the millennium, they'll be putting these just-elected politicians to a deservedly severe test.

Review & Outlook

Starr Wars

The spectacle of James Carville assessing the character of Kenneth Starr is almost too much to behold, but since Shakespeare's time and before, the court jester has been used to deliver deadly serious messages. When Mr. Carville reacted to Paula Corbin Jones with quips about dragging $100 bills through trailer parks, of course, Bob Bennett and his "tabloid trash" comments were not far behind.

So as a newly elected Bill Clinton reshuffles his cabinet, the campaign is also under way to drag his independent counsel into the mud. The President himself signaled this intention back in August when he condemned "the abuse of the special-counsel law" in a CNN interview. Later, while dangling a pardon in front of Susan McDougal, he told PBS's Jim Lehrer that it was "obvious" Mr. Starr was out to get him.

On November 3, just two days before the election, Mr. Carville took the campaign to besmirch Mr. Starr into the booster stage on CNBC's Tim Russert show. He launched a nearly incoherent tirade accusing Mr. Starr of being in bed with tobacco lawyers, the Washington Post, Pat Robertson, "scumbag" Senate Whitewater Committee counsel Michael Chertoff, three federal judges, two United States Senators and a partridge in a pear tree. But Mr. Carville did manage to get the important message out: "If I was the attorney general, I would have dismissed him."

The same day on "Meet the Press," Senator Christopher Dodd endorsed Mr. Carville's remarks. Mr. Starr's dismissal "certainly ought to be under consideration, in my view, because he's crossed the line politically," Senator Dodd said. And Mr. Carville was back at it the day after the election, telling this newspaper that he was "inclined to raise money, run full-page ads and run television ads" to portray Mr. Starr's investigation as a "partisan, right-wing" witch hunt.

Now of course, Mr. Starr's official charter specifically says he's to investigate possible involvement of the President and First Lady in the banking matters on which he's already convicted their former business partners. Investigating the President is what he is *supposed* to do. A report also is due on events surrounding the death of Deputy White House Counsel Vincent Foster. At the request of Attorney General Janet Reno, Mr. Starr's mandate has been expanded at least three times—to cover the Travel Office affair, the FBI files dispute, and whether White House Counsel Bernard Nussbaum committed perjury. Other matters also may be under investigation—sealed to the public, but known to the White House. Now there is talk of an independent counsel for the Indonesian funds flap, with perhaps Mr. Starr being assigned Whitewater-related aspects, such as payments to former Associate Attorney General Webster Hubbell.

Kenneth Starr

Clearly Mr. Starr is big trouble for the President's second term, and all sorts of options for dealing with him must be before the Whitewater defense team—at least five lawyers in the White House counsel's office, plus Mr. Bennett and his big law firm plus David Kendall and his big law firm. The easy course, having a Democratic Congress slowly pinch Mr. Starr's funding, is no longer an option. So after Tuesday's election, what remains?

The most effective parry would be a raft of pardons, leaving no one for Mr. Starr to investigate. This would be a jolly way to start a new term, rending the President's new credibility, forever marring Mr. Clinton's bid to be more than an asterisk in the history books. The use of presidential prerogatives to obstruct justice might even trigger an actual effort to impeach. In any event, the problem is where to stop. If you start with a pardon for Hillary, the logic of protection takes you to Maggie Williams and on down the line to already-convicted Susan McDougal.

The independent counsel law allows the Attorney General to dismiss a counsel for "good cause." This may, or may not, have something to do with the embarrassingly public way Janet Reno has been proclaiming she'd like to stay in the job. While Ms. Reno is pliant, her most likely replacements, Commerce Secretary Mickey Kantor or Deputy Attorney General Jamie Gorelick, seem more likely hatchetmen. In any event, an Attorney General would have to submit a report to Congress and the Special Division of the U.S. Court of Appeals that appointed Mr. Starr specifying the facts found and the grounds for his removal. Mr. Starr would have the opportunity to obtain judicial review of his dismissal. If it were upheld, the Special Division would appoint a replacement. (Our nominee would be soon-to-be-former Congressman William Clinger.) Dismissal would only buy time, in short, but that is not nothing.

Just what sins could be alleged against Mr. Starr, Mr. Dodd and Mr. Carville don't bother to specify. Obviously he avoided election-eve indictments, like the ones delivered by Lawrence Walsh in 1992. His probe has been notably careful, winning a raft of guilty pleas and a big conviction, though one relatively minor courtroom loss. His integrity recently was endorsed by Abner Mikva, President Clinton's own former counsel. Even the hometeam Arkansas Democrat-Gazette has complained about Mr. Clinton's comments. "Not since Richard Nixon has a president of the United States launched so public a campaign against a special counsel," the paper wrote. "Whatever happens before a grand jury, Mr. Clinton has begun trying his case in public."

The Administration's bashing of Mr. Starr is bad enough merely as a public relations gambit, but also lays a basis for even rasher steps. Mr. Clinton's first term was marked at times by a hubris that led it into perilous political waters, and he will be asking for trouble if he lets himself get carried away by Tuesday's victory.

Review & Outlook

Asides

Reno Watch

And so it begins. With most of the Clinton Cabinet going quietly—Labor Secretary Robert Reich nicely publicizing his exit as an act of family values—the birds of the Beltway are now gathering up in the low branches to watch Attorney General Janet Reno try to survive. Only yesterday, the President's invisible aides squeezed off a few rounds at Ms. Reno for the apparent affront of saying she'd continue "if the President wanted me to stay." We don't doubt that the palace politics of the second term are going to be interesting, and perhaps somewhere out there is another Edward Levi to provide bedrock credibility. Other than Ms. Reno herself, we doubt

Janet Reno

there is anyone else currently at Justice who would do that. And perhaps a Republican such as William Weld can be coaxed into the limelight. But if post-Clinton-I credibility is the goal, why not ask back former Deputy Attorney General Philip Heymann, who still doesn't have a full answer to his famous question: "Bernie, are you hiding something?"

Editorial Feature

Kenneth Starr on Civic Virtue And Whitewater

The following remarks were made by Independent Counsel Kenneth Starr in a meeting on Monday night sponsored by the Economic Club of Detroit.

I want to begin by talking about something that we don't hear much about these days: civic virtue. The phrase has a kind of fussy sound, something out of the era of quill pens and powdered wigs. And, as a matter of fact, it is a concept that the framers of our Constitution took very seriously, and—despite their many differences and disagreements regarding policy and politics—agreed upon.

The framers were realists about human nature. Men are not angels, as James Madison wrote—that's why our constitutional structure is permeated with checks and balances. Although these checks and balances sometimes make it difficult for the government to move forward expeditiously, they also circumvent abuses of power by officials who, as Madison and his colleagues knew, may not be angelic.

But—and this is important—the framers believed that people are not invariably scoundrels, either. They knew that a democratic government demands a degree of civic virtue. It demands this virtue on the part of elected officials and on the part of the citizens who choose the officials. Civic virtue must transcend party (or, as the framers would phrase it, "factions") and the vagaries of opinion and interest that inure to democratic governance. If people lack "sufficient virtue . . . for self-government," Madison wrote, then "nothing less than the chains of despotism can restrain them from destroying and devouring one another."

What did Madison and his colleagues mean by civic virtue? They meant that individuals, as they pursued their self-interested goals, would feel a commitment to justice, to civility, and, above all, to truthfulness. Without those traits, the individual cannot be a true citizen. And without virtuous citizens, the framers believed, self-government will ultimately self-destruct. In the 1990s as in the 1790s, civic virtue is an essential canopy over our public square. . . .

This brings me to my topic for today: "Whitewater—A Perspective From Little Rock and Washington." The conventional wisdom is that Whitewater is unfathomably, eye-glazingly complicated. As Tony Snow of the Detroit News puts it, "Whitewater, with all its complexity, makes even the most devoted news hound woozy."

The details of the various matters that have been labeled "Whitewater" do have some Byzantine twists and turns. At heart, though, it's not difficult. I propose to offer a brief summary, one that I hope won't make anyone woozy.

The story has its roots during the 1992 primary season, when a New York Times report raised questions about Whitewater Development Corporation, a real estate partnership between then-

Susan McDougal

Gov. and Mrs. Clinton and James and Susan McDougal. The presidential campaign commissioned a report by James Lyons, a Denver attorney, which found no wrongdoing by any party to the Whitewater investment and concluded that the Clintons had, in fact, lost money on the deal. Whitewater, as a public issue, essentially disappeared for more than a year and a half. Then, in December 1993, published reports stated that Whitewater files had been removed from the White House office of Vincent W. Foster Jr. shortly after his death in July of that year.

With public interest renewed in Whitewater, the president in early 1994 asked the attorney general to appoint an independent counsel. She selected Robert Fiske. Later, I was appointed to the position when the independent counsel statute was reauthorized by Congress.

As Bob Fiske and I discovered, Whitewater is about several related things. It is, at its origins, about lying—false statements and fraud—that contributed to the demise of a federally insured savings and loan in Little Rock, Madison Guaranty, co-owned by James and Susan McDougal. It is about lying and fraud to secure loans for wealthy and influential people from another financial institution chartered by the Small Business Administration to aid economically and socially disadvantaged small businesses.

Let me be more specific. Whitewater is about, among others, Susan McDougal, co-owner of Madison Guaranty and one of four partners in Whitewater Development. At trial the evidence established that using false and fraudulent information, Susan McDougal borrowed $300,000 from a federal program designed to benefit disadvantaged small businesses. The loan, ostensibly, was to finance her advertising business. She walked into the loan office, signed a few papers, and took home

The conventional wisdom is that Whitewater is unfathomably, eye-glazingly complicated. At heart, though, it's not difficult.

$300,000. According to her attorney, she said when she was handed the check, "Gee, this is fun. Can I come back tomorrow?"

That $300,000 went in a lot of directions. According to Mike Patkus, the FBI agent who carefully followed the paper trail, some of it went to pay Susan McDougal's clothing bills. Some went to renovate her house. Some went to pay her tennis club dues. Some was used to further her brother's political campaign. Some ended up on the account of Whitewater Development, and the balance went to other personal debts. Not one penny of the $300,000 aided a disadvantaged small business; and, not one penny was repaid.

This case—involving fraud and false statements—was tried before 12 men and women from the Eastern District of Arkansas. That Little Rock jury convicted Susan McDougal, along with her ex-husband. She was convicted on four felony counts, by her peers from Arkansas who sat through a three-month trial. The judge—Judge George Howard Jr.—imposed a two-year prison sentence. Since the trial, Ms. McDougal has refused to testify before a grand jury in Little Rock seeking to get to the bottom of Whitewater. She is now incarcerated for contempt of court.

That is part of the story. Whitewater is also about lawyers, judges, politicians and business people who, like Susan McDougal, borrowed money through lies and deceit for one purpose and used it for anoth-

the highest professional and ethical standards, especially an investigation into possible public corruption or violation of the public trust. Ralph Waldo Emerson once remarked of someone, "The louder he talked of his honor, the faster we counted the spoons." So I'm not going to do that. Instead, I want to make three points about this investigation.

First, I am enormously aided by a superb, highly professional team. I have recruited highly experienced lawyers, mostly from the top ranks of the Justice Department and U.S. Attorney's offices. We have also called on skilled investigators from the FBI and the IRS. They are, in every sense of the word, professionals. They are battle-tested public servants who are following the standards of their professions as they set about unearthing the facts and analyzing the law. These are not partisans. They are not spin doctors. They are professionals in a system built on law, not on politics.

Second, every major decision in our office entails careful, collegial deliberation. We meet and hash out each significant prosecutorial question, including each possible indictment. The individual attorneys have their respective areas of primary responsibility, but everyone participates actively in these deliberative discussions. We operate, to an extraordinary degree, on broadly shared professional judgments.

Finally, I want to stress that we are conducting a law enforcement investigation. Our principal function is to determine whether prosecutable crimes have been committed. We must leave to others—to congressional investigators, journalists and, ultimately, citizens—the task of making judgments about those Whitewater allegations that do not result in actions called for by the independent counsel statute.

I earnestly wish I could give you a final report on our investigation today. As much as I enjoy life in Little Rock, I would rather be home with my wife of 26 years and our three children. But we are not yet at that stage. I can tell you that we are making very substantial progress on all fronts, with active grand jury inquiries under way in Washington and Little Rock.

The investigation is at a critical juncture now, and we are proceeding as expeditiously as possible. We will continue to do so in the interests of justice and fairness to all concerned—not only to the subjects of the investigation but ultimately to the American people.

Letters to the Editor

In Whitewater, Clintons Are Clean

In response to "Kenneth Starr on Civic Virtue and Whitewater" (editorial page, Nov. 13), the reprinted remarks of the independent counsel to the Economic Club of Detroit:

I do not wish to comment on the questionable propriety of a prosecutor speaking publicly (again) concerning a pending criminal investigation that he is conducting. Nor do I challenge Mr. Starr's right to make pious proclamations about "civic virtue." I do, however, challenge his reckless if not deliberate mischaracterization of a report I prepared for then-Gov. and Mrs. Clinton in March 1992.

Mr. Starr states that my report "found no wrongdoing by *any* party to the Whitewater investment and concluded that the Clintons had, in fact, lost money on the deal" (emphasis added). This characterization is only half true; I did conclude, with the aid of an independent financial investigation conducted over several weeks, that the Clintons had in fact lost money in Whitewater Development Co. Also, based on the available evidence and material, I concluded that the Clintons were passive investors in Whitewater Development and had assumed a substantial personal financial risk, including personal liability for corporate loans totaling more than $200,000.

The scope of my analysis was limited to these areas. I was not asked nor could I have determined whether other parties to the Whitewater investment (i.e., the McDougals) had engaged in any wrongdoing. Mr. Starr's statement to the contrary is simply untrue, and Mr. Starr knows it or should know it. He need only have talked to his "highly experienced lawyers" and "skilled FBI investigators," who have sent me repetitive document subpoenas and had me testify about my report on two separate occasions, one at great length. Frankly, all he really had to do is read the report himself. As we lawyers say, it speaks for itself.

Mr. Starr also fails to mention that the Resolution Trust Corporation (later the Federal Deposit Insurance Corporation) engaged the respected law firm of Pillsbury, Madison & Sutro to undertake an extensive investigation of Whitewater Development Co. as part of the RTC's investigation of possible civil claims against individuals and entities associated with Madison Guaranty Savings & Loan Association. Their report—conducted over about two years and at a cost of almost $4 million—reached the same conclusions as I did: The Clintons were passive investors, were personally at risk, and lost substantial funds in Whitewater Development. In reviewing the $300,000 loan to Susan McDougal, which Mr. Starr references in his remarks, the Pillsbury firm concluded unequivocally as follows:

"The evidence does not suggest that the Clintons played any role with respect to the transactions discussed above [i.e., the $300,000 loan and its proceeds]." (Pillsbury report, Dec. 13, 1995, page 45.)

Further, the Pillsbury report stated:

"Therefore, on this record, there is no basis to assert that the Clintons knew anything of substance about the McDougals' advances to Whitewater, the source of funds used to make those advances, or the source of the funds used to make payments on bank debt. In particular, there is no evidence that the Clintons knew anything of substance about the transactions as to which the RTC might be able to establish liability as to people other than the Clintons." (Pillsbury report, page 77.)

Finally, and perhaps most importantly, Pillsbury reported:

"On this record, there is no basis to charge the Clintons with any kind of primary liability for fraud or intentional misconduct. This investigation has revealed no evidence to support any such claims, nor would the record support any claim of secondary or derivative liability for the possible misdeeds of others." (Ibid, page 77.)

In view of these findings and this uncontroverted evidence exonerating the Clintons, one wonders what Mr. Starr's definition of "civic virtue" really is. More particularly, where is his commitment to justice, civility and truthfulness, which James Madison and his colleagues maintained that civic virtue requires?

JAMES M. LYONS

Denver

REVIEW & OUTLOOK

Clinton's Masons

The election is over, which means the Clinton masons can return to building the biggest stonewall in the history of American politics.

At one end of the stonewall, the Clinton Justice Department one week after the election came up with a blanket argument whereby the White House doesn't have to answer any pending Congressional subpoenas: It claims that after a Congress adjourns, its subpoenas cease to have any legal effect.

This is quite something. Observers specializing in the study of the Clinton stonewalls will recall that we have analogized them to Dean Smith's famous, clock-killing four-corner offense at North Carolina. This latest gambit might be called the Cinderella offense, by which subpoenas become pumpkins at the adjournment bell. Clinton Justice wants to force new subpoenas to be issued by the *next* Congress, a procedure that could take two to three months. But by then no doubt new legalistic boulders would be rolled into place against the details of those subpoenas. This one could get interesting.

Meanwhile, at another point on the Great Wall of Refusal, the Clinton National Security Council now refuses to let Congress look at 33 of 36 trade documents that were improperly removed from the Commerce Department and stored for months in a safe at the Small Business Administration.

The trade documents in dispute were removed from the late Secretary Ron Brown's office by his special counsel, Ira Sockowitz, who moved to a new job at the SBA, where he made a special request for a safe to store them. Observers specializing in the fund-raising activities of the Democratic National Committee will recall that the documents are under subpoena as part of a Freedom of Information Act lawsuit brought by Judicial Watch, a watchdog group whose efforts set in motion the surfacing of John Huang and the Asian contribution pipeline. This in turn has given us what might be called the DNC's Perfect Act of Contrition Strategy: "We took all this money which somehow turned out to be illegal but we *sincerely* gave it back and we've all said five Hail Marys so everything's OK now." Last week saw the latest trip to this confessional, as the DNC announced it was returning that famous $450,000 contribution made by an Indonesian gardener with ties to the Lippo Group, Mr. Huang's former employer.

The documents in the SBA safe concern negotiations for large sales of satellite and telecommunications technology to China, Russia and India during the time Mr. Huang worked at Commerce. Congressional investigators have been blocked for weeks from seeing the classified documents to determine their possible relevance to their investigations of potential misbehavior at Commerce.

Earlier this month, Alan Kreczko, the NSC's legal adviser, instructed the SBA not to allow any Congressional review of the documents, even by Rep. Larry Combest, the chairman of the House Intelligence Committee. Mr. Kreczko noted that while a Congressional committee is investigating why Mr. Sockowitz took the documents from Commerce, it "is not clear why the committee needs access to the text of those documents for its inquiry." This sophistry prompted Rep. Combest and four other House committee chairmen—William Clinger of Government Reform, Jan Meyers of Small Business, William Thomas of House Oversight and Donald Manzullo of an exports subcommittee—to write White House Counsel Jack Quinn in protest.

They note that if the White House is in fact invoking executive privilege as the reason for withholding the documents—the only real reason to issue such a refusal—it will have to provide a detailed index of the documents and reasons why each is covered by executive privilege. So far none has been provided and "only then can we assess the validity of the executive privilege claim," they wrote.

A fishing expedition? How can you call it a fishing expedition after all the record-sized fish that have been getting pulled from these waters? Recall that the last time the White House claimed executive privilege was over 2,000 pages of documents relating to the Travel Office firings. They were turned over just before the House planned to vote Mr. Quinn in contempt. And as it turned out, one memo among the 2,000 pages led to Filegate—a big fish called Craig Livingstone and the discovery that the White House had gotten its hands on some 900 FBI files on Republican appointees.

Before the election, a lot of people across the political spectrum, viewing the Administration's stonewall masons at work, asked what these people could be hiding. Having run out the clock once, the White House now hopes interest will wane, even as it argues that subpoenas are pumpkins and privilege is in the eye of the document holder. Congress, in short, is being told to get lost. In the new spirit of the times, it should refuse.

Journal writer Micah Morrison disclosed the existence of a 331-page White House report detailing a right-wing "conspiracy" to plant negative stories about the Clintons in the mainstream press by utilizing a sinister-sounding "media food chain." The story became a pressroom sensation. "Its silliness aside," a Journal editorial observed, "the 'food chain' report has to be seen as the nastiness it is. It's part of a generally successful Clinton effort to provoke criticism of members of the press who are reporting the Clinton scandals."

Editorial Feature

Consensus, the Enemy of News

By ROBERT L. BARTLEY

In 1922 Walter Lippmann wrote a very wise book called "Public Opinion." In one of its most penetrating sections he discusses the dilemma of the newspaper editor, even more excruciating for today's network news producer, of trying to give meaning to the gushing reality of a day's events. Of the multitude of events taking place on any given day, how does he sort out which deserve attention, which can be ignored, and which top the news? Lippmann's answer was that the only way an editor can deal with the torrent is to carry in his head pre-existing patterns, what Lippmann called stereotypes, to apply to events as they come by.

These stereotypes or preconceptions exert a powerful influence on news coverage. To take a trivial example, back when Gerald Ford was president, he bumped his head getting out of a helicopter, and the stereotype quickly became clumsiness; so a whole series of slips and bumps was reported instead of overlooked. With no pre-existing stereotype, Vice President Dan Quayle might have been forgiven for following instead of correcting a card misspelling the word potato. But given the pre-existing stereotype of simple-mindedness, the episode more or less blew him out of American politics. In analyzing the press, the most intriguing and most penetrating question is, where do these stereotypes come from?

In the case of editorialists and commentators the answer is clear enough. We wear our stereotypes on our sleeves, they are on display every day, and the reader can credit or discount as he or she chooses. Editorialists apply an intellectual agenda, an ideological one if you will, and this sometimes allows them to recognize the importance of developments that don't strike the interest of reporters relating yesterday's events.

In the case of reporters and editors who are supposed to be objective, the development of news stereotypes is much more mysterious. But it doesn't take much exposure to the process to understand that a very large part of it, especially in the hothouse of the Beltway press corps, involves looking over your shoulder at your colleagues, which is to say your putative competitors in finding news. Social interactions within the press corps, what Tom Bethell of the American Spectator has christened "the hive," are a principal explanation for the rise and fall of stereotypes of what is "news" to be covered and what is not.

So a consensus of supposed competitors tends to hold sway over such concepts as "objectivity" and "fairness" and "balance." Often the operative definition of these matters concerns "being tough" equally on both sides, usually defined in terms of political parties rather than ideas. The notion is to put a thumb on one side of the scale, and then offset it by putting a thumb on the other side of the scale. It calls for an almost divine sense of justice on the part of the press, and leaves a rather small place for the concept of, hey, this is new and interesting. It's news.

Within this consensus there are of course honorable exceptions, reporters and editors who think for themselves. But let me assure you that independence of thought is much easier if you are a step or two out of the mainstream—a tabloid, say, or an editorialist.

For like any other group, the mainstream press corps unwittingly develops pressures for conformity. There is nothing especially calculated or particularly sinister about this. It is simply the group dynamics familiar to psychology and sociology. Among teenagers we call it peer pressure. Examples of social controls in the newsroom range from snide comments to keep mavericks in place to invitations to the right cocktail parties and breakfasts in Washington. If you step out of the mainstream, you will find it harder to win such recognitions as membership in the elite Gridiron Club or a Pulitzer Prize. And if you confront or challenge the mainstream, you have to be willing to endure criticism from colleagues, in particular the criticism that if you depart from the prevailing stereotype you are no longer "objective," that instead of following "the news" you are promoting someone's agenda.

Now, About Whitewater

Which brings me to a topic I propose to discuss in greater detail, our editorial-page coverage of Whitewater and related Clinton administration scandals.

To critics of our Whitewater coverage, I have a simple reply: It's news, stupid. Here we have the president of the United States under investigation by a specially appointed prosecutor. We have the death of one close associate of the president and first lady, and the jailing of another. We have serial resignation by White House counsels. We have revelations about the first lady's implausible commodities profits, and subpoenaed billing records appearing in the family quarters of the White House. We have the White House security office traducing FBI files while being run by a former bar bouncer and political operative. We have suspect political contributions raised by a long-time associate of an Indonesian billionaire. Laying aside for a moment the names of the personalities, it is a compelling drama—an ongoing, real-life Tom Clancy novel.

The question, that is, is not why we're covering it on the editorial pages of The Wall Street Journal. The real question is why the mainstream press isn't covering it far more extensively than it has.

Everything on my little list of dramas has of course been duly reported by the press, and much more besides. But as reported in the mainstream press, somehow the whole was less than the sum of its parts. "Where is the outrage in America? Where has the media gone in America?" Bob Dole asked on the presidential stump. This echoed an earlier William Safire column, "Absence of Outrage"—"Ennui is in; outrage is out."

Or to put it in terms of Lippmann's stereotypes: Looking back over the extensive coverage on our editorial page, we have been interpreting these events in terms of a stereotype that might be described as, more corner-cutting by an ethically challenged administration. No such stereotype ever caught on in the mainstream news coverage. The events—the Foster death, the Hubbell conviction, the commodity profits, the Travel Office firings, the billing papers, the FBI files, the Indonesian fund-raising—have been treated as unconnected and discrete, with no common theme. So while some revelation might raise a storm, it blows quickly by.

You can argue, I suppose, that the corner-cutting theme or stereotype is simply false, that these are indeed discrete, accidental events. It is certainly true that when this very same stereotype was applied to the Nixon administration in Watergate, our editorial page played a cautionary role, some said a defensive one. As it happened, in this I was taking deathbed advice from Alexander Bickel, the leading constitutional scholar of the time, and I've always thought that this was an honorable role—making the prosecution prove its case, and standing by to say with the "smoking gun" tapes, yes, now, he should resign.

The Post's Pulitzer nominating letter by Managing Editor Howard Simons said Woodward and Bernstein reported Watergate "in spite of a silent majority in the rest of the media."

Yet it surely seems to me that the corner-cutting theme is as justified by events in Whitewater as it was in Watergate. I've recently reviewed The Washington Post's submission for its Watergate Pulitzer, and it seems rather thin gruel compared to what we already know about Whitewater, with a lot of headlines about Donald Segretti, an unimportant campaign trickster. I don't mean to take anything away from the Post, which was certainly on the trail of much skullduggery; it is also only fair to note that throughout the 1972 campaign the Post was alone in its coverage. The Post's Pulitzer nominating letter by Managing Editor Howard Simons said Woodward and Bernstein reported Watergate "in spite of a silent majority in the rest of the media." In all likelihood, the Post coverage was instrumental in persuading Judge John Sirica to impose the provisional 40-year sentences on the Watergate burglars, which led to uncovering the cover-up. With the judge's initiative in January 1973, the "corner-cutting" stereotype quickly developed, the Pulitzer jurors decided the Post was right all along, and the rest is history.

Watergate, for that matter, set a fashion in press coverage that prevailed until now. The mainstream press was quick enough to make connections among discrete events in, say, the confirmation hearings of John Tower for secretary of defense. Or to find corner-cutting reaching close to the top in the Iran-Contra hearings. It was willing to entertain the "October Surprise" accusations that are now seen to be pure myth. While the early appointment failures of the Clinton administration created a stereotype of "bumbling," it never approached the consuming fire of the Clarence Thomas or Robert Bork confirmation hearings. Having lived through these experiences, those of us who admit to having opinions need feel no embarrassment about holding the Clinton administration to what we thought was the established pattern. And indeed to ask why supposedly objective news coverage refuses to connect the dots.

In the closing days of the political campaign, the press did bestir itself about the Indonesian political contributions. A Journal editorial had raised the now-infamous Riady and Lippo connections back in March, and during the campaign, coverage of them was led by Mr. Safire, a conservative commentator, and, I'm proud to say, newshounds in the Journal's Washington bureau. This story did reverberate through the press, but the operative stereotype had to do with money in politics, about the agenda of campaign finance reform. So past and already reported Republican misdeeds had to be pushed into the reporting to match Democratic ones, and the disproportions minimized—avoiding, indeed obscuring, the issue of character.

The mainstream media's news judgments on Whitewater puzzle others a step or two outside the American media consensus. Christopher Wood, New York bureau chief of The Economist, puzzled over this on our pages in departing America in 1994. He remarked on the media keeping "a genteel distance" from the first couple's Arkansas background as "not fit conversation for polite company." So the story was coverage by Internet mail groups and talk radio: "A media elite centered on Washington and New York talks to itself while the rest of thinking America listens to the radio and draws its own conclusions."

A Problem for Publishers

A double standard in connect-the-dots stereotypes is often perceived as "press bias." Bob Dole of course struck this theme in the final days of his campaign. In September 1996, the Roper Voters & Media study found that 53% of respondents felt media coverage of the campaign was generally balanced. Some 31% felt it favored Democrats, while only 9% thought it favored Republicans. Among Democ-

tion is usually proposed along some such line as, can we lure back younger readers with more color and splashier graphics? There is even a new fad of "civic journalism," which so far as I can tell is editing a newspaper through focus groups. No one much seems to notice that a large hunk of the audience has run off with Rush Limbaugh.

Whether there is a cure for this I do not know. We are not likely to change the kind of people who go into journalism. But I think we can ask for more self-awareness of the problem this creates. And I think we can ask editors and reporters to be more conscious of the need to think for themselves. When they look over their shoulders, they shouldn't see colleagues who sit in judgment, but competitors to be outwitted in finding the next scoop.

Mr. Bartley is editor of the Journal. This article is based on a speech he delivered on Nov. 11 as Minow Visiting Professor in Communications at the J.L. Kellogg School of Management and the Medill School of Journalism, Northwestern University.

Letters to the Editor

Partisans Disguised As News Reporters

Robert Bartley's extended treatment of the press bias issue ("Consensus, the Enemy of News," editorial page, Nov. 27) was helpful both for re-examining the perspective that informs modern journalism and for pointing to the solution. "Consensus" is a thoroughly predictable consequence of a profession that has committed itself to what Walter Lippmann called the "cardinal ideal" of "objective testimony." If any element of the press dissents from the prevailing judgments, what else can be concluded except that the dissenters "lack objectivity"? But in fact, contrary to Lippmann's expectation, partisanship did not go away; it just went underground, disguised as news reporting.

On the other hand, Michael Barone is on to something, as Mr. Bartley reminds us. Yes, the coverage would be different if the "media [were] divided, as the voters usually are, between the two parties." But that is not all. The political debate would be more "open and robust," that one-time goal of so-called "nonpartisan journalists." The Republicans would be less intimidated by the New York/Washington media axis and would pay more attention to the varied opinion that in fact exists in the country.

We need to disenthrall ourselves of the childish notion that the political partisans who are invariably attracted to political journalism are not governed by their principles in their selection of facts

place some Democratic eminence he thinks deserving, like a George Mitchell.

No, the complaint against Ms. Reno concerns her administration of the independent counsel law, which provides for a system of court-appointed counsels to investigate criminal allegations involving certain high-ranking government individuals. Specifically, the complaint is that Ms. Reno has sought the appointment of too many independent counsels (four, a record for a presidential first term) and agreed too often (five times at least) to jurisdictional expansions of the counsel that most interests the Clintons, Whitewater counsel Kenneth W. Starr.

This complaint against Ms. Reno doesn't come with specific details as to what's wrong with her judgments under the Watergate-inspired independent counsel statute, first enacted in 1978 and reauthorized three times since. It is hard to see how Ms. Reno—or any other attorney general—could have decided many independent counsel issues differently than she has. The fact is, the law permits an attorney general very little discretion.

Janet Reno

Under its terms, an attorney general must commence a "preliminary investigation," usually lasting 90 days, if the allegation is specific and from a credible source—even if the elements of a crime, including state-of-mind evidence, are lacking. During this investigation, the attorney general may not convene grand juries, plea bargain, grant immunity, or issue subpoenas—as a prosecutor might in the ordinary case.

If, thus handicapped, the attorney general is not able to conclude at the end of the preliminary investigation that there are "no reasonable grounds to believe" that further inquiry "is warranted," then he must ask for a court-appointed counsel. And the request will be honored: The law requires a special panel of three judges from the D.C. Circuit Court of Appeals to name a counsel once application is made. The statutory provisions regarding expansion of an existing counsel's jurisdiction are also biased in its favor.

Arguably, Ms. Reno did not have to ask for an independent counsel to investigate whether Housing Secretary Henry Cisneros lied about the size of the payments he made to a former lover. On the other hand, Ms. Reno was probably wrong to turn down a request by Donald Smaltz, the independent counsel investigating former Agriculture Secretary Mike Espy, for an expansion of his jurisdiction.

On balance, however, Ms. Reno has made the calls that any attorney general would have felt compelled to make. Even the decision that apparently sticks most deeply in White House craws—the recent referral to Mr. Starr of whether former White House counsel Bernard Nussbaum made false statements to Congress—is fairly demanded by the law. How could Ms. Reno have conscientiously decided that there are *no* reasonable grounds for further investigation of an allegation that a crime *may* have been committed?

The wonder is that a president so skilled in political maneuvers should be allowing his aides to whisper to the media against Ms. Reno. Their complaint guarantees that congressional Republicans would be keenly interested in her departure. And anyone Mr. Clinton names to succeed her would face a skeptical Republican Senate, some of whose members might try to condition confirmation upon a promise of good-faith application of the independent counsel law. Though such a promise could not be binding, for constitutional reasons, there is a precedent of sorts: In 1973, Elliot Richardson's promise to name a special prosecutor in Watergate secured the confirmation vote of Sen. Ted Kennedy.

Of course, the White House campaign against Ms. Reno may have another purpose: to influence her handling of current requests for a counsel to investigate Democratic fund-raising from foreign sources. Ms. Reno already has turned down two requests on grounds that they were too vague, as indeed they were, and she is now reviewing a more detailed request even as the press uncovers more information about "Indogate." But if White House aides think they can persuade Ms. Reno that by doing the president's bidding she can keep her job, they may be underestimating her. Bear in mind that she has shown independence in some past dealings with the White House—a characteristic not admired by some who work there.

Beyond the matter of Ms. Reno's future is the future of the independent counsel statute, scheduled to expire in 1999. The White House complaint against Ms. Reno must be understood as less about her administration of the law than the law itself. It's worth pondering whether Mr. Clinton, who took office as a devout believer in the independent counsel law—theretofore an enfeebler of Republican presidencies—will seek major changes in it or even oppose its renewal. And what will be the Republicans' view of the law, especially if in 1998 they retain control of both houses of Congress? Will they express their traditional opposition to the law by letting it lapse, or will they dispense with principle now that a Democratic presidency finally has had to experience its costly impact?

Mr. Clinton's bridge to the 21st century is going to have a lot of sections that deal with present and perhaps future independent counsels, and with the independent counsel law itself.

Mr. Eastland is a fellow at the Ethics and Public Policy Center in Washington. He is author of books on the presidency and the independent counsel statute.

REVIEW & OUTLOOK

A Test for Justice

With Friday's decision not to name an independent counsel in the Indogate campaign-finance flap, Attorney General Janet Reno puts her career prosecutors at Main Justice on the line. That's all to the good, we think. The performance of the Public Integrity Section of the Criminal Division in this matter will be seen as an important test of the Justice Department's credibility and independence, particularly, as now seems inevitable, tensions mount over other investigations into the Clinton Administration.

Senator John McCain and other top Republicans wrote Ms. Reno requesting an independent counsel probe into the campaign-finance activities of John Huang, a former executive with the Lippo Group, an Indonesian investment giant with longstanding ties to Bill Clinton and Arkansas. Mr. Huang served in the Commerce Department in 1994, then bounced over to fund-raising at the Democratic National Committee in 1995. Since September, the DNC has had to return nearly half the $2.5 million Mr. Huang raised in murky circumstances from interests linked to South Korea, Indonesian gardeners and Buddhist monks, among others. Senator McCain also wanted an independent counsel to look into the connection of the President and Vice President to all this.

In a letter to Senator McCain declining to name an independent counsel, Deputy Assistant Attorney General Mark Richard wrote that there was no "specific and credible allegation of criminal conduct against the President, the Vice President, or any other high-ranking executive branch or campaign official." Lower-ranking officials, such as Mr. Huang, are not covered by the independent counsel statute, Mr. Richard noted, but a task force had been created within Public Integrity "to explore fully the range of allegations and issues that have been raised." He also left open the possibility of later seeking an independent counsel, if more "specific and credible information" about individuals covered by the statute is discovered.

In declining to name a counsel, Ms. Reno is not on entirely firm ground. A President, of course, is a "covered individual" under the statute, and Mr. Clinton had plenty of contact with Mr. Huang and

Janet Reno

his former boss, Lippo Group scion James Riady. Pre-election, the spin control concocted by senior aide Bruce Lindsey was that the meetings were mere "social visits." Post-election, it emerged that policy issues had been discussed at the meetings. Of particular interest, as well, is a September 1995 meeting at which Mr. Huang and Mr. Riady lobbied President Clinton and Mr. Lindsey for Mr. Huang's transfer from Commerce to the DNC. A few days later, Mr. Huang met with Mr. Lindsey and deputy White House chief of staff Harold Ickes, and the transfer deal was sealed.

Again, the big question is whether Public Integrity is up to the task. One looming question is whether it will look at Mr. Lindsey's links to both Mr. Huang and the 800-pound gorilla in the Whitewater mists—former Associate Attorney General Webster Hubbell. While awaiting sentencing to prison for fraud in 1994, and under pressure to cooperate with Independent Counsel Kenneth Starr, Mr. Hubbell was paid a large sum—variously reported at between $100,000 and $250,000—by Lippo for services as yet unspecified. But he also was on the phone to Mr. Huang, according to Commerce Department phone logs. These are dots that need to be connected to complete the picture.

What might Mr. Hubbell be able to illuminate? The installing of Clinton friend Paula Casey as U.S. attorney in Little Rock, the improper handling of Resolution Trust Corp. criminal referrals into Madison Guaranty, the destruction of Madison files at the Rose Law Firm and the disappearance of documents in Washington, the search of Vincent Foster's office, and the possible perjury of top Administration officials.

We have long expressed doubts about the independent counsel statute. But Kenneth Starr, currently under attack from many quarters, is doing his appointed duty. The larger question in any reconsideration is, how well are the traditional system's other parts—Justice, Congress and the press—doing their jobs?

Justice can claim some notable aggressiveness in prosecuting Democrats while a Democrat reigns at the White House—Dan Rostenkowski and Mel Reynolds come to mind—and some recent lapses, including U.S. Attorney Eric Holder's decision not to prosecute Ira Magaziner for perjury.

As to the public's right to know, that has become a journalistic cliché honored largely in the breach. This week's New Republic cover story by William Powers on the extensive, and largely successful, White House effort to shut down serious media investigation of the Clintons is instructive reading, as is ex-Timesman John Corry's press essay in the current American Spectator.

Meanwhile in Congress, investigators such as Senator D'Amato and others worry about being portrayed in press coverage as "partisan" or "political." Our worry, however, is that the *benefits* of political tension and competition around an issue such as Whitewater are being undervalued by both Beltway politicians and the press.

Maybe Clinton Two will provide a new start at getting at the truth. If traditional political and legal institutions can show themselves capable of treating the system's most serious fevers, so much the better. If ultimately they show themselves no longer inclined to do the job, then we all will be revisiting this subject in the none too distant future.

Editorial Feature

Notable & Quotable

Excerpts from a discussion last Sunday on "Meet the Press," hosted by Tim Russert:

Mr. Russert: You heard Senator Moynihan say that "Kenneth Starr is an independent counsel. Let him do his job." James Carville has been outspoken on this program and other places, saying, "No, no. Ken Starr is a political animal. He's going to politicize this whole process. Any indictment will be political and we have to educate the public about all that." Is that smart politics for the president's side?

Jack Germond (Baltimore Sun): I think so. And I think if they have Carville do it, in particular—people like Carville, people outside the White House, directly. The fact is there's a lot of reason to believe that Starr is a very partisan Republican. And that's his history. And if he's going to come at them, particularly on matters sort of extraneous to the original topic of the investigation, they're going to have to make the case that this is political. I'm talking about for political reasons. I'm not talking about—I don't care whether this is valid or not. I'm saying that this is what you do. And so I think it is smart politics . . .

David Broder (Washington Post): I could not disagree more, Jack.

Mr. Germond: But you believe in good government, David. I don't have that problem.

Mr. Broder: I think if Carville makes his public appearances in the same style that he did on your program last week, Tim, this is going to be totally counterproductive. I mean, he was barely in control of himself. If indictments issue—and I emphasize the word "if"—this is going to be a very, very serious constitutional challenge for the country. And the last thing we need is some guy who is barely in control of his own voice and emotions out there yattering about how it's all political. The White House and whoever is indicted is going to have to respond substantively, and if they try to make the case that the indictments have no validity because of some alleged partisanship on the part of this former solicitor general and federal judge, I don't think the country's going to buy it.

Review & Outlook

Asides

International Thriller

We've long held that the Democrats were masters of the ageless strategy that the best defense is a good offense. And so on Tuesday, Senate Minority Leader Tom Daschle announced that his party is ready this very minute to enact campaign finance reform. "There's no need to wait to do meaningful legislation," he said. Wait a minute. We want to know what that Ron Brown event at the Island Shangri-La Hotel was all about. This quite amazing affair, disclosed in yesterday's Wall Street Journal, featured a few words from Secretary Brown, on a trade mission at the time, to Hong Kong's wealthiest elites, while various Democratic fund-raisers commingled and reportedly worked side deals. A number of the Hong Kong guests, no doubt appalled, declined the entreaties. We suppose this has something to do with campaign finance reform, but the Clinton-Gore Democrats increasingly sound like characters out of some Robert Ludlum international melodrama. Let's hold the law until we get to the end of the story.

Editorial Feature

Frittering Away an Electoral Victory

Bill Clinton may have had the traditional honeymoon for victorious presidential candidates but he has spent it in political Siberia.

On the one-month anniversary of the president's decisive reelection, congressional Democrats, and more than a few within his own administration, are despondent over Mr. Clinton's performance. In recent weeks, the consensus about the president—that off the campaign trail he remains a huge disappointment—has been fortified by:

Politics & People

By Albert R. Hunt

• policy gaffes, the most serious being the president's embrace of the popular constitutional amendment mandating a balanced budget. This was a flip-flop that stunned congressional Democrats; the next day he flipped back to his original position.

• a poorly planned Asian trip that distracted from the planning and promotion of a second term. "How many Americans even know the president was in Australia?" asks one leading Democrat.

• constant fumbling and dissembling on campaign financing that is turning an embarrassment into a mushrooming scandal.

• endless foot-dragging on filling at least seven cabinet posts, including secretary of state. The president, who for months has known there would be these vacancies and that he would be reelected, appears, at best, indecisive and, at worst, unable to figure out where and with whom he would like to lead the country.

The bottom line one month after he won 379 out of 538 electoral votes: The agenda is being set more by Republican critics and the media than by the White House. That is particularly galling because with Congress out of session and with the usual honeymoon following a presidential victory, this was supposed to be Mr. Clinton's time.

Instead the most dominant story has been the various fund-raising scams perpetrated by the Clintonites with Lippo, James Riady and other Indonesian connections. In part this scandal has grown because it entails some genuinely questionable—perhaps illegal—activities. It's also more than a little self-inflicted. There has been a notable lack of candor, suggesting something to hide. And while in Australia the president even went to the absurd lengths of comparing his plight to that of Richard Jewell, the Atlanta security guard falsely suspected of planting the bomb at last summer's Olympics.

The president's problems are compounded by his unwillingness to reach out. At a Democratic congressional leadership meeting earlier this week, both Senate Minority Leader Tom Daschle and House Minority Leader Dick Gephardt said

Bill Clinton

they had no idea what was going on or who might be picked for top cabinet posts; they've been kept almost totally in the dark.

These difficulties have been exacerbated by a senselessly long transition at the top of the White House. North Carolina businessman Erskine Bowles was tapped as the next chief of staff four weeks ago. But Leon Panetta, who is returning to California, is staying on the job until Jan. 20.

Indeed even the few positive moves that the president has made since Nov. 5 have had their own fallout. The critical selection of Mr. Bowles, a talented adult who brings the sort of managerial skills normally not essential to the top White House staff job but mandatory with this president, was a good one. But the president's failure to even tell his longtime loyal supporter, Harold Ickes, that he wasn't going to get this job, which he coveted, engendered a backlash from both sides of the political spectrum.

The biggest failure of the past four weeks has been the inability to deliver on what once was advertised as a quick succession of nominations to help plan and lead a second Clinton administration. Mr. Clinton, by most accounts, has been terminally indecisive in this process, unable to deliver on the urgings of close confidants to move more quickly.

A key figure in all this is Vice President Gore, who has more than passing interest in the political success of a second Clinton term. (Fritz Mondale recently was asked privately about the now-routine assertions by Mr. Clinton that Al Gore is the "best vice president in history." The former vice president reportedly said he agreed—Gore was first, followed by Jefferson and then Mondale.)

But for all the vice president's influence, informed insiders vehemently deny that he has been given a mandate to select the domestic team for the second administration. There are at least five domestic cabinet posts that have to be filled and while some nominees—Rep. Bill Richardson (D., N.M.) and Bill Daley of Chicago, perhaps Andrew Cuomo or an African-American mayor—seem likely, the precise lineup remains jumbled.

And top Clinton advisers want him to move first on the all-important selection to succeed Warren Christopher as his secretary of state. The president not only vacillates, but the range of the seriously considered—from the serious and sober George Mitchell to the brilliantly egotistical and self-promoting Richard Holbrooke—is so diverse it suggests that Mr. Clinton has little idea of what he really wants to do in foreign policy anyway. The front runners du jour are retiring United Nations Ambassador Madeleine Albright and Sen. Sam Nunn (D., Ga.).

In several discussions, the president has ventured that with a Republican Congress stymying domestic initiatives, his legacy may be determined by his foreign policy decisions. There's only one problem: he doesn't seem to know what he wants to do.

Likewise the president has vacillated on defense, leaving two exceptionally able possibilities—retiring Sen. Bill Cohen (R., Maine) and CIA director John Deutch—twisting in the wind. A few days ago, The Wall Street Journal's Michael Frisby reported that after months of consideration the list of potential nominees to these key national security posts was now being expanded. And one key insider says there now is serious talk of getting Secretary William Perry to stay on through the middle of next year.

Clinton defenders say once these appointments are made and

the budget and policy pronouncements are forthcoming, none of the current carping will matter. This president, they note, has shown remarkable resiliency; whatever political problems he has today pale next to the depths of exactly two years ago when he was virtually written off by most of the Washington cognoscenti following the Republican congressional takeover in 1994.

Perhaps. But the Clinton comeback, as impressive as it was, would have been impossible without the stunning ineptitude of House Republicans. This time the loyal opposition will be led by the more secure and sure-footed Trent Lott. And given the blown opportunities of the past month, it may be much tougher to recover this time.

Editorial Feature

Carville's Fury Shows You Reap What You Sow

James Carville's ranting about independent counsel Kenneth Starr isn't getting the full political credit it deserves.

President Clinton's most offensive defenseman has already done what countless others have tried and failed to do: Get Washington thinking that the independent prosecuting institution created after Watergate is a bad idea.

Potomac Watch

By Paul A. Gigot

"There've been four 'Nightlines' on independent counsels," Mr. Carville bragged to reporters this week. "I've made my point."

Sure enough, on that very same Tuesday evening, ABC's Ted Koppel broadcast a thoughtful program on how horrible it is to be the target of a prosecutor whose only task is to investigate *you*. The Koppel show, in turn, cited a long, sympathetic piece in Vanity Fair that gave fulsome play to Clinton officials who've racked up big legal bills without yet being indicted. This is sympathy I don't recall seeing for Ed Meese or Ted Olson during their Reagan-era ordeals.

The New Republic is also suddenly alarmed, saying "the need to reform the special prosecutor system has reached a critical point." Assorted liberal columnists have had similar revelations.

Forgive those of us who've written about this for years, but we told you so: We said the ethics demons would return to haunt those who unleashed them. If President Clinton had taken our 1993 advice not to reauthorize the special-counsel law, he wouldn't have to worry about Mr. Starr now. His tawdry political motives notwithstanding, Mr. Carville's fury at least has the virtue of proving that in politics you reap what you sow.

The ironies of Mr. Carville's rage are even richer than his speaking fees. The loud Louisianan is now trying to taint as "political" an institution created expressly to be removed from politics. Or at least that was the thinking after Watergate. Richard Nixon had fired Archibald Cox, so the Democrats who then ran Congress wanted an institution outside of (Republican) executive control.

During the 1980s, Democrats fine-tuned this law into a lethal political weapon. Congress produced "reports," which triggered the appointment of counsels, which created a culture of permanent ethical attacks. This culture reached its apogee, or nadir, when Lawrence Walsh indicted Caspar Weinberger four days before the 1992 election.

Recall, too, that the counsel law expired in December 1992, and most Republicans were ready to let it die. (One ironic exception: Bill Cohen, then a Maine senator and now Mr. Clinton's defense nominee.) But Mr. Clinton reinstated it as a favor to Hill Democrats, who

James Carville

thought they'd never lose power. White House spinmeister George Stephanopoulos explained to me at the time that the Clinton team wasn't worried because it was going to set "the highest ethical standards in history."

Attorney General Janet Reno even stumped for the law before Congress. She had already appointed her own Whitewater counsel, Robert Fiske. But by signing the new law, Mr. Clinton turned over the power to appoint a prosecutor to an independent three-judge panel. The judges then chose Mr. Starr, dumping Mr. Fiske. So maybe Mr. Carville should attack Mr. Clinton for making Mr. Starr possible.

Another irony is that Mr. Starr's presence helped Mr. Clinton win re-election. Like all special counsels, his probe is hidden behind grand jury rules of evidence. Mr. Starr became a kind of shield against political (as opposed to criminal) accountability. He made Senate hearings less important, because he would have the last word on wrongdoing. Whenever the president was asked about Whitewater, he could say the special counsel was looking into it. And unlike Judge Walsh, Mr. Starr—a "rabid partisan," says Mr. Carville—didn't indict anyone before the election.

Which explains why Mr. Carville has unleashed his tirade now, *after* the election, when the White House fears Mr. Starr will finally act. It's Mediscare all over again: The facts don't matter as much as the ability to sow public (and later, jury) doubt with punchy epithets. That's why Mr. Carville's idea of an argument is to call Mr. Starr "Pat Robertson's cigarette lawyer."

Mr. Carville clearly has the president's blessing for his assault, because Mr. Clinton could shut him down with a simple word of disapproval. White House spokesman Mike McCurry can barely keep a straight face when he says "the president's private views are private." If Mr. Clinton had the courage of Mr. Carville's conviction, he could always fire a special counsel, according to the Supreme Court. And if the president believes Mr. Starr is running nothing but a vendetta, he *should* fire him. But that would entail paying a large political price, with echoes of Nixon. It's so much easier to unleash your court jester to pursue a sound-bite assault.

So excuse those of us who were right from the beginning if we don't show much sympathy for Mr. Carville and his friends now. The timing of their independent-counsel conversion reeks of bad faith. If they feel the same way when the law expires in a few years, then we can talk. But their purpose now is to change the law they wrote in the middle of the game. A president is sworn to uphold that law—even a president whose political agents now want us to believe that the law should apply to everyone except this president.

Editorial Feature

ABC's Tainted Pundit...

By Byron York

Last week ABC News announced it has hired departing presidential aide George Stephanopoulos as a contributor to "This Week,"
"Good Morning America" and other programs. The network seemed
delighted with its catch. Mr. Stephanopoulos is "one of the best
known and most articulate presidential advisers this country has
ever seen," news President Roone Arledge said. "His vast knowledge of Washington politics and policy will be an enormous asset to
ABC News."

The announcement created some confusion about Mr.
Stephanopoulos's role. A press release issued by ABC last Wednesday stated that he "will serve both as a political analyst and as a
correspondent." Vice President of News Joanna Bistany now says
Mr. Stephanopoulos will be just an analyst; he will not report news
or question guests on "This Week." Ms. Bistany says his role will be
similar to that of ABC contributor William Kristol, who was Dan
Quayle's chief of staff. "We want a mix of voices," she says, adding
that Mr. Stephanopoulos "won't do anything that has any appearance of conflict."

ABC's clarification—intended to defuse accusations of bias—
misses a serious issue. The administration Mr. Stephanopoulos
served is still in power, and many investigations touching on his
conduct and that of his former colleagues are under way. Independent Counsel Kenneth Starr's probe of Whitewater, Filegate and

events leading up to the firings of the Travel Office staff seems incomplete. The following is Mr. Stephanopoulos's exchange with a lawyer from the House Government Reform and Oversight Committee:

Q: Do you remember how you were first notified that there was a problem in the White House Travel Office?

A: Not really, no. I might have had a passing conversation with Jeff Eller.

Q: Do you recall the circumstances of that conversation?

A: No.

Q: OK. Do you remember what he said to you?

A: Not specifically. It was something, I suppose, about there being trouble in the Travel Office.

Q: Did he describe where he had received that information from?

A: I don't remember.

Q: OK. There are some notes which Mr. Eller had recounting a conversation where it said he had seen you in a driveway. Do you recall seeing Jeff Eller in a driveway, I believe the White House driveway, one morning?

A: I probably saw him in the White House driveway every day.

Q: OK. Specifically, these notes recount that he had talked to you about problems in the Travel Office and one of the quotes was, "These guys are crooks." Do you recall having—Mr. Eller saying that to you?

A: I don't recall that specific conversation. . . .

Q: Were you aware—did you attend any meetings prior to the firings concerning the White House Travel Office matter?

A: I don't think so. I may have been in a room when it came up, but I don't think so.

Mr. Stephanopoulos has been questioned about these issues before the Whitewater-Travelgate-Filegate grand jury. Although prosecutors are forbidden by law from revealing what went on before the grand jury, Mr. Stephanopoulos is free to tell his ABC audience what he was asked and what his answers were.

It's important to point out that the issue is not biased reporting or one-sided punditry. Of course Mr. Stephanopoulos is biased, and ABC will presumably match him with a counterbalancing conservative. Rather it is a question of journalistic ethics. Mr. Stephanopoulos's firsthand knowledge of events in the current White House puts his fellow journalists at ABC in an untenable position: Either they ask him about things he likely won't talk about, or they stifle their journalistic instincts and don't ask questions that should be asked.

It's not a very good choice. Sometime—probably soon—CBS, CNN and NBC will be glad they lost the bidding war for George Stephanopoulos.

Mr. York is an investigative writer for The American Spectator magazine.

Editorial Feature

... And the Networks' Whitewater Whitewash

By L. BRENT BOZELL III

On Election Night several leading journalists suggested that because the American people don't understand and are tired of the many Clinton scandals, Republicans should drop their investigations and get back to the business of government. But what if I were to tell you the public has never been given the news about most of these scandals?

If you are a typical political junkie, you probably know all about these scandals because you read The Wall Street Journal or the Washington Post or the Washington Times. Maybe you watch the weekend TV talk shows, or listen to Rush Limbaugh or any of the other radio talk show hosts who discuss them virtually every day. Maybe you draw your information from Time and Newsweek, or the American Spectator and National Review, or the Nation and the New Republic, or PBS and "The 700 Club," or the Internet.

So how can the average American not get news about the scandals? Because the average citizen doesn't read, listen to or watch any of the above. A study of the 1992 campaign by the University of Michigan's Center for Political Studies found that 50% of voters paid no attention to newspaper articles about the campaign, and 77% paid no attention to magazine articles. This month the Pew Research Center released a survey showing that while the audiences for radio (19%) and on-line services (10%) have increased, once again television is the leading source for news for a whopping

REVIEW & OUTLOOK

The Money Trie

So President Clinton's legal defense fund sent back $640,000 raised by Yah Lin "Charlie" Trie, once an owner of a Little Rock Chinese restaurant and now an international entrepreneur operating out of Arkansas, Beijing and Washington's Watergate complex. In assessing this latest revelation, keep in mind the President's vow on CNN in August about the legal expenses of his friends and aides. "I'm going to do everything I can to help raise the money," he said, "if it's the last thing I ever do."

Michael Cardozo, executive director of the Presidential Legal Expense Trust, knows that he has a high-visibility operation. He succeeded in keeping the suspect contributions secret through the election campaign, but knows they would eventually have faced public scrutiny. We happen to sympathize with middle-class aides facing big legal bills, and indeed have suggested that Congress appropriate money for the defense of the President and others in the executive branch—as, over the President's objections, it paid legal bills for Travel Office victim Billy Dale.

One good reason is that when funds are privately raised, it gets hard to distinguish between a legal defense fund and hush money. This was precisely our point last March, when we raised the issue of payments by the Lippo Group to Webster Hubbell for unspecified legal work between his resignation as associate attorney general and his conviction as a swindler. Lawyers representing Independent Counsel Kenneth Starr made it entirely clear at Mr. Hubbell's sentencing that he'd not redeemed plea-bargain promises of cooperation. After receiving Lippo money, that is, he took a hang-tough attitude toward investigation of the President. With Mr. Hubbell now finishing his prison term in a halfway house, we still do not know how much he was paid or for what.

Nor do we know who is buying top-of-the-line counsel for Craig Livingstone, the former bar bouncer and political operative ousted as security chief at the Clinton White House after traducing some 900 FBI files. Mr. Livingstone is represented by Miller Cassidy, the Washington criminal defense boutique where Deputy Attorney General Jamie Gorelick formerly toiled—for example representing Clark Clifford and Robert Altman in their efforts to get reimbursed for *their* legal bills in the BCCI case. Mr. Livingstone announced he was starting his own defense fund, but has resisted attempts to plumb his financing.

Charlie Trie

Now comes Charlie Trie, with $640,000 to spare. Mr. Cardozo says he showed up in March with two large manila envelopes stuffed with $460,000 in checks and money orders, and came back in April with another $179,000. Fund officials became suspicious when they noticed some of the money orders were sequentially numbered and in the same handwriting, although supposedly they were from donors in different cities. The money was returned, Mr. Cardozo says, "to protect the integrity of the trust." Investigators hired by Mr. Cardozo traced most of the donations back to a Taiwan-based Buddhist organization that operates meditation centers in thirty countries, including the United States.

It also happens that Mr. Trie's activities intersect on several fronts with Lippo's John Huang, whose Commerce Department phone records show calls to both Mr. Trie and Mr. Hubbell. Earlier this month, our Marcus Brauchli and Craig Smith reported that Mr. Trie and former Lippo executive Antonio Pan pressured guests for donations at a dinner for Commerce Secretary Ron Brown held at Hong Kong's luxurious Island Shangri-La Hotel.

Mr. Trie now runs a trading company, Daihatsu International. In public data bases we've perused, it shows up only in an Arkansas

Editorial Feature

White House Heat
On Whitewater Beat

By MICAH MORRISON

Bill Clinton's Whitewater problems are due to a "media food chain" through which conservative philanthropist Richard Scaife engineers a "media frenzy"—at least according to a White House report running 331 pages. The notion: Mr. Scaife's funding of the Western Journalism Center and publication of the Pittsburgh Tribune-Review introduces "conspiracy theories and innuendo," which are then picked up by the likes of the American Spectator magazine and London's Sunday Telegraph. From there they enter the "right-of-center mainstream media," such as the Washington Times and this editorial page. Then Congress looks into the matter and "the story now has the legitimacy to be covered by the remainder of the American mainstream press as a 'real' story."

Chortling over his newly disclosed power, Mr. Scaife asks, "Now that George Stephanopoulos is going to ABC, does that mean he'll be working for me?" Yet the report from the White House counsel's office—entitled "Communication Stream of Conspiracy Commerce" and coupling a series of brief analyses with a large package of press clips and Internet gleanings—demonstrates the extremes of White House press management. Lanny Davis, the new White House special counsel for scandals, says the report was created "in response to press inquiries and provided to journalists who asked." Mr. Davis complied with this newspaper's request for a copy, but declined to respond to questions.

A version of the report was posted on the Internet by an ostensibly independent group of Clinton defenders, the Back to Business Committee. The committee, chaired by former Democratic National Committee vice-chairwoman Lynn Cutler, lists a board of advisers that includes former Reps. Tony Coelho and Robert Drinan, S.J.; Dukakis campaign manager Susan Estrich; Carter administration officials Jody Powell, Anne Wexler and Andrew Young; as well as Arthur Coia, president of the court-supervised Laborer's International Union.

White House attempts to manage press coverage of "Whitewater" are especially interesting now, because a new round of press skepticism about the administration is clearly under way, propelled by the controversy over Indonesian campaign contributions and the abrupt departures of a slew of administration officials responsible for damage control. There has also been increased attention to the relative lack of press coverage of the scandals, most prominently in a November article on the Paula Jones case by Stuart Taylor Jr. of American Lawyer magazine and in a Dec. 16 New Republic cover story, "Scandal-shy," by William Powers. But these articles only scratched

---

One of the striking things about press coverage of Whitewater is the number of star reporters who, for one reason or another, are no longer on the beat.

---

the surface of the Clinton administration's extraordinary efforts to block, blunt and beat down reporters on the scandal beat.

One of the striking things about press coverage of Whitewater is the number of star reporters who, for one reason or another, are no longer on the beat. Investigative reporter Douglas Frantz quit the Los Angeles Times over its handling of a December 1993 Troopergate story that he co-authored with Bill Rempel. ABC's Jim Wooten took himself off the scandal beat after the network killed a Troopergate-related story, Mr. Powers reported. Washington Post reporter Michael Isikoff left the paper after a bitter internal dispute over the Paula Jones story; he continues to report scandal stories for Newsweek, a sister publication.

At Time magazine, investigative journalist Richard Behar was involved in a dispute with Arkansas powerhouse Tyson Foods over a report linking the company to cash payments allegedly destined for then-Gov. Clinton. Mr. Behar eventually left for sister publication Fortune, though he reports that Time stood behind him even when Tyson yanked a large advertising contract. Even the tabloid New York Post let reporter Christopher Ruddy go; he now details discrepancies in the investigation of Vincent Foster's death for Mr. Scaife's Tribune-Review.

Survivors on the Whitewater beat report, both on and off the record, that life is uncomfortable. Surrogates for the president—including White House spokesman Mike McCurry, ABC-bound presi-

Media Food Chain?

MARTIN KOZLOWSKI

dential aide George Stephanopoulos, and private attorney David Kendall—complain to news executives and lobby to kill stories. And in what Mr. Powers called a chilling "divide-and-conquer approach," whispering campaigns about allegedly shoddy work are launched in an effort to convince reporters to ignore the work of their colleagues. The New Republic story added that a particular target has been Susan Schmidt, a widely admired reporter for the Washington Post.

Jeff Gerth of the New York Times, who broke the original Whitewater story in 1992 and who, along with other Times reporters, revealed Hillary Clinton's now famous commodities trades, has been an abiding White House target. "For a long time, the White House thought if they could just neutralize Gerth, the whole scandal thing would go away," says a White House reporter from a rival newspaper. "In private, they would just savage the guy." By contrast, Jerry Seper of the Washington Times, who also provided early ground-breaking coverage of the scandals, says he escapes pressure because the White House strategy is to ignore him.

Recently, Mr. Gerth and fellow Timesman Stephen Labaton reported on White House visits by Lippo Group scion James Riady.

They wrote that presidential aide Bruce Lindsey "was the central figure behind the White House's decision to call the meetings social calls, ignoring the counsel of two White House lawyers." The White House explanation was false; after the election, it emerged that Mr. Riady had discussed trade policy toward Indonesia and China with Mr. Clinton at these meetings, and on one occasion had successfully lobbied for the transfer of now-suspect fund-raiser John Huang from a post at the Commerce Department to the Democratic National Committee.

The Times story directly quoted former White House lawyer Jane Sherburne as warning against the false description of the meetings. According to reporters and others, White House aides immediately launched personal assaults on the two Times reporters in off-record remarks. Then pro-Clinton TV talking head and Time magazine columnist Margaret Carlson attacked Messrs. Gerth and Labaton by name in the Dec. 16 Time, linked reporting on the Indonesia controversy to liberal *bete noir* Rush Limbaugh, and cited anonymous sources "close to Sherburne" saying that the White House lawyer "felt she had never been overruled or lied to by Lindsey and that the Times had torqued up a conflict."

Actually, the meticulous Gerth-Labaton report had not used the words "lied" or "overruled." (The latter was used in a Times editorial, and certainly seems a legitimate opinion to draw from the facts of the case.) Time then ran a letter from New York Times Washington bureau chief Andrew Rosenthal and an editor's note setting the record straight. While such sniping may seem minor, reporters view attacks like Ms. Carlson's as a kind of drip-drip water torture to try to undermine the credibility of journalists working the story.

The Columbia Journalism Review conceded in another editor's note that an attack it had made on Mr. Gerth had also been in error, inaccurately describing how he obtained one of the first interviews with Whitewater witness David Hale. That mistake occurred in a May-June 1994 article by Trudy Lieberman. (Just recently, the magazine has named a high-powered new editor, Marshall Loeb, formerly of Fortune.) Ms. Lieberman's article, "Churning Whitewater," closely parallels parts of the White House "conspiracy report."

In particular, Ms. Lieberman breathlessly flayed "the frenzied media" for listening to information from partisan sources such as Citizens United, and its one-time Whitewater investigator, David

Bossie. Of course reporters listen to such sources, and then seek independent confirmation before passing stories up the "food chain." Mr. Bossie's information, much of it in documents, checked out so often he moved on to become a congressional investigator, though still frequently under attack. In the same recent issue that defended Mr. Powers against a White House attack on his article, the New Republic also demanded that Mr. Bossie, in a new position with a House oversight committee, be fired for news leaks—perhaps the only known example of a publication demanding that someone be fired for telling the truth to journalists.

Writers with a history of criticizing conservatives have recently been asking questions about The Wall Street Journal's coverage of Arkansas housewife Linda Ives, whose crusade for answers to the unsolved deaths of her son Kevin and his friend Don Henry was detailed here April 18. Indeed, this editorial page first learned of the "conspiracy report" from Philip Weiss, a writer on assignment for the New York Times Magazine, who cheerfully acknowledged that he had discussed the Ives case with White House officials and had been given a report on "the conspiracy feeding frenzy."

Mrs. Ives alerted this page that Mr. Weiss had called. Mr. Weiss "wanted to know what journalists I was talking to," the Arkansas housewife recalled. "Mark Fabiani, the White House spokesman, had sicked him on me, he said. I found that curious. What would the White House want with me?" Mrs. Ives had gone through essentially the same experience several months earlier with a producer from CBS's "60 Minutes." When her teenage son and his friend were run over by a train in August 1987, the state medical examiner ruled the death "accidental," saying the boys had fallen asleep on the tracks after smoking marijuana. A second autopsy called it murder; one local prosecutor who developed information suggesting air-drops of drugs might be involved was run out of the state, while a second prosecutor is now himself the subject of a federal drug-corruption probe. Mrs. Ives says that "60 Minutes" had been interested in the story as an example of "Clinton bashing," but killed the report after listening to her account.

New Yorker writer David Remnick, on assignment for a forthcoming PBS documentary segment on this page and The Wall Street Journal Editor Robert L. Bartley, also asked about the Ives case. His question concerned the relevance of the story to Bill Clinton—the answer to which is that Gov. Clinton's support of state medical examiner Fahmy Malak was highly controversial, and that President Clinton's hand-picked U.S. attorney in Little Rock, Paula Casey, now has authority over the drug-corruption probe involving public officials entangled in the case. Although the Little Rock FBI forwarded Ms. Casey the train deaths file 18 months ago, she has taken no action on it.

ABC News also has had a series of battles with the White House over the Clinton scandals. In 1994, when the network was set to run a story including Gov. Clinton's use of state troopers to procure women, Mr. Clinton's private attorney David Kendall flew to New York to lobby against the piece. White House officials suggested that ABC correspondents look into reports that the main source for the story, Arkansas State Trooper L.D. Brown, had murdered his mother. The ugly allegation was false, but the ABC story never ran.

In June, the White House launched a furious blitz at ABC executives to block former FBI agent Gary Aldrich from appearing on "This Week With David Brinkley" to discuss his book on White House mores. ABC didn't back down, but NBC's "Dateline" and CNN's

---

In 1994, when ABC was set to run a story including Gov. Clinton's use of state troopers to procure women, Mr. Clinton's private attorney David Kendall flew to New York to lobby against the piece.

"Larry King Live" cancelled plans to interview Mr. Aldrich. "We killed it," Mr. Stephanopoulos later boasted.

Last January, ABC correspondent Jackie Judd and investigative producer Chris Vlasto were working on a story about the political nature of Sen. Alfonse D'Amato's Whitewater Committee. The White House, Ms. Judd recalled, "instantaneously produced a D'Amato packet." The D'Amato "Ethics Sampler" recounted allegations of the senator's influence peddling and supposed mob ties. "The packet was given to us without any conditions," Ms. Judd said, "so it became part of the story." White House spokesman Mike McCurry was furious that the derogatory information was attributed to the White House. According to several people familiar with the incident, Mr. McCurry complained to network executives, and in an angry call to Mr. Vlasto, he screamed: "You're never going to work in this town again!"

More recently, there have been charges that IRS audits of certain 501(c)3 nonprofit organizations have been politically motivated. Joseph Farah, a former editor of the Sacramento Union, says the Western Journalism Center that he runs is being audited after it was the only news outlet mentioned in a White House "action plan" on how to deal with Administration scandals. In a meeting, the Center's accountant questioned why IRS examiners wanted documents "related to the selection of Christopher Ruddy as an investigative reporter and how the topic [of Whitewater] was selected." According to Mr. Farah, IRS Field Agent Thomas Cederquist said, "Look, this is a political case, and it's going to be decided at the national level." The IRS denies it has any political motives behind its audit decisions.

Nonetheless, the Landmark Legal Foundation this week announced it will monitor complaints about IRS audits. It points to published reports that the National Rifle Association, the Heritage Foundation and other conservative groups are also the targets of IRS investigations. The conservative American Center for Law and Justice has gone further and sued the IRS. It contends the agency singled out a conservative New York church and revoked its tax-exempt status because it engaged in politics by taking out a 1992 newspaper ad that criticized Bill Clinton. Center attorneys claim Methodist and Episcopal churches frequently raise money for liberal candidates, but are never sanctioned.

There are also concerns about the privacy of IRS records. Last Sunday, Rep. Charles Rangel, the ranking Democrat on the House Ways and Means Committee, announced on "Face the Nation" that he had "been in touch with the IRS" and that it was conducting "an ongoing investigation" of charitable groups associated with Speaker Newt Gingrich. Rep. Bob Barr, a former federal prosecutor, has fired off a letter to Attorney General Janet Reno. "Taking Rep. Rangel at his word, he has violated section 6103 of the Internal Revenue Code, which prohibits the disclosure of confidential tax information, and is a felony." Presumably the IRS made it clear to Mr. Rangel how important it is that such information be kept confidential.

Many of those concerned about the IRS can't be dismissed as partisans. Shelley Davis, who served for seven years as the IRS's first and only historian, says that Commissioner Richardson, a friend of First Lady Hillary Clinton and frequent contributor to Democratic candidates, has politicized the agency. In her new book, "Unbridled Power: Inside the Secret Culture of the IRS" (HarperCollins), she notes that only two outsiders have ever been brought in to fill senior positions at the IRS. She told us this insularity has created a "paranoid culture of secrecy" within the agency, which is largely "untouchable because of its power."

Christopher Bergen, the editor of the tax practitioners' journal Tax Notes, accuses the IRS of having "a bunker mentality." "It may even be an agency in danger of going out of control," he told the National Journal. Such concerns prompted Congress to create the National Commission on Restructuring the IRS, which meets today in Washington. Commission members come from both the government and private sector and are charged with finding ways to "ensure the IRS is effective and user-friendly."

An essential element in reforming the IRS is to erect greater safeguards that the tax laws are administered without regard to the prejudices of any sitting Administration. When President Clinton sends up a new nominee to replace Commissioner Richardson, we hope Congress makes clear it wants the new head of the IRS to follow the example of Johnnie Walters, the Nixon IRS commissioner, who scrupulously avoided mixing politics with 1040 forms.

name, we were up to "Who Is Webster Hubbell?—IV." Mr. Hubbell is now a convicted felon. Yet, as Mr. Morrison reported, we find one of our Foster press critics assigned by the New York Times Magazine to second-guess our coverage of the Linda Ives train death story.

The list goes on: Gennifer Flowers couldn't be believed because she took money for her story, but the Arkansas troopers confirmed it. Paula Jones could be dismissed as something dragged up from a trailer park. Yet her complaints concern not only the original sexual harassment but libel by agents of a sitting President. And also libel by a private person, trooper Danny Ferguson, whom superlawyer Bob Bennett will argue is somehow also protected by the President's asserted immunities.

Every White House tries to manage the news, of course, but this one shows the same lack of compunction or inner restraint that runs like a thread through the whole corpus of Clinton scandals. At least in its reaction to the conspiracy report, and in cases such as the recent Newsweek Paula Jones story, the mainstream press seems to be recovering its nose for news.

Spreading Erosion

A week before President Clinton's second inauguration, the United States Supreme Court found itself hearing arguments over whether the dignity of the President is so momentous that until he leaves office the courts can't take up allegations that he made gross sexual advances. The Paula Jones case marked both the President and the High Court.

"For the second Clinton term," the Journal asked on inauguration, "how about stability? The first Clinton term was among the most tumultuous Presidential administrations ever. Scandals rained down like some four-year Biblical torrent." These scandals had not prevented the President's re-election, but the flood spread through the American government, eroding away at institution after institution.

Controversy continued to swirl around the independent counsel and campaign finance laws. But as the foreign-contributions issue was plumbed, American foreign policy decisions on China and Indonesia came under a cloud, and Asian-Americans felt they'd been unfairly stigmatized. In other developments, the Internal Revenue Service, the subject of some question for its UltrAir investigation in the wake of the Travel Office firings, was hit by new questions. And the Central Intelligence Agency had to answer questions about its involvement in Mena Airport in a remote section of Arkansas.

But the true litmus test for the second term, as the Journal noted, would be in the Department of Justice. The editors wrote: "Clinton crony Webster Hubbell's inexplicable ascendancy at Justice in the early days of the Clinton term roused, as much as anything, our interest in the new Administration from Arkansas and its connections. Between Mr. Hubbell's fall and the recent Arkansas-based details of the Indogate fund-raisers, we feel vindicated in raising those early concerns."

Indeed, by the end of January, Mr. Hubbell would be back in the news. At an acrimonious press briefing, President Clinton repeatedly denied having any advance knowledge of Mr. Hubbell's employment by the Lippo Group, now suspected of paying the Arkansas insider "hush money" on behalf of the Administration. The problem, the Journal noted, was that just a week earlier the White House spokesman "had to backtrack from the previous White House line that no one knew about the Lippo hiring until reading about it in the newspapers." The backtrack occurred when the Associated Press reported that in November 1994, 16 months before a Journal editorial first made public Mr. Riady's payments to Mr. Hubbell, this employment connection was well known to top Clinton aide Bruce Lindsey.

REVIEW & OUTLOOK

Above the Law?

An air of unreality hung over the ornate Supreme Court chambers yesterday as the Justices heard arguments about whether the Paula Jones case should be delayed until the defendant is no longer President of the United States.

Here were Robert Bennett and Walter Dellinger—Bill Clinton's $475-per-hour defense lawyer and the acting Solicitor General of the United States—making high-minded arguments about the separation of powers and the Constitution. Now to be sure, we are sympathetic to the concern raised by Mr. Clinton's defenders—and endorsed during questioning by several Justices—that the Presidency shouldn't be at the mercy of some county judge somewhere. But these arguments, coming from this particular source, reflect such rampant hypocrisy about the condition of the legal system in America today that it's simply hard to take his lawyers' arguments at face value.

Paula Jones

The President's central contention was that he somehow enjoys de facto immunity for unofficial acts. There is no precedent to suggest anything of the sort. Several Presidents—Teddy Roosevelt, Harry Truman, John F. Kennedy—faced civil suits over private matters. As the 8th Circuit U.S. Court of Appeals ruled in turning away this argument: the Constitution "did not create a monarchy." The relevant case here, *Nixon v. Fitzgerald* (1982), gives the President protection only within the "'outer perimeter' of his official responsibility." Chief Justice William Rehnquist noted yesterday that *Fitzgerald* doesn't block Paula Jones's claims.

Even Mr. Dellinger didn't seem to take this argument very seriously. He conceded at one point that a pressing matter—such as a child custody case—ought to be dealt with before a President left office. Thus Mr. Clinton's principle here seems to be: Delay only those suits that will embarrass me. And indeed Justice Sandra Day O'Connor suggested that his immunity claims may be as rooted in "political damage control" as "constitutional balance."

The President's expediency in this instance is surpassed by that of his feminist supporters, many waving law degrees, who all of a sudden have discovered distinctions and nuance in the sexual harassment codes. Susan Estrich and others booing Paula Jones's complaint now suggest that a woman's complaint of harassment can't be taken at face value. This was the subtext of the argument advanced by Mr. Clinton's lawyers that delaying the Jones case for another four years wouldn't damage anyone. After all, it's only a "he-said, she-said," case, right? No doubt Justice Thomas, who maintained an eloquent silence yesterday, will be interested to see how standards of proof and reputation are suddenly higher than a Coke can.

Robert Bennett

The final and crowning hypocrisy here is the new-found concern of the President and his defenders with runaway litigation. In his brief, Mr. Bennett wrung his hands over the prospect of the President falling victim to a "frivolous but embarrassing claim." He made this plea for prudence and balance on the very same morning that news reports appeared that plaintiff's lawyers in the Texaco case are asking for $29 million of the settlement, plus expenses, and that Morgan Stanley has been hit with a copycat suit for offensive e-mail.

Mr. Bennett shuddered over the Leader of the Free World suffering the same fate as corporate defendants and getting caught up in endless depositions, interrogatories, motions and so forth. Similar concerns were expressed by a lengthy list of law professors—led by Yale's Akhil Amar—who filed an amicus brief for Mr. Clinton.

Welcome to the team, fellas. We've been complaining for years about the civil justice system and the obscene costs it imposes even on defendants who are ultimately judged innocent. But wasn't this system created in the first place by all those liberal legal thinkers who now want us to believe that it's gone too far? If they were really worried about the litigation explosion, presumably these eminent thinkers would join us in calling for adoption of the English rule (loser pays) and limits on punitive damages, the "deep pockets" rule and junk science in court. Don't hold your breath. As with the feminists, there's no rethinking here of first principles by the purveyors of liability, only an expedient argument that says Bill Clinton should be exempt from the standards they've inflicted on everybody else.

If the Justices ultimately decide that Mr. Clinton's isn't above the law, the President will get the pleasure of experiencing firsthand the legal system created by his pals in the plaintiff's bar. So perhaps the next time Congress sends up civil justice reform, the President will think twice before vetoing it.

Editorial Feature

Lippo's Chinese Connections

By Peter Schweizer

The many questionable contributions to the Democratic Party and President Clinton's legal defense fund are as much about U.S. national security as they are about White House influence peddling.

Questions swirling around former Deputy Assistant Commerce Secretary John Huang, the Lippo Group of Indonesia and the fundraising activities of Charles Yah Lin Trie may well be linked by the shadow efforts of the Chinese military to influence U.S. foreign and military policy. Both the Democratic Party and the president's legal defense fund have returned vast contributions, yet considerable security damage will continue to occur unless the matter is fully investigated.

The most recent revelation concerns the fact that Charlie Trie arranged for President Clinton to meet with Wang Jun, a Chinese arms merchant, at a Feb. 6, 1996, White House coffee social. Mr. Wang is chairman of Poly Technologies, which is owned and run by the Chinese People's Liberation Army. Poly Technologies is a front company under China's General Staff Department's Equipment and Technology Department, and the Chinese Commission of Science, Technology and Industry for National Defense. The latter, known as Costind, is in charge of military research and development, testing and production. Among Costind's more important state functions is control of the technical and professional work at the PLA's strategic missile force.

Almost all high-level Costind officials have military rank. PLA Gen. Ding Hennggao has been the director since June 1985 and has the bureaucratic rank of a minister. Four of the five deputy directors of Costind are lieutenant generals. Costind and front companies such as Poly Technologies, Yuanwang Group Corporation, New Era Corporation and Galaxy New Technology Corporation have three important functions.

First, they manage arms sales to countries such as Iran, Iraq, North Korea and Pakistan. Second, they acquire advanced dual-use technologies to assist in modernizing the PLA. Finally, they serve as conduits for intelligence operations. The U.S. Defense Intelligence Agency reports that these organizations are "key to supporting the uniformed services and China's industrial base and to acquiring military and dual-use technology." DIA officer Nicholas Efitimiades identified Poly Technologies as a cover for such activities in his book "Chinese Intelligence Operations."

The PLA's links extend to the Lippo Group; Costind, through the Yuanwang Group Corp. and New Era Corp., has run several joint ventures with Lippo. Recently, Lippo and a U.S. firm, Entergy Corp., signed a $1 billion deal to build a nuclear power plant in China. The deal was negotiated with help from the U.S. Commerce Department and Costind, which also runs the Chinese nuclear research program.

Given the PLA's link to these fund-raising scandals, what could it possibly be after? The most direct answer is access to high technology, particularly so-called dual-use technologies, which have both civilian and military applications. The Commerce Department, where Mr. Huang worked, is responsible for licensing exports of U.S. dual-use items. And by any measure, the Clinton administration has been very willing to grant the PLA access to such critical technologies.

On Sept. 14, 1994, the Commerce Department approved the export of machine tools to China, "despite the strong warnings from U.S. military and intelligence officials," notes South Carolina Rep. Floyd Spence, chairman of the House National Security Committee. The machine tools were to be used to produce parts for commercial aircraft that would be built in China under a contract with McDonnell Douglas. According to the General Accounting Office, however, some of the more sophisticated machine tools were shipped to the Nanchang Aircraft Co., which produces fighter aircraft and cruise missiles for the PLA. As the principal deputy assistant commerce secretary with a strong interest in Asian commercial affairs, Mr. Huang would have played a significant role in this decision.

Even after officials became aware of this diversion, the wheels of enforcement moved very slowly. The Commerce Department did not formally investigate the export-control violations until six months after they were first reported, the GAO noted in a recent report.

The Commerce Department's Los Angeles field office recommended that Commerce issue a temporary denial order against the PLA's China National Aero-Technology Import & Export Association and its subsidiaries. Commerce rejected that recommendation; the Los Angeles office subsequently referred the case to the Department of Justice for consideration. An investigation is pending.

In April 1994 the Commerce Department created a new general license category, allowing nearly all dual-use telecommunications items to be exported to civilian customers in China without licenses. AT&T sold advanced asynchronous transfer mode and synchronous digital hierarchy telecommunications equipment without review to HuaMei, a joint venture partly owned by Galaxy New Technology; several members of its board are PLA officers. Pentagon officials warned Commerce that such dual-use technologies would be enormously beneficial for the Chinese military in sharing intelligence, imagery and video among several locations, as well as in command and control of military operations. Again, the warnings fell on deaf ears.

These and other possible links between PLA-managed companies and the White House and Democratic Party fund-raising occur alongside the Clinton administration's inaction in the face of dangerous activities by the Chinese military. In addition to passing sensitive ballistic-missile and nuclear-weapons-related technologies to rogue states, the PLA is operating under the assumption that the U.S. is a rival, not a friend. In 1993 the PLA High Command published a textbook titled "Can the Chinese Army Win the Next War?" In it, the U.S. is identified as the "principal adversary"; most of its war scenarios center on armed conflict with America.

Mr. Schweizer is co-author, with Reagan administration Defense Secretary Caspar Weinberger, of "The Next War," just released by Regnery.

Editorial Feature

What if Paula Jones Had Sued a CEO?

The Supreme Court heard oral arguments Monday on whether Paula Jones's sexual harassment lawsuit should be handled differently from all other cases—that is, delayed for seven years. Whatever the court rules, Bill Clinton has already received preferential treatment. Just imagine if Mr. Clinton were president not of the whole country but of a donut factory. A secretary accused him of luring her to a hotel room, grabbing her, dropping his pants, and demanding sexual satisfaction. Once she filed suit, what would Bill-the-donut-guy do?

Rule of Law

By Max Boot

(A) Stonewall by claiming he has "no recollection" of being "alone in a hotel with her."

(B) Offer to settle.

(C) Go to trial and lose a seven-figure punitive damages verdict.

There's a good chance the answer would be (D), all of the above. The likelihood of that outcome would be even greater if the charges were filed not against an obscure donut-maker but against somebody as prominent in the business world as Mr. Clinton is in politics. The mind boggles at what would happen if, say, Jack Welch or Lou Gerstner faced pants-dropping accusations. Suffice it to say, the ensuing uproar would make the Texaco Tapes tempest look insignificant by comparison.

But far from paying much of a cost, financial or political, Mr. Clinton has so far gotten a virtual pass in the Paula Jones case. Though the press is starting to wake up to the story—it was on Newsweek's cover last week—only this newspaper has dared to print the explicit complaint filed by Ms. Jones. There's been no wolf pack of feminists tearing apart the alleged harasser. And the fact that the justices even accepted Mr. Clinton's appeal before a verdict is pretty extraordinary. The court turns down roughly 99% of appeals and almost never takes an unresolved case.

This kid-gloves treatment is especially glaring in light of what Mr. Clinton is accused of doing. Stuart Taylor Jr. has already noted in the American Lawyer that the charges against Mr. Clinton are more substantiated, not to mention more substantial, than those against Clarence Thomas. What hasn't been pointed out yet is that Paula

> *Paula Jones's accusations are far more serious than those that routinely result in big-bucks verdicts against private-sector defendants.*

Jones's accusations are also far more serious than those that routinely result in big-bucks verdicts against private-sector defendants.

Consider some of the biggest sexual harassment cases. A secretary won $6.9 million (later reduced to $3.8 million) from law mega-firm Baker & McKenzie. Among other charges, she accused a partner of dropping some M&M's down her blouse pocket and asking her, "What's the wildest thing you've ever done?" Then there's the $50 million award against Wal-Mart (reduced to $5 million). Among the store's sins was not disciplining a supervisor who referred to women as "goddamn dummies." And now the Equal Employment Opportunity Commission has filed a $150 million class action suit against Mitsubishi because male workers at its U.S. plant scrawled obscene graffiti in men's bathrooms and made crude remarks about women. (Rough language in a factory? Shocking!)

Smaller, and weirder, examples proliferate. A 14-year-old girl in the San Francisco Bay Area recently won $500,000 for sexual harassment because when she was in sixth grade, boys would direct "obscene gestures" her way. An Atlantic City, N.J., female police sergeant won $1.3 million, in part because on one occasion a sanitary napkin marked with sergeant's stripes was hung from the ceiling while she conducted roll call. Unpleasant, sure, but a far cry from pants-dropping.

All these defendants were snared due primarily to two changes in the law. First, the burden of proof has been dramatically lowered. Proving sexual harassment under Title VII of the 1964 Civil Rights Act used to require showing that a supervisor had made a put-out-or-get-out demand. Then in *Meritor Savings Bank v. Vinson* (1986), the Supreme Court wove out of whole cloth the "hostile environment" standard, which allows a plaintiff to collect for anything that would offend a "reasonable person's" sensibilities. In *Harris v. Forklift Systems* (1993), the court held that conduct didn't even have to be "psychologically injurious" to be actionable. It is this standard that makes plaintiffs like Paula Jones prime candidates for compensation. And, despite the protestations of Clinton cronies, the lack of a "pattern" of harassment—a usual requirement under the law—may not matter much. The EEOC informs us that "a single, unusually severe incident of harassment may be sufficient to constitute a Title VII violation."

The second change that's opened the sluice gates to sexual harassment cases is the lifting of limits on damages. The 1991 Civil Rights Act, which might as well be called the Anita Hill Act, for the first time allowed plaintiffs to collect compensatory and punitive damages in federal employment discrimination cases; previously only back pay and attorney's fees were available. Although damages in federal sexual-harassment suits are capped at $300,000, the sky's the limit in many state courts. This has set off gold-rush fever among the plaintiff's bar. If Ms. Jones were suing anybody other than the president, she would have had to beat off the ambulance chasers with a broom. "This case is something I could work with and present to a judge or jury in an attempt to recover adequate compensation," confirms Los Angeles plaintiff's lawyer Carla Barboza.

Given this obliging legal climate, no wonder sexual harassment claims are skyrocketing. And so are payouts: Jury Verdict Research estimates that the median compensatory damage award in sexual harassment cases increased to $120,000 in 1995 from $70,000 in 1991. Plus, one-third of all these cases result in punitive damages. All of this is imposing fearsome costs on American business. Not only soaring settlements and legal fees, but also payments to the "diversity" industry that is offering companies "protection" (in the Al Capone sense) from this racket.

If anything good comes out of the Paula Jones case, it should be to focus public attention on this area of the law. Most would agree that boorish bosses who make put-out-or-get-out demands should be aggressively prosecuted. But a "hostile environment"? That's a different story. Conflating the two is like saying there's no difference between rape and a wolf whistle.

Who knows, now that Hillary's husband is in the frying pan, perhaps the lefty lawyers who ignited this blaze in the first place will see the need to douse the fires of discrimination law. Naw. The den mothers of the left are willing to give Bill-the-prez a pass because of all the goodies he can deliver for them. They wouldn't care about Bill-the-donut-guy. To them, he'd be just another fat, male chauvinist who should be squeezed until he oinks.

Mr. Boot is deputy features editor of the Journal editorial page.

REVIEW & OUTLOOK

Daring Doolittle

It's worth paying attention to a member of Congress, left or right, willing to stand athwart political convention yelling stop. So let's now say a nice word about California Republican Rep. John Doolittle's proposal to fight the Pamplona bulls of the Beltway on campaign finance reform.

Because the current campaign rules didn't stop dubious contributions to Democrats from emigre Indonesian gardeners last year, the sages of Washington are now saying we need even more rules. This follows the Common Cause-Ralph Nader model of "reform," which has dominated our campaign laws since Watergate. It is a regulatory vision of politics: Government can and should decide how Americans elect their government. The fact that all of this hasn't worked so far only means that government hasn't been trying hard enough.

Enter Mr. Doolittle, who wants to break the Common Cause monopoly on what constitutes reform. His bill, which he plans to introduce soon, would eliminate most current rules and nearly all limits on campaign contributions, in return for requiring full public disclosure of who gave how much to whom. This might work.

Unlike the Common Cause model, it doesn't dream the impossible dream of purging money from politics. Mr. Doolittle recognizes that campaign giving and spending are forms of political speech under rulings by the U.S. Supreme Court. And he understands that much of the perversity of current campaign practice flows from the previous attempts to make money go away.

For example, the current limit on individual donations to candidates—$1,000—was passed in 1974. If it had been indexed for inflation, that limit would be about $5,000, but it has never been changed. So a Presidential nominee must spend most of his time raising the $20 million or so it takes to be credible in the primaries. This is why the only Presidential candidates tend to be either the well connected (Bob Dole, Phil Gramm), the well heeled (Steve Forbes), or those who can live off the ground (Pat Buchanan). Many potential candidates are simply put off by the fund-raising burden (Colin Powell, Dick Cheney). In the name of creating more political competition, in short, our current laws in reality constrain it.

John Doolittle

The Doolittle idea would help competition by making it easier for challengers, Presidential and Congressional, to raise money. A handful of backers would be able to give a candidate at least a fund-raising base. This is how Democrat Gene McCarthy started his improbable, but historic, Presidential run in 1968 against a sitting President of his own party—before the Watergate-era reforms would have made such a challenge impossible. Today more House and Senate seats would have competitive challengers.

But wouldn't fat cats simply buy their own candidates? With disclosure, candidates would have to face the political consequences of the money they accept. If tobacco money was involved, say, then an opponent would be free to make that a campaign issue. It was today's minimal disclosure laws, for example, that got the press corps looking into fund-raisers at Buddhist temples. Democrats arguably paid a political price for those disclosures late in the election campaign. Vice President Gore this week is lamely admitting the obvious: uh, yeah, he knew all along the event had some connection to "finance." If the Federal Election Commission became an agency of disclosure, instead of a feckless regulatory bureaucracy, its existence might even be justified.

In any event, it's hard to imagine a worse system than today, when unions and the NRA, among others, can run "independent expenditures" in campaigns with almost no disclosure, but very real influence on Congressional votes later. Eliminating limits would make the special interests arguably *less* influential, not more.

The Doolittle proposal probably won't become law soon, at least not as long as President Clinton embraces the Common Cause model. But here and there we notice a turn among political elites toward daring Doolittle. The Columbus Dispatch and Cleveland Plain Dealer have recently broken out of the usual big newspaper regulatory mold. And David Broder, the ultimate barometer in good-government intentions, has gone on record calling today's campaign limits "ridiculous, given television and campaigning costs." He says he'd raise the personal contributions limit to "$50,000. Maybe even go to $100,000."

The phony populists who want more regulation still have the upper hand, but Mr. Doolittle is showing the country there's a rational alternative. If nothing else, he may give the Beltway bulls a reason to think before they further ruin our politics.

REVIEW & OUTLOOK

Clinton II

For the second Clinton term, how about stability?

The first Clinton term was among the most tumultuous Presidential administrations ever. Scandals rained down like some four-year Biblical torrent.

At the same time, Clinton I witnessed the Democratic Party moving, kicking and screaming, toward the political center. It opened

Bill Clinton

with national health care and closed with the signing of a welfare-reform bill ending a national entitlement. Future historians and Administration memoirists will explain whether this shift was a product of the rankest political calculation to win re-election, as defrocked adviser Dick Morris suggests in his new book, or at some level the result of a larger recognition of reality.

This is Inauguration day, so in the spirit, we'll ponder the possibility of the latter. And indeed, the initial portents are pretty good.

The new chief of staff, Erskine Bowles, has received good notices from key Senate Republicans so far. As well, Mr. Clinton managed to attract a White House Counsel of the caliber of Charles Ruff, who in a more perfect world would have been in this hot seat four years ago. Bruce Reed, the fellow who urged Mr. Clinton to sign the welfare bill for the right reasons, is now domestic policy adviser. Send in the pros. The arrival of these folks simultaneous with the departure of

George Stephanopoulos and Harold Ickes is on its face a net gain in general White House gravitas.

Madeleine Albright at State may turn out to be the best appointment Mr. Clinton ever made for the wrong reasons. While Ms. Albright may not have published as often as other members of the foreign affairs fraternity, we suspect this daughter of Czechoslovakia understands the way the Communist mind works better than most of them did; and so conceivably the relationship with China will be more clearly managed this time around. We want to believe that Defense is in good hands, though Senator Cohen's test will be whether he maintains, or abandons, his traditional support for building missile-defense systems.

If a true litmus test for the second term exists, it is probably the Department of Justice. Clinton crony Webster Hubbell's inexplicable ascendancy at Justice in the early days of the Clinton term roused, as much as anything, our interest in the new Administration from Arkansas and its connections. Between Mr. Hubbell's fall and the recent Arkansas-based details of the Indogate fund-raisers, we feel vindicated in raising those early concerns. Especially so considering the resignation of Philip Heymann, the department's ethical lodestone. Now many of the first-term problems, for example the DNC's Asian fund-raising operation, are locked inside the legal or judicial pipelines. Justice will be involved.

We don't know what caused Mr. Clinton to keep Janet Reno, but he did. Mickey Kantor has left. Deputy Attorney General Jamie Gorelick, by our lights a troublesome figure despite her administrative abilities, has resigned. But Ms. Reno is impaired by illness, Ms. Gorelick is now a lame duck, and "acting" designees fill several other important posts. The problem is empty chairs, and how Mr. Clinton fills them will be a sharp test of the initial indications of a new seriousness.

Robert Rubin will remain at Treasury, where he was chiefly responsible for the appointment of Alan Greenspan and thus Mr. Clinton's re-election. The new appointments suggest he will have the company of other figures of substance, especially important if the first-term scandals mushroom into crises. In policy matters, first-term initiatives were undercut by Mr. Clinton's famous "permanent campaign," a source of constant, deserved doubt about his real motives. Now he can tell the pollsters to go home. The second term is about governance.

And that means making choices. One of the more interesting stories bubbling out of the Gingrich cauldron is that many recently elected Democrats and centrists are sick of it and want to govern. Mr. Clinton absolutely must decide whether he wants to lead these people or be part of the 1970s mob burning down the system as it retreats. For example, will his new budget truly try to control entitlements or in fact feed them? Who will he put at the head of the line for education reform—the unions or the kids? On the personal side, will he apologize to Paula Jones and Billy Dale? In striving for a landmark, as Richard Nixon was the President to open China, Bill Clinton could be the one to reform Social Security or build a serious missile defense.

As we noted, Mr. Clinton inevitably will have to deal with some of the problems born in the first term. But the office of the Presidency affords its holder an array of powerful tools to accomplish good or ill. Standing on the doorstep of a second term, Bill Clinton has the rare luxury of holding the opportunity and the means to affect how he will be remembered.

Editorial Feature

Democrats Change Their Minds On Independent Counsel Law

In a little noticed comment last month, President Clinton said the independent counsel law had had "enormous costs" and should be reassessed. A week later, the president said that "this special counsel thing ought to be reviewed . . . because the costs outweigh the benefits."

Mr. Clinton's comments indicate his interest in major revision of the independent counsel statute. Many other Democrats and their media allies hold the same view. Yet before this reform train leaves the station, it's worth noting that until the Clinton presidency, few Democrats were critical of the law. Indeed, Democrats were generally supportive of "this special counsel thing"—so long as it was directed at Republican presidencies.

Rule of Law

By Terry Eastland

The law, of course, is a product of Watergate. In response to President Nixon's firing of Archibald Cox, whom the Justice Department had appointed to probe Watergate, Congresses controlled by Democrats spent the middle 1970s searching for a statutory means of providing for "special prosecutors" with enough independence to prosecute executive-branch crime. Title VI of the Ethics in Government Act of 1978, signed by President Jimmy Carter, established procedures to trigger the court appointment of a prosecutor whom the president cannot easily discharge.

The law would have been enacted earlier had the Ford administration supported it. But Attorney General Edward Levi had warned that the law would create opportunities for "actual or apparent partisan influence in law enforcement; publicize and dignify unfounded, scurrilous allegations against public officials; result in the continuing existence of a changing band of multiplicity of special prosecutors, and promote the possibility of unequal justice."

This was not the view of most Democrats back then. Persuaded that Republican presidencies were especially prone to misconduct, few Democrats seemed to think that Democratic presidencies might be candidates for special counsel investigations. That view was shaken when the first two individuals subjected to special counsel probes were Carter aides Hamilton Jordan and Tim Kraft. Both investigations, though duly required by the law, were plainly unjustified. But the Carter administration soon passed from the scene, and the 12 years of Republican presidencies commenced.

> *Mr. Clinton would cut a more credible figure on the need for reform if he admitted his party's essential role in establishing the very system he now complains about.*

During those years, Republicans continued to object to the law even as congressional Democrats ensured its vitality by pressing for its reauthorization in 1983 and again in 1987. By 1987, moreover, Democrats on Capitol Hill saw how the statute could be used to weaken Republican presidencies. In renewing the law, Congress added provisions that in effect required *more* independent counsel investigations. Congressional Republicans managed only the triumph of defeating measures that would have made the law permanent.

In 1992, the law was again up for renewal. Thanks to their increasing irritation with Iran-Contra Independent Counsel Lawrence Walsh, Republicans were even more opposed to reauthorization. The law expired, and it was not until the summer of 1994 that the Democratic Congress revived it. But during the 1992 campaign, the essential dynamic of independent counsel politics continued, with Democrats led by then vice presidential candidate Al Gore calling for counsels to investigate various Republican "scandals," most notably "Iraqgate."

The current vehicle for the Democrats' reform of the law that they originated and have perpetuated is a bill already introduced by

Rep. John Conyers (D., Mich.). It proposes that the attorney general initiate investigation of an allegation when a crime actually "has been" committed. This is what the statute provided before the 1987 reauthorization, when Democrats pushed through an amendment requiring investigation when a crime merely "may have been committed." Also, so that the attorney general may have more information in reviewing the merits of an allegation, the bill would give him or her subpoena authority—authority explicitly denied by the 1983 reauthorization.

The Conyers bill also would strengthen the attorney general's hand in deciding whether "there are reasonable grounds to believe that further investigation is warranted"—in which case the attorney general must ask for a counsel. The 1987 reauthorization, seeking to constrain the Reagan Justice Department's discretion in reviewing allegations, included a provision preventing the attorney general from ending an investigation unless there is "clear and convincing evidence" that the accused lacked criminal intent. The Democrats want to relax their own standard by requiring only "a preponderance of the evidence." Another provision in the Conyers bill would require coverage of only a handful of high-level officials, including the president and vice president.

All these provisions would result in the appointment of many fewer independent counsels. (There have been at least 17 under the statute.) The rest of the bill's key provisions may be described as inspired by Whitewater: One would limit the law's concern to crimes committed in office, not beforehand; others would establish criteria for counsels that essentially embody James Carville's wild objections to the appointment of Whitewater Independent Counsel Kenneth Starr.

The Conyers bill notwithstanding, Congress isn't likely to review the independent counsel law anytime soon. Hearings now would be premature, inasmuch as 1997 is likely to see significant actions by current independent counsels. Besides, there is no urgency: The law isn't scheduled to expire until the summer of 1999.

Nonetheless, criticism of the statute is bound to continue, with Democrats taking the lead. Mr. Clinton himself would cut a more credible figure on the need for reform if he admitted his party's essential role in establishing the very system he now complains about. And, at least privately, he should be pleased that congressional Republicans have not been as aggressive on independent counsel matters as con-

Yet even after decades of experience in the political process, Mr. Hwang was somewhat taken aback when, at the behest of John Huang, he shared the president's table at a July Century Plaza fundraiser with people who didn't seem to be residents of this country but simply representatives of Taiwanese, Indonesian and other Chinese diaspora businesses.

"A lot of the people at the table didn't even speak English," Mr. Hwang, a lifelong Republican, notes. "The newer they are, the more ignorant they are about the process. That's why they blew it."

John Huang

Mr. Hwang's assertion about his community's fund-raising naiveté—particularly in raising cash from noncitizens—is widely accepted by many in Los Angeles's half-million-strong Chinese-American community. In contrast to the widespread notion of John Huang as a kind of Asiatic Maurice Stans, he is widely viewed by his many acquaintances as nothing more than an unwitting victim of the collision between Chinese political custom and the unrelenting greed of the Clinton fund-raising machine.

President Clinton's promise of personal access at the highest levels—amplified by messengers like Mr. Huang—resonated strongly with both diaspora businessmen and Chinese-American entrepreneurs, most of whom personally tilt Republican. Vincent Diau, former city editor of the Chinese Daily News, located in the Asian enclave of Monterey Park, says Mr. Huang's success in raising money from the Asian business community reflected not so much enthusiasm for the President's policies but the traditional desire to secure *guanxi* (connections) with well-placed officials. Some of those who gave money to Mr. Clinton also supported Bob Dole; like Mr. Hwang, many have supported both right-wing Republicans and leftish Democrats, depending on the practical necessities.

"Chinese tradition stresses great importance on personal relationships, and there is a tendency to mix that up with public policy," Mr. Diau says. "*Guanxi* dominates everything in Taiwan, China, here."

In this context, the prominent role of the Jakarta-based Lippo Group, John Huang's longtime employers, in the growing Clinton re-election funds scandal becomes all the more understandable. Although they are only 5% of Indonesia's population, ethnic Chinese control roughly 75% of that nation's business assets. Over the past century, this success has invited repeated persecutions, most painfully when tens of thousands of Chinese were slaughtered in the aftermath of the mid-1960s coup that brought the current Suharto regime to power.

"The Indonesian Chinese are particularly sensitive," the banker Mr. Hwang observes. "In Indonesia, the only way they can grow is to make political ties. If not, they are dead. The Chinese are hated in these countries, and they know if things go wrong, they'll get killed."

In America, mercifully, the stakes are not often that high. Yet Asian businesspeople—who have been prime investors in California's burgeoning economic recovery—are acutely aware that federal, state and city officials possess the power to make life miserable for both them and their businesses. To most, it seemed simply good business to burn some cash at the elaborately decked-out Clinton altar rather than risk a nasty regulatory surprise later on.

This proclivity to seek influence has made Asian-Americans exceedingly liable to the kind of suggestive wooing that is hallmark of the Democratic Party under Clinton. But this should not shock anyone, since newcomers to America—such as the Irish in the 19th century and the Jews and Italians earlier in this century—also often gravitated to unscrupulous politicians who promised them both respect and influence for money. Wealthy Jews, for example, often found the Democrats attractive because, in large part, they felt unwelcome in the WASP-dominated GOP.

Ultimately, these same immigrants later learned more about how to use and, in some places, dominate the political system, as the Italians did in much of New York state or as the Irish did in Massachusetts. A similar maturation will likely also occur among Asians, whose numbers and economic power are increasingly palpable, and not only in California.

This recent progress makes particularly poignant the fate of John Huang, a self-effacing middleman whose stated lifelong goal has simply been to accelerate Asian immigrants' integration into American political life. Today, for his effort, Mr. Huang sits stoically in his Glendale, Calif., home, with only the support of friends and Hillary Clinton's assurance of support to bolster his courage.

Not surprisingly, many of Mr. Huang's longtime acquaintances increasingly doubt the efficacy of the Clintons' backing. They are painfully aware of the first family's poor record of support for those onetime operatives left behind in their various financial and political schemes.

"Some of us don't understand why Clinton has such a low profile on this scandal and John is taking all the responsibility," observes Mr. Diau, now a business manager. "John says the Clinton family supports him, but nothing's being done. Clinton's reputation in the community has really suffered. *Guanxi* is supposed to go both ways."

Mr. Kotkin, a fellow at the Pepperdine Institute for Public Policy and the Pacific Research Institute, is the author of "Tribes" (Random House, 1993).

REVIEW & OUTLOOK

Politics and the IRS--II

The White House's voracious media food chain is alive and chewing. On Sunday Oklahoma Senator Don Nickles, chairman of the Finance Subcommittee on Taxation and IRS Oversight, said he would conduct hearings into whether the Clinton Administration has been using the IRS for political purposes. Senator Nickles told "Fox News Sunday" (itself increasingly a valuable source of new information about Washington politics) that "the IRS has the responsibility to conduct audits, but not just against political enemies or political adversaries." Under food-chain theory, this means Mike McCurry has to take the subject seriously now.

Just last Thursday the White House press secretary was asked about news reports that a surprising number of conservative non-profit groups are the targets of Internal Revenue Service audits. "I'm not aware of any credible news organization that's reported anything like that," Mr. McCurry sniffed. The fact that conservative groups are currently the target of IRS audits has been reported recently by the Chicago Tribune, Washington Times and in Journal editorials. Come to think of it, the logic of media food-chain theory would suggest that Mr. McCurry address the substance of these stories as we bring them up, rather than refuse to until they reach the mainstream reporters standing in front of him or a congressional committee run by a member of the GOP leadership.

As to the details, up to a dozen conservative groups, by their own admission, are being scrutinized by the IRS. Both the Tribune (the city of Chicago apparently having been relegated beyond the main-stream) and the Times called around to prominent liberal groups and couldn't find any who were being audited. Just last weekend, the Public Broadcasting System program "TechnoPolitics" aired its own story on the IRS audits. Host Jim Glassman, a columnist for the Washington Post, noted that National Review, the American Specta-tor and Oliver North's Freedom Alliance have all been the subject of IRS probes. Other groups currently undergoing audits include the Heritage Foundation, Citizens Against Government Waste, the Na-tional Rifle Association and the Western Journalism Center.

* * *

As background reading for the impending hearings, we commend to the White House the nearby article [page 291] by Wall Street Jour-nal reporter Elizabeth MacDonald, which details the politicization of the IRS during the Kennedy Administration.

Meanwhile, the New York newspaper Newsday has uncovered a curious chain of events which indicate yet another possible prong in the politicization of the IRS. Rep. Charles Rangel, the ranking Democrat on the Ways and Means Committee, recently revealed that five nonprofit groups linked to Speaker Newt Gingrich are the subject of IRS investigations. On December 23, Mr. Rangel issued a press release stating that the groups were IRS targets, and specifically named the Abraham Lincoln Opportunity Fund. Then on January 5, Mr. Rangel announced on CBS that he had been "in touch with the IRS on this issue" and that it was conducting "an ongoing investigation" of the groups.

The problem here is that the Abraham Lincoln group wasn't offi-cially notified it was being audited until it received a certified letter from the IRS dated January 7, two days after Rep. Rangel announced it to the world on CBS. A further problem is that Rep. Rangel may have violated the Privacy Act. Section 6103 of the IRS code makes it a felony to publicly reveal confidential IRS information.

Naturally Mr. Rangel is trying to explain himself. "I had not seen the release, nor had I approved it," he says, an admission of over-sight failure that got Speaker Gingrich into a tad more hot water re-cently. Mr. Rangel's press secretary, Emile Milne, says he "in-ferred" from news reports and a letter from Deputy IRS Commissioner Michael Dolan that the groups were being investigated and wrote a "stupid" release. But the news reports mentioned possible IRS audits of two groups, not five, and Mr. Dolan's letter mentions no groups by name but merely states there are about 50 investigations of tax-exempt groups in which political activity is an issue. "Of course, Mr. Rangel has no inside information," Mr. Milne told us. But no explanation yet for Mr. Rangel's comment on CBS that he had been "in touch with the IRS on this issue."

The IRS denies political motives in selecting groups or individuals for audit. The agency's Mr. Dolan says that when it comes to auditing tax-exempt groups the IRS "largely" relies "on issues raised in media reports and third-party communications," which strikes us as an odd basis for such decisions. It would appear to follow that such third parties could systematically file reports on groups with opposing views and skew the political mix of IRS audits. Perhaps the Nickles hearings will shed some light.

*   *   *

This of course is not the first time that mainstream Washington has been around the IRS track with the Clinton White House. Concerns surfaced in 1993 when the White House's report on the Travel Office affair admitted that former associate White House counsel William Kennedy had told the FBI that if it didn't start a criminal investigation of the Travel Office, he "might have to seek guidance from another agency, such as the IRS." Eight days later, after the Travel Office workers were fired, three IRS agents began an audit of UltrAir, the charter company that was the subject of unfounded rumors about using kickbacks to secure Travel Office business. The audit lasted two years and cleared UltrAir of any wrongdoing.

Congressional investigators probing the Travel Office firings later found notes relating to the affair in which a White House attorney said IRS Commissioner Margaret Milner Richardson was "on top of it." Ms. Richardson says she doesn't recall any such reference, and a GAO report claimed no interference. Nonetheless, shortly after Travel Office Director Billy Dale was fired from his White House job, he got audited.

Ms. Richardson has announced her impending resignation. A self-described "yellow dog Democrat," Ms. Richardson is a friend of First Lady Hillary Clinton. While IRS commissioner, she flew to the Democratic convention in Chicago to see President Clinton's acceptance speech. Ellen Miller of the liberal-leaning Center for Responsive Politics said the trip "suggests politicization." Charles Lewis of the liberal Center for Public Integrity said her presence at a partisan convention "sort of underscores our tax collecting agency is run by the Democrats, and that is something you don't need to underscore, even as a spectator."

This Thursday and Friday the Commission on Restructuring the IRS meets in Washington. It is co-chaired by Democratic Sen. Bob Kerrey and GOP Rep. Rob Portman. Commission member Grover Norquist, president of Americans for Tax Reform, plans to make taxpayer rights an issue. Mr. Norquist supports a rule requiring that any IRS official who initiates an audit file a letter stating the reason for the audit and whether it originated from an outside complaint. At a minimum, such letters should be available to Members of Congress on behalf of constituents (as opposed to grist for Sunday morning political grenades).

We suppose it's possible that the IRS's auditing of a dozen or so conservative groups, against none reported for liberal organizations, could turn out to be the work of some lone phone-caller to the agency's powerful enforcement division. But given this White House's habit of discovering new information after a second or third try, maybe the IRS's audit trail of late is something that should be checked out.

Letters to the Editor

No Improper Contacts With the IRS

The allegations concerning me in your editorials ("Politics and the IRS," Jan. 9 and "Politics and the IRS—II," Jan. 28) are totally without merit. Let me be clear: Neither I nor any member of my staff has received any confidential taxpayer information from the IRS concerning the House Speaker Newt Gingrich's use of tax-exempt organizations for political purposes. In fact, I did not have access to protected tax information, under Internal Revenue Code section 6103, during the 104th Congress. Accordingly, it would have been impossible for me to violate the law as implied in your editorial. I have never asked for nor have I received information from the IRS that is not publicly disclosable.

Your editorial hints that I may have impermissibly contacted the IRS concerning its investigation of tax-exempt organizations controlled by the speaker and his associates. Chairman Archer and I both have contacted the IRS concerning this matter, and the following are the details of those contacts:

Last September, Chairman Bill Archer wrote to IRS Commissioner Margaret Milner Richardson stating that he had read media accounts that the IRS was auditing a college course taught by Speaker Gingrich. Chairman Archer's Sept. 4, 1996, press release announcing his letter stated, "Archer . . . wrote to the IRS today inquiring whether Gingrich was singled out for the audit."

In response to Rep. Archer's letter to the IRS, I also wrote Commissioner Richardson asking that the IRS respond immediately to the chairman's request so that the IRS could resume its function of enforcing our tax laws and avoid any political cloud that might hover over that institution. I did ask, in my letter, whether there was *publicly disclosable* information indicating that Speaker Gingrich was not being singled out for audit. The IRS's response to me is a matter of public record.

On Jan. 3, 1997, I also wrote Commissioner Richardson asking for copies of the tax returns filed by several tax-exempt organizations controlled by the speaker and his associates. These tax returns are not confidential information protected under Section 6103 of the Code, but are publicly disclosable under Section 6104 of the Code.

Your editorial makes much of the fact that a press release from my office mentions the Abraham Lincoln Opportunity Foundation. As I have stated for the record, that release was a mistake. That's all it was. However, the details of the use of that foundation by the speaker and his associates for political purposes were set forth in media reports long before my office issued that press release. Specifically, a Los Angeles Times article on June 25, 1996, clearly sets forth serious allegations of tax violations involving that foundation. The press release was not based on any information from the Internal Revenue Service but was based on inferences drawn from media reports. It may have been untimely, but public media reports have since indicated that it was correct.

Let me repeat, I have not asked for, nor have I received any information from the IRS that is not public information. Any question over the appropriateness of the IRS investigation should be answered by the bipartisan decision of the Ethics Committee to submit its voluminous record to the IRS to assist it in its investigation.

REP. CHARLES RANGEL (D., N.Y.)

Washington

Editorial Feature

The Kennedys and the IRS

By Elizabeth MacDonald

These days, you can't pick up a newspaper without seeing the smoking wreck of another politician's career crashed on the rocks of our nation's tax system. We now know all about House Speaker Newt Gingrich's widely publicized abuses of tax-exemption laws. Disclosures continue to leak out about Richard Nixon's attempts to use the Internal Revenue Service to attack his political enemies. But few are aware that President John F. Kennedy and Attorney General Robert Kennedy systematically used the IRS to muzzle both right-wing and left-wing groups.

John F. Kennedy

Over the past few years, the IRS has released hundreds of its documents to John Andrew, a relentlessly curious historian at Franklin and Marshall College in Lancaster, Pa. The documents obtained by Prof. Andrew—the basis for a book he's writing, due out from Rutgers Press this spring—add to earlier congressional disclosures and work by others showing that the Kennedys were far worse than Nixon in their manipulation of the IRS. These abuses show how the tax agency's vast powers often tempt presidents of both parties to use it as a stick to beat opponents over the head.

To be sure, the government must guarantee that tax-exempt nonprofit groups adhere to the law. However, these documents show that the Kennedys targeted non-exempt activist groups. And the auditing was done at behest of politicians, not the professionals at the IRS. "If the president is interested in a particular program, you would certainly in some instances give attention to some area he's interested in," says Mortimer Caplin, IRS commissioner under President Kennedy. "I am comfortable with that as a commissioner, though you prefer to be left alone. But if the president should call, and you feel that he has a reasonable request, you will be compliant."

In the Kennedys' defense, it should be noted that using the IRS for intelligence gathering didn't become illegal until the 1970s. And in the early 1960s, some right-wing organizations *were* threatening the stability of the government. Army Maj. Gen. Edwin A. Walker tried to indoctrinate troops with his radical-right views. But lots of what irked Jack Kennedy was simply politics as usual, often of the hardball variety. Numerous Protestant fundamentalist ministers criticized the president for his Catholicism. Many right-wing groups, like

---

The documents show that the Kennedys targeted non-exempt activist groups. And the auditing was done at the behest of politicians, not the professionals at the IRS.

---

the Young Americans for Freedom, attacked him for the Bay of Pigs fiasco. The president publicly railed against the right in two speeches in the fall of 1961. "They find treason in our churches, in our highest court, in our treatment of water," he bellowed.

Behind the scenes, the Kennedys mounted a counteroffensive. In early 1961, documents show, the Kennedys planted family friend Carmine Bellino, a certified public accountant, in the IRS Office of Chief Counsel, gave him the title of "special consultant to the president," and demanded that he have access to tax returns. IRS memos argued that the president was "entitled to all information relative to his control over the executive branch."

That fall, Attorney General Kennedy turned to Walter Reuther, president of the United Auto Workers, and civil rights attorney Joseph Rauh Jr. for help. On Dec. 19, 1961, Reuther and Rauh sent the attorney general a 24-page memo headlined "The Radical Right in America Today." The memo writers advocated "deliberate Administration policies and programs to contain the radical right from further expansion" and "to reduce it to its historic role of the impotent lunatic fringe."

The memo writers advised the Kennedys, among other suggestions, to use the IRS to probe possible right-wing tax violations. They noted that several radical-right groups had federal tax-exempt status. "Prompt revocation in a few cases might scare off a substantial part of the big money now flowing into these tax-exempt organizations," they noted.

Recently, Mr. Caplin has publicly said, "We had no 'enemies list' or 'Dean's list' or any other type of political list." However, IRS documents show that Commissioner Caplin sent numerous memos to Attorney General Kennedy and other administration officials about this investigation, dubbed the "Ideological Organizations Audit Project."

In the fall of 1961, the papers show, the IRS commissioner assigned his assistant, Mitchell Rogovin, to run the audit program. On Dec. 20, 1961, Rogovin forwarded to Dean J. Barron, the IRS audit director at the time, a list of 18 organizations to investigate. In late 1961, the IRS launched the first phase of the Ideological Organizations Audit Project.

In January 1962 the audits began. A May 14, 1962, memo from Commissioner Caplin to Henry Fowler, undersecretary of the Treasury, listed at least 12 right-wing organizations and 10 left-wing groups targeted. "We recognized the sensitivity of just going after [the] right wing, so we wanted to add both left- and right-wing groups for balance," Mr. Caplin says in an interview. "It's unclear who selected these groups, though. Many left-wing groups had already been given a difficult time during the Eisenhower years. They had already been audited. So, we scraped the bottom of the barrel to find groups that had not already been audited."

IRS documents list seven non-exempt right-wing groups: the National Indignation Convention, the Conservative Society of America, Americans for Constitutional Government, the John Birch Society, Robert Welch Inc., the All-American Society and the Conservatives. Five exempt right-wing outfits were also targeted: the Christian Crusade-Christian Crusaders Inc., Fred Schwarz's Christian Anti-Communist Crusade, H.L. Hunt's Life-Line Foundation, the National Education Program of Harding College and Billy James Hargis' Christian Echoes Ministry Inc. of Sapulpa, Okla.

Three non-exempt left-wing groups were added: the Common Council for American Unity Inc., the Kenderland Colony Association and the Fair Play for Cuba Committee. The IRS later added the Fund for Social Analysis. Ominously, Lee Harvey Oswald pamphleteered as a member of the Fair Play for Cuba Committee, a group that supported Fidel Castro. In addition, seven exempt liberal-leaning groups made the list: the American Veterans Committee, League for Labor Palestine, Inc., the Anti-Defamation League of B'nai B'rith, the Bressler Foundation, the Zionist Organization of America, the League for Industrial Democracy, the Freeman Charitable Foundation, and a group referred to only as "Gilbert."

On top of all this, IRS memos note that in March 1962 the agency had requested "that examinations be made of six large corporate taxpayers who are alleged financial backers of extremist groups" in New York and San Francisco.

Confidential IRS documents show that the president was delighted with the program. On July 11, 1963, IRS Commissioner Caplin sent the president's deputy counsel, Myer Feldman, a status report on the project. The IRS recommended yanking the tax-exempt status of three right-wing groups: the Christian Anti-Communist Crusade, Life-Line Foundation and Christian Echoes Ministry. The IRS left alone nine left-wing groups. It cannot be determined who the corporate taxpayers were, nor what happened to them or the other groups. Additionally, IRS memos note a plan to target up to 10,000 groups of all stripes, but it's unclear whether that ever came to pass. "The thinking was, the further we reached out, the more neutral the program would be," explains Mr. Caplin.

Soon after, the president urged the IRS "to go ahead with [an] aggressive program on both sides of center," according to a penciled note on an IRS memo. By the fall of 1963, the IRS had rolled out the second phase of the Ideological Organizations Audit Project. This time, the IRS cracked down on 24 outfits—19 right-wing and five left-leaning groups, though Mr. Feldman later got the Daughters of the American Revolution and the Zionist Organization of America deleted from the list. Other reports show that Robert Kennedy suggested to Rogovin that the Justice Department could be called in to defend the IRS in case any of these groups sued the agency.

At the end of the second phase, the IRS recommended that 14

right-wing and one left-wing group lose their tax-exempt status. In 1966, three more right-wing groups lost their tax-exempt status; the IRS kicked another four (including one left-wing group) out of non-profit-land in 1967. No names were disclosed, though, and the information peters out after this point.

Getting even this much out of the IRS wasn't easy. IRS historian Shelley Davis resigned in protest in 1995 because agency officials had been stonewalling Prof. Andrew's requests and even shredding some documents. The agency was so alarmed about the historian's demands that it sent two security officials to interrogate him in the summer of 1995. Even now, the IRS hasn't turned over many of the relevant files. For instance, a 65-page report describing how the Kennedys and the IRS set up this audit project sits buried in the agency files. In typical arrogant fashion, the agency told Prof. Andrew that this report is exempt from the Freedom of Information Act.

No wonder the IRS didn't want this information to come out. It doesn't want the public to realize that the line separating the agency's auditing decisions from politics has often been more like a sieve than a firewall.

Ms. MacDonald, a Journal reporter, covers accounting in the New York bureau.

Leach's question about whether information was conveyed to Arkansas officials in the 1980s, the report states that "interface with local officials was handled by the other federal agency" involved in the joint Mena exercise, sidestepping the issue of what Mr. Clinton knew.

The Clinton White House has gone to great lengths to discredit the Mena story. It figures in the notorious White House conspiracy report and was denounced by former Whitewater damage-control counsel Mark Fabiani as "the darkest backwater of right-wing conspiracy theories." Beltway pundits tend to dismiss Mena as an excess of the Clinton critics. But in Arkansas the campaign is more vicious. With a passive press having long ago abandoned the field, Mena investigators such as former Arkansas State Police investigator Russell Welch and former IRS agent Bill Duncan were stripped of their careers after refusing to back away from the case. Mr. Leach's CIA report provides some vindication for the two Arkansans.

Mr. Leach's full report is not likely to resolve all the questions surrounding Mena, but it might provide important details about that "other agency" and related mysteries. In Arkansas, meanwhile, the Little Rock FBI office is following leads in a sensitive drug-corruption probe involving the Linda Ives "train deaths" case and allegations of Mena-related drug drops. The big drug-corruption question is what network encompassed the Barry Seal operation. The answer could come by following the money on some of the smaller questions, such as whether those CIA contracts for "aviation-related services" went to one of Seal's front companies at Mena. But in forcing an admission from the U.S. intelligence community, Mr. Leach already has performed an important service: He's demolished the notion that nothing happened at Mena.

Mr. Morrison is a Journal editorial page writer.

Letters to the Editor

Balderdash From the CIA

While Micah Morrison's account of the Mena airport matter was sound in most respects ("Mysterious Mena: CIA Discloses, Leach Disposes," editorial page, Jan. 29), I would like to add a point or two about his discussion of the CIA's report on Mena. As I noted in my syndicated column last fall, the CIA's declassified summary of the report released on Nov. 8 was misleading. In fact, after comparing the summary with congressional testimony dating back to 1988, I described the summary as "lawyerly balderdash." In the declassified summary of the report, the CIA is at pains to understate its knowledge of Barry Seal, the pilot, who flew arms flights out of Mena beginning in 1984. The report claims that there is "no evidence" that the CIA ever knew Seal's "true identity." As I reported when the report came out, a Drug Enforcement Administration officer, Ernest Jacobsen, testified in 1988 to the House Subcommittee on Criminal Activity that in May 1984 four CIA officials met with DEA officials regarding Seal's impending flights. They knew exactly Seal's identity. Later in his testimony Jacobsen describes an actual meeting between Seal and the CIA officials.

There is another matter about which the CIA's report is unnecessarily vague, namely its knowledge of the plane Seal used in these flights. The plane, a C-123K, slipped from the hands of Southern Air Transport (the well-known CIA front) landing right into Seal's lap. After he had flown his last flight, the plane returned to Southern Air Transport and met a spectacular demise in Nicaragua after Sandinista fire brought it down, revealing one Eugene Hasenfus on the CIA flight to resupply the Contras.

Now we know that Seal was bringing cocaine back into the country after resupplying the Contras. In its Nov. 8 report the CIA is adamant that it never engaged in drug trafficking or money laundering or "arms smuggling" from Mena. Again the CIA is serving up lawyerly balderdash. No one accuses the CIA of secreting arms into Nicaragua to avoid paying duties on them, which is what smuggling is. And as for drug trafficking and money laundering, I know of no evidence that the CIA was engaged in either activity. The lawyerly deceits that the CIA continues to employ with respect to its activities at Mena do not inspire confidence in the agency.

One other point. As recorded in the prologue to my biography of Bill Clinton, "Boy Clinton: The Political Biography," the other federal agency that the CIA admits to having worked with at Mena is the National Security Agency. NSA's project was called RAPPORT. It is time the Department of Defense comes clean on that project.

R. EMMETT TYRRELL JR.
Editor-in-Chief
The American Spectator

Arlington, Va.

REVIEW & OUTLOOK

Who Is Bruce Lindsey?

Coverage of the President's Tuesday press conference focused on his defense of having coffee with contributors and his new-found ardor for campaign finance reform. Frankly, we don't think Presidential coffees should be outlawed, though we do wonder whether superlawyer Bob Bennett totaled up the 103 coffees over the past two years before telling the Supreme Court the President is too busy to defend himself in the Paula Jones case.

Bruce Lindsey

Kathy Kiely of the Arkansas Democrat-Gazette noticed something else: "Of all the questions, only one seemed to rattle him—a question about his old Arkansas friend, Webb Hubbell." She added, "In the course of a twelve-sentence answer, Clinton denied seven times—in increasing unequivocal terms—having any advance knowledge of Hubbell's employment by the Lippo Group." Lippo, readers will remember, is the Indonesian conglomerate that paid Mr. Hubbell between $100,000 and $250,000 for unspecified services after resigning from the Justice Department but before his felony conviction by Independent Counsel Kenneth Starr. The President blasted as "irresponsible" critics who have suggested that strings were pulled to get Mr. Hubbell funds that would buy his silence in the Whitewater probe.

Precisely what Mr. Clinton said regarding Mr. Hubbell's employment by Lippo was this: "We did not know anything about it. . . . I knew nothing about it—no—none of us did—before it happened. And I personally didn't know anything about it till I read about it in the press."

All of which, and especially the "none of us," raises the question, who is Bruce Lindsey? He's an old Arkansas hand and deputy White House counsel. At another acrimonious press briefing yesterday, White House spokesman Mike McCurry insisted that the President's answer was consistent with Mr. Lindsey's. "No, you're misreading the transcript. Go back and look at it and you'll get it right," he told a dubious press corps.

The problem is that just last week, Mr. McCurry had to backtrack from the previous White House line that no one knew about the Lippo hiring until reading about it in the newspapers. The Associated Press dug up a deposition by Mr. Lindsey acknowledging he knew about Mr. Hubbell's new job as early as November 1994, sixteen months before this page first made it public knowledge. Mr. McCurry's exegesis of the Presidential transcript was: Yes, Bruce Lindsey knew early on, but strictly after the fact. And he never told me, so I read it in the press.

Oh.

Mr. Lindsey seems to have this kind of problem recurrently. After the election, the White House also had to reverse its description of the many White House visits by Lippo scion James Riady as "social calls." This turns out to have been White House disinformation put out during the campaign to avoid admitting that substantive business was discussed. Mr. Lindsey, who sat in on meetings about returning money to former Little Rock restaurateur Charlie Trie, was the architect of the campaign lie. Jeff Gerth and Stephen Labaton of The New York Times revealed that Jane Sherburne and Mark Fabiani, members of the White House counsel's office handling Whitewater, had recommended telling the truth.

Another instance of Mr. Lindsey withholding information from his boss is even more intriguing, especially in terms of the investigations being conducted by Mr. Starr. On October 6, 1993, the President met in the White House with then Arkansas Governor Jim Guy Tucker, with a follow-up meeting on November 18 in Seattle. On October 8, the Resolution Trust Corp. forwarded criminal referrals asking the

Justice Department to investigate Madison Guaranty Savings & Loan, the start of the case in which Mr. Starr ultimately convicted Mr. Tucker. Mr. and Mrs. Clinton were also named as witnesses or beneficiaries of illegal activities. Mr. Lindsey admits he learned of the impending referrals after a September 29 "heads up" from Treasury Counsel Jean Hanson to White House Counsel Bernard Nussbaum.

Mr. Lindsey says he told the President about the referrals on October 4 or 5. He told Congress he didn't mention any specific targets. Subject to correction by a McCurry exegesis, we take this to mean the President's senior aide told him about the referrals without saying that they included the President's name and his wife's, and certainly not the Governor with whom he was about to meet. Somewhere it was said that the Clinton-Tucker meeting was about the Arkansas National Guard.

On Monday, even before the President's press conference, Chairman Dan Burton of the House Oversight Committee asked the President to remove Mr. Lindsey from the task of gathering White House documents that Congressional investigators requested concerning the fund-raising controversy. After all, Mr. Lindsey had participated in the meetings in question, Rep. Burton pointed out, and may have a conflict of interest.

Yes, a walking one.

Rot Spreads

By early February 1997, the Clinton scandals started to envelop Vice President Al Gore, who was emerging as a major player in the campaign-finance affair. Defending his role as "solicitor in chief" of the 1996 campaign, Mr. Gore insisted that "no controlling legal authority" indicated that fund-raising calls made from his office were illegal. Matters went from bad to worse for the Vice President when news reports linked several associates to shakedowns of poor Indian tribes for donations and, at the end of March, a trip to China was met with sharp criticism.

Former National Security Adviser Anthony Lake lost his nomination as Director of Central Intelligence, but a Republican Senate confirmed Alexis Herman as Secretary of Labor despite her involvement with fund-raising as a White House aide. In the Congress, Senator Fred Thompson and Rep. Dan Burton struggled to put their respective campaign-finance probes on a sound footing. Independent Counsel Kenneth Starr admitted a "beaut" of a mistake with his attempted resignation but emerged with only minor damage. Delay and stonewall continued in Washington and Arkansas.

At the Justice Department, Attorney General Janet Reno continued to resist calls for an independent counsel for campaign finance. In April, as reporters closed in, the White House revealed that the Clintons and top advisers had met in 1994 to discuss funds for Webster Hubbell, then under pressure to cooperate with the Whitewater investigation. The White House portrayed the payments as help to an old friend. "The alternative explanation," the Journal wrote, "is a conspiracy to obstruct justice, hatched in the March 1994 meeting with the Clintons, Harold Ickes, Bruce Lindsey, and David Kendall, personal attorney to the Clintons. The key question is one of motive: charity, or hush money?"

REVIEW & OUTLOOK

Second-Term Stall

Preparing for a now-likely filibuster of appropriations for Senator Fred Thompson's campaign-finance hearings, Democrats are complaining about the size of the $6.5 million request. The cost of the inquiry, though, simply reflects the Clinton stonewall. By constantly resisting requests for evidence, even to the extent of subpoenaed billing records turning up in the White House family quarters, the Clintons managed to stall any resolution of Whitewater right past the Presidential election.

Tom Daschle

The second-term stall is now under way. Under the leadership of South Dakota's Tom Daschle, Senate Democrats are dragging their feet on the campaign finance front, fretting about costs measured in millions, not the usual billions, and noting with alarm that Senator Thompson may someday run for President. Democrats on the Governmental Affairs Committee, headed by Ohio's John Glenn, have picked as their special minority counsel a master of legislative maneuvering, Michael Davidson, former counsel to the Democratic majority. On the broader Whitewater front the stall continues apace, with Independent Counsel Kenneth Starr facing new obstacles in his quest for the truth.

The leading example is of course Susan McDougal, who this week begins her sixth month in the lockup for refusing to testify before a

Little Rock grand jury. Ms. McDougal's jail time is mounting: up to another year on the contempt citation, two years on the Whitewater fraud convictions, and up to seven more years if convicted in Southern California on separate charges of defrauding conductor Zubin Mehta and his wife. To go free on the contempt charge, she only needs to tell the truth.

Ms. McDougal clammed up before the grand jury when asked what Bill Clinton knew about an illegal $300,000 loan, and whether he told the truth in his videotaped testimony at last year's fraud trial. The $300,000 at issue came from David Hale's government-backed Capital Management Services; some $50,000 of it went to the benefit of the Whitewater Development Corp. If Governor Clinton knew about the loan, he could be party to a conspiracy to defraud the taxpayer. If President Clinton knew about the loan, he perjured himself in sworn testimony from the White House.

David Hale

Mr. Hale, now in prison following his own Whitewater plea, claimed that then-Governor Clinton asked him to make the loan. Jim McDougal, reversing his trial testimony in an interview with James Stewart of the New Yorker, now says that Bill Clinton was present at a meeting with Mr. Hale where the $300,000 loan was discussed. He also said his wife was having an affair with the Governor at the time, which she denies.

So silent Susan sits atop an explosive issue for the Clinton Presidency. As months pass without her answering the questions that could win her freedom, we find ourselves wondering if she is the smartest clam in America, or the stupidest. We also wonder about her attorney, old Arkansas hand Bobby McDaniel. He lost the big case, got his client jailed on contempt, and he can't even get her moved back to a local jail from California after a judge ruled in her favor on the transfer. While he's now signed up three high-powered Houston lawyers to aid in her defense, he has not served this client well.

Another master of the stall is Webster Hubbell. After resigning as Associate Attorney General, he pleaded guilty to two felonies and agreed to cooperate with the Starr probe. He proved uncooperative, but is about to complete his sentence. But Mr. Starr now wants to know what services Mr. Hubbell rendered for the $100,000 to $250,000 paid to him by Mochtar Riady's Lippo Group before he went to jail. Last week, Mr. Starr summoned former Los Angeles Airport Commission head Theodore Stein to Little Rock to explain what Mr. Hubbell did for a $24,750 "consulting services" fee received in the same period. Mr. Stein, a Democrat, says he hired Mr. Hubbell on the recommendation of Los Angeles Deputy Mayor Mary Leslie, a Clinton fund-raiser. Mr. Starr may succeed in bringing new indictments against Mr. Hubbell, but the second term clicks away.

Mr. Starr was also in court the other day concerning Mr. Clinton's successor as Governor of Arkansas, Jim Guy Tucker, who was convicted with the McDougals in one Whitewater case. A second case

Jim Guy Tucker

against Mr. Tucker, though, may win the stall championship. It was delayed first by Clinton crony Judge Henry Woods in a decision that was overturned by the Eighth Circuit Court of Appeals. With Mr. Tucker's liver transplant delaying the case until June, co-defendant John Haley now seeks to sever his case, seeking a speedy trial after fighting the charges for 19 months all the way to the Supreme Court.

Mr. Tucker could hold a key to the Washington phase of Mr. Starr's inquiry. In October 1993, Governor Tucker met with President Clinton in the White House, just days after the President was informed by senior adviser Bruce Lindsey of confidential criminal referrals by the Resolution Trust Corp. to Justice asking for an investigation into Madison Guaranty. Among the figures named in the referrals: Jim Guy Tucker, and Bill and Hillary Clinton. Another Clinton-Tucker meeting followed in Seattle. Did President Clinton illegally tip off Mr. Tucker to the impending criminal probe, and were any promises exchanged?

Obviously Mr. Starr would like to have the testimony of Jim Guy, Webb and Susan, but at some point he will have to decide whether to go ahead without their cooperation. Last week, Pete Yost of the Associated Press reported that Mr. Starr's team had completed a lengthy memo evaluating evidence against the President, Mrs. Clinton, and senior government officials in the Whitewater, Travel Office and Filegate affairs. Most of the memo, Mr.

Yost reports, "details material involving the first lady." Also last week, the prosecutors asked for a further delay in sentencing Mr. McDougal, because of the "voluminous" amount of "new and important information" he has provided.

Mr. Starr's criminal probe will grind on, but meanwhile Senator Thompson is charged with oversight, that is, determining and informing the public on how our government works. Whitewater is not about some land deal in the Ozarks, but about abuses of power in the White House, whether in covering up the Madison referral, or firing Travel Office employees or going berserk seeking campaign contributions. These are important questions, and if Senator Daschle mounts a filibuster it will be up to Majority Leader Trent Lott to make clear what is happening, and up to normally thoughtful Democrats such as Senator Glenn to draw a line on partisan

Fred Thompson

defensiveness. It would not be a good thing for our democracy if these issues were left unresolved, stalled through a second term.

Editorial Feature

Starr's Exit Doesn't Preclude More Indictments

By TERRY EASTLAND

White House officials are elated over the news that Whitewater Independent Counsel Kenneth W. Starr will leave this summer to become dean of the Pepperdine University Law School. Mr. Starr would not be leaving, they believe, if he were about to bring an indictment against the president. Ergo, he must have decided against it.

But only Mr. Starr knows what he has decided, and it could be that he has not come to a conclusion. Assuming he hasn't, the question of whether to indict Mr. Clinton is not simply whether he committed prosecutable crimes. For even if that is the determination, the difficult question remains whether the Constitution permits the prosecution of a sitting president. On the other hand, there is no question that Mr. Starr has the authority to report what he learns about Mr. Clinton and Whitewater to Congress and the public. Thus, Mr. Starr could decide to leave the judgment on Mr. Clinton to the political process.

The Constitution does not expressly provide for a sitting president's immunity from prosecution. But Article I, section 3, clause 7 provides that any "Party convicted [upon impeachment] shall nevertheless be liable and subject to indictment, trial, judgment and punishment, according to law."

This clause precludes an officer convicted upon impeachment from avoiding subsequent criminal prosecution by claiming double jeopardy. But does the sequence in the clause in which prosecution is treated mean that there is immunity to prosecution before the impeachment process is concluded? If that is the intention of the clause, then the Constitution has been violated on each of the several occasions in our history when civil officers subject to impeachment have been prosecuted while still in office. These officers have mostly been judges, but the most famous was Vice President Spiro Agnew.

The best case for presidential immunity acknowledges this history while maintaining that the president is unique among officers subject to impeachment, and therefore should be spared prosecution. In the Agnew proceedings, the Justice Department, represented by Solicitor General Robert Bork, made precisely this argument. Observing that "the nation's Chief Executive [is] responsible as no other single officer is for the affairs of the United States," Mr. Bork contended that his prosecution would more seriously impair the functioning of government than would the prosecution of any other impeachable officer. The president should not be taken from his du-

Kenneth Starr

ties, Mr. Bork said, "unless and until it is determined [in an impeachment trial] that he is to be shorn of those duties by the Senate."

This remains the position of the Justice Department under Mr. Clinton—it is indicated in a footnote in the government's brief in *Clinton v. Jones*, the civil immunity case now before the Supreme Court. But while the argument is a strong one, it is not conclusive. Under Article II, the president has the duty to "take care that the laws be faithfully executed." This clause gives him complete authority over the execution of the laws, including the power to control prosecutions. The president's take-care authority is often said to be inconsistent with the idea of prosecuting an incumbent president. But the take-care clause does not direct how the president should exercise this authority. It is therefore possible to think that a president might agree to allow, say, an outside lawyer armed with a prosecutorial mandate to investigate criminal allegations concerning himself. This may seem odd—why would any president agree to be investigated by someone who can bring criminal charges? But political considerations forced President Nixon in 1973 and President Clinton in 1994 to agree to such an arrangement.

Asked to void an indictment of a president, the courts might decline to do so on grounds that under the Constitution the president may allow himself to be prosecuted, noting that the same constitutional authority that permits the president to allow his own prosecution also enables him to stop it. Such a decision would leave it to the president to decide his own legal fate. Thus, the president could order the prosecutor to end the case against him. Given his take-care authority, the president—whether guilty of felonies or not—should prevail in this kind of battle. But the political price could be costly, with removal via impeachment a strong possibility.

While these considerations underscore why any sitting president would fear an indictment, they also explain why a prosecutor probing a president might decide against seeking one. Again, Watergate bears recalling.

Watergate Special Prosecutor Leon Jaworski concluded that the Constitution left open the possibility of indicting a sitting president. But he decided that Nixon, though guilty of prosecutable crimes, shouldn't be charged. Assuming that Nixon would contest his indictment in the courts, Jaworski didn't want to risk protracted litigation and a Supreme Court decision wiping out the time and effort he had spent trying to prosecute the president. Jaworski also reviewed the possibility that Nixon might challenge an indictment by ordering him to end the prosecution; he decided not to put his work at risk from that angle, either. Jaworski also concluded that considerations involving the presidency and our constitutional system counseled against prosecution: The nation is not well served if an indicted executive is receiving ambassadors or commanding the troops abroad. And the impeachment process does enable Congress to effect a sitting president's removal from office.

Jaworski wound up naming Nixon as an unindicted co-conspirator, an option of less risk to his investigation, to the presidency and to the nation. He also advised the House of Representatives of information relevant to impeachment—a course of action the independent-counsel law now requires of those like Mr. Starr who serve as counsels.

Though the news of Mr. Starr's departure has allowed Bill Clinton to catch his breath, Whitewater is not over, not yet. Mr. Starr will have a successor who can take over the team Mr. Starr put in place. And the odds daily increase that a prosecutor will be assigned to the

Asian money case. For a good while longer, if not for the balance of his term, Mr. Clinton will have to employ defense lawyers and hope that his scandal-ridden presidency can avoid, remote as these dangers may seem to some, the Scylla of indictment and the Charybdis of impeachment.

Mr. Eastland is a fellow at the Ethics and Public Policy Center and author of "Ethics, Politics, and the Independent Counsel."

REVIEW & OUTLOOK

Money Laundering Alert

Some of the biggest crimes of the 21st century, as we have noted in our observations on the BCCI case, will be global financial crimes. While money moves across national frontiers at the speed of light, methods of policing corruption and money laundering across borders remain back in the Stone Age.

Aficionados of such matters have been watching a test case unfold in a Manhattan courtroom these past three months. The bankers are Venezuelan. The bank in question is in Puerto Rico. Manhattan District Attorney Robert Morgenthau put them on trial in New York, charging them with defrauding Latin American depositors of some $55 mil-

Robert Morgenthau

lion. On Wednesday, a jury agreed with Mr. Morgenthau. It convicted Orlando Castro Llanes, and his son and grandson—Orlando Castro Castro and Jorge Castro Barredo—on grand larceny charges involving multimillion-dollar thefts of money on deposit at their Banco Progreso International de Puerto Rico.

Defense attorneys for the Castros had lambasted the District Attorney for operating way outside his jurisdiction, since Puerto Rico banks are supposed to be supervised by the Federal Reserve Bank of New York. To win his jurisdictional argument Mr. Morgenthau used records showing that checks and electronic transfers had passed through New York banks. In a statement yesterday, he pointedly noted that "individuals who perpetrate fraud through financial transactions in New York will be held accountable."

From the start of the Castro case, as well, the scent of more sinister dealings has hung in the air. While Mr. Morgenthau has repeatedly declared that money laundering charges were not at issue in the Castro trial, he also has conceded in published reports that his office first began studying Venezuelan banks because of concern that laundering operations there might be connected to New York drug imports.

Last April, Peter Truell of the New York Times reported that an investigator for the newsletter Money Laundering Alert had obtained evidence of as much as $3 billion in suspicious transfers from a Castro bank in Venezuela to the New York offices of Madrid-based Banco Atlantico. But the investigator's findings, strongly suggestive of money laundering, were rejected by the editor of the newsletter, Charles Intriago. Mr. Castro, it turns out, is an old friend of Mr. Intriago's, as well as a founding partner of Money Laundering Alert.

Mr. Intriago, in turn, is well acquainted with the Clinton White House. A big Democratic Party contributor, he got the help of Florida super fund-raiser Charles (Bud) Stack in arranging a meeting between President Clinton and Mr. Castro at the White House. "Mr. Castro and his supporters in Caracas have used a photograph of that occasion, which has been reproduced in Venezuelan newspapers, to back their contention that Mr. Castro has friends in high places," Mr. Truell reported.

Mr. Clinton proposed Mr. Stack for a seat on the 11th Circuit Court of Appeals, but the nomination foundered last year. Mr. Intriago says that he bought out Mr. Castro's share in his enterprise in 1992, and that the findings of his investigator were flawed—that's why they were never presented to authorities; his newsletter remains highly respected in the field.

Yet it remains true that another White House visitor traded on a photograph with President Clinton back in his home country, and has now been found to be an international banking criminal.

REVIEW & OUTLOOK

Independence of the Counsels

Kenneth Starr no doubt did some damage to himself and his investigation with last week's flip-flop decision to resign as independent counsel. Pepperdine University will have to wait longer than the Clinton Administration for closure. When by week's end Mr. Starr had changed course, held a news conference to explain himself and gone back to work, much of the damage appeared to have been mitigated. Whatever else, all agree there is serious work to do here.

Still, the episode should raise questions in the minds of serious people about the function of the independent counsel statute and the unique court officer it creates. For instance, our reading would be that in the main Mr. Starr returned after seeing the discomfort his departure created among his own staff. He has spoken at length in past days about the cohesiveness and professionalism of the staff, and it seems clear in retrospect that he greatly underestimated the importance they attach to his role.

In his few public comments over the past year, Mr. Starr has made clear his view of the Office of Independent Counsel as a microcosm of the Justice Department or a regional U.S. Attorney Office, operating with the culture of professionalism that survives routine transitions at the top. Yet it is not quite so. The Office of Independent Counsel is a work in progress, both legislatively and administratively. The Justice Department or a U.S. Attorney work on lots of cases simultaneously, while an independent counsel generally has one big, all-consuming case.

An administrative leave-taking, say, for family reasons, is less obtrusive for the manager of many cases, but what happens when an independent counsel wants to resign or needs to be removed? William Rehnquist's opinion upholding the independent counsel statute admonished the Special Division of the U.S. Court of Appeals, which appoints independent counsels, not to get involved in the management of investigations. With whom, then, beyond his own sphere

Kenneth Starr

can an independent counsel talk when a real need arises, personally or professionally? For now, hardly anyone. This is a problem Congress might want to grapple with as it reconsiders the statute.

Meanwhile, developments proceed apace. On Sunday, the Los Angeles Times reported that Mr. Starr has completed a detailed report into the events surrounding the death of Deputy White House Counsel Vincent Foster. Mr. Starr, according to the news report, will conclude that Mr. Foster died by his own hand in Fort Marcy Park, and that there was no subsequent coverup.

We should make clear, given assiduous White House efforts to drop us into the farthest reaches of the Foster conspiracy swamp, that we're on record as accepting Robert Fiske's conclusion. In commenting on the release of his report back in July 1994, we said, "Barring some unimaginable new disclosure we find no reason to doubt that the former deputy White House counsel committed suicide in Fort Marcy Park." Still, it is scarcely surprising that conspiracy theories abound when, in the death of a sensitive official, there are no crime scene photos, no autopsy X-rays, a missing bullet and so on. The investigation was clearly botched, and Mr. Starr's report will be of great service if it dampens some of the lingering questions.

We've long expressed doubts about the extra-legal character of the independent counsel, but it is now what events and history have left us for dealing with wrongdoing in high places. In recent weeks, we have had a cascade of stories and revelations about the wild fundraising practices of the Clinton Democratic National Committee—starting with John Huang and the Lippo Group and spreading to high-rolling coffee klatches at the White House. This in turn has led to calls for a new independent counsel separate from the Starr organization.

There seems an inevitability to the appointment of an independent counsel to plumb the fund-raising. As Senator Moynihan remarked to the New York Post last week by way of concluding that a counsel was necessary: "Everyone has Chinese arms merchants to lunch, don't you?" Still, we hope the events of the past week with Mr. Starr strike a cautionary note. This well may be the institution we have to work with, but recent events show it's an institution still evolving. At this juncture, we all should hope for the best.

A series of labyrinthine maneuvers last year seems to have left the Riadys only more beholden to China.

The family, while sitting on a stack of properties worth maybe $12 billion, has been running into liquidity problems. One headache was their showcase—perhaps too showcase—shopping and residential complex, Lippo Karawaci, an hour outside Jakarta. China Resources and Mr. Li came to the rescue, each pumping in $26 million for 5.5% of the project.

The family also seems to have been backing out of its Indonesian corporate empire, Lippo Group, in favor of China. Late in 1995, depositors yanked $500 million out of Lippo Bank on rumors of bogged-down property loans. In a hurry, the family launched a series of rights issues on the Jakarta market, raising $324 million.

Next, they pushed through a drastic restructuring of their role in the Lippo Group. According to estimates by Kleinwort Bentson, these arrangements enabled family members to withdraw some $384 million from their listed businesses, cutting their stake in the empire with which they have long been associated to as little as 3.7%.

Mochtar Riady

All this is believed to have been aimed at freeing up money to bolster their mainland projects. The Riadys, more than ever, are placing their chips on China.

Now, of course, a Riady whispering in his ear didn't turn Candidate Clinton around on China's MFN trade status; Mr. Clinton's ascension to executive responsibility did that. But everything else speaks for itself: The Riadys' sprinkling of cash into Clinton campaign coffers; their placing one of their own operatives, former Lippo exec John Huang, in the Commerce Department and later the Democratic National Committee; the record of Mr. Huang's many contacts with Chinese officials.

These are the coils within coils in which the overseas Chinese have always operated. In situations where the rule of law is often absent or unreliable, they have made their way through *guanxi*, or connections. And, to a remarkable degree, people like the Riadys and Mr. Li have been the driving engine of Asia's prosperity. But their practices feel odd when imported here.

Yet friends and acquaintances from Bill Clinton's Arkansas days have been industrious in selling their own connections to Asia's wealthy. And Mr. Clinton has allowed them to use the White House as stage and himself as prop. The DNC has dealt itself in for a cut. Policy personnel have been detailed to give earnest attention to the donors' thoughts on world affairs. It all looks bad for U.S. prestige in Asia, the other pillar of the region's post-war success.

The Riadys probably are not the Chinese agents some would make them out to be. It would be foolish, though, not to recognize that such people are interested primarily in the care and feeding of their business empires. And they have cast their future, as measured in dollars, with China.

Editorial Feature

Lesssons From Lippo

By PETER SCHUCK
And BRUCE BROWN

Lawmakers, anxious to condemn foreign corporate money seeping illegally into the 1996 campaigns, are rushing to support a ban on political contributions to federal candidates from legal immigrants who are permanent residents of the U.S. This would be a bad solution to a nonproblem, and it may even be unconstitutional.

Federal law already forbids contributions from foreign governments, foreign corporations and temporary visitors from abroad. A Federal Election Commission rule further forbids these groups from making expenditures, even those that are independent of any particular candidate's campaign. In contrast, legal resident aliens, like citizens, have always been permitted to contribute to campaigns up to statutory limits and to make unlimited independent expenditures. However, Sens. John McCain (R., Ariz.) and Russell Feingold (D., Wis.) have co-sponsored a bill that would extend the ban on contributions to resident aliens. (If the bill succeeds, the FEC may then bar aliens' independent expenditures as well.) Similar legislation is pending in the House, and President Clinton endorsed the idea in his State of the Union message. Even if the McCain-Feingold bill fails for other reasons, the ban on resident-alien contributions could pass separately.

Campaign reformers have targeted immigrants because of recent revelations that foreign companies, notably Indonesia's Lippo conglomerate, may have funneled cash to the Democratic National Committee through resident aliens. But the true lessons of the Lippo affair are different. First, bans on foreign contributions are always

John McCain

easy to circumvent; only a U.S. citizen is needed as a front. Second, buying access is not the same as influencing policy. So far, the alleged Lippo money seems to have purchased only the appearance of influence. Most important, the best regulator of campaign contributions is public disclosure, especially the immediate, accessible kind that today's technology permits. After all, it was news coverage of the Lippo link that fueled the current public indignation and debate. (Similarly, public outcry following this week's disclosures about the Clintons' use of the Lincoln Bedroom will be heard by politicians.)

Resident aliens cannot vote. But it does not follow that they should be barred from contributing to campaigns. The Supreme Court has held, wisely, that campaign contributions amount to activity protected by the First Amendment (although contributions may be regulated to limit corruption). It has also held that resident aliens' First Amendment rights are fully protected. They can leaflet, demonstrate and otherwise seek to influence policy, just as citizens can. To treat resident aliens differently by proscribing an important category of their speech might well violate the Constitution. Even if the Constitution would permit such a ban,

Russ Feingold

however, the more important question is whether Congress should adopt it in the first place.

Resident aliens now constitute about 4% of the U.S. population. Like the citizens that many of them will become, they work, pay taxes, serve in the military and contribute in many other ways to the quality of American life. Their political and other speech enriches our national discourse. It is in our interest, not just theirs, that public policy seriously consider their needs. This interest is especially vital now that Congress has rendered resident aliens more vulnerable by excluding them from many safety-net programs.

Prohibiting legal residents' contributions would also reduce the private cash flows on which robust, competitive campaigning now depends. Incumbent politicians, of course, wish to make their lives easier and more secure by reducing the amount of money they must raise while limiting their potential challengers' funding. But the democratically vital purpose of reaching voters requires spending more money, not less, on political campaigns. It is true that less private funding might be required if Congress were to provide free TV spots and public financing of campaigns. But incumbents, who are now re-elected about 95% of the time, already enjoy immense advantages. The only public financing system worth having is one that does not further limit challengers' opportunity to raise and spend funds.

Unfortunately, we can't trust Congress, which for 23 years has declined to raise campaign-contribution caps, to set funding limits high enough so that new candidates can amass the money needed to mount a credible challenge. Like other proposals that seek to reduce the amount of money spent on campaigns, a ban on resident aliens' contributions would reduce political competition while enabling lawmakers to pose as anti-Lippo reformers. This would create a double windfall for incumbents. No wonder they are so eager to pass it.

Mr. Schuck, a Yale law professor, is a visiting professor at New York Law School this semester. Mr. Brown is a reporter for Legal Times.

Editorial Feature

No, Everybody Doesn't
Do It Like Bill Does

"Yes, pursue all 3 and promptly—and get other names at 100,000 or more 50,000 or more—ready to start overnights right away."

> — PRESIDENT CLINTON, IN A NOTE TO FUND-
> RAISING FINAGLER HAROLD ICKES

"I did not have any strangers here. The Lincoln Bedroom was never sold."

> — MR. CLINTON,
> EXPLAINING THAT NOTE

Mr. Clinton's smooth evasion this week brings to mind the Marx Brothers' famous line, "Who are you gonna believe—me or your own eyes?" It also begs the question of whether political Washington will finally drop its mantra that "everybody does it."

Potomac Watch

By Paul A. Gigot

For months now Mr. Clinton has made this "moral equivalence" spin his campaign-finance defense. It's brilliantly Clintonian: denying personal responsibility by passing it off on "the system." If everyone is accountable, then no one in particular is, least of all this president.

So every time someone blames "the system," or "all politicians," he in effect gives Mr. Clinton a personal alibi. Even some of the same reporters who uncover his misdeeds end up giving him political cover. "Pox-on-everyone" reformers like Common Cause become his closet ally. No wonder the latest CNN-USA Today poll shows 63% of Americans believing he's done nothing worse than any other recent president.

The spin has also worked to slow Congress's campaign-finance probe. Republicans fear, understandably enough, that the media and Common Cause won't distinguish between legal contributions made

by honest Americans and dirty White House bedsheets. John Huang, the Commerce legend, may take the fifth and dodge the klieg lights. But Joe Citizen will testify sincerely and could get tagged as sleazy.

This helps explain why many Republicans would just as soon deep-six Tennessee Sen. Fred Thompson's too-wide-ranging probe and turn the whole thing over to another independent counsel—which may now be inevitable anyway. But this might also help Mr. Clinton by burying most evidence for months, if not years, behind grand jury secrecy rules. Congress would be giving up on its role of educating voters.

Richard Nixon

All the more so because the more we learn about the 1996 campaign, the more we're discovering how truly remarkable the Clinton White House was. Everybody doesn't do it like this one did. What this week's documents show is a White House so intent to raise money any way possible that normal ethical restraints simply vanished.

All politicians raise money, but even in this "system" most of them raise it without inviting Chinese arms dealers to "coffee." Everybody doesn't return more than $400,000 gathered illegally from Indonesian gardeners who've suddenly moved back to Jakarta, out of subpoena range. Everybody doesn't hire Commerce officials who could end up seeking immunity from congressional committees.

And every president hasn't treated the White House like an Ozarks Bed and breakfast: George Bush's records show only 273 sleepovers and just a few by big donors. Mr. Clinton had 938, more than four a week, lots of them fat cats--and those are the ones they're admitting to.

"I almost feel like a chump," says Boyden Gray, Mr. Bush's White House counsel, contemplating what he might have gotten away with under the Clinton standards. "The White House is a great place to raise money, but we had a rule you just didn't do that."

The point here isn't partisan, because as more facts emerge it's clear the only recent White House that compares to this one is Richard Nixon's. Only "Nixonian" captures the essence of the amazing exchange this week between a reporter and spokesman Mike McCurry regarding the intent of the White House coffees:

Q: "But then they were eventually used for fund-raising, though not technically being fund-raisers?"

Mr. McCurry: "Technically, not used for fund-raising, but they became an element of the financial program that we were trying to pursue in connection with the campaign."

Q: "But isn't that really a—the distinction without difference?"

Mr. McCurry: "No, because the law is what counts. . . . It's that the law goes to the question of solicitation, and that's the issue."

It's almost enough to make you feel sorry for Mr. McCurry, who isn't that ethically obtuse. But to defend his boss he has to resort to a line that says if there's no felony, there's no problem. If Mr. Clinton isn't indicted, then he can't have done anything wrong.

It's yet more evidence of how this president has, to adapt Pat Moynihan's phrase, defined political deviancy down. From Paula Jones to Whitewater to renting the Lincoln Bedroom, Mr. Clinton has so degraded the expectations Americans have for politicians that almost nothing shocks them anymore. Under this new Clintonian standard, not only do the political ends (re-election) justify any means (sleazy fund-raising), but those same means are then invoked to justify new, supposedly idealistic ends (campaign "reform").

As audacious as it all is, he'll continue to get away with it as long as the press and everyone else holds "the system" more accountable than a sitting president.

REVIEW & OUTLOOK

'My Counsel Advises Me...'

Watching Vice President Gore explain his White House campaign solicitations—"I understood what I did to be legal and appropriate. I felt like I was doing the right thing."—we kept thinking about Newt Gingrich.

Speaker Gingrich, after all, got socked with a $300,000 fine for signing a letter prepared by his lawyers that misstated some facts concerning what may or may not have been a tax code violation with no criminal penalty. What would he have had to pay, we wondered, if he'd been guilty of the Vice President's offense, using his federal office to make phone calls soliciting contributions?

Al Gore

For despite the Vice President's legalistic defense, his admitted actions appear to be in direct conflict with a federal felony statute. As 18 U.S.C. 607(a) states: "It shall be unlawful for any person to solicit or receive any contributions ... in any room or building occupied in the discharge of official duties ... any person who violates this section shall be fined not more than $5,000, or imprisoned not more than three years, or both."

As laws go, that's pretty straightforward. Abner Mikva, who must be relieved he left his job as White House Counsel in late 1995 before this and so many other storms broke, spelled out the clear meaning in an April 27, 1995, legal admonition: "Campaign activities of any kind are prohibited in or from Government buildings. This means fund-raising events may not be held in the White House; also, no fund-raising phone calls or mail may emanate from the White House."

Mr. Mikva now tells Newsweek that "any Philadelphia lawyer knows you don't raise money in a government office." Certainly Members of Congress are painfully aware of that. One former Senator told us that he became "physically ill" after he made a fund-raising call from his office to a donor who was about to leave for an overseas trip. "I just knew what my opponent and the Ethics Committee could do to me if that ever came out," he recalls. From the day they arrive on Capitol Hill, members are told they must leave their offices and walk down the street to party campaign offices if they want to raise money. Mr. Gore must have done that many times over the 16 years he served in both houses.

A Congressional watchdog group did file a compliant with the Senate Ethics Committee after GOP Senator Phil Gramm told the Journal in 1995 that he sometimes made campaign calls from his office using a private credit card. He escaped without a Gingrich-style fine when the ethics committee dropped the matter after advising him that using a private credit card doesn't absolve the offense, that "applicable law" prohibits the use of Senate offices for campaign activities.

In his press conference, Mr. Gore repeatedly insisted he'd broken no law. He said, for example, that the Mikva memo "was addressed to White House employees other than the president and vice president" so it didn't apply to him. However, that position is flatly contradicted by a January 17, 1979, legal opinion from Jimmy Carter's Justice Department. An opinion from Assistant Attorney General John Harmon's Office of Legal Counsel held that both the President and the Vice President were covered by the statute prohibiting fund-raising in federal buildings.

Vice President Gore insisted seven different times during his news conference that he had been advised by "my counsel" that "no controlling legal authority" or case indicates that his fund-raising calls were illegal. Yesterday, the Vice President's office told us there is no written legal opinion to that effect. When asked if one would be prepared we were told: "I don't think you should expect one."

Counsel Abner Mikva, who wrote while in office in 1995 that campaign fund-raising "of any kind" (including phone calls) was prohibited in government buildings. This president has a history of legalistic cuteness when asked hard questions, so it will be interesting to learn whether a White House or Justice Department lawyer actually approved the use of the White House to raise campaign funds and what the rules really were.

One of the oft-cited "lessons of Watergate" is that politics and ambition can corrupt the presidency. Post-Watergate presidents have therefore installed a cadre of highly sensitized lawyers in the Office of Counsel to the President to keep corruption, sleaziness and questionable legal practices out of the White House and away from the president. Generally led by a politically astute Washington vet-

> *Instead of preventing the shipwreck, the White House lawyers are finding excuses for the captain.*

eran, this office, with an occasional assist from the Justice Department's Office of Legal Counsel, sounds the alarm when politics or private agendas threaten the integrity of the presidency, and crafts legal guidelines to protect the president, his family and his subordinates from questionable practices and associations.

Something curious has happened to the counsel's office. Mr. Clinton is now on his fifth counsel. As reported in this paper Friday, the office has become the "nucleus of the Clinton damage-control effort," a "clearinghouse . . . for information that gets disseminated by friends and allies on the airwaves," and is "joined at the hip" with the president's outside private attorneys. Instead of preventing the shipwreck, these lawyers are finding excuses for the captain.

The metamorphosis apparently began as soon as Mr. Clinton took office. Vincent Foster, a Hillary Clinton law partner appointed as deputy White House counsel, reportedly spent most of his energy before his suicide dealing at taxpayer expense with the Clintons' personal tax returns and Whitewater files. Another Hillary Clinton partner, William Kennedy, was installed as an associate counsel and promptly became involved in the controversial White House Travel Office firings and the misuse of the FBI to damage the reputations of career Travel Office employees. Today, one of the two deputy counsels is Bruce Lindsey, another Arkansas crony, approved last year by a federal judge for designation as an unindicted co-conspirator in one of the Whitewater cases.

Presumably some of the lawyers in the counsel's office still try to keep the president out of trouble. If so, no one seems to be paying any attention. Former special counsel Jane Sherburne explained to the National Journal that she had been hired, not by the counsel, but by former Deputy Chief of Staff Harold Ickes, who was revealed last week as the de facto head of the Clinton-Gore re-election and fund-raising drives. She and Mr. Ickes assembled a Clinton "defense team," including special associate counsel Mark Fabiani, to orchestrate the response to charges against the first family. There was no ambiguity in her job description: "the objective was re-election . . . the goal was to get him re-elected." While Ms. Sherburne and Mr. Fabiani (now replaced by Lanny Davis) were nominally in the White House Counsel's office, they reported directly to campaign impresario Mr. Ickes.

Shortly after taking office, Ms. Sherburne compiled a 12-page "Task List." One task was listed as: "Hubbell—monitor cooperation," a reference to Webster Hubbell, yet another former Hillary Clinton law partner and Mr. Clinton's No. 3 person in the Justice Department. Mr. Hubbell was facing jail for bilking his former law firm and clients and was a potential cooperating witness for Independent Counsel Kenneth Starr.

The Los Angeles Times reported last week that White House aide Marsha Scott was tapped for the "monitoring" job. She frequently visited Mr. Hubbell at a Little Rock "safe haven," serving "as a line of communication between Hubbell and Mrs. Clinton . . . tell[ing] him what they were doing for him." Fortunately for Mr. Hubbell, in the midst of his legal difficulties he received a large sum of money from Mr. Clinton's Indonesian Lippo Group allies for unspecified legal services. He became a noncooperative (well-monitored?) witness and is now refusing to have any further dealings with investigators.

Lawyers perform entirely legitimate functions when they defend their clients from accusations. And it is certainly not inappropriate for White House lawyers to respond to legal attacks on an incumbent president. (Whether they should be paid by the public to serve in the campaign to re-elect the president is another matter, which perhaps Congress will investigate.) But, most of all, the White House needs lawyers with the skill, courage and clout to build the walls around the presidency that will prevent that office from being misused by anyone, even the president.

The documents from Mr. Ickes's files show that Mr. Clinton was so consumed by the re-election campaign that a White House aide explained in writing in January 1996 that certain presidential responsibilities would be "truncated or eliminated" so that the president could devote more time to "political fund-raising." We know what happened to the last lawyer-president who took personal day-to-day control of his re-election and who bent the laws and his lawyers to his personal will. Mistakes were made. Laws were broken. Congressional and special-prosecutor investigations were launched. Indictments were returned and convictions were obtained. Articles of impeachment were issued. And the president resigned.

Mr. Olson, a Washington attorney, was a Reagan administration assistant attorney general for the Office of Legal Counsel.

Editorial Feature

Indictments in the Executive Branch

By JOSEPH E. DIGENOVA

Can the president of the United States be indicted? The question is of more than academic concern now. Every day brings fresh revelations of potentially criminal conduct by Bill Clinton, Al

Richard Nixon

Gore and their aides, in matters ranging from Whitewater to Filegate. The latest scandal, of course, concerns whether Messrs. Clinton and Gore traduced campaign fund-raising laws in order to win re-election last year.

To borrow a phrase from Mr. Gore, there is no controlling legal authority on whether the president can be indicted for criminal conduct before being impeached by the House, tried by the Senate and removed from office (there's no question a president can be indicted *after* being impeached). On its face, there doesn't seem to be any reason why the president can't be held liable for violating the law. One can roam through the criminal statutes—indeed through the Constitution itself—and nowhere find an addendum stating that a certain act is "unlawful, except when committed by the president of the United States."

Nevertheless some eminent legal scholars have taken the position that the president is above the law. Robert Bork, when he was solicitor general under President Nixon, declared on behalf of the Justice Department that a president had to be impeached and removed from office before being indicted. By contrast, the Justice Department declared that Vice President Spiro Agnew could be criminally prosecuted, but the issue was never resolved because Mr. Agnew pleaded guilty.

Then the grand jury investigating Watergate was instructed by prosecutors not to indict Nixon. Instead Attorney General John Mitchell was indicted while Nixon was named as an unindicted co-conspirator. Nixon challenged the grand jury's power even to do that. The Supreme Court first granted his request for review of the grand jury's action but later refused to take up the case. The court certainly never said anything suggesting that the president was immune from criminal prosecution. Indeed, the justices ordered the White House tapes turned over to Judge John Sirica, declaring that in criminal trials the jury was entitled to "every man's evidence." So there is no Supreme Court decision prohibiting the indictment of a sitting president.

While the Nixon Justice Department took the view that the president couldn't be indicted, the House Judiciary Committee, which draws up articles of impeachment, had a different perspective. A memorandum of law drawn up for the committee during Watergate states: "The Constitution itself provides that impeachment is no substitute for the ordinary process of criminal law since it specifies that impeachment does not immunize the officer from criminal liability for his wrongdoing." Significantly, the committee did not say that such a criminal charge had to await the president's removal from office.

It's possible to imagine many circumstances where such a delay would be unthinkable. Let us suppose that one day a president, tired of the constraints of security, secretly leaves the White House in a car and strikes and kills a pedestrian. Suppose, further, the president was drunk at the time. Does anyone argue that justice must await his impeachment and removal? Impeachment might not even be warranted since this is not the type of "high crime or misdemeanor" contemplated by the drafters of the Constitution.

Obviously criminal misconduct would be harder to prove in Whitewater, Filegate or the assorted other Clinton scandals. Neither Kenneth Starr nor any other independent counsel should indict Mr. Clinton or anyone else unless he finds clear evidence that would convince a jury that the defendant committed a crime. But neither should any independent counsel be reluctant to prosecute based on some vague concept of presidential immunity.

The Bork position, as previously noted, has no basis in law. Nor is it particularly convincing as a matter of policy. Yes, the president is the chief enforcer of the laws, so it would be somewhat odd for him in effect to indict himself. But this is precisely why the independent counsel was created. Independent counsels are not appointed by the White House, so presumably they should be free to pursue criminal charges against the president if his actions warrant it.

Nobody should underestimate the upheaval that a prosecution of the president would cause. But we went through it once before, in Watergate, and survived. The nation, in fact, could conceivably benefit from the indictment of a president. It would teach the valuable civics lesson that no one is above the law. As an appeals court told Mr. Clinton in the Paula Jones case, the Founders created a presidency, not a monarchy.

Mr. diGenova is a former U.S. attorney and independent counsel.

REVIEW & OUTLOOK

Illegal Ends

Somewhere along the line—Georgetown, Oxford, Hot Springs—Bill Clinton picked up some moral philosophy. Such as, the end justifies the means, currently being put out as a defense of the DNC fund-raising frenzies.

"I would remind you," Mr. Clinton instructed the White House press corps last week, "that we knew that we had a very stiff challenge. We were fighting a battle not simply for our re-election, but over the entire direction of the country for years to come, and the most historic philosophical battle we've had in America in quite a long time."

This is the fellow who signed the Republicans' welfare reform bill, who shoved aside White House liberals to pursue Dick Morris's rightward political strategy, who in his acceptance speech and campaign expropriated as many conservative-to-moderate GOP positions as he could get his arms around. A historic philosophical battle?

The private sector has plenty of people who live in alternative realities of their own devising, and in a tolerant society, we try to give them a wide berth. Public life, however, is about mainly one thing—the law—the rules that all consent to abide by and enforce so that life can be civil. It has been the contention of this page since its earliest editorials on the Clinton Presidency—Who Is Webster Hubbell?—that this coterie from Little Rock came to Washington not with any recognizable legislative purpose, but to *game the system.*

Gaming the system is what they'd been doing their entire lives. Whitewater's significance, it should now be plain, was never the arcane details of a land deal in the Ozarks, but that the future President of the United States spent years pushing the edge of the envelope with the likes of Jim and Susan McDougal. This milieu and its mores gave birth to the likes of Charlie Trie, Mark Middleton and whoever thought to rent the Lincoln Bedroom—all of it more or less defensible because of this "most historic philosophical battle."

Instead, it still looks to us like a culture long habituated to cutting every corner and—as bad—not a smidgen of propriety about any of it. The danger, however, is that at this level it all sits in the public mind, fermenting as nothing more than an unprecedented gross-out by what are, after all, just pols. But in fact the most important Clinton people aren't "just pols"; they are the highest legal officers in the land. And from the Administration's earliest days, at least since Travelgate, the time and energies of these high legal officers have been dedicated to what can be called obstruction.

Congressional subpoenas were flouted, White House memories collapsed at hearings, Cabinet officers gave the White House "heads up" alerts about agency investigations, and files denied to exist later made miraculous appearances. Now the fund-raising scandals have arrived at a moment that has the President and the Vice President attesting that "we had to be aggressive and strong within the law" even as John Huang and Mark Middleton plead the Fifth, and Charlie Trie and Pauline Kanchanalak get out of the country.

If Mr. Clinton believed it was all legal or, in the Gore formulation, not subject to any "controlling legal authority," then one might expect the President to instruct these panicked fund-raisers to come forward and tell all they know. Instead, his instinct is to ride out day after day of revelations, letting the system live on the edge of a legal cliff.

However repugnant the stories, so long as the White House is able to define these events as a debate over the arcana of campaign finance, nothing will come of it, other than public contempt for American politics. That is, it poses no danger to Mr. Clinton. But in fact the true seriousness of these events was suggested in a March 6 story by Jeff Gerth and Stephen Labaton of the New York Times.

Messrs. Gerth and Labaton reported that Webster Hubbell, in the interim period between departing the Justice Department and his conviction for overbilling law clients, received more than $400,000 and that much of that came from the Riady-controlled Lippo Group of Indonesia. The report indicated that the Whitewater independent counsel's office was looking into whether any of this money was intended as hush money for Mr. Hubbell. We ourselves raised this same concern last March 1 in an editorial, "Who Is Mochtar Riady?" And for that matter, no one has explained who or what is paying for Craig Livingstone's costly Beltway lawyer's fees.

Let us then revisit Mr. Clinton's news-conference musings on the underlying morality. It would be one thing to solicit unsavory money from whomever for an important political campaign—or as Mr. Clinton would have it, questionable means to an honorable end. But to solicit funds for obstruction of justice would be an illegal end.

In more traditional terms, the first duty of the Presidency is to see that the laws are faithfully executed. It would be naive not to recognize that nearly all presidencies have at some point seen fit to squeeze the law for some larger, often disputed purpose. But we are certainly not so naive to believe that what has been going on the past four years constitutes any recognizable interpretation of faithfully executing the laws.

The fund-raising flap is just one piece of a larger problem with the Clinton Presidency. It is not all "just politics." It is about obligations to the spirit of the laws that up to this point all politicians, even the most imperfect, acknowledged as their primary duty. Not any more. Now, on any given day, the law is what Bill Clinton, Al Gore, Mike McCurry, Ann Lewis, Bob Bennett or, it now seems, Janet Reno wish it to be. It is a philosophy for getting by, perhaps, but not likely to work well as governance.

REVIEW & OUTLOOK

FBI FIB?

It's only Wednesday, but the week has already heard the thud of the Arapaho shoe and the FBI shoe. The White House fund-raising story is starting to resemble a centipede.

The Cheyenne-Arapaho tribes coughed up $107,000 for the Democratic National Committee, in hopes that it would help get back some of their tribal lands. The Washington Post reported that long-time Al Gore fund-raiser Nathan Landow wanted to represent the tribes, for 10% of the royalties on mineral rights on the lands involved. Also involved was Peter Knight, Clinton-Gore campaign chairman, who wanted a $100,000 retainer plus $10,000 a month for lobbying representation. Mr. Landow denies it; he only sent a contract but didn't mean it. Mr. Knight says it was his partner. The Clinton-Gore Administration is also in the clear; instead of allowing the contribution to affect policy, it stiffed the tribes.

Then the FBI made history by issuing what surely must be its first-ever public correction of a Presidential news conference. Mr. Clinton said he didn't know anything about intelligence reports about the Chinese trying to buy up American politicians. He said FBI agents had briefed senior staff members at the National Security Council, but the briefing agents "for whatever reasons, asked that they not share the briefing, and they honored the request."

The FBI issued a statement flatly denying the President's version of events, and then Presidential spokesman Michael McCurry did another round saying the NSC staffers stood by their story, and that the FBI statement was "in error." With all these high authorities flatly disagreeing with each other, what's a poor onlooker to believe?

Oh well, the Administration needs a break. Why not just suspend disbelief: Yes, the FBI agents went to the White House with the message: The Chinese are trying to buy up American politicians, but please don't pass the word to the politicians.

Editorial Feature

Golden Gore Touch Turns to Velcro

Several years ago, when Clinton confidant Webster Hubbell faced imprisonment and big legal bills, Democratic moneyman Nathan Landow tried to arrange a favorable real estate deal involving a Washington office building for the former top Justice Department official.

Several other well-heeled Democrats also tried to help the beleaguered Mr. Hubbell; this has drawn the attention of special prosecu-

Politics & People

By Albert R. Hunt

tor Kenneth Starr, who questions whether Mr. Hubbell's limited cooperation with Mr. Starr's investigation of the president was influenced by all the help Mr. Hubbell received from the president's associates.

What sets Mr. Landow apart, however, is that he and Bill Clinton actually have a hostile relationship. But Mr. Landow is close to Vice President Albert Gore. Political observers who know him say it's highly doubtful that Mr. Landow would have done this out of personal kindness rather than political calculation; Mr. Landow, the former Maryland Democratic Party chairman, did not return phone calls. Late yesterday, the vice president's office said Mr. Gore did not know of Mr. Landow's offer to help Mr. Hubbell.

This all may be perfectly innocent, but it's another reminder that Albert Gore, widely viewed as the Democrats' front-runner for 2000, has a lot at stake in the mushrooming Clinton investigations. This crystallized last week with the Washington Post report that the vice president was known in the White House as the "solicitor in chief" for shaking down fat-cat contributors during the 1996 campaign. There then followed what only can be called a disastrous press conference at which Mr. Gore tried to explain it all.

The upshot is that the Albert Gore who only a few weeks ago seemed to possess most of Bill Clinton's strengths—intelligence, political savvy and a bevy of heavyweight advisers—with none of his character weaknesses, is now viewed differently. Democratic insiders now worry that he may get swept up in the fund-raising controversies and the new doubts that have surfaced about his political judgment and advisers.

This week's Wall Street Journal/NBC News poll shows the vice president slipping in public approval, with his negatives rising to

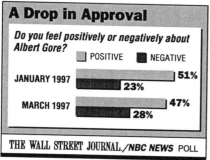

A Drop in Approval

Do you feel positively or negatively about Albert Gore?

POSITIVE · NEGATIVE

JANUARY 1997 — 51% / 23%

MARCH 1997 — 47% / 28%

THE WALL STREET JOURNAL./*NBC NEWS* POLL

near record levels. Pollsters Peter Hart and Robert Teeter say Mr. Gore "has paid a price" for his role in the fund-raising controversies. Indeed, they suggest he may be more hurt by recent revelations than the president is: "Unlike Bill Clinton, this currently is the only story that the public has to connect with Al Gore; there is no alternate arena in which his performance can be assessed."

To be sure, the headlines of the moment may exaggerate the vice president's problems. There has been considerable fanfare about Mr. Gore making fund-raising solicitations from the White House. But former White House Legal Counsel Abner Mikva, who warned the president's staff against fund-raising from the White House, says this prohibition clearly didn't apply to the president or vice president; there is well-documented precedent for that distinction, he says.

Mr. Gore's predecessor, Dan Quayle, has sniped at Mr. Gore, but that rings hollow; Mr. Quayle himself was no slouch with GOP contributors, including more than a few who were affected by the decisions of his Council on Competitiveness. Moreover, while Mr. Gore may have made some errors in judgment, his basic integrity is acknowledged even by detractors.

The vice president can also find comfort from the experience of another predecessor. Ten years ago Vice President George Bush was thought to be in deep trouble because of his involvement in President Ronald Reagan's Iran-Contra scandal. But Mr. Bush not only survived but went on to capture a hotly contested GOP presidential nomination the next year and win the presidency.

Thus, almost any odds-maker on Democratic politics still would rate Mr. Gore the clear favorite for his party's nod in 2000. Still, inevitability isn't associated with the vice president any longer. Republicans and Democrats alike see some considerable chinks in Mr. Gore's political armor, including:

•The prospect of resurrecting his pedestrian performance as a national candidate in 1988, when he was on his own, not the running mate of a charismatic candidate. Mr. Gore's pitiful press conference last week—with his ludicrous defense that there was "no controlling legal authority" that says he violated any law—brought back those memories. Some Capitol Hill Democrats this week drew parallels to Bob Dole, a great indoor politician who got lost when he went out on his own.

•The diminished value of one of Mr. Gore's greatest strengths, fund-raising. Even if the current system isn't changed, the vice president's every effort now will be carefully scrutinized and his associations with questionable money men like Mr. Landow may become liabilities.

•Whether the vice president possesses the requisite political judgment and top-notch advisers. The decision to hold the news conference last week was, aside from the successful decision to debate Ross Perot during the Nafta fight, the highest-stakes political decision of Mr. Gore's vice presidency and it was a calamity. It's also worth remembering that on matters ranging from the no-holds-barred fund-raising scams to signing last year's welfare bill, the nefarious Dick Morris had few better allies inside the Clinton White House than Mr. Gore.

It's still premature to assess presidential politics three years away. And few would deny, no matter his current woes, that the vice president enjoys considerable institutional advantages; it is rare in modern politics for a vice president to be denied his party's nomination.

But supporters of other possible contenders—House Democratic Leader Dick Gephardt, Sen. Bob Kerrey and former Sen. Bill

Bradley—are openly talking these days about the vice president's vulnerabilities. Asked about 2000, the Iowa Democratic Party chairman earlier this week told the New York Times that "at this point, it's anyone's race." The vice president may not be as weak as that suggests, but he's not as strong as he seemed several weeks ago.

Personally, Mr. Gore, friends say, has been taken aback by the virulence of the attacks on him, and upset that White House efforts to drum up verbal support from congressional Democrats hit a stone wall.

Last week the vice president did stop in at a party one of his pals, former Rep. Tom Downey, was throwing for House GOP Budget Chairman John Kasich. He bumped into Rep. Charlie Rangel, the politically astute New York Democrat. Not surprisingly, the talk turned to Mr. Gore's press conference. "You did as well as you could with the material you had," Mr. Rangel noted. That's about as good as it gets these days for Albert Gore.

Letters to the Editor

I've Had No Dealings With Webster Hubbell

The statement in Albert Hunt's March 13 Politics & People column that I tried to arrange a real estate deal for Webster Hubbell is totally false and without foundation. The only Washington office building in which I have an interest, the one Mr. Hunt referred to in his telephone conversation with me, has been owned by the same partnership for more than 20 years, and there never has been any consideration of any involvement of Mr. Hubbell or any other person at any time. We would be happy to make any records or correspondence pertinent to this property available to you for your inspection.

I barely know Mr. Hubbell and have never had a discussion with him concerning business of any kind, nor have I participated in any group that has done so. Mr. Hunt's suggestion to the contrary is patently wrong and, I might note, without a designated source identified in his column. Given the extraordinary amount of interest in Mr. Hubbell's activities since leaving the administration, trying to connect my business with any issues pertaining to Mr. Hubbell is both unfair and dead wrong.

NATHAN LANDOW
Landow & Co.

Bethesda, Md.

Review & Outlook

Nothing Personal

One of the charms of the Clinton Presidency has been its audacity. Only a President with remarkable nerve, for example, would now be daring the U.S. Senate to promote two senior members of his White House staff to the Cabinet amid a still growing scandal over White House campaign finance. The only thing more remarkable would be if the Senate went along.

We say this not because we have anything personal against the two nominees, Anthony Lake for CIA and Alexis Herman for Labor. In a

Anthony Lake

normal Presidency, they'd deserve normal Senate deference. But considering the political moment of this unfolding scandal, these nominations are less about the individuals than about the character of this Presidency. Their nominations are an in-your-face challenge to the advise and consent powers of the Senate.

Though both nominees are trying to keep their distance from the campaign-finance web, they both sat in the highest White House councils. As National Security Adviser in Mr. Clinton's first term, Mr. Lake was the chief coordinator of a foreign policy more preoccupied with domestic politics than any in memory. Ms. Herman ran the White House office of public liaison, which is tasked with the care and feeding of political supporters. These are not innocent bystanders.

Just in the last week, we learned that FBI officials tipped off two NSC underlings last June about Chinese government intentions to influence U.S. politics. Mr. Lake says he was never told because the FBI advised the pair to keep it to themselves. The FBI replies that its agents told the NSC no such thing—and why would they tell the NSC if not to have the information influence official policy? Stranger still, one of those FBI agents assigned as liaison to the NSC, Edward Appel, is now quitting the White House for undisclosed reasons.

Attorney General Janet Reno also now says she tried to tell Mr. Lake about the Chinese tie last May but couldn't get him on the phone. Maybe Ms. Reno would have had better luck if she'd tried talking to Sandy Berger, then Mr. Lake's deputy and now successor as NSC adviser, who we know attended the weekly White House campaign strategy meetings all last year. This is unheard of among foreign-policy advisers, who usually try to distance themselves from campaign work. With so many new and odd developments, the Senate can be forgiven if it doesn't take White House explanations at face value.

Alexis Herman

We're sympathetic to those who say that Mr. Lake, with his intelligence and experience, is about as good as we're going to get from this administration. But Jim Woolsey was a first-rate CIA chief, until he proved too independent for this President. The CIA is a secret enforcement agency where such independence is vital, especially in an Administration as given to corner-cutting as this one. With the FBI now publicly feuding with Mr. Clinton over who knew what and when about Chinese influence, it stretches belief that a member of his White House responsible for China policy would now go to run the CIA, in charge of intelligence that might bear directly on the China-campaign connections.

Ms. Herman's case is almost as egregious from the point of view of domestic politics. Her office played a role in hosting the notorious White House coffees, though she now claims she herself didn't. Even if that's true, we know she was a former aide and confidant to Ron Brown, the late Commerce Secretary whose department is at the center of campaign-finance suspicions. Who knows what we might learn about the quid pro quos that came out of John Huang's Commerce shop?

Ms. Herman is also a proven expert in the art of gaming the political system, another hallmark of this Presidency. Her political prominence in Washington, D.C., won her an invitation in the 1980s to join a real estate partnership without making any personal investment, giving her a freebie ownership stake now worth more than $500,000. To be sure, it must have been hard to resist such offers, since even the government gave them a stamp of approval, but it's then also hard to imagine Ms. Herman as a spokesman for average working folk at Labor.

More important than these cases, however, is the credibility of this Presidency. Amid story after new campaign story, Mr. Clinton maintains he did nothing wrong—indeed he insists that what he did was right, because for the good of the country he had to defeat the Republicans. He also pledges complete cooperation with all investigators, even as his fund-raisers take the Fifth before Congress or have fled the country. If he is serious about cooperating, why doesn't he implore John Huang and the rest to explain everything they know?

If Mr. Clinton wants his nominees confirmed, he can always show he's serious about coming clean. Until he does, for a Republican Senate to confirm White House staff nominees would be to give him a free pass. It would only confirm what most of the public seems to believe about the fund-raising scandal, which is that all politicians are equally sleazy. If Republicans give Mr. Clinton a pass on these nominees, it will be a sign that they do not take their duties seriously.

REVIEW & OUTLOOK

Integrity of the Institutions

Perhaps the real legacy of the Clinton Presidency will be that it forced all of us to think hard about what is appropriate and what is not appropriate in the running of a modern political system.

The story of late has been mainly about the role of money in politics. Our sense, though, is that something larger came to the surface this week with the failure of Anthony Lake's nomination to be CIA director and the related tales of a National Security Council staff and CIA struggling to weigh their duties against the demands of Democratic political operatives.

Now before we all get too high-minded about this subject, let's recognize some realities. Anyone who has read Presidential memoirs knows—because the Presidents themselves frankly admit—that even the most sensitive policy decisions are often measured against political effect. And as well, the career staff in sensitive agencies such as the CIA or FBI assuredly do not operate in some fog oblivious to these realities; they know when elections are held.

That said, anyone who has served in a position of responsibility in Washington stretching back through the postwar years has understood that some line exists between proper and improper political pressure on the national security and law enforcement bureaucracies. We now learn that the chairman of the Democratic National Committee called NSC staffer Sheila Heslin to insist that she drop objections to Roger Tamraz, the pipeline entrepreneur and contributor with connections to some of the BCCI crowd, getting in to "see" the

President. And, even more breathtaking, that this Clinton campaign pol ordered up an intelligence file for her from the CIA. Surely this is way beyond any recognizable norm.

But the Clinton White House had made it routine.

This has to be one of the most troubling aspects of the Clinton tenure, its across-the-board willingness to subvert national agencies charged with law enforcement and security concerns. Specifically, the FBI, the Secret Service, the National Security Council, the Central Intelligence Agency and most likely the Internal Revenue Service. Again, the reality is that all these agencies have experienced serious runs at their integrity by past Presidents. The Clinton innovation is to have made it banal.

Early in the first term, assistant White House Counsel William Kennedy called the FBI, demanding to know "within 15 minutes" what the agency would do about accusations that had been made against the Travel Office by Clinton friends and travel-agency entrepreneurs Catherine Cornelius and Harry Thomason. And if the answer was nothing, Mr. Kennedy was prepared to bring in the IRS. The IRS shortly began a two-year audit of the Travel Office airline, UltrAir.

In the Filegate scandal an irresponsible White House aide, Craig Livingstone, asked the FBI for, and got, files on several hundred former Bush aides. When the Filegate issue emerged, White House aide Tony Marceca, a Democratic activist, falsely said the Secret Service provided outdated lists. Earlier, in 1993, when the Secret Service withheld passes from about 12 White House employees because of drug-use concerns, it dropped the holds after the Administration set up a twice-a-year testing program for the aides.

Now, within a week, we have the FBI, the NSC and the CIA all embroiled with this White House over their proper functions. In an incredible display of recrimination, the FBI and White House accused each other of misrepresenting the agency's warnings to the NSC about Chinese contributors. Then in the middle of this spitting match came leaks last week that the government's most sensitive monitoring operation, the National Security Agency, had passed along communications intercepts early last year to the FBI regarding possible Chinese interest in making campaign contributions. In this wake, a senior FBI agent serving as liaison to the NSC "retired."

Then on Monday came this paper's front page story about the Democratic Party chairman seeking to enlist both the CIA and NSC staffer Sheila Heslin in the effort to place $177,000-giver Roger Tamraz in front of . . . of what? The President, or the candidate?

As widely reported, the Bill Clinton story is one of a "permanent campaign," a career in which no discernible line exists between public service, as commonly understood, and political gamesmanship. And all who come within this orbit are understood to be on call for political jobwork—a heads up, a free pass, an I-don't-remember. That is why Tony Lake's nomination arrived with a taint that couldn't be rubbed out. It is why Janet Reno's thoughts on independent counsel produce suspicion.

We have a flexible and resilient system. But when it becomes evident that the prevailing mores now allow the routine compromise of the system's institutions and those who work within them, then perhaps the time has arrived for a lot of people to start reframing, publicly, the right boundaries of political behavior in Washington.

Editorial Feature

The Vice President:
Mr. Clean or the Godfather?

Last week's column about Vice President Al Gore's problems, chiefly from the fund-raising controversies, produced such an intense reaction that it's worth revisiting.

Several conservatives praised it, saying it's about time I write about the money-and-politics shenanigans. Where were they a couple months ago on Newt Gingrich?

Mr. Gore's supporters were outraged; most were civil; a few were

Politics & People

By Albert R. Hunt

not. They argued that the press was engaged in a McCarthyite tirade against him.

They objected to my assertion that the vice president has been harmed by his high-pressured fund-raising tactics in the last election, the kind the Washington Post has reported got him dubbed "the Solicitor-in-Chief." Gore supporters took particular umbrage at my linking him to an effort by Gore fund-raiser Nathan Landow to help Webster Hubbell, even though that column reported that the vice president's office said he had no knowledge of that deal.

In a letter appearing in the Journal today [page 349], Mr. Landow flatly denies my report that he tried to arrange a real estate deal for Mr. Hubbell, the former Clinton Justice Department official who faced financial problems and a prison term. Here is the context of that report.

I called Mr. Landow twice in the two days before last week's column ran; he didn't call back until after the column appeared. He then said he barely knew Mr. Hubbell, never had any "official" conversation with him nor ever even discussed any business arrangements for him with anyone. Subsequently, he acknowledged that Mr. Hubbell spent a weekend at the Landows' Maryland Eastern Shore home, but says it was as the guest of his son-in-law and daughter.

The next day Mr. Landow called and said he knew my "source" was Michael Berman, a Washington lobbyist with close ties to the White House. Mr. Landow recalled that Mr. Berman once had asked him to help Mr. Hubbell, maybe to include him in a real estate deal. But Mr. Landow also recalled that he had forcefully rejected this suggestion. (Mr. Berman, who has been open about his efforts to help the troubled Mr. Hubbell—and whom I spoke to about this for the first time Monday night—says of this: "I have absolutely no memory of that whatsoever.")

Actually, it was an investor with Mr. Landow in a Washington office building who told me that he was asked by Mr. Landow to sell his interest to Mr. Hubbell; he volunteered this information but asked that his name not be used. When told this, Mr. Landow acknowledged he had inquired with the other investors in the building about selling their interests and in one such conversation "could have mentioned Webb Hubbell's problems." But he insisted he never discussed a business deal for Mr. Hubbell and offered affidavits and documents to show how hard that would have been. The investor said he rejected the explicit Landow overture and nothing came of it.

This isn't the only story that has rankled Mr. Landow and the Gore team. Ten days ago the Washington Post reported that two poverty-stricken Indian tribes said that Mr. Landow and Peter Knight, a close Gore confidant and manager of the Clinton-Gore presidential campaign last year, sought, at expensive rates, to represent the tribes, which are trying to get back their native lands.

The Cheyenne and Arapaho Indian tribes of Oklahoma, which separately were shaken down for $107,000 in contributions to the Democratic National Committee, told the Post that Mr. Landow had touted his and Mr. Knight's access to the administration to get the contract; the Indians further were warned, they claimed, that there was no chance to get the land if they didn't use these well-connected Democrats. Mr. Knight has been quoted as saying that although his firm was involved in the negotiations, he was going to stay out; Mr. Landow says that the story misrepresented his role, that no threats were made and that he has demanded a retraction.

Mr. Gore's supporters complain it's highly unfair to cite him in these stories, as he wasn't involved. They miss the point. It would be McCarthyism if the vice president or Speaker Gingrich were linked to a friend who championed transvestite Teamsters; it's clear such activity doesn't represent their views or philosophy.

But ideas are different from the political money culture, to which cozy connections are central. Peter Knight brought in $2.9 million in billings to his law firm in 1995, vastly more than he brought in before Mr. Gore was elected in 1992. Does anyone think there's not a connection? Or does the vice president believe the Cheyenne and Arapaho Indians would have come last December to Nathan Landow, a longtime Gore fund-raiser, if Bob Dole had been elected?

> '*There is a sharp contrast between what the president has stood for and does stand for now, on the one hand, and an extremist agenda fueled by special-interest lobbyists in the Republican Congress on the other hand. . . .*'
> Vice President Albert Gore on PBS's "The MacNeil-Lehrer Newshour," April 3, 1995

The Gore camp still complains about the Washington Post piece by Bob Woodward earlier this month that documented how the vice president—"the Solicitor-in-Chief"—has the most formidable fund-raising network in America, often using heavy-handed and otherwise questionable tactics. In fact this piece—with the sole flaw of going a little easy on Dan Quayle by comparison—was brilliantly reported, full of the specifics of many examples.

The fund-raising horror stories seem endless. The Michael Frisby-David Rogers piece in Monday's Wall Street Journal detailing how the White House ignored security warnings and gave presidential access to a shady international oil financier—who not so coincidentally is a big Democratic donor—was the catalyst for the withdrawal of Tony Lake's nomination as CIA director.

Where is the outrage of the vice president over this episode, or the one involving the Oklahoma Indians? The White House, without question, sold access; where is Mr. Gore on that? Does he regret, as the Washington Post reported, calling an executive in the fall of

1995 with "a sense of urgency" that an immediate big donation was essential to help a major Democratic National Committee advertising campaign extolling President Clinton?

No informed observer, as I wrote last week, questions Mr. Gore's basic integrity. But the political money system, much of which revolves around the Washington fund-raising and lobbying axis, is sleazy. Looking ahead, Mr. Gore, more than any other politician, is the Godfather of that system, which he hopes will catapult him into the presidency in 2000. At the same time he advertises his personal integrity, and freely criticizes Republican fealty to big-money interests.

There is an inherent conflict between these two realities. The role of the press in covering the vice president is to scrutinize carefully which side he comes down on.

REVIEW & OUTLOOK

Democrats Slow Investigation

Yesterday's close defeat on the House floor of GOP attempts to fund an investigation of campaign-finance scandals shows how high the political stakes have become. Democrats felt they had to defeat the budget of the House Government Reform and Oversight Committee, fearful that since its well-funded investigation—unlike the Senate's—doesn't have to end by this December, many damaging revelations could be pushed into an election year. Eleven Republicans went over to join the Democrats.

Essentially, the Democrats have taken a page from the White House's famous stalling tactics—stonewall documents, delay cooperation until the clock runs out. But of course it is not possible to simply acknowledge any such strategy, so the smoke screen behind which they cloaked this consisted of charges on the House floor that the committee's budget represented some sort of "slush fund." They also repeated innuendoes against Rep. Dan Burton, the chairman of the Government Reform and Oversight Committee, who is conducting the probe.

These accusations were transmitted via that part of the media known to be working the moral-equivalence beat, which grinds down all significant distinctions to "they all do it."

On the eve of yesterday's vote, Rep. Burton was accused of shaking down a lobbyist for Pakistan for a campaign contribution. Like most such stories that belly-flop into the middle of a big vote, it should be viewed with caution. Mark Siegel, the lobbyist who made the accusations, is a former official of the Democratic National Committee, which is itself at the heart of the fund-raising scandals. Indeed, several news organizations passed on the last-minute story before it found a home on the front page of the Washington Post. In any

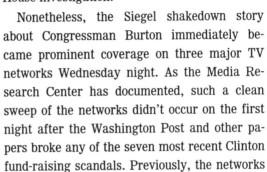

event, it is hardly cause for blowing up the House investigation.

Nonetheless, the Siegel shakedown story about Congressman Burton immediately became prominent coverage on three major TV networks Wednesday night. As the Media Research Center has documented, such a clean sweep of the networks didn't occur on the first night after the Washington Post and other papers broke any of the seven most recent Clinton fund-raising scandals. Previously, the networks

Dan Burton

also elevated a story that Rep. Burton had played a round of golf with the chairman of AT&T, a government contractor. This heinous act of socializing took place at a charity tournament that Mr. Burton had paid his own way to.

There are in fact commentators in Washington who really do understand the difference between venial and mortal sin, but given the stakes of the Clinton scandals, any such helpful nuance is consciously ignored.

And of course the dispute is entirely political. The root of Mr. Burton's problems is not his fundraising habits, but his refusal to define "fairness" the way Rep. Henry Waxman, the ranking Democrat on his committee, wants him to. Mr. Waxman has demanded the committee allot one-third of its budget to the minority—up from Mr. Burton's proposed 25%. The hallowed Watergate committee allocated far less than a quarter of its

Henry Waxman

staff to the minority. The Iran-Contra Congressional probe employed 51 Democratic staffers and only nine GOP staffers.

Mr. Burton responded to Mr. Waxman's demands that the House probe's scope include fund-raising problems in Congress by noting that House Rules require that such matters be handled by the same Ethics Committee that Democrats were happy to use against Speaker Newt Gingrich: "Fairness does not mean finding the same number of Democrats and Republicans to investigate, particularly when to do so requires exceeding the charter of this committee, which is oversight of the Executive Branch."

The outcome of the House's vote yesterday effectively slows down Congress's efforts to find out just what the Clinton White House's fund-raising apparatus was doing. Accordingly, more than anything else, the Democrats' attempts to push the Burton committee off the rails make one thing about the events since the Inauguration very clear: The stakes have become very high.

REVIEW & OUTLOOK

Asides

Still a Crime

Believe it or not, it turns out that lying to federal investigators is still a crime. That appears to be the clear lesson of the conviction on Friday of Tyson Foods lobbyist Jack L. Williams. The Williams conviction was brought by the office of Independent Counsel Donald C. Smaltz, charged with investigating the financial affairs of former Agriculture Secretary Mike Espy. Mr. Williams faces up to five years in prison. Sometimes in Washington, it really isn't just "all politics."

Editorial Feature

Let's Hear Reno's Reasoning On an Indogate Counsel

We will soon know more about whether Attorney General Janet Reno intends to call for the appointment of an independent counsel to investigate possible fund-raising violations involving the White House and the Democratic National Committee. On March 13, the Republicans who control the Senate Judiciary Committee formally asked her to seek such an appointment. By law, she must respond within 30 days.

Ms. Reno has been resisting calls for an independent counsel for months. Last fall, as news of the fund-raising irregularities came

Rule of Law

By Terry Eastland

out, she assembled a task force of Justice Department lawyers and FBI agents to look into the mess. Since then, in response to the many calls for a counsel (some coming even from Democrats), she has offered the formulaic response that the statutory criteria for an independent counsel have not been met.

By this, she means that there is no specific, credible allegation of wrongdoing against either a high-ranking official in the executive branch who is "covered" by the independent counsel statute, or against a "noncovered" person who should be probed by a counsel because a Justice Department investigation would present a conflict of interest.

Ms. Reno hasn't indicated whether her task force has come across information requiring a preliminary investigation—or a "p.i." as it's dubbed within her building. The statute requires the Justice Department to conduct a p.i. if there is evidence of wrongdoing by a covered official. At the end of 90 days, if the attorney general is unable to conclude that there are no "reasonable grounds" to investigate further, she must ask a special panel of judges to name an independent counsel. In the case of a noncovered person, it's up to the attorney general to decide whether to initiate a p.i. and ask for a counsel.

Ms. Reno's task force has been looking at the White House fundraising coffees featuring Mr. Clinton; Vice President Al Gore's solic-

itation of contributions from his office; the acceptance by the first lady's chief of staff of a check made out to the DNC; and the foreign contributions made to the DNC. For all anyone on the outside knows, there could be a p.i. now under way.

In her response to the senators' letter, Ms. Reno is obligated to say whether there is or will be a preliminary investigation. She also has a duty to the public, which already has learned a great deal about the White House-DNC fund-

Janet Reno

raising abuses, to explain her enforcement decisions under the independent counsel law.

Earlier this month Mr. Gore admitted that he made phone calls from his office soliciting contributions to the DNC that helped sustain the Clinton-Gore re-election bid. Federal criminal law bars any person from soliciting contributions for federal campaigns on federal property "occupied in the discharge of official duties." Ms. Reno has declined to say whether Mr. Gore violated this law, but she has said that the law itself does not apply to the solicitation of "soft-money"— funds that go to a political party, not a specific candidate. Her implication is that Mr. Gore and anyone who might have done what he did—including the president—would not have broken the law.

Ms. Reno's view of the law may very well be correct. But it's not at all clear that an attorney general has the power to make that determination. The authority to interpret and apply the law in a case involving a covered person such as Mr. Gore would appear to lie with a duly appointed independent counsel. Is Ms. Reno claiming this authority? And if so, on what legal basis?

Ms. Reno has discretionary power to ask for a counsel. She used it in seeking a counsel in Whitewater, telling the appointing judges that a Justice Department investigation of James McDougal and others associated with the Clintons "would present a political conflict of interest." She also invoked it in the case of Anthony Marceca, the Army detailee accused of making false statements to the FBI in the files scandal. And she used it in the case of Bernard Nussbaum, the former White House counsel accused of making contradictory statements concerning the role of Hillary Clinton in hiring Craig Livingstone.

In explaining the potential conflicts, Ms. Reno said that a Justice investigation of Mr. Marceca would involve "an inquiry into dealings between the White House and the FBI" and that one of Mr. Nussbaum would involve "an inquiry into statements allegedly made by a former senior member of the White House to the FBI concerning the role of the First Lady in a controversial personnel decision."

A Justice investigation of allegations against noncovered persons involved in the fund-raising (such as Harold Ickes or John Huang) would seem to present conflicts of interest similar to those Ms. Reno perceived in Whitewater and related matters. A thorough Justice inquiry would have to probe friends of Mr. Clinton—such as the Riadys and Charlie Trie—in whose donations the president had a profound personal interest. Not to mention that a Justice investigation could be damaged by the increasing tension between the FBI and the White House.

Of course, Ms. Reno is free to do as she wishes—that is what discretion means. But if she decides against invoking her discretionary authority in this case, especially given her previous uses of it, a sense of obligation to the rule of law should prompt her to explain why.

The explanation might be as simple as this: "The president directed me to use my discretionary authority to ask for a counsel in Whitewater, and he now has directed me not to use that authority in this matter."

With this speculation I am getting ahead of the story. But bear in mind that the attorney general serves at the pleasure of the president. And that, as this newspaper reported some weeks ago, the president has made phone calls complaining to Democratic senators about Democratic calls for a counsel in the case at hand. Mr. Clinton clearly does not want another independent counsel, especially not one that would nibble at the White House, the Democratic Party and their big contributors into the next century, and who would be less controllable than an attorney general.

For these reasons, Mr. Clinton is unlikely to leave the decision about an independent counsel to Ms. Reno. The question for the attorney general is whether she will go along.

Mr. Eastland is a fellow at the Ethics and Public Policy Center in Washington.

REVIEW & OUTLOOK

The Quiet American

Back when the DNC and Ron Brown were targeting Asia, do you imagine that anyone piped up to say: "You know, before we unleash John Huang and Charlie Trie on Asia, should we worry at all that

Al Gore

this might cause policy or diplomacy problems for us with the Chinese some day?" Some day arrived this week, as Vice President Al Gore flew to Asia to do some explaining and hang around a few deals.

In Tokyo, Mr. Gore's press secretary, incredibly, barred reporters from covering Mr. Gore's speech to the American Chamber of Commerce on the rather lame grounds that it was a "working meeting." Once in Beijing, the staffers continued to banish journalists—and shift the blame to the Chinese, which is implausible considering the usual urge of Chinese leaders to bolster their legitimacy in the world's eyes by appearing next to visiting dignitaries. The local state-controlled media have given prime coverage to the visit.

The moment of maximum discomfort arrived during an obligatory champagne toast with Chinese Premier Li Peng, still remembered for his role in the 1989 Tiananmen massacre. As Mr. Gore half-heartedly raised his glass, his mind might have been swimming with campaign-2000 TV commercials by the opposition, juxtaposing footage of this toast with a voice-over of charges about Chinese-directed campaign contributions.

And in fact Mr. Gore entangled himself by first saying the contributions scandal wouldn't affect U.S.-Chinese relations; then, discomfited by the implications, had aides tell reporters that he'd told Li it *would* be "serious" if the allegations were proven true.

With all the baggage Mr. Gore had to carry into China, this visit was different in interesting ways from past Clinton emissaries. One example was the Vice President's hesitancy at attending signing ceremonies for a $685 million order for Boeing aircraft and a $1.3 billion deal for a new GM plant. What a difference from the grand style of late Commerce Secretary Ron Brown, who blew through China in August 1994—executive supplicants in tow, the Secretary raking in glory for $6 billion worth of contracts. Those were the good old days.

The message Beijing's chess masters may glean from this week's tour is that America's China policy now sits in check. Li Peng chastised the U.S. for not playing "a more positive role in international affairs," and reportedly told Mr. Gore that Taiwan is to be the key issue in bilateral relations. That could be a prelude for further pressure on the U.S. to reduce its arms sales to Taiwan and back away from pledges to help defend the island against attack.

Beyond Taiwan, other issues require clear thinking and freedom of maneuver. They include the future treatment of Hong Kong, China's alleged transfers of nuclear and ballistic missile technology to rogue states, and the disputes between China and its neighbors over their competing claims to regions of the South China Sea.

The Gore visit is hardly an encouraging prelude to forthcoming summits between Presidents Bill Clinton and Jiang Zemin. It will take enormous skill for the U.S. to shape and pursue a policy that both improves the relationship while maintaining a tough line on the serious issues that divide China and the U.S. But like some permanent, damp fog, the embarrassments of the campaign gift scandals will permeate this relationship for four years. That is the real cost of the White House/DNC decision to lower the bar on standards of acceptable political conduct.

REVIEW & OUTLOOK

Missing Witnesses

So we learn that after a Whitewater strategy meeting with the President and the First Lady, then chief of staff Mack McLarty and current chief of staff Erskine Bowles set out to funnel money to Webster Hubbell, at the time facing charges of bilking his law partners and under pressure to cooperate with the Whitewater investigation. Independent Counsel Kenneth Starr took the Hubbell payments to a Little Rock grand jury this week.

In its pre-emptive disclosures, the White House sought to portray the payments as help to an old friend. The alternative explanation is a conspiracy to obstruct justice, hatched in the March 1994 meeting with the Clintons, Harold Ickes, Bruce Lindsey and David Kendall, personal attorney to the Clintons. The key question is one of motive: charity, or hush money? A jury may ultimately have to decide, but the surrounding circumstances provide plenty of reason to put the question.

From its first days, indeed, the Clinton Administration has been stonewalling investigation of misdeeds in Arkansas and beyond. When the Resolution Trust Corp. moved to reopen investigation of the Whitewater S&L, Madison Guaranty, the White House got a "heads-up" from the Treasury, and the President quickly held a meeting with one of the apparent targets, then-Governor Jim Guy Tucker. As the ethical carnage moved from the Travel Office firings to the Vincent Foster papers to the current furor over foreign political contributions, we have witnessed a ceaseless blizzard of belated revelations, denied documents, amnesiac aides and disappearing witnesses.

Of these, Mr. Hubbell is merely the most prominent. After resigning as Associate Attorney General, he pleaded guilty to two felonies in a scheme to defraud his former Rose Law Firm colleagues. He pledged to cooperate with the independent counsel, but at sentencing Mr. Starr pointedly declined to recommend a sentence reduction. While Mr. Hubbell was in prison, he was frequently visited by one of the President's top aides, old Arkansas chum Marsha Scott.

WANTED

Webster Hubbell Susan MacDougal

Charlie Trie Craig Livingstone

FOR TESTIMONY

Through 1994, Mr. Hubbell was reaping the benefits of White House business solicitations, detailed on page one yesterday by our Glenn Simpson. In all, the about-to-confess felon took in more than $500,000 for legal work, as opposed to $310,000 he reported for his last year at the Rose Law Firm. A big chunk, about $100,000, came from Indonesia's Lippo Group in a June 1994 payment. That month, Lippo honcho James Riady met with President Clinton and his aides at least five times. On June 23, Mr. Riady met with Mr. Hubbell for breakfast, went to a meeting at the White House, and met Mr. Hubbell again for lunch.

Among those stepping up to help Webb was former Commerce Secretary Mickey Kantor, whose old law firm represents Lippo in the U.S.; he contributed to an education fund for Mr. Hubbell's children. Mr. Kantor also lined up Democratic Party bigwig Bernard Rapoport, who put Mr. Hubbell on his payroll at $3,000 per month for six months. Mr. Hubbell also received funds in 1994 from tycoon Ronald Perelman, Washington lobbyist Michael Berman, and James

Wood, who became U.S. envoy to Taiwan. Also pitching in was lobbyist Jack Williams, who got two of his clients, Pacific Telesis and Mid-American Dairymen's Association, to hire Mr. Hubbell. Mr. Williams, who counts Arkansas's Tyson Foods among his biggest clients, was convicted last month of making false statements in the probe of former Agriculture Secretary Mike Espy. A Tyson Foods spokesman says the company did not make any payments to Mr. Hubbell.

*   *   *

Mr. Hubbell's fate contrasts sharply with that of witnesses who have cooperated with the course of justice. An Arkansas jury believed David Hale told the truth in court, and convicted Governor Tucker and the Clintons' former business partners, James and Susan McDougal. For confessing his own crimes, Mr. Hale is serving the longest jail sentence handed out in a Whitewater case. He continues to provide the independent counsel with valuable information, and Mr. Starr recently petitioned the court for a reduction in his sentence. Arkansas prosecutors, however, have hit him with a criminal insurance fraud claim that in any normal state would have been reduced to a civil penalty months ago.

Or consider the case of Don Denton, a former Madison vice president who testified that Mr. McDougal had pushed for a fraudulent loan; he later made headlines when he told federal regulators that he had warned Hillary Clinton, then a Rose Law Firm lawyer representing Madison, that a loan arrangement might be improper. He was fired from his job as manager of Little Rock Municipal Airport by a politically connected board. Similarly, the Little Rock Board of Directors revoked municipal Judge Bill Watt's pension after his testimony at the Tucker trial. We reprint nearby an excerpt of that testimony concerning what would appear to be efforts to encourage resistance by potential witnesses.

*   *   *

Scant wonder, it would seem, that there is such a long roster of unwilling or simply missing witnesses. Ms. McDougal, in a spectacular example, continues to defy a Little Rock grand jury with her silence about what then-Governor Clinton knew about illegal loans, even though she will go on trial May 6 in Los Angeles on embezzlement charges unrelated to Whitewater. Her husband, meanwhile, has become Mr. Starr's latest star cooperator, and it will be instructive to watch his fate.

In the contributions controversy, meanwhile, a long list of witnesses have fled the country. Congressional investigators would like to talk to Mr. Riady, for example, but he is in Asia and is not returning to the United States anytime soon. The Indonesian gardeners who donated $200,000 to the Democratic National Committee have long since returned to Jakarta. Pauline Kanchanalak, whose $253,000 in contributions had to be returned by the DNC, has decamped to her native Thailand. Little Rock restaurateur Charlie Trie, big fund-raiser and recipient of wire transfers from the Bank of China in Hong Kong, has apparently taken up residence in Beijing.

A most intriguing potential witness, former White House personnel security chief Craig Livingstone, is under tutelage of a high-powered Washington attorney. Mr. Livingstone, you may recall, reached prominence as the marauder of some 900 FBI files. He also was one of the first to be notified of the death of Mr. Foster and to visit the morgue to identify the body. He was as well one of the earliest visitors to Mr. Foster's office the day after his death, and a Secret Service officer testified Mr. Livingstone exited the White House that morning with a briefcase and binders. Mr. Livingstone, a former bar bouncer, is without visible means of support. Who, it is only logical to ask, is raising funds for *his* lawyer?

All of these roadblocks in the course of justice may be mere coincidences, we suppose, but it looks to us like a pattern of conduct. It may have started as a little land deal in the Ozarks, but as a little lie leads to a string of bigger and more implausible ones, it has come to involve misuse of the powers of the President of the United States to subvert his first duty, seeing that the laws are faithfully executed.

Editorial Feature

On Resisting Cooperation

*On March 26, 1996, at the trial of then-Arkansas Gov. Jim Guy Tuck-
er and Madison Guaranty Savings & Loan owners James and Susan Mc-
Dougal, Municipal Judge Bill Watt testified about his approach to
Whitewater witness Don Denton, a former vice president of Madison, on
behalf of a group of lawyers linked to David Kendall, personal attorney
for Bill and Hillary Clinton. Jack Lassiter, the attorney mentioned
below by Judge Watt, had represented Webster Hubbell (during plea
bargaining with the independent counsel), as well as other Whitewater
figures. The Little Rock Board of Directors later revoked Mr. Watt's municipal pension, and the politically appointed Municipal Airport Commission fired Mr. Denton from his job as an airport manager. Here are
excerpts from Mr. Watt's testimony:*

Prosecutor Jackie Bennett: All right, sir, did you have occasion to
run into Mr. Don Denton at that time?

Mr. Watt: Yes, sir, at the base of the escalator or somewhere near
the entrance to the airport.

Q: Did you have a conversation with Don Denton?

A: We did. Up the escalator and down through security and over to
either the first or second gate on the right when you go through security at Little Rock Airport.

Q: All right, sir. Tell the jury about that conversation with Mr.
Denton. . . .

A: I was acquainted with Mr. Denton on a first-name basis. We
had known each other for some time, so the conversation I had with

him going up the escalator, down the hall . . . was that basically, "Don, are you getting hammered the same way everybody else is in town on all of this stuff that's going on," referring to Whitewater.

And I also indicated to him, "I don't know who are your lawyers, don't know what you're doing, but it seems like everybody in town has lawyers and everybody has out-of-town lawyers and there's lawyers out of Washington, and in fact if you need any help, there's people you need to call; if you've got the opportunity, you could call my lawyer, if somebody that's around you needs any assistance, to call, to talk to, to find out what everybody is doing, you could feel free to call him." I said, "Jack Lassiter is representing

Don Denton

someone in the case." I'm not sure if I made a reference to any particular client of Mr. Lassiter. [I] mentioned that a Mr. Kendall, I think his first name is David, but I probably just said Mr. Kendall, is representing some of the Clinton interests out of Washington and on at least one occasion that we had been in contact with them.

Q: Who is "we," sir?

A: My attorney, my counsel.

Q: And who was your counsel at the time?

A: Mark Hampton.

Q: You mentioned Jack Lassiter a moment ago. Was Jack Lassiter also your attorney, sir?

A: No, sir, he was not my counsel. There was consideration as to whether or not I was going to retain him. It really depended on where we were butting heads with the independent counsel's office. . . .

Q: What was Jack Lassiter's relationship with David Kendall?

A: I don't know of a formal relationship. I don't know what the status of that relationship is.

Q: Did you understand there to be some informal relationship?

A: I knew that Mr. Lassiter was in contact with Mr. Kendall or others in Washington concerning various other parties, or potential parties to all this.

Q: All right, sir. And what did you tell Don Denton at that time?

A: Other than a discussion concerning the lawyers and that type of thing, I indicated we were basically butting heads, that we were arguing, that we absolutely were in a total adversarial position. Obviously I was not happy with the Office of Independent Counsel or anybody else, and I made the comment to Mr. Denton that they wanted us to tell a lie on Mr. Tucker or anyone else. . . .

Q: Had there ever been an occasion in which anybody, either at the independent counsel or the FBI, had encouraged you to tell a lie about Jim Guy Tucker?

A: No one has asked me to tell a lie.

Q: All right, sir. So your statement to Don Denton on that day was, itself, a false statement?

A: It was—excuse me?

Q: Your statement to Don Denton on July 24, 1995, in which you told him that you understood that we, the independent counsel, had wanted you to tell a lie about Jim Guy Tucker was a false statement.

A: If you take it as a definite statement, yes, I said it seemed like that that's what they were wanting us to do, and yes, it would have been false based on the fact I had not been asked to lie. . . .

Q: Sir, in connection with the conversation you had with Don Denton at the airport on July 24 in which you described lawyers, both in Washington, D.C., for the president and in Little Rock, teaming up and exchanging information, and in which you falsely stated that the independent counsel had tried to get you to lie about Jim Guy Tucker, were you trying to recruit Don Denton into the group of people who were resisting cooperation with the independent counsel?

A: I was making sure that Don knew if he made the decision to resist, that he had avenues available to him to call and at least would have a place to start.

REVIEW & OUTLOOK

Cynical Bubbling in Washington

The way the Indogate hearings story has developed lately, it appears the Beltway's capacity for inciting public loathing of the American political system is pretty much limitless.

Going back months to when the name "John Huang" first appeared in the newspapers, the story has been overwhelmingly about the fund-raising practices of the Clinton-Gore campaign, which, like some gelatinous organism, appears to have absorbed the Democratic National Committee into its circulatory system. The story's particulars—the coffee klatches, the unvetted Runyonesque characters, the Lincoln Bedroom rentals—have reached such grandiloquent proportions as to cry out for some public accounting. Which is why Janet Reno is under pressure to call for a special prosecutor.

But if you thought this is essentially what the Indogate story was about, pay heed to what the Beltway is trying to turn it into.

Today, both the Senate and House committees investigating the campaign finance scandals will have a showdown over expanding the probe's scope. House Democrats will argue that Rep. Dan Burton's Government Oversight Committee should also look at the "improper" campaign activities, which Senator Fred Thompson's committee has agreed to fold into its mandate.

This everyone-does-it strategy has been developed from desperation by the Democrats, who assume they'll be abetted by a local press corps still wandering the land in search of the campaign-finance Grail. Many Republicans, despite majority status, are acceding simply because they haven't yet developed the courage or character to stand up to it.

In Senator Thompson's committee the Democrats are complaining that the committee hasn't yet acted on their demands to subpoena 11 groups that often work with Republicans, such as the Christian Coalition and Americans for Tax Reform. In other words, the Democrats are saying no investigation of John Huang, Charlie Trie or drug-dealer donors will be permitted unless Ralph Reed is placed on the pyre as well.

Republicans have been complicit in this mindless equivalence. The Thompson investigation was "broadened" at the insistence of at least six Senate Republicans who revolted against Majority Leader Trent Lott at a private luncheon a month ago. The six (Olympia Snowe and Susan Collins of Maine, John McCain of Arizona, Sam Brownback of Kansas, Jim Jeffords of Vermont and Arlen Specter of Pennsylvania) argued that in the name of "balance" Congress should probe any and all practices viewed as "improper," a notion empty of meaning.

Capitalizing on this senatorial courtesy, Senator Robert Torricelli claimed on Fox News Sunday that "some of the worst abuses of the '96 campaign" were committed by 11 Republican-leaning groups. "The biggest change in 1996 was not the presidential campaign. It was millions of dollars in independent expenditures," intoned Mr. Torricelli.

As blood sport, it no doubt would be vastly entertaining to watch the Democrats and Republicans perform ritualistic mutual assured destruction before the hearings' cameras. A day devoted to Arthur Coia would be particularly entertaining. This is the head of the Laborers Union, who was named in a 1994 Justice Department RICO complaint as having "associated with, and been controlled and influenced by, organized crime figures." A week after Hillary Clinton spoke to the Laborers convention in February 1995, Mr. Coia convinced Justice to drop the RICO complaint and leave him in charge of cleaning up the union. In 1995 and 1996, the Laborers Union gave the Democratic Party a total of $2.3 million.

Yes, a great political bonfire could indeed be lit beneath "improper" campaign behavior, with endless column inches and headlines poured on like gasoline. The evidence suggests this is the course that the Senate has set for itself, with Senators from both parties given equal time to condemn the sinners dragged to testify before them. Thus will they immunize one another.

Which means it falls for now to Rep. Burton's committee in the House to remain focused on the big story. Anyone paying attention to Indogate the past few months knows it is in a class by itself, as presumably at the time was Watergate. Now, as then, there is a large difference between political gamesmanship and compromising the integrity of the government's primary institutions. If Washington can't handle this kind of distinction anymore, the level of public cynicism about all politics is going to bubble a lot higher than it already has.

Editorial Feature

Burton's Accuser: The View From Pakistan

By Husain Haqqani

KARACHI, Pakistan—Democrats in Washington are questioning the ethics of Republican Rep. Dan Burton's alleged tactics in attempting to secure campaign contributions from U.S. citizens of Pakistani origin. The case against Mr. Burton is based on claims

by Mark A. Siegel, a former lobbyist for the government of Pakistan, that he was "shaken down" for contributions of "at least $5,000" last year. As proof, we are offered a memo in which Mr. Siegel says he complained to his client about Rep. Burton's behavior.

For most Pakistanis, the episode raises many more questions about Mr. Siegel's conduct as a lobbyist than about Mr. Burton's as a congressman. Contributions from Pakistani-Americans to congressional candidates do not violate U.S.

Dan Burton

law. Mr. Siegel has said nothing to indicate that the Pakistani government in Islamabad or its embassy in Washington broke any rules. What he is doing is using his relationship with his former client to try to score points in a partisan U.S. domestic dispute.

The timing of Mr. Siegel's allegations is significant. As Rep. Burton probes alleged Democratic campaign fund-raising abuses, what could be better than to subject him to similar allegations? That in doing so he might himself be abusing the privileged relationship with his former client seems to be of no importance to Mr. Siegel, described by the Washington Post as "a longtime Democratic activist."

Last week Mr. Siegel testified before a federal grand jury about alleged campaign-finance abuses; two weeks earlier, the Washington Post reported, unnamed Democratic congressional sources released a memo Mr. Siegel purportedly wrote last year to an aide of former Prime Minister Benazir Bhutto. There is widespread doubt in Pakistan about the memo's authenticity.

The memo is said to have been written on July 25, 1996. But to this day the Pakistani Embassy in Washington knows nothing about it except what's been in the papers. As a lobbyist, Mr. Siegel worked with

---

If a memo from Pakistan's lobbyist was not seen by the prime minister, her principal secretary or her ambassador, how are we to be sure that it was ever sent?

---

the embassy and should have sent it a copy of any memo he sent to Islamabad. Officials then responsible for handling correspondence in the Pakistani Prime Minister's Secretariat say they did not receive the memo described in the Washington Post. Ms. Bhutto does not recall having seen such a memo—but then Mr. Siegel does not claim she did.

Yet if a memo from Pakistan's lobbyist was not seen by the prime minister, her principal secretary or her ambassador, how are we to be sure that it was ever sent? What is certain is that Mr. Siegel can not have expected to advance his client's interests and earn his large fees through the transmission of such a memo, especially one that left no trace on the memory of any of the key figures on the client's side.

Exposing the truth here matters a great deal in Islamabad. For one thing, the name of Pakistan and the Pakistani community in the U.S. has been dragged in by the Democrats in an effort to cast aspersions on the character of a Republican opponent. Moreover, even if the information in the July 25 memo is accurate, Mr. Siegel betrayed the confidence of his client, the Pakistani government, by not protecting its contents. Had he been an attorney representing a client, there would be a perfect case for disbarment. Unfortunately, lobbyists play by much looser rules.

Mr. Siegel's relationship with Pakistan has always been a troubled one. In 1988 he launched his lobbying business, around the time Benazir Bhutto became prime minister of Pakistan for the first time. Until the election, he worked for Ms. Bhutto on a pro bono basis. Under U.S. law, he was required to register as a foreign agent with the Justice Department, but he did not do so until after his appointment as a fully paid lobbyist. This oversight caused Ms. Bhutto some embarrassment when the Justice Department pointed out Mr. Siegel's failure to register, which was then reported in Pakistani newspapers. But all that was nothing compared with the full-blown controversy involving Mr. Siegel that erupted near the end of Ms. Bhutto's first term of office.

Benazir Bhutto

In the early 1980s, Islamabad had a subtle but effective lobbying operation in Washington as part of the close relationship with the U.S during the Afghan war. Presidents Reagan and Bush supported economic and military aid to Pakistan, and a low-key congressional lobbyist, Denis Neill, secured appropriations approval from a Democratic Congress. During this same period, Mr. Siegel was busy opposing appropriations for Pakistan on the grounds that it was under martial law. When news of this was made public in Islamabad in 1988, it caused quite a stir. So did the disclosure that Mr. Siegel had an unimpressive record as an international lobbyist: Apart from Pakistan, the government of tiny Aruba was his firm's only international client. Ms. Bhutto's parliamentary opponents questioned Mr. Siegel's selection as the country's lobbyist.

In 1990, soon after Ms. Bhutto's government was dismissed by the Pakistani president on charges of corruption and mismanagement, Mr. Siegel too lost his job. Along with the other concerns, the incoming government found out that Mr. Siegel—the man Ms. Bhutto had hired to represent all Pakistan—had issued a press release condemning the president of Pakistan for dismissing Ms. Bhutto, while Mr. Siegel was still on Islamabad's payroll. Mr. Siegel got his job back in 1993, when Ms. Bhutto returned to office. He lost his lucrative contract once more last November, when Ms. Bhutto's government was again dismissed on corruption charges.

Conflicts of loyalty, it seems, have been a trademark of Mr.

Siegel's career. His loyalty to Ms. Bhutto made him disloyal to his client—the government of Pakistan, which he condemned for dismissing her. This time, his loyalty to the Democratic Party has led him to betray his former client again, dragging the name of Pakistan into a controversy this nation has nothing to do with.

Ironically, it is Mr. Siegel's bogeyman, Rep. Burton, who has been a loyal and effective voice for Pakistan. Mr. Burton has supported Pakistan on issues including aid to India and ending the military embargo against Islamabad. Pakistani-Americans have donated voluntarily to his campaigns for this reason.

As a lobbyist, Mr. Siegel was being paid to win support in Congress for Pakistan. His job demanded that he lend a helping hand to congressmen favorably disposed to his client. For him now to express surprise that a Republican would ask him, a Democrat, for fund-raising help is not only unfair. It makes him appear grossly incompetent, or worse. If being a Democrat was more important than the money he was making as a lobbyist for Pakistan, Mr. Siegel should have resigned as lobbyist the day the Republicans gained control of Congress.

As Americans get down to examining campaign fund-raising abuses by their politicians, perhaps they should also look at the abuses of lobbyists working for foreign governments. Before he accuses Mr. Burton of shaking him down for campaign contributions, Mr. Siegel should explain why he took money from poverty-stricken Pakistan for lobbying services not adequately rendered.

Mr. Haqqani was press secretary to Prime Minister Benazir Bhutto. He has also served as Pakistan's secretary for information and broadcasting and ambassador to Sri Lanka.

Letters to the Editor

A Personally Motivated Attack on Me

I respond as the subject of Husain Haqqani's April 9 editorial-page commentary ("Burton's Accuser: The View From Pakistan").

Mr. Haqqani's piece does not reflect the record. For example, during the time I first served as the lobbyist for the government of Pakistan from 1988 to 1990, Pakistan became the third-largest recipient of foreign aid from the U.S., behind only Israel and Egypt, an extraordinary achievement in light of the end of the war in Afghanistan. During my second tenure as lobbyist for the government from 1993 to 1996, we were able to achieve the first adjustments to the Pressler Amendment, a statute that had been law since 1985 and caused sanctions against Pakistan since 1990. The successful passage of the so-called "Brown Amendment"—the lobbying strategy that I designed and helped to execute with others in Washington on the prime minister's behalf—not only provided for the resumption of U.S.-Pakistan bilateral cooperation in areas like economic development, anti-terrorism and international drug trafficking, but also allowed for the delivery of $368 million in Pakistani military equipment being held in the U.S. under the sanctions, including Orion aircraft and Harpoon missiles, and repatriation to Pakistan of $124 million that had been held since September 1990. Mr. Haqqani's suggestion that I was ineffective in the performance of my duties would seem to be belied by the results of my efforts.

Mr. Haqqani is also incorrect on the matter of documents surrounding the Burton affair. On July 25, 1996, I received a memorandum from Zafar Hilaly, an aide to Prime Minister Bhutto: "We were distressed to know from the Embassy that Congressman Dan Burton says that you were unable to keep certain promises regarding fund-raising for his re-election campaign and that you are also very un-helpful in other matters. So much so that you are no longer 'persona grata' in his office. This is most upsetting as he is a good friend of Pakistan. I would welcome your comments for onward transmission to the P.M." My response was immediate, and was reviewed in a process involving several people on my staff. Not only was the mem-orandum sent, it was thoroughly discussed in New York City in a long conversation between Mr. Hilaly and myself at the Waldorf Towers on Oct. 3, 1996.

Mr. Haqqani suggests that it is legitimate for a strong supporter of Pakistan to expect and to receive large contributions from the Pak-istani-American community, and apparently that there is nothing in-appropriate about Mr. Burton's involving the Pakistani Embassy and the government in Islamabad in his fund-raising schemes. This would seem to be the kind of quid pro quo policy/fund-raising link that is currently being investigated in the Senate and by a special task force of the Justice Department. It would seem appropriate that the House Committee on Government Reform and Oversight, chaired by Mr. Burton, should also turn its attention to these problematic for-eign entanglements in U.S. political affairs, as well as the fund-rais-ing abuses that are inherent when members of Congress threaten economic retribution against lobbyists who do not contribute to polit-ical campaigns.

Although Mr. Haqqani identifies himself as Benazir Bhutto's press secretary (a position he held for a short time before being fired by her in 1994), he is far better known for his long and enthusiastic ser-vice to the Pakistan Muslim League's Nawaz Sharif and the man in charge of the disinformation campaign against Prime Minister Bhut-to from 1988 to 1990, which aimed at destabilizing her government. One element of that disinformation campaign, for which Mr. Haqqani personally apologized to me in February 1994, was a bar-rage of anti-ethnic attacks against me in the press and the parlors of Pakistan.

I am surprised that you chose to publish an inaccurate and per-sonally motivated attack that failed to address the most significant issues raised in the situation with Mr. Burton: Did a member of Congress solicit campaign contributions from a lobbyist for a foreign government, and when the member was unsatisfied with the level of contribution, did he cut off access to his own office and threaten the lobbyist's access to other members of Congress and involve a foreign embassy in pressuring the lobbyist to contribute? Additionally, perhaps Mr. Burton should also appear before the grand jury and testify under oath as to these events, as I did.

MARK A. SIEGEL

Chevy Chase, Md.

Editorial Feature

The Witch Hunt in the House

Rep. Dan Burton can be an engaging fellow. Overcoming a poor childhood with an abusive father, he's a plain-speaking, conservative Republican congressman.

But the 58-year-old Indianan is ill-suited to his current task: To lead a House investigation into campaign-financing misdeeds by President Bill Clinton. Mr.

 **Politics & People**

By Albert R. Hunt

Burton espouses fringe views and theories; he also has poor judgment and an erratic staff. And he is embroiled in his own campaign-financing scandal, which could prove dreadfully serious.

The House Government Reform and Oversight Committee will vote today on the nature and scope of these hearings. The Republican leadership has two objectives: To cut up the president and to avoid anything that might bring pressure to change the sordid campaign-financing system that's so advantageous to incumbents. Many at the White House, meanwhile, privately relish Mr. Burton's role, figuring it will discredit serious inquiry into some outrageous conduct.

The biggest losers will be taxpayers. The Burton-led circus, which could cost between $6 million and $12 million, will overlap the more substantive Senate hearings. "My goal is not to get Bill Clinton," Mr. Burton insists in an interview. But he quickly adds that he possesses information that "strongly indicates illegal activity took place."

If Sen. Fred Thompson, who heads the Senate inquiry, makes that assertion, take notice. But it is hard to take Rep. Burton seriously given his background. He is obsessed with the late White House lawyer Vince Foster's suicide; he once even conducted a mock shooting in his backyard in hopes of proving that Mr. Foster was murdered. Although Whitewater independent counsel Kenneth Starr is expected soon to join all other relevant law enforcement authorities in concluding that Mr. Foster committed suicide, Mr. Burton says he still doesn't believe it. A few years ago the same Mr. Burton advocated mandatory AIDS testing of every American.

He also has little regard for fairness. The blizzard of allegations he's leveled include charges that the White House is employing "hard drug users," but he's never substantiated that. The more than 100 subpoenas that he has issued include one for all visitors to the residential portion of the White House since 1993; what's he going to do with all of Chelsea Clinton's friends?

Mr. Burton's staff is worse, particularly David Bossie, a 31-year-old wacko who once helped write a book entitled "Slick Willie: Why Americans Cannot Trust Bill Clinton." A few months ago Mr. Bossie duplicitously obtained a Democratic fund-raiser's phone logs from another House committee and leaked them.

Chairman Burton insists he was outraged and will fire Mr. Bossie if he does this again; few take this seriously. This wild-eyed conspiratorialist—"Ollie North without the judgment," in the words of one participant—inflames all of Mr. Burton's already incendiary instincts. (Rep. Burton seeks to downplay Mr. Bossie's clout, citing his "influential" committee counsel—but then forgets his last name.)

Republican members, ranging from moderate Rep. Chris Shays to conservative Rep. Mark Sanford, say the inquiry must include congressional fund-raising abuses to avoid becoming a partisan witch hunt. Chairman Burton and the GOP leadership are adamantly against this.

Such an inquiry not only would deflect from the get-Clinton plan but also could be exceedingly embarrassing. In addition to the many House fund-raising scams, Mr. Burton has his own problems. The most serious involve foreign policy-related contributions, the sort that are at the core of the most significant charges against the Clinton campaign.

Mr. Burton has parlayed his position on the House International Relations Committee to rake in big campaign contributions even though he has a safe seat, winning 75% of the vote last November. While championing their causes he has raised money from Puerto Rican-Americans, Cuban-Americans and most successfully from Sikhs, Kashmiris and Pakistanis in this country who like his anti-India and pro-Pakistan positions.

Mark Siegel, formerly the top lobbyist for the government of Pakistan, charges that Mr. Burton shook him down for contributions last year. When he didn't deliver enough, says Mr. Siegel, a long-time Democratic Party activist, the Indiana lawmaker threatened him, even complaining to the Pakistani ambassador.

Mr. Burton has called Mr. Siegel a "liar," and charges that this "is a transparent attempt by the Democrats to stop my investigation . . . I will not back down one foot." Yet the FBI is investigating and a grand jury has already convened.

Dan Burton

The evidence that Mr. Siegel offers is compelling. Documents from last July show that a top aide to then-Prime Minister Benazir Bhutto faxed Mr. Siegel that her government "is distressed" to learn that he was unable to keep "certain promises regarding fund-raising" to Mr. Burton and therefore is "no longer 'persona grata' [sic]" in the congressman's office. That conforms to a conversation that Siegel associate Brian Sailer says he had with Mr. Burton about that time in which the Indiana congressman railed about Mr. Siegel not delivering enough money; therefore, Mr. Sailer says, the congressman declared Mr. Siegel "persona non gratis [sic]."

Mr. Siegel, in a memo to Islamabad written July 25, 1996—months before any of the Clinton fund-raising scandals arose and before Mr. Burton ascended to the chairmanship of the Government Reform and Oversight Committee—laid out the case of Mr. Burton's shakedown that Mr. Siegel is now apparently telling the grand jury. Moreover, three other lobbyists who worked with Mr. Siegel, including Mr. Sailer, a Republican, tell the same story, and presumably will do so before the grand jury.

Mr. Burton's version—on the advice of counsel he now refuses to elaborate—doesn't hold up. On occasion he has dismissed the notion that he sought fund-raising help from the Pakistani lobbyists. Yet in 1995 Mr. Siegel actually signed a $500 contribution from a pro-Pakistani group. Under other questioning, Mr. Burton has admitted that he mentioned "in an offhand" manner to the Pakistani ambassador that Mr. Siegel had failed to deliver on fund-raising promises. The most plausible explanation for this admission—the frank Mr. Burton does little in an "offhand" way—is that he wanted to punish Mr. Siegel by costing him his job.

The Hobbs Act explicitly prohibits congressmen from extorting lobbyists and others for campaign contributions. Although rarely invoked, Stanley Brand, an expert on this law and a counsel to many Democrats, says of the allegations against Mr. Burton: "On its face this is a very heavy one."

And Republican Rep. Shays acknowledges, "If this isn't resolved soon, it's going to cause serious problems for this committee." Even if Mr. Burton steps down or is forced out, this ill-advised—and costly—investigative escapade should be curtailed. Otherwise taxpayers will be treated to a multimillion-dollar travesty that would make the late Joe McCarthy proud.

Toward Accountability

In the spring of 1997, as skirmishes continued in Washington over slowly growing campaign finance probes, the original Whitewater issues re-emerged in various judicial forums. In April, convicted Whitewater felon James McDougal received a light sentence after Independent Counsel Kenneth Starr testified that Mr. McDougal's cooperation had resulted in new "information on a wide range of matters," including "documents and witnesses." Later that month, an Arkansas judge approved the extension of a Whitewater grand jury after Mr. Starr filed a notice calling for further investigation of "perjury, obstruction of the administration of justice, concealment and destruction of evidence, and intimidation of witnesses."

In an editorial titled "Whitewater and Watergate," the Journal noted that while there were many differences, Watergate, like Whitewater, was about abuse of the powers of the Presidency. " 'Obstruction of justice,' the term Independent Counsel Kenneth Starr invoked in extending the Whitewater grand jury in Little Rock, resonates with themes from the Watergate epic a generation ago. When the House Judiciary Committee voted up the bill of impeachment that led to Richard Nixon's resignation, count one was obstruction."

On May 2, the White House unexpectedly announced it was going to the Supreme Court to overturn a previously sealed Eighth Circuit Court of Appeals ruling that notes government lawyers took in Whitewater-related conversations with Hillary Clinton were not protected by attorney-client privilege and must be turned over to Mr.

Starr. "The Eighth Circuit, like Judge Royce Lamberth in Washington, seems to be increasingly impatient with representations from Clinton Administration lawyers," the Journal observed. The appellate court had "also ordered the Paula Jones case to go forward, writing that the Constitution 'did not create a monarchy.'" The Supreme Court, which had been instrumental in Watergate in *U.S. v. Nixon*, now had Whitewater on its docket, as well as the Jones case.

REVIEW & OUTLOOK

Pepperdine Scores

Kenneth Starr, already No. 1 draft choice at Pepperdine Law School, ran up a huge number of yards yesterday for the Independent Counsel probe into Whitewater. It is hard to come to any other con-clusion from what happened at the sentencing of convicted Whitewater co-conspirator Jim Mc-Dougal. The judge could have given McDougal 84 years for his conviction on 18 felonies. Instead he said from the bench he was taking into ac-count the defendant's "co-operation," and hand-ed down a three-year term.

Ken Starr

Whitewater was bubbling yesterday with the McDougal sentencing, Janet Reno's refusing an independent counsel for campaign contributions and fallout from the indictment of Dan Harmon (see page 395). Earlier, of course, we had Hillary Clinton's assertion that the only people who still thought Whitewater amounted to any-thing probably also believed in UFOs and the Hale-Bopp comet. Just slightly below this level of visibility the past few weeks was a series of news articles detailing how White House aides excavated some $500,000 worth of business for the soon-to-be-convicted assistant at-torney general Webster Hubbell. This caused much speculation—de-rided by the White House—that the purpose of these jobs was to keep Mr. Hubbell's mouth shut about Whitewater.

Most notably joining Mr. Hubbell on this side of the Whitewater divide so far has been Susan McDougal, Jim's wife, who sits in jail because she refuses to speak to a grand jury about Mr. Clinton's Whitewater involvement. Beyond this, Ms. McDougal is facing possible conviction at a May trial on charges that she swindled $150,000 from conductor Zubin Mehta in California.

Now, it appears, at least two parties to the Whitewater real estate deals have talked. First David Hale's testimony led to the convictions of Jim and Susan McDougal and of the sitting governor of Arkansas, Jim Guy Tucker. Now Jim McDougal himself; Mr. Starr said yesterday the defendant had talked with the IC's staff on "a wide range of matters, including matters heretofore unknown to us, including matters known to only a few individuals."

While Mr. McDougal has been widely viewed as an unreliable witness, Mr. Starr pointedly noted that the McDougal contribution to the case now includes "documents and witnesses." Some of the fruits of his contribution were presented to the sentencing judge under seal.

What all this suggests is that the Starr investigation has suddenly moved to a higher level of seriousness for all parties. It is important to note that at this juncture the legal exposure for the Clintons no longer has to do with land deals in the Ozarks, but lives on in obstruction of justice, false statements or even perjury. They are exemplified by the questions Susan McDougal refused to answer: Did President Clinton know of David Hale's illegal loans to her Master Marketing, and did the President testify truthfully when he gave his White House deposition for her trial?

No doubt Susan's former husband has now answered these questions. More importantly, he seems to have offered leads that have persuaded the prosecutor and judge that his testimony is more than the latest change in his bipolar moods. In remarks outside the courtroom afterward, Mr. Starr pointedly noted that the Independent Counsel's investigative mandate extends to Mr. McDougal, Hillary Clinton and Bill Clinton. Connect these dots, and you have the latest in a series of bad days for the first couple.

Editorial Feature

Big News From Arkansas

By MICAH MORRISON

LITTLE ROCK, Ark.—To Whitewater aficionados the exciting news of the moment is neither the Jim McDougal sentencing hearing showing his cooperation with the prosecutors nor Janet Reno's decision not to appoint an independent counsel on campaign contributions. Rather, it's last Friday's indictment here of Dan Harmon.

Mr. Harmon served as prosecuting attorney for Arkansas's Seventh Judicial District from 1990 until his abrupt resignation in July 1996. Earlier, he had insinuated himself as a volunteer investigator and later special prosecutor in the controversial "train deaths" murder case of teenagers Kevin Ives and Don Henry, unsolved since 1987. A federal grand jury charges that Mr. Harmon (and two associates, Roger Walls and William Murphy) "operated the Seventh Judicial District Prosecuting Attorney's Office as a conduit to obtain monetary benefits to themselves and others, and to participate and conceal criminal activities."

Distributing Cocaine

Mr. Harmon faces two counts of conspiracy to distribute cocaine and two counts relating to the production of methamphetamine. Also four extortion counts and a count under RICO, the Racketeer Influenced and Corrupt Organizations law. Plus one count of witness tampering and another of retaliating against a witness, for physically attacking Arkansas Democrat-Gazette reporter Rodney Bowers last May.

The defendants are not directly connected with President Clinton. However, the Harmon indictment is the clearest charge yet that during Gov. Clinton's tenure certain Arkansas law enforcement officials were dealing in drugs. The new charges were brought to the grand jury by Paula Casey, Mr. Clinton's hand-picked U.S. attorney for the Eastern District of Arkansas, who says that an FBI and IRS investigation is continuing. Mr. Harmon vigorously denies the charges, saying they are the result of "a federal bureaucracy that's out of control."

Mr. Harmon knows something about being out of control. In March 1996, two months prior to allegedly assaulting Mr. Bowers, he

---

The Harmon indictment is the clearest charge yet that during Gov. Clinton's tenure certain Arkansas law enforcement officials were dealing in drugs.

---

briefly kidnapped and threatened to kill Holly DuVall, his estranged wife. She had been arrested on drug charges in November 1995, and was thought to have cooperated with the corruption probe. In her condominium, police found an evidence package that was supposed to contain two pounds of pure cocaine and be locked in the safe of Mr. Harmon's drug task force. It proved to contain a silicon-based substance.

Mr. Harmon has a long and colorful career in Arkansas law enforcement. In 1980, he was running unopposed for a second term as prosecuting attorney when he abruptly withdrew and declared personal bankruptcy. He came back from political oblivion with the train deaths case. When Ives and Henry were found dead on railroad tracks southwest of Little Rock in August 1987, Gov. Clinton's medical examiner, Fahmy Malak, quickly ruled the deaths "accidental," saying the teenagers had fallen asleep after smoking too much marijuana. After a public outcry, a second autopsy concluded the boys had been murdered, and Mr. Clinton's solicitude for Dr. Malak in this and other cases became a subject of controversy. Gov. Clinton named Department of Health Director Joycelyn Elders to head a commission to review Dr. Malak. She cleared him of improprieties and recommended a raise. Dr. Malak was eased out of office on the eve of Mr. Clinton's 1992 presidential run.

Shortly after the death of the boys, Mr. Harmon approached Linda Ives, Kevin's mother, to help with the investigation on a volunteer basis. Later he persuaded a judge to name him special prosecutor to supervise the investigation. In 1990, he was elected again as the local prosecutor. But meanwhile, he'd come under scrutiny in a 1989 corruption probe alleging drug distribution, money laundering and political payoffs. In June 1991, then-U.S. Attorney Chuck Banks cleared Mr. Harmon, saying there was "no evidence of drug-related misconduct by any public official."

Dan Harmon

Mrs. Ives is not impressed with the current indictment. She's conducted a decade-long campaign over the airwaves, and lately the Internet (http://www.idmedia.com); her account was elaborated in a story on this page on April 18, 1996. She charges that Mr. Harmon was at the murder scene and that "high state and federal officials" had participated in a coverup. "I firmly believe my son and Don Henry were killed because they witnessed a drug drop by an airplane connected to the Mena drug smuggling routes." She scornfully notes that the current indictment only goes back to August 1991, two months after U.S. Attorney Banks cleared Mr. Harmon in the earlier probe. "Are we to believe Dan Harmon was clean in June, but dirty in August?"

Mrs. Ives might be dismissed as a grieving mother grasping at straws, but in charging that Mr. Harmon was involved in the boys' murder she has found some allies among investigators. One of them is Jean Duffey, who in 1989 headed a Seventh Judicial District drug task force. Ms. Duffey left the state when Mr. Harmon filed charges against her, later found to be baseless. "We had witnesses telling us about low-flying aircraft and informants testifying about drug pickups" in the area of the train deaths, Ms. Duffey said last year. She also says that a local official told her she was "not to use the drug task force to investigate any public officials."

Someone else who believes Linda Ives is former Saline County Detective John Brown, who reopened the case in 1993 and found a new witness he says saw Mr. Harmon on the tracks the night the boys died. Detective Brown's work caught the attention of the FBI's new top man in Little Rock, Special Agent I.C. Smith. A storied figure in the bureau, Mr. Smith was sent to Little Rock in August 1995 by Director Louis Freeh. The Harmon indictment is part of a new interest in public corruption by investigators under Mr. Smith and Ms. Casey.

Money Laundering

Earlier last week, Ms. Casey also indicted Arkansas lawyer Mark Cambiano on 31 money laundering and conspiracy counts. The indictment said the $380,000 Mr. Cambiano allegedly laundered had come from a methamphetamine ring, and that $20,000 of it went to the Democratic National Committee and $9,770 to President Clinton's inaugural fund. Ms. Casey said that although Mr. Cambiano laundered the money, he was not involved in drug trafficking, and that there was no reason to believe those receiving the contributions knew of their tainted origins. Mr. Cambiano denies the charges. The allegations arose from a drug investigation that resulted in guilty pleas from Willard Burnett, alleged leader of the ring, and Carl Poteete, former Conway County sheriff.

Whether or not the Smith and Casey investigations proceed to further revelations about the "train deaths" and Mena, the signs of a shifting landscape are unmistakable. Exhibit One: Dan Harmon.

Mr. Morrison is a Journal editorial page writer.

REVIEW & OUTLOOK

FBI Leadership

With news swirling about the Federal Bureau of Investigation, it might be an apt time to review the last change of leadership there. It took place, you probably do not recall, on the most tempestuous weekend of the Clinton Presidency.

FBI Director William Sessions, under fire over expense accounts and the deportment of his wife, had already tendered his resignation,

Louis Freeh

pending a replacement. But on Saturday, July 17, 1993, he was told to resign immediately or be fired. Bearing the message was Attorney General Janet Reno, Deputy Attorney General Philip Heymann, White House Counsel Bernard Nussbaum and now notorious Associate Attorney General Webster Hubbell. On the way out of the meeting, Mr. Sessions stumbled on the curb and broke his elbow. His replacement, former FBI agent and New York Judge Louis Freeh, was announced the following Tuesday morning.

"It had taken strenuous argument from Nussbaum to persuade Clinton not to name his old friend and fellow Rhodes Scholar Richard Stearns to the post," James B. Stewart reports in his book "Blood Sport." Mr. Stearns is a judge on the Massachusetts Superior Court, and that fateful Monday our own columns had reviewed his résumé: "Judge Stearns and President Clinton were war protesters together as Rhodes Scholars at Oxford. Judge Stearns was

REVIEW & OUTLOOK

Whitewater and Watergate

"Obstruction of justice," the term Independent Counsel Kenneth Starr invoked in extending the Whitewater grand jury in Little Rock, resonates with themes from the Watergate epic a generation ago. When the House Judiciary Committee voted up the bill of impeachment that led to Richard Nixon's resignation, count one was obstruction.

Watergate was not about a two-bit burglary, that is, but about the abuse of the powers of the Presidency. The committee charged that the President, "in violation of his constitutional duty to take care that the laws be faithfully executed, has prevented, obstructed, and impeded the administration of justice." Seeking to cover up the initial misdeed, President Nixon and his highest aides dug themselves ever deeper into a legal morass that led the President to disgrace and the aides to jail. The final "smoking gun" tape-recorded the President issuing instructions to induce the CIA to get the FBI to call off its investigation of the burglary by claiming bogus national security concerns. With this revelation, the President's last support vanished and he left office.

Mr. Starr's filings this week [page 413] ring similar chords, talking of "extensive evidence of possible obstruction of the administration of justice," of resistance to subpoenas, of "grand jury litigation under seal" over privileges and documents, of *in camera* citations to the court. It calls for further investigation of "perjury, obstruction of the administration of justice, concealment and destruction of evidence, and intimidation of witnesses."

These parallels are all the more ironic because Hillary Rodham Clinton served on the legal staff of the Watergate Committee. Former White House Counsel Bernard Nussbaum also worked for the House Watergate Committee, while the minority counsel to the Senate investigation was Senator Fred Thompson, now heading the Senate inquiry into the Clinton campaign contributions scandal.

Rep. Bob Barr makes some sport at Mrs. Clinton's expense alongside [page 410] by citing the 1974 staff memo on grounds for impeachment. The Georgia Republican has written Judiciary Chairman Henry Hyde to officially request the start of an impeachment inquiry. Rep. Hyde has said he's started staff studies "just staying ahead of the curve" and not for serious action "unless we have what really amounts to a smoking gun."

Bill Clinton

Rep. Barr, a former U.S. Attorney, makes the legal case that in Whitewater and the campaign funds scandal we are dealing with potential impeachment material. Even as a legal case, of course, there remains no small matter of proof. Were the payments to Webb Hubbell really hush money, for example, and were the Rose Law Firm billing records intentionally withheld while under subpoena? And to what extent was Bill Clinton personally involved—in Watergate phraseology, "what did the President know and when did he know it?"

*   *   *

While Mr. Starr is obviously digging in these fields, we have no reason to believe he's reached the mother lode. The Watergate impeachment case, after all, was built on the testimony of John Dean, Mr. Nixon's White House Counsel. Even then, it had to be cinched by tape recordings. Mr. Starr can't even get the cooperation of Susan McDougal. The Arkansas Democrat-Gazette, recently on an anti-Clinton roll, cites Webb Hubbell's Camp David visit while editorializing, "If only Richard Nixon had been less stiff, he might still be jollying John Dean into silence—and Watergate would have stayed the name of another Washington apartment complex."

Writing recently in the New York Times, Watergate survivor Leonard Garment also remarked that President Clinton "seems infinitely elastic, positive and resilient." By contrast President Nixon's morose defensiveness was shaped by his "prize collection of emotional scars" from the Alger Hiss case. Even more important, "Mr. Clinton has not been a central participant and target in a debate as polarizing as the conflict over the Vietnam War." President Nixon's

Richard Nixon

resignation, and the impeachment of President Andrew Johnson, came at already impassioned turns in the nation's history. Today's mixture of contentment and cynicism insulates a President from scandal.

In a recent Watergate symposium, Mr. Garment also made the point that we should not expect Presidents to have normal personalities. "The presidential gene," he said, "is filled with sociopathic qualities—brilliant, erratic, lying, cheating, expert at mendacity, generous, loony, driven by a sense of mission. a very unusual person. Nixon was one of the strangest of this strange group."

No President is likely to meet the clinical definition of a sociopath; what psychiatrists call an "anti-social personality," a complete obliviousness to the normal rules of society, is evident in early adolescence and will to lead to jail rather than high office. Sociopaths, the textbooks tell us, are seemingly intelligent and typically charming, though not good at sustaining personal or sexual relationships. They lie remarkably well, feel no guilt or remorse, and are skillful at blaming their problems on others. A most striking feature is, as one text puts it, "He often demonstrates a lack of anxiety or tension that can be grossly incongruous with the situation."

Childhood symptoms are essential to this clinical diagnosis, and Bill Clinton's experience in Hope and Hot Springs, while troubled, supports no such speculation. Yet clearly he has "the presidential gene," perhaps even more so than Richard Nixon. And this catalog of traits is ideally suited to, say, finding some way to overcome seemingly impossible election odds, or withstanding the onslaught of scandal. As Mr. Garment summarizes the present outlook, "The country is in for a year or more of dizzy, distracting prime-time scandal politics. But I wouldn't hold my breath waiting for the ultimate political cataclysm."

*   *   *

While we take this as the most likely outcome, our judgment is that in fact Mr. Clinton is guilty of essentially the same things over which Mr. Nixon was hounded from office—abusing his office to cover up criminal activity by himself and his accomplices, and misleading the public with a campaign of lies about it. From the first days of his Administration, with the firing of all sitting U.S. Attorneys and Webb Hubbell's intervention in a corruption trial, we have seen a succession of efforts to subvert the administration of justice. The head of the FBI was fired, and days afterward a high official died of gunshot wounds, and the investigation ended without crime scene photos or autopsy X-rays. Honorable Democrats like Phillip Heymann have fled the Justice Department, leaving it today nearly vacant; White House Counsel have committed serial resignation. Yet Mr. Clinton remains President and still commands respect in the polls. Handled with enough audacity, it seems, the Presidency is a powerful office after all.

There is even a school of thought, implicit in talk about "more important" work for the nation, that the coverup *should* succeed. Yet as we look back on Watergate, the nation went through a highly beneficial, even necessary learning experience. Whitewater carries a similar stake, simply put: learning how our government operates, whether laws are being faithfully executed. With sunshine, citizens can make their own judgments, and have plenty of opportunity to express them, starting with the 1998 mid-term elections. But it is essential that the investigators—Mr. Starr, the FBI, Senator Thompson, Rep. Dan Burton and newly vigilant members of the press—get moral support against the deterrent attacks to which they've uniformly been subjected.

Whitewater did not prevent Mr. Clinton's re-election, though the scandal was much more advanced than Watergate was during Mr. Nixon's 1973 landslide. When President Nixon left we wrote that he had so severely damaged his own credibility he could no longer govern. We do not know how Whitewater will finally end, but we are starting to wonder whether we ultimately understood Watergate.

Letters to the Editor

Clinton's 'Sociopathic Features'

This is in response to your April 25 editorial "Whitewater and Watergate," in which you say that Nixon adviser Leonard Garment has made the point that we should not expect presidents to have normal personalities. Mr. Garment said, "The presidential gene is filled with sociopathic qualities—brilliant, erratic, lying, cheating, expert at mendacity, generous, loony, driven by a sense of mission, a very unusual person. Nixon was one of the strangest of this strange group."

Your editorial also states: "No President is likely to meet the clinical definition of a sociopath. . . ."

Many of us in the psychiatric profession, regardless of our political persuasion, have been most curious about these psychological characteristics of President Clinton. We have followed him for years, examined his early history, and have noted a pattern that's quite recognizable throughout his Arkansas years and his years in the presidency. We believe that he has more than the average number of "sociopathic features" that could be expected to exist in a president. We also see consistency. You will recall the description of him as being "a liar in the past, a liar now and always will be a liar" on some CNN program. But we see that he has the capacity to charm. For that matter, "will charm your pants off." That would include your wallet, your change purse, and anything else that is significant on your person.

One of the characteristics of a sociopath is that he looks rather poorly on paper, but in person is extremely effective, both provocative and convincing. Mr. Clinton, like all "good sociopaths," externalizes every event that is negative and takes credit for every event that turns out positive. Sociopaths are wonderful blamers. They are always ready to identify fault elsewhere. Mr. Clinton measures the atmosphere around him with a very effective wet finger in the air. He doesn't act unless he has a very good idea that what he wants will occur.

But most significant is the fact that he talks a good story as to whom he cares about and what he plans "for you"; in reality he cares only for himself. He chooses people who perpetuate his myth and, not surprisingly, he disappoints them, frustrates them and betrays them, leaving them wondering how in the world they got into this mess.

Yes, a sociopathic president is dangerous. The danger is not only what he will do in the White House, especially when it comes to foreign policy, but how he affects the reputation of the office. Trust in the office of the presidency may never be the same.

Irwin S. Finkelstein, M.D.

Linda R. Finkelstein

Mesa, Ariz.

*   *   *

June 13, 1997

Character Assassination

The response of your correspondents, Dr. Irwin S. and Linda R. Finkelstein, to your April 25 editorial "Whitewater and Watergate" cannot stand unchallenged. Be it noted at the outset that I have always shared most of the views to be found in your pages, and certainly could never be considered a supporter of the Clintons. That said, let me take issue with both the text and some of the obvious misapplications of the diagnostic nomenclature and clinical practice that seem to have inspired their communication to you.

Addressing a truncated statement drawn from your editorial, to wit, "No President is likely to meet the clinical definition of a sociopath. . . ." the Finkelsteins suggest that "many of us have been most curious about these psychological characteristics of President

Clinton. We have followed him for years, examined his early history, and have noted a pattern that's now quite recognizable. . . . We believe that he has *more* than the average number of "sociopathic features than could be expected to exist in a president." The writers then proceed to offer us further putative characteristics of a sociopath and presumably their application to the president's behaviors and character structure. What they do not provide are some requisite qualifiers, for example that the so-called true sociopath is rather rare in any population, and is more likely than not to be a loner, misfit and hardly in receipt of the social skills one needs to succeed in this world, never mind to be the president of the United States.

They also should be aware of the serious difficulties involved in making such a "diagnosis," especially when there is no possibility of making those necessary kinds of clinical observations that only the interactive setting of the clinical interview can provide. Likewise, your correspondents should be aware that the grouping of erstwhile character traits or subjectively honed observations of behavior into a personality disorder is a tentative exercise at best, having very limited epistemological validity. The glib use of diagnostic rubrics is a kind of psychiatric name-calling that has been around for a long time. It is most unbecoming whenever it is used and only serves to decrease the credibility of the field.

To engage in such sophomoric rhetoric is absolutely inappropriate professional behavior in my view. It is as dangerous as it is dilettantish. It serves only to depreciate a profession and a discipline that deserves to be taken seriously, but only when we acquit ourselves in a serious manner.

J. GORDON MAGUIRE, M.D.
Training and Supervising Analyst
Institute for Psychoanalysis
Chicago

* * *

This type of pseudo-scientific character assassination disguised as objective psychiatric diagnosis has no place in serious public discourse. It is impossible to make a valid diagnosis at long distance, without formal examination of the supposed patient, and indeed it is unethical to do so and to proclaim the results in public. When Barry Goldwater was running for president, an unscrupulous publisher solicited such opinions from anti-Goldwater psychiatrists, some of whom were foolish enough to cooperate with this mud-slinging exercise. The uproar in the professional community at that time was instantaneous and gratifying. Let us not indulge in such dirty politics again. It slanders the president and makes the profession of psychiatry look ridiculous. Criticize the president's actions and comments—don't take cheap shots hiding behind so-called professional objectivity.

HENRY KAMINER, M.D.
Past President, N.J. Psychiatric
Assocation
Past President, N.J. Psychoanalytic Association
Tenafly, N.J.

* * *

The American Psychiatric Association's Code of Ethics expressly prohibits such gratuitous statements. Specifically, "The Principles of Medical Ethics with Annotations Especially for Psychiatry," Section 7.3 states:

"On occasion psychiatrists are asked for an opinion about an individual who is in the light of public attention, or who has disclosed information about himself/herself through public media. In such circumstances, a psychiatrist may share with the public his/her expertise about psychiatric issues in general. However, it is unethical for a psychiatrist to offer a professional opinion about that specific individual unless he/she has conducted an examination and has been granted proper authorization for such a statement."

Assuming that Dr. Finklestein has not examined Mr. Clinton, or if he has examined him, has not obtained his permission for release of medical information, then Dr. Finklestein's comments appear to represent a violation of the Ethical Code of our profession.

PETER B. GRUENBERG, M.D.
Chair, Ethics committee
American Psychiatric Association
Beverly Hills, Calif.

Editorial Feature

Mrs. Clinton's Defense of Impeachment

Dear Mrs. Clinton:

In February 1974 the staff of the Nixon impeachment inquiry issued a report produced by a group of lawyers and researchers assigned with developing a scholarly memorandum setting forth the "constitutional grounds for presidential impeachment."

You were a member of that group of lawyers and researchers, barely, I am sure, able to conceal your dislike for President Nixon. Within the year, Nixon would leave office disgraced, having witnessed articles of impeachment voted against him by the House Judiciary Committee, based in part on your report.

Hillary Clinton

I must give you and your colleagues credit. You did not appear to have let personal animus influence your work product, at least not the final, published report. In fact, the report you and your colleagues produced appears objective, fair, well researched and consistent with other materials reflecting and commenting on impeachment. And it is every bit as relevant today as it was 23 years ago.

I presume—but I must ask whether—you stand by your research and analysis today. You said in 1974 that impeachment, as understood by the framers of our Constitution, reflected the long history of the term used at least since late-14th-century England: "one of the tools used by the English" to make government "more responsive and responsible" (page 4 of your report).

You also noted then—clearly in response to those who mistakenly claimed impeachment presupposes or requires a violation of criminal law—that British history, to which our Founding Fathers turned for guidance, clearly envisaged impeachment as a tool to correct "corruption in office" that "alleged damage to the state," and was "not necessarily limited to common law or statutory . . . crimes" (page 7).

You quoted James Wilson, who at the Pennsylvania ratification convention described the executive (that is, the president) as not being above the law, but rather "in his public character" subject to it "by impeachment" (page 9).

You also—quite correctly—noted then that the constitutional draftsmen chose the terms describing the circumstances under which a president could be impeached very carefully and deliberately. You noted that "high crimes and misdemeanors" did not denote criminal offenses in the sense that prosecutors employ such terms in modern trials. Rather, in your well-researched memorandum, you correctly noted that the phrase "high crimes and misdemeanors" was substituted for George Mason's less precise term in an earlier draft of the Constitution: "maladministration" (page 12 of your report). Not only that, but your further research led you to quote Blackstone's "Commentaries on the Laws of England" in support of your conclusion that "high crimes and misdemeanors" meant not a criminal offense but an injury to the state or system of government (page 12). I applaud the extent and clarity of your research.

You even note that the U.S. Supreme Court, in deciding questions of intent, must construe phrases such as "high crimes and misdemeanors" not according to modern usage, but according to what the framers meant when they adopted them (page 12 once again). Magnificent research!

Even Alexander Hamilton finds a place in your research. You quote from his Federalist No. 65 that impeachment relates to "misconduct of public men, or, in other words, from the abuse or violation of some public trust" that is "of a nature . . . *political* [emphasis in original]" (page 13 of your report).

Finally, in bringing your research forward from the constitutional drafting documents themselves, you find support for your properly broad interpretation of "high crimes and misdemeanors" in no less a legal scholar than Justice Joseph Story. I was in awe of your use of Justice Story's "Commentaries on the Constitution" (1833) supporting your proposition that "impeachment . . . applies to offenses of 'a political character' . . . [that] must be examined upon very broad and comprehensive principles of public policy and duty" (pages 16 and 17 of your report). I could not have said it better.

You even note that the specific instances in which impeachment has been employed in our country's history "placed little emphasis on criminal conduct" and were used to remove public officials who had "seriously undermined public confidence" through their "course of conduct" (page 21).

Mrs. Clinton, when I first raised the notion last month that the House should take but the first step in determining whether impeachment might lie against President Clinton for a pattern of abuse of office and improper administration of his duties, little did I realize your scholarly work 23 years ago would provide clear historical and legal basis and precedent for my proposition.

Amazingly, the words you used in your report are virtually identical to those I use today. For example, you said in 1974, much as I did in my March 11, 1997, letter to Judiciary Chairman Hyde, that "[i]mpeachment is the first step in a remedial process" (page 24 of your report) to correct "serious offenses" that "subvert" our government and "undermine the integrity of office" (page 26).

Thank you, Mrs. Clinton, for giving Congress a road map for beginning our inquiry.

Sincerely,
BOB BARR (R., GA.)
Member of Congress

Editorial Feature

Starr's Motion to Extend Grand Jury

Portions of a motion filed this week by Independent Counsel Kenneth W. Starr to extend the term of the Arkansas grand jury looking into the Whitewater affair by six months. Judge Susan Webber Wright granted the motion.

24. This grand jury has also heard extensive evidence of possible obstruction of the administration of justice relating to the matters within the Independent Counsel's jurisdiction. That portion of the investigation cannot be completed by May 7, 1997.

25. The conduct of the overall investigation has been delayed in some respects by a failure of persons and/or entities to make timely or complete production of documents pursuant to grand jury subpoena.

26. There have been efforts by some persons and entities to challenge grand jury subpoenas through the filing of motions to quash, or resisting compliance even in the face of a motion to compel by the Independent Counsel. This has led to grand jury litigation under seal, some of which is ongoing.

27. In addition, there have been assertions of privileges which, in some instances, the Independent Counsel believes are unfounded and invalid, and which have been or will be the subject of additional grand jury litigation.

28. Some witnesses and entities have refused to be interviewed and/or to produce documents voluntarily, taking the position they

will not testify or produce documents absent a subpoena.

Conclusion

The Independent Counsel has been vested with jurisdiction to fully investigate and prosecute certain matters. This includes authority to investigate and prosecute federal crimes that may arise out of the above described matters, and all related matters, including perjury, obstruction of the administration of justice, concealment and destruction of evidence, and intimidation of witnesses. This grand jury has dedicated much time to these important matters. It would impede and further delay the investigations of these matters if this grand jury were discharged and a new grand jury had to be summoned.

For all these reasons, and for those reasons which have been made known to the court *in camera*, it is respectfully requested that the Court issue an Order Extending the term of this grand jury an additional six months to November 7, 1997.

Respectfully submitted,
KENNETH W. STARR
Independent Counsel
By: W. Hickman Ewing, Jr.
Deputy Independent Counsel

Editorial Feature

A Pattern of Stonewalling

By William F. Clinger

As the former chairman of the House Government Reform and Oversight Committee, I have watched with a great interest and sympathy the efforts of my successor, Rep. Dan Burton (R., Ind.), to get the Clinton administration to comply with his legitimate requests for information and documents. At issue this time is the investigation of questionable White House fund-raising activities and related national security issues. It is clear—as it often was during my tenure—that the administration is consistently resisting Congress's oversight efforts and denying the public its right to know the facts.

We are seeing the same pattern of dissembling, stonewalling and lack of cooperation that I endured for four years, first as ranking GOP member and then as chairman of the committee. This pattern was established during the Clinton administration's first months in office.

In conjunction with the first lady's effort to reform the health care system, a number of task forces were established. Many members of these task forces were not full-time federal employees, yet notices of the meetings were never published, and the meetings were closed to the public. The Federal Advisory Committees Act mandates that advisory panels that make policy recommendations to the president must advertise their proceedings and open them to the public if nongovernmental individuals are members. Yet when my committee requested the names of the people serving on the task forces, then-

White House Counsel Bernard Nussbaum told me: "Congressman, I don't have to give you that information, and I'm not going to give you that information, and you can't make me give you that information."

This open defiance of the committee's legitimate requests continued throughout my tenure:

- Commerce Secretary Ron Brown refused to explain discrepancies in his financial disclosure statement despite repeated requests.

- A "damage control" unit was established in the White House by Special Counsel Jane Sherburne, who reported directly to Deputy Chief of Staff Harold Ickes rather than to the White House counsel. Apparently, the sole purpose of this unit was to deny the committee as much information as possible and drag out document production as long as possible.

- The White House counsel's office, under four successive counsels, refused to comply with repeated requests for documents related to the firing of the White House Travel Office employees.

'Congressman... I'm not going to give you that information, and you can't make me give you that information.'

In fact, then-White House Counsel Jack Quinn sat in my office a little over a year ago and informed me he would go to jail before turning over certain Travelgate documents. Unknown to us at the time, these documents, which the president asserted were "privileged," included the White House request to the FBI for Billy Dale's file seven months after Mr. Dale was fired in the 1993 Travel Office purge. This single document led to the discovery that hundreds of FBI files of Reagan and Bush appointees had been inappropriately gathered at the White House. FBI Director Louis Freeh called this an "egregious violation of privacy."

Mr. Quinn finally turned over 3,000 pages of documents, which the White House had spent months trying to withhold, on the morning the House scheduled a floor vote to hold Mr. Quinn in contempt if he didn't turn over the documents.

These are just a few examples of the stonewalling and defiance that have characterized the Clinton administration from the start and which continued up to my last days in office. Now this modus operandi continues in response to Chairman Burton's requests.

When the committee first opened its Travelgate hearings, I said: "If senior White House officials will bend the rules over so seemingly inconsequential an issue [as the White House Travel Office] and then spend two years keeping the true story from coming out, what lengths might they go to, to frustrate oversight of areas of far more serious consequence?" Now we are learning how the White House responds when serious national security matters are the subject of oversight.

The first hints of what is turning out to be a pattern of massive fund-raising abuses emerged in October 1996, when I first wrote Mr. Quinn asking for information about the activities of John Huang. His answer was conveniently delayed until after the election, and six months later the White House still hasn't fully responded.

In the passing months, key figures in this investigation, like John Huang and Webster Hubbell, have taken the Fifth Amendment, and others, such as Charlie Trie and DNC contributor Pauline Kanchanalak, have fled the country. With revelations that the Chinese Embassy in Washington may have been involved in funneling foreign funds into the 1996 campaign, serious matters of national security are at issue. The past patterns of obfuscation and hide-and-seek games with documents must not continue. The matters at issue simply are too serious.

For more than four years the president has promised cooperation with investigations—but his actions have been quite another story. As one who has walked this walk and listened to the president talk the talk, I encourage my former colleagues to continue aggressively pursuing the information to which Congress is entitled. You must expect that the Clinton administration will resist you at every step, but the issues at stake require the vigilance of serious congressional oversight and members of Congress committed to getting the facts to the American people.

Mr. Clinger, a Pennsylvania Republican, retired from Congress last year.

Editorial Feature

And the Pattern Continues

From an April 29 House floor speech by Rep. Dan Burton, chairman of the Government Reform and Oversight Committee:

After weeks of seemingly good-faith negotiations with White House lawyers in which the committee prioritized its requests, the White House refuses to provide all documents to the committee. For weeks, the White House counsel said documents would be forthcoming once a document protocol was adopted, yet the committee's April 10 adoption of a document protocol was met with continued White House resistance. The White House proposed an alternative document protocol, essentially putting control of subpoenaed records into the hands of the White House that is being investigated. . . .

I was optimistic after my first meeting with the White House counsel in February that the White House's actions during the last Congress of delaying and withholding documents in the Whitewater, FBI files and Travelgate investigations would not be repeated. Yet now, six months into this investigation, and a month after the deadline for compliance with the committee's March 4 subpoena, the president is repeating the same dilatory tactics of the past. . . .

Last week, we sent the White House two narrowly targeted subpoenas for documents dealing only with John Huang and the Riady family—nothing else. These documents were first requested by the committee over six months ago. Mr. Huang is being investigated for alleged illegal activities involving foreign governments and interests while a federal employee at the Department of Commerce, and [for] his DNC fund-raising practices. Of the $3.4 million Huang raised for the DNC campaign during the last election, the DNC has pledged to return nearly half of that.

These two subpoenas were a real test case of whether the White House was going to cooperate with Congress or not. The deadline was yesterday and the White House has not produced the documents. My staff has spent hours working with the White House to respond to its concern.

... My predecessor, Chairman Clinger, issued the first request for Mr. Huang's documents on Oct. 31, 1996. Six months, numerous letter requests and three subpoenas later, the committee has yet to receive all documents from the White House pertaining to John Huang. ...

Mr. Speaker, the main purpose of a congressional investigation is to illuminate facts, not hide them. Congressional investigations are, by their nature, far different from a judicial inquiry where a grand jury conducts all matters secretly. Public disclosure of the facts is the essence, and in large part the purpose, of congressional oversight. The American people have a right to know the facts in this matter. The president committed to provide all documents. I hope that all members will join me in asking the president to keep his word and comply with our subpoenas and produce all documents to our Committee.

REVIEW & OUTLOOK

Closing In

"And so all I can do is keep smiling, keep cooperating and answer the questions that are asked of me. . . ."

—PRESIDENT CLINTON
ON "FACE THE NATION," APRIL 27

Yes, keep cooperating. But resist subpoenas all the way to the Supreme Court. And hide the meetings with and money for Webb

Hubbell. And let Susan McDougal know you think that she and her lawyer will figure out the right thing to do. While the White House damage-control team tried to hide the latest revelations under the budget agreement news, Whitewater continues to pound.

On Friday the White House announced it was going to the Supreme Court to overturn a previously sealed appellate court ruling that it had to deliver notes government lawyers took of conversations with Hillary Clinton. In a 2-1 decision, the Eighth Circuit Court of Appeals overturned a ruling by U.S. District Court Judge Susan Webber Wright that said the notes were protected by attorney-client privilege. The court majority held that Mrs. Clinton was not the client of government-paid lawyers, so the privilege did not apply.

Hillary Clinton

The White House has already delivered similar notes for other staff members without raising attorney-client objections; but Counsel Charles Ruff drew the line at Mrs. Clinton. The dissenting judge, Richard Kopf, also agreed that attorney-client privilege might be overcome. But he raised procedural safeguards, observing that on the Watergate Nixon case, the Supreme Court insisted that before dismissing executive privilege, courts should hold a hearing on whether prosecutors really needed the material, and then examine it in camera before delivering it to the prosecution.

The Eighth Circuit majority, Pasco Bowman and Roger Wollman, brushed this aside: "the strong public interest in honest government and in exposing wrongdoing by public officials would be ill-served by recognition of a governmental attorney-client privilege applicable in criminal proceedings inquiring into the actions of public officials. We also believe that to allow any part of the federal government to use its in-house attorneys as a shield against the production of information relevant to a federal criminal investigation would represent a gross misuse of public assets."

The Eighth Circuit, like Judge Royce Lamberth in Washington, seems to be increasingly impatient with representations from Clinton Administration lawyers. Judge Bowman also ordered the Paula Jones case to go forward, writing that the Constitution "did not create a monarchy." As High Court Justices receive the appeal on attorney-client privilege, of course, they already have the Jones case before them. If they are also impatient, they can conclude that the purpose of appeal is to delay with endless procedural arguments, and simply deny certiorari and let the Eighth Circuit decision stand.

When the notes are ultimately unsealed, they should make interesting reading. While it's not easy to imagine Mrs. Clinton revealing big secrets even to her lawyers, the subjects of the notes are intriguing. One set was taken at breaks in and after Mrs. Clinton's January 1996 grand jury testimony on the sudden appearance of Rose Law Firm billing records in the family quarters of the White House. The other concerns a July 1995 meeting with Mrs. Clinton, her private attorney David Kendall, White House attorney Jane Sherburne and others about Mrs. Clinton's activities in the aftermath of the death of Deputy White House Counsel Vincent Foster.

*　　*　　*

Also on Friday, the White House yet again readjusted its story line on Mr. Hubbell, disclosing four previously unreported meetings with the Clintons after he resigned as Associate Attorney General and before starting his jail term for defrauding his former Rose Law Firm colleagues. Mr. Clinton previously had acknowledged only two contacts with Mr. Hubbell in this time, when he was collecting fat fees from various Friends of Bill. Mr. Hubbell turned famously uncooperative with the independent counsel probe, and Mr. Starr is exploring, among other things, whether fees paid to him constitute hush money.

Webb Hubbell

The newly revealed visits include a private July 1994 meeting with Mrs. Clinton, and a May 1994 visit including a group of Arkansas insiders—Mr. Foster's widow, Lisa, Sheila Anthony and Marsha Scott, who also visited Mr. Hubbell several times in prison. The Washington Post reported on Saturday that unreleased White House phone records show additional calls between the President and Mr. Hubbell. Also on Saturday, the Kansas City Star reported another Hubbell contract, this one for $90,000 from Sprint to lobby for a European venture; Rep. Dan Burton speculates that the total Hubbell take may reach $1 million.

Yesterday the New York Times knocked another rock out of the Hubbell stonewall concerning who knew what when. "Everybody thought it was just some sort of billing dispute with his law firm," Mr. Clinton said at an April 3 photo session. "And that's all anybody knew about it." The White House reiterated this line yesterday, without really denying the Times report that Mr. Kendall knew Mr. Hubbell was in deep legal trouble even prior to his resignation. Also that Tyson Foods general counsel Jim Blair, who helped with Mrs. Clinton's commodity trades back in the 1980s, has testified that he came to the White House to warn the Clintons that Mr. Hubbell "needed to resign as quickly as possible."

* * *

Meanwhile in Los Angeles, Whitewater felon Susan McDougal is slated to go on trial today on charges of embezzling $150,000 from conductor Zubin Mehta and his wife. Mrs. McDougal, of course, is already serving time for contempt in refusing to answer questions before a Whitewater grand jury. One question was whether then-Governor Clinton knew about the illegal Master Marketing loan at the heart of Mr. Starr's inquiry; another was whether President Clinton told the truth in testimony at the trial in which an Arkansas jury convicted her, her husband and Governor Jim Guy Tucker. Barring help from an Eighth Circuit reversal, and if convicted in Los Angeles, she may face more than a decade in jail. Asked on "Face the Nation" whether he'd ask her simply to tell the truth, Mr. Clinton said, "It's none of my business. She has a lawyer. And it would be very wrong for me to inject myself in this."

Even during budget week, the waves have been building. Keep an eye on the weather glass; the storm may be closing in.

In Court

On May 27, 1997, the Supreme Court issued a unanimous opinion declaring that the Paula Jones sexual harassment suit against the President could go forward, rejecting a White House appeal that the case be delayed until after Mr. Clinton left office.

Although sympathetic to executive branch prerogatives, the Journal was critical of the Clinton Administration's frequent attempts to "put itself above and beyond legitimate inquiries and even laws," citing disputes over secrecy in Mrs. Clinton's health-care task force, the Travel Office affair, stonewalls of Congressional committees, removal of documents from Vincent Foster's office, Filegate and Indogate. "While these columns have defended the official capacities of the executive branch against Congressional incursions, there is simply no precedent in our modern history for the assertion of personal Presidential political and legal non-obligation by the Clinton Administration. If this philosophy of refusal stands, if the stonewalls of Congress and federal judges succeed, there is no question that future White House lawyers will study them and cite them as established precedents for similar feats of noncompliance."

Within a month of the Jones ruling, in another sharp blow to the White House, the Supreme Court declined an Administration request to hear its appeal of a Eighth Circuit Court ruling that notes government lawyers took in Whitewater-related conversations with Hillary Clinton were not protected by attorney-client privilege and must be turned over to Kenneth Starr. The Justice Department, meanwhile, seemed increasingly to be under White House sway, filing an amicus brief on behalf of the Clintons in the notes case. And U.S. Attorney Eric Holder, nominee for Deputy Attorney General, continued to fight with District Judge Royce Lamberth in a case involving the late Commerce Secretary Ron Brown, a Holder friend.

On Capitol Hill, investigators progressed unevenly toward new hearings. Rep. Dan Burton got new subpoena powers despite Democratic objections, but Senator Fred Thompson failed to get immunity for key figures in the Buddhist Temple fund-raiser hosted by Vice President Gore. Democrats sought to equate some Republican contributions with the Democratic ones, and to broaden the topic into the morass of all campaign funding. The Republicans, however, did not control assets such as the Lincoln Bedroom, Air Force One or U.S. Navy ships off the Taiwan Strait.

With further court proceedings on the original Whitewater mess still in store and Mr. Starr adding seasoned public-corruption prose-cutors to his staff, the campaign finance issue turned on whether the illegal contributions were the result of a conspiracy hatched in the Oval Office.

Editorial Feature

Ken Starr, Not Hillary Clinton, Is the 'Client' Here

The Clinton administration, while professing "full cooperation" with independent counsels and congressional investigators, has been waging an extended battle to avoid surrendering key documents. That struggle hit the headlines most recently when the Eighth Circuit Court of Appeals ordered the White House to give Whitewater Independent Counsel Kenneth Starr the notes taken by government lawyers at meetings attended by Mrs. Clinton. The administration argued that the notes were protected by attorney-client privilege. Continuing its program of "full cooperation," the administration says it will appeal the decision to the Supreme Court.

Rule of Law

By Douglas R. Cox

The court's ruling is correct and should withstand further review; but as Mr. Clinton has already demonstrated with both Congress and the courts, disclosure delayed can be disclosure effectively denied. Evidently, the temptation to seek further review, and thus further delay, was too great to resist.

The attorney-client privilege is an important common-law doctrine designed to preserve client confidences. The theory underlying the privilege is that such confidentiality is necessary to encourage clients to seek candid legal advice.

The administration sought to assert the attorney-client privilege with respect to two sets of lawyer's notes. The first set was taken by

Miriam Nemetz, an associate counsel to the president, at a meeting attended by Mrs. Clinton, Jane Sherburne (another government lawyer), and Mrs. Clinton's personal attorney. The second set was taken by Ms. Sherburne during meetings attended by Mrs. Clinton, her personal attorneys, and another government lawyer. Thus, both sets of notes were taken by government lawyers—lawyers whose salaries were paid by the taxpayers and who did not have an attorney-client relationship with Mrs. Clinton.

It is well-established that the attorney-client privilege "belongs" to the client, not to the lawyer, and that it is the client who decides whether to assert or waive the privilege. The administration argued that the White House was the client at these meetings, and Ms. Nemetz and Ms. Sherburne its attorneys; it accordingly sought to defeat the grand jury's subpoena by asserting the attorney-client privilege on behalf of the White House. But when Mr. Starr subpoenaed the notes, he was acting on behalf of the executive branch; when Ms. Nemetz and Ms. Sherburne took the notes, they too were acting on behalf of the executive branch. The administration was reduced to the circular argument that the executive branch can assert the attorney-client privilege against itself.

The court described its task as deciding "whether a governmental attorney-client privilege exists at all in the context of a federal criminal investigation." It concluded that in such circumstances there is no government attorney-client privilege. The court's conclusion accords with the reality that government attorneys represent the government, not a particular individual or group of individuals.

Moreover, those who believe that a government attorney-client privilege does or should exist should also agree with the court's conclusion that the notes must be produced. Any such privilege would plainly belong to the United States; so the question becomes who represents the United States in the face of an independent counsel subpoena.

In the course of an ordinary federal criminal investigation, the president as the head of the executive branch would decide how to respond to a subpoena. If the Justice Department decided to seek the notes of a government lawyer, the president would either waive any privilege and order the notes produced, or instruct Justice to direct its investigation elsewhere.

But that's not the case here. For better or for worse, the independent counsel law places a portion of the executive branch's prosecutorial power in the hands of the independent counsel. The independent counsel is just that—independent, which means that he operates outside direct presidential supervision. Put another way, for the limited purposes of his investigation, the independent counsel exercises the decision-making authority ordinarily exercised by the president. As a result, the independent counsel is the government "client" to whom any government attorney-client privilege belongs, and it is his decision whether to assert any privilege.

The role of Ms. Nemetz and Ms. Sherburne as government attorneys is significant for another reason. Ordinarily, if a client shares a purported confidence with her attorney in the presence of others, the privilege will be deemed to be waived. Here, Mrs. Clinton was not meeting privately with her attorneys. The court could have concluded that the communications were not privileged in the first place.

> *The Eighth Circuit's ruling is correct and should withstand further review.*

Nonetheless, the administration argued that the notes should be deemed privileged because some disclosures to groups of attorneys representing different clients may properly remain privileged where the clients share what the courts call a "common interest." But there could be no "common interest" between Mrs. Clinton and the government. Mrs. Clinton's personal interest is to avoid prosecution and jail; the government, and the lawyers who represented it at the meetings, could not have a legitimate interest in forestalling or defending against a potential future prosecution brought by the government. Mrs. Clinton and the government thus had conflicting interests; there was no "common interest" to protect Mrs. Clinton's disclosures to individuals who were not her personal lawyers.

The independent counsel, as the court was careful to note, did not seek to invade Mrs. Clinton's attorney-client relationship with her own, private, lawyers: Only notes taken by government lawyers have to be surrendered to Mr. Starr.

Moreover, a government lawyer's duty to the government, and not to an individual, is well-recognized. Any official who has concerns about individual criminal exposure is routinely advised to hire a private lawyer—as Mrs. Clinton did here. Her own acts demonstrate her awareness that Ms. Nemetz and Ms. Sherburne did not represent her, and that the attorney-client privilege did not apply to communications she made to them.

Of course, this entire dispute would end tomorrow if the Clinton administration acknowledged the public interest in having the Whitewater investigation concluded on a full factual record, and declined any further stratagems or claims of privilege its lawyers might concoct. But that outcome is plainly unacceptable to an administration that defines "full cooperation" with investigators to include fighting disclosures all the way to the Supreme Court.

Mr. Cox, a Washington attorney, served in the Office of Legal Counsel during the Bush and Reagan administrations.

Letters to the Editor

Mena, Drugs and the Train Deaths Case

Micah Morrison's April 15 article, "Big News From Arkansas," reported ex-prosecutor Dan Harmon was indicted for running his office as a criminal enterprise. Just as newsworthy is the absence of any reference in the indictments to what I believe, based on my investigation, to be Mr. Harmon's involvement in the murders of Kevin Ives and Don Henry, the nationally known train deaths case.

Under the Racketeer Influenced and Corrupt Organizations law, Mr. Harmon could be charged with crimes committed up to 10 years ago, but his indictment only goes back to August 1991. Just two months before that, in June 1991, then-U.S. Attorney Chuck Banks cleared Mr. Harmon of drug-corruption allegations strikingly similar to the ones he now faces. The obvious question arises: Is current U.S. Attorney Paula Casey protecting Mr. Banks? It's hard to ignore that the August 1991 starting date of Mr. Harmon's indictment shields Mr. Banks from the appearance of impropriety and excludes evidence related to the train deaths.

In 1990, as head of a drug task force in the area, I gathered a significant amount of evidence against Mr. Harmon, as well as evidence connecting drugs and public officials to the train deaths. I was stunned when Mr. Banks cleared Mr. Harmon and all other public officials in 1991. I believe that, in this regard, the years of covering up the train deaths case continues.

Mr. Morrison has eloquently unraveled the complex story surrounding the train deaths, but in one case he left the wrong impression. He wrote, "Ms. Duffey left the state when Mr. Harmon filed charges against her, later found to be baseless." I'm not so easily intimidated.

In 1990, my task force uncovered too much. I was brutalized by an Arkansas media that supported Mr. Harmon, who was running for and won our district's prosecutor position. Mr. Harmon immediately subpoenaed the evidence I had against him and other public officials. But to protect witnesses, I refused to comply. Circuit Judge John Cole then issued a felony warrant for my arrest, and my family was warned from two law enforcement agencies that I was going to be killed. Discredited, defeated, and threatened, my husband and I moved our family to Texas.

I didn't understand the power of the political machine back then, but after being persuaded by the FBI to assist in an investigation they opened in 1994, I learned of connections to the CIA, Mena, and drug-smuggling. I finally understood; to solve the train deaths case would be to expose the crimes of Mena, and no government agent who has come close to doing either has survived professionally.

The Arkansas media have mostly realized their misjudgment of me, with the exception of the Arkansas Democrat-Gazette. The most important paper in the state either ignores or ridicules the facts surrounding the profoundly disturbing train deaths case. I pray Micah Morrison and The Wall Street Journal will continue to expose the deep-rooted corruption in Arkansas. People deserve to have sources of information that will not back away from the truth.

JEAN K. DUFFEY

Pasadena, Texas

REVIEW & OUTLOOK

Home Alone

With Janet Reno rattling around empty offices at the Justice Department like Macaulay Culkin in "Home Alone," few appointments are more critical than the nomination the Senate Judiciary Committee takes up today—that of Eric Holder Jr. as Deputy Attorney General.

Eric Holder

Mr. Holder's confirmation is expected, but we hope that Senator Orrin Hatch and his committee establish a record giving him the opportunity to explain his part in the controversies during his tenure as U.S. attorney for the District of Columbia. Some of these—his expressed personal debt to the late Ron Brown, his decision not to prosecute Ira Magaziner when he was referred by Judge Royce Lamberth for possible perjury, his separate argument with Judge Lamberth over a Freedom of Information suit concerning Mr. Brown's records at the Justice Department—were detailed in these columns April 30.

Now there is a new dust-up over Mr. Holder's request that the IRS not audit the tax returns of some 800 District Police Officers. This again concerns Judge Lamberth, who is presiding over the trial that precipitated the request and who called it "both disturbing and troubling." The officers had been clients of an accountant indicted for fraud, conspiracy and tax evasion. Some attorneys speculate that Mr. Holder was concerned about precluding a basis for impugning the testimony of officers in criminal trials; he and Justice issued a joint statement saying that after six months he withdrew the request except for about 20 officers. Given the position Mr. Holder is about to assume, the committee and the public deserve a fuller explanation.

Even more urgently, in our view, Mr. Holder should be asked whether he feels a responsibility to recuse himself from remnants of the investigation the Ron Brown Independent Counsel passed back to Justice with the Secretary's death. Legal Times reported in its May 5 edition that one remaining portion of the probe "now appears to be reaching critical mass." This concerns political contributions by officers and employees of Dynamic Energy Resources Inc., a company founded by Brown allies, Democratic fund-raiser Nora Lum and her husband Eugene. The Lums gave stock in the company to Mr. Brown's son Michael, and the company bought into the Oklahoma gas business in 1993. The Lums' activities were the subject of Peter Boyer's recent New Yorker article and a PBS documentary.

Legal Times reports that one of its sources appeared before a grand jury in April, and speculates that a vigorous investigation of this case could prove that the Public Integrity section of Justice is awake after all. The Oklahoma deal also touches Presidential buddy "Mack" McLarty; another recipient of the Lums' political generosity was Senator Teddy Kennedy. In a tribute after Secretary Brown's death, Mr. Holder said he "played a substantial role in my becoming a U.S. attorney. He's the guy who made the phone calls. . . ." Mr. Holder should elaborate this relationship, and whether he will recuse himself from Brown cases.

Jamie Gorelick

We had similar problems with the last Deputy Attorney General, Jamie Gorelick, who as a private attorney has represented Clark Clifford and Robert Altman in their attempt to get the trustee for First American bank to reimburse them for legal fees in the Bank of Credit & Commerce International case. We were glad to publish Ms. Gorelick's letter saying she had recused herself from all BCCI matters, though it seems to us that the appropriate forum for putting on record such statements about highly publicized cases would be confirmation hearings.

Too often these hearings are overly clubby. Ms. Gorelick, for example, went before a committee headed by Senator Joseph Biden, whom she had personally represented. At her earlier hearings as Pentagon General Counsel, Chairman Sam Nunn invited her up afterward to answer some questions without a public record. Secretary of the Navy John Dalton had part of his confirmation hearing in executive session, presumably to discuss his failed savings and loan and perhaps his subsequent employment by Little Rock's Stephens Inc.

Too, it is no accident that Ms. Reno is home alone at Justice. Philip Heymann resigned after arguing with White House Counsel Bernard Nussbaum over limitations on the search of Vincent Foster's office. Webster Hubbell went to jail. Mr. Holder took his present office as a result of the Clinton Administration's unprecedented demand for immediate resignations of all U.S. attorneys. The Administration has had five White House Counsels and three CIA Directors. It fired one FBI Director and is now embroiled with another.

It is scarcely a surprise that a U.S. Attorney for Washington has been involved in controversy, but Senators owe Mr. Holder an opportunity to explain himself instead of letting suspicions fester. And given the record of this Administration, real scrutiny of law-enforcement appointments is something they owe the nation.

Letters to the Editor

The Clinton Scandals Have a Special Trait

Bill Clinton's numerous scandals are frequently compared with past presidential scandals, which "are as common in history as Tiger Woods fans are today." In this vein, Richard Nixon's Watergate and Ronald Reagan's Iran-Contra scandals keep surfacing alongside every new revelation of the Clintons' wrongdoing. This strengthens the notion that there is really nothing extraordinary about the current president and his wife. They just do what other presidents have been doing, which, in turn, reinforces popular cynicism about the political process in general and this presidency in particular.

This vague and diffused public cynicism could become the ally of the Clintons' own focused and calculating cynicism, and in the end save the Clinton presidency. The losers would not only be the American people, but ultimately the American system of government, which relies for its continued existence on the willingness of the governed as well as the governing to accept and submit to the principles of the Founding Fathers.

Comparing the current developments in the White House with the Nixon and Reagan scandals is also misleading. Ronald Reagan and, to a considerable extent, Richard Nixon were pursuing policy goals that they deemed beneficial to the U.S. Both were frustrated by what they perceived as endless and partisan congressional bickering and obstruction, which led them to opt for non-democratic and, yes, unlawful shortcuts. Contrast this with the Clintons and their actions back in Arkansas in an uncompromising and systematic preparation for conquering the highest office of this country. This president's foreign-policy record is a disaster, while his domestic policies are a sequence of unprincipled waverings geared toward what serves Bill Clinton, not what serves the long-term interests of the U.S.

ELISABETH TAMEDLY LENCHES
Associate Professor of Economics
Pepperdine University

Culver City, Calif.

REVIEW & OUTLOOK

Jones 9, Clinton 0

No doubt many of our readers passed part of the Memorial Day weekend watching the playoffs for the Stanley Cup or National Basketball Association. They play rough all right, but it's not the law of the jungle; every now and then a referee blows the whistle to restore civilization. Yesterday a referee finally intervened in our increasingly free-for-all domestic politics: The Supreme Court blew the whistle on the Clinton Presidency.

In a unanimous 9-0 slam dunk, the Court ruled that Paula Jones's sexual-harassment suit may proceed against Bill Clinton while he is still in office. Writing for the Court, Justice John Paul Stevens said: "The high respect that is owed to the office of the chief executive, though not justifying a rule of categorical immunity, is a matter that should inform the conduct of the entire proceeding."

Paula Jones

We're grateful to the Court for that useful phrase—categorical immunity. It has been our impression these past four years that "categorical immunity" was the Clinton Administration's philosophy of life.

The Jones case and yesterday's decision are of course about the status of the President's *unofficial* conduct; specifically, as described in the Court's summary of the case, that "petitioner made 'abhorrent' sexual advances to her." This to be sure is an explosive matter for Mr. Clinton, and for some days now the issue will be whether this one event, the Paula Jones case, will do lasting political damage to the President.

More than fair enough. The woman who was initially vilified by the President's press secretary, his lawyer Bob Bennett and a sneering James Carville—this woman with big hair, a tiny Southern voice and no Yale law degree—has nine Supreme Court Justices saying she's entitled to the decency of a response from Bill Clinton.

So are a lot of other people.

However dramatic the Jones case, the stark truth is that from its earliest days the Clinton Presidency has asserted that it's beyond the reach of, not accountable to or immune from all manner of established processes in our government. There is nothing extraordinary about the Paula Jones case. *It is the norm.* Categorical immunity has been standard operating procedure.

Bill Clinton

When back in 1993 a physicians' group asked to know the members of Hillary Clinton's secret health care task force—which was undertaking an unprecedented reorganization of the U.S. health system—the Administration refused. Ruling against the Administration, an angry Judge Royce Lamberth said it "submitted meritless relevancy objections in almost all instances."

Time after time in the years since, this Administration has sought to put itself above and beyond legitimate inquiries and even laws. With Congress, the most notable refusals have involved Travelgate (with preposterous claims of executive privilege to the Clinger committee), Filegate and now Indogate. A succession of investigating committees issued subpoenas for documents, and those subpoenas were invariably refused right up to the point of contempt of Congress.

Lest it all be written off as "partisan," let's understand the origins: The GOP Congress didn't invent these scandals; the press uncovered them, and the committees followed up. Nothing partisan caused one Deputy Attorney General to resign after accusing a White

House Counsel of withholding pertinent information from the Justice Department.

There have been White House stonewalls over White House passes for past drug abusers, over Hillary Clinton's Rose Law Firm billing records (materializing later in a Lourdes-like apparition), over Vincent Foster's missing diary, and over Asian campaign contributions and fund-raisers who fled to China rather than appear in court. Next, the Supreme Court must turn its attention to whether to accept a case asserting attorney-client privilege for (1) the First Lady, a "functional equivalent" of a government official, (2) in conversations with government-paid lawyers (3) concerning private business concerns (4) arising from matters predating her husband's election.

Serious tensions and conflicts have always existed among the branches of government, and occasionally—rarely—it has fallen to the Supreme Court to resolve them. While these columns have defended the official capacities of the executive branch against Congressional incursions, there is simply no precedent in our modern history for the assertion of personal Presidential political and legal non-obligation by the Clinton Administration. If this philosophy of refusal stands, if the stonewalls of Congress and federal judges succeed, there is no question that future White House lawyers will study them and cite them as established precedents for similar feats of noncompliance.

If balance is preserved, American history will owe a debt to Paula Jones. The object of James Carville's kiss-off—"Drag a $100 bill through a trailer camp and there's no telling what you'll find"—took her complaint to the Supreme Court. To a man and woman, the Court said yesterday that Bill Clinton has to start providing some real answers, that he doesn't have categorical immunity after all.

Editorial Feature

How Congress's Subpoena Power Works

Congress's authority to impose contempt sanctions was demonstrated once again last week. In response to a subpoena for documents relevant to a House investigation into campaign finance abuse, the White House had withheld 2,000 pages of documents and had censored others on the ground of attorney-client or attorney work-product privilege. But after Rep. Dan Burton (R., Ind.) scheduled a vote of the House Government Reform and Oversight Committee to cite White House Counsel Charles Ruff for criminal contempt, an agreement to produce the documents was swiftly reached. Last year a similar measure convinced then-White House Counsel Jack Quinn to comply with a request by the same committee to turn over documents concerning the White House Travel Office firings.

Rule of Law

By John C. Yoo

Congress's power to compel members of the executive branch to obey its legitimate requests for information has long been deemed critical to the functioning of our democracy and has been upheld by the Supreme Court. In the early days of the Republic, Congress enjoyed unchecked power to sanction individuals at its own discretion. In 1796, for example, the House of Representatives itself tried and convicted a man for attempting to corrupt two congressmen; the House even imprisoned the guilty man itself.

In 1857 Congress limited its own powers by enacting a law that established the modern power of criminal contempt. The law imposes a fine of not more than $1,000 and jail time of up to one year for willful refusal to appear or to answer questions before a congressional hearing.

If an individual refuses to cooperate, the law requires that the congressional committee first vote to hold the person in contempt. The committee's inquiries must further an independent legislative purpose related either to legislation, possible legislation or oversight into government administration.

The Supreme Court has interpreted the statute to require that the committee's investigation be authorized by the full House or Senate, and that the investigation actually rest within the delegated authority. The statute demands that the questions be "pertinent" to the investigation, and that the relationship between the question and the purpose of the inquiry be proven at trial beyond a reasonable doubt. A witness must be informed of this relationship with the same notice and lack of vagueness that is required of all criminal laws. The defendant must have acted willfully, another fact that must be proven at trial beyond a reasonable doubt.

If the full House or Senate approves a contempt citation, the speaker of the House or the president of the Senate is obliged to refer it "to the appropriate United States attorney, whose duty it shall be to bring the matter before the Grand Jury for its action." Although Democrats who sought to use the contempt power against the Reagan administration argued that the U.S. attorney *must* begin grand jury proceedings, such a requirement is surely unconstitutional. The president and his subordinates have the exclusive discretion to bring or to decline to bring prosecutions for violations of federal law.

Prosecutorial discretion allows the president to order the U.S. attorney not to initiate contempt of Congress proceedings against an executive branch official, even if that official is withholding information from Congress. Such an order is essentially unreviewable by the courts; a president could decline to prosecute not only because he believed his subordinate had a legitimate reason to refuse to answer questions, but also because he simply wanted to protect a trusted aide.

If the latter seems unlikely, examine the case of Ira Magaziner, who apparently misrepresented the truth (as lying is called these days) to federal Judge Royce Lamberth concerning Hillary Clinton's health care task force. Using a procedure similar to the contempt of Congress law, Judge Lamberth referred possible contempt of court and perjury charges to Eric Holder, the U.S. attorney for the District of Columbia. Mr. Holder refused to prosecute Mr. Magaziner. Mr. Clinton has since nominated Mr. Holder for the No. 2 job at the Justice Department. While the two events may be unrelated, they suggest the pressures that a president can bring to bear to prevent an unwanted contempt prosecution.

Even if the U.S. attorney were to bring a case before the grand jury, a conviction is not foreordained. The 1857 contempt statute requires that a federal court try the case. A defendant would be entitled to all of the protections of the Bill of Rights that apply in any crimi-

> *After Rep. Burton scheduled a vote to cite White House Counsel Charles Ruff for contempt, an agreement to produce the documents was swiftly reached.*

nal proceeding. He would have the right to a jury trial in a jurisdiction, the District of Columbia, whose inhabitants have experienced little reluctance to engage in jury nullification and who have voted more than 85% Democratic in the last two presidential elections. Finally, the president could pardon any official convicted of contempt of Congress, just as he could anyone else convicted of a federal crime.

Despite all of these safeguards against abuse of Congress's criminal contempt power, its overuse can raise difficult separation of powers problems. The public good will suffer if government officials must worry about paying fines and spending time in jail whenever they make a policy decision that the House or Senate may disagree with.

Congress, especially a Republican Congress, ought to be wary of using criminal penalties to fight a separation-of-powers dispute, especially when the individual officials involved honestly believe that they are pursuing the national interest. During the 1980s Republicans fought against abuse of the contempt power when congressional Democrats used it in the case of EPA Director Anne Burford to force the disclosure of law enforcement documents. Similar abuse of the independent counsel statute by congressional Democrats led to the investigation of Theodore Olson for his actions as assistant attorney general in advising the president to invoke executive privilege in the Burford case.

For the first 125 years of the contempt statute, neither the House nor the Senate ever voted to use the law against a presidential claim of privilege. It was congressional Democrats in the Burford controversy who first invoked it in a dispute over information.

As with the independent counsel statute, Democrats again are experiencing the bitterness of reaping what they have sown. It is unfortunate that a Republican Congress must take advantage of such precedents to press their investigation. The extreme measure of criminal contempt, however, has become necessary to handle an administration that provokes conflicts with Congress when neither national security, diplomatic or law enforcement information is at stake.

Mr. Yoo, general counsel to the Senate Judiciary Committee from 1995-96, is an acting professor at Boalt Hall School of Law, the University of California at Berkeley.

REVIEW & OUTLOOK

Paula's Aftershocks

Washington reporters had been complaining lately, and even writing articles, about the dullness of the news landscape. Who'd have thought the Supreme Court, led by bow-tied Justice John Paul Stevens, would shock the Beltway with a decision that registered, oh, about 9 on the political Richter scale.

The unanimity against the President's position surprised almost everyone, but then, they were surprised with the Tucker and McDougal convictions, too. Neither should have been a surprise to people following these affairs closely. Yes, 9-0 would have been brash to predict, but not a bad bet given the evident temper of the federal judiciary these days and the behavior of the Clintonites in the first term. So a second-day survey of the wreckage around 1600 Pennsylvania Avenue seems in order.

The apology. Wags have been having sport suggesting the precise wording of any apology Mr. Clinton might proffer to Ms. Jones. But maybe there's a way for the President to avoid this abjection. He could instead ask James Carville and Robert Bennett to apologize to Paula Jones.

Mr. Bennett, the President's lawyer for the Jones case, tried to undermine Ms. Jones early on by calling her allegations "tabloid trash." This set the tone for the media offensive against her by the President's surrogates. The White House press office called it a "cheap political trick."

But the best was yet to come. Lawyer Bennett in fact got close to working out a settlement with Ms. Jones's lawyers. It collapsed, however, when recoiled at the haymaker delivered by Mr. Clinton's ragin' Cajun, James Carville: "Drag a $100 bill through a trailer camp, and there's no tellin' what you'll find."

This is very rough stuff. The game was to demolish Ms. Jones's standing in the court of public opinion. Some reporters have acknowledged that it largely succeeded. We may never know what happened in the Excelsior Hotel, but we know what James Carville and Bob Bennett did to Paula Jones in public. This is a known Clinton tactic: smear opponents. The whole batch of them participated in it, and they all ought to have to apologize to her.

James Carville

Another aftershock to ponder: the federal judiciary. If Paula Jones had said in her complaint, "I made love to the President in a space ship," does anyone think that the lower courts or the Supreme Court would have dignified it by allowing the case to move forward? Somehow, she keeps winning.

We suspect that one of the more underexplored subjects of the Clinton Presidency has been its rocky relationship with the federal judiciary, especially the D.C. circuit. Somehow appeals court Judge Royce Lamberth has borne the brunt of some extraordinary courtroom effrontery by the Clintonites—first with the health-care task force case and recently with the DNC's representation of John Huang and friends. Stiffing and stonewalling the opposition, as we detailed here yesterday, is standard operating procedure for this Administration. Our view is that the bench is not insensitive to this sort of behavior, and looking beyond the Jones case, this White House faces the prospect of a lot of time in front of the D.C. circuit's judges.

Bob Bennett

To be sure, the Court's 9-0 decision was an embarrassing legal defeat for a Beltway superlawyer, and it's a real blow to Mr. Clinton's stature all over a town that calibrates power carefully. But Mr. Bennett earned his fee; his litigious delaying tactics worked, pushing this awfulness onto the far side of the Presidential election.

The Jones case is having a big impact because its details are easy to comprehend. But it's important not to miss the ramifications on the Clintonites' side. Their strategy was familiar—do whatever it takes to win. It's the same strategy, virtually acknowledged, behind the campaign contributions. Someday, the courts, including the Supreme Court, may tend to these matters as well. By then, the results may not be so shocking.

Editorial Feature

Jones v. Clinton: Credible Case, Bad Decision

The Supreme Court's painstakingly reasoned unanimous decision permitting Paula Jones to pursue her sexual harassment suit against President Clinton is a reminder why the court needs a few experienced politicians.

Tuesday's well-intended verdict sounds eminently reasonable: No man, however powerful, is beyond the reach of the law. But the court's rationale is politically naive and its conclusion could set a dangerous precedent.

Politics & People

By Albert R. Hunt

It would have been far better if the court had permitted discovery to continue but postponed any possible trial until after the president's term ends. This may be a moot point—the president's lawyers could yet drag out the deliberations to avoid a trial for several years, or there could be a settlement. But postponement would have addressed the fear of immunity for the powerful yet not encouraged future suits against presidents.

Paula Jones's case isn't frivolous; Stuart Taylor meticulously documented it late last year in American Lawyer, finding "clear proof" that an incident involving then-Gov. Clinton and Ms. Jones, a young state employee, occurred in Little Rock in 1991.

Specifically, she alleges a state trooper brought her to a hotel room where the governor propositioned her in a lewd manner. The president has said he doesn't recall meeting her. However, the accounts of top Clinton aides on his use of troopers for liaisons in general and the account of the trooper in this case yield ample reason to believe those broad outlines.

It also seems likely that Ms. Jones, under the tutelage of conservative enemies of the president, has embellished her story. Her professed naiveté, claiming she willingly went up to his room thinking it might mean a better job, strains credulity. Several women very familiar with the former governor's sexual proclivities say in interviews that the Jones version of Mr. Clinton trying to force himself on an unwilling innocent doesn't ring true. Finally, her charge that after rejecting his overtures she then was discriminated against in her lower-level state job seems a post facto concoction by her lawyers.

Still, there plainly is enough here to bring an action. But the original district court decision permitting most pre-trial proceedings to advance, including testimony and depositions from potential witnesses, yet to delay any actual trial until the end of the president's term, would have fulfilled most equal-justice-under-the-law concerns and avoided some dangerous political pitfalls.

The high court underestimates the unique nature of the presidency. A powerful member of Congress can be incapacitated by legal problems—witness former Rep. Dan Rostenkowski a few years ago—and the legislative branch doesn't ground to a halt. Similarly, a judge can hand over duties to another judge.

But the burdens of the presidency aren't so easily shared. Actually the White House spin doctors have done a disservice in insisting Mr. Clinton has been minimally affected by his legal problems; those more intimately involved with these matters suggest the president sometimes spends an inordinate amount of time on them. Much of this is unavoidable, but a trial in the Jones case could add substantially to that burden.

The court drew a distinction between earlier decisions that gave a president immunity from civil action resulting from official acts and suits resulting from nonofficial acts, such as Ms. Jones's complaint. Justice Stevens dismisses the fear of this producing frivolous charges by noting the "paucity of suits against sitting presidents for their private actions." Separately the court reasoned that nonserious charges could be dismissed, that a district court could handle such problems or, if necessary, Congress could pass a law providing a president stronger protection.

There are a lot of ifs there. Justice Breyer, in a concurring opinion that often reads more like a dissent, said he was "less sanguine," noting the number of civil suits filed in federal district courts have increased fourfold in recent decades.

"The threat of actions could well discourage much unneeded litigation," Justice Breyer agreed, but added, "some lawsuits (including highly intricate and complicated ones) could resist ready evaluation and disposition; and individual district court procedural rulings could pose a significant threat to the president's official functions." The majority opinion suggests it would be easy to schedule convenient times for a president in any trial. Who's going to explain this to Saddam Hussein or the North Koreans?

Paula Jones

There are three underlying political messages in Tuesday's decision. One is the power of sexual harassment; no one, including Supreme Court justices, wants to appear insensitive on this. Another is the confidence in the brotherhood of federal judges to be entrusted with the president's fate. Finally, the judges assume these are less dangerous times than the Depression, or the Cold War; it's harder to imagine this decision coming 20 years ago.

Undeniably, the high court has left the president with a set of bad options. A settlement likely would be seen as a tacit admission of culpability. Prolonged proceedings might delay a trial but also will keep the story in the news. A trial, even if Mr. Clinton won—a distinct possibility—would be incredibly embarrassing.

The president's defenders insist all this stuff turns the public off; the electorate never thought Mr. Clinton was an angel when it voted for him in 1992 and again in 1996. Further, he has been very well served by his adversaries: congressional critics like Sen. Al D'Amato (R., N.Y.) and Rep. Dan Burton (R., Ind.), residents of ethical greenhouses who throw stones; the pitiful former FBI agent Gary Aldrich, who has more problems with supposed sources than anyone since Janet Cooke; and Ken Starr's inept stewardship as independent counsel.

Nevertheless, the cumulative effect—Whitewater, Paula Jones and, most serious of all, the fund-raising scandals—inevitably undermines the president's credibility. The argument that these are all right-wing crazies out to get him diminishes in the face of a unanimous Supreme Court decision, though not decided on the merits. That is a pleasant prospect for his frustrated political enemies.

Someday, however, five or 10 or 15 years from now, when a personal action is brought against a Republican president some of these critics may rue the day the Supreme Court that reached this decision didn't include a former governor, a former senator or a former attorney general who really understands the realities of high-level politics.

Letters to the Editor

Justice Doesn't Need Politicians

Al Hunt's Politics & People column is frequently entertaining or amusing, if nothing else. But pedestrian? Ill-conceived? Politically naive? Rarely. But his tortured analysis of the Supreme Court's decision in *Jones v. Clinton* ("Jones v. Clinton: Credible Case, Bad Decision," May 29) displays all three: pedestrian thinking, ill-conceived conclusions, and political naiveté. His suggestion that the court "needs a few experienced politicians"—incredible though that observation reads—is laughable.

Dear Mr. Hunt: beyond the activities going on at both ends of Pennsylvania Avenue, we have (stay with me on this) a *third* branch of our government. It's called the judiciary. Fortunately, its role in our form of government is apolitical, an essential ingredient in our system of checks and balances. The "underestimation" of the political consequences of the court's decision that he derides misses the point completely and precisely. In a society that embraces the rule of law (for further instruction on this point, observe developments unfolding in Hong Kong), as ours does, we don't expect the courts to "estimate" the political fallout. We don't want that to be taken into account at all. Plainly, we demand that our courts altogether ignore partisan, political fallout in their decision-making.

ALFRED J. T. BYRNE

Richmond, Va.

* * *

Surely Mr. Hunt feels the court was correct in curbing President

Nixon's assertions of privilege in the Watergate saga? But it's lots different when the shoe's on the other foot and your favorite liberal is being skewered by his own disgusting treatment of women and all the NOW ladies are turning a deaf ear. It's okay when Bill and Teddy do it. If a Republican inhabited the White House today, Patricia Ireland would be leading the charge to run him out of town on a rail.

DAVID A. YOUCK

Onarga, Ill.

* * *

Mr. Hunt's words, "But the original district court decision permitting most pretrial proceedings to advance [but not the trial] . . . would have fulfilled most equal-justice-under-the-law concerns and avoided some dangerous political pitfalls." Politically dangerous for whom? Not the people, as in government of the people, by the people, and for the people. Why satisfy only most of a basic principle of our justice system? What overriding concern justifies not meeting equal justice for all? How can that idea be supported without saying some are more equal than others because of politics?

Has Mr. Hunt forgotten which party was not satisfied with the original district court opinion? Who insisted on appeal? Now that the president's very expensive lawyer has lost his argument twice, there is no opportunity to say, "I would like to go back and take Door Number One instead."

Mr. Hunt's efforts to discredit Mr. Starr and Mr. Aldrich near the end of his essay get much too close to childishness. If the facts are not in your favor, try name calling and throwing stones.

The final gem was ". . . a unanimous Supreme Court decision, though not decided on the merits." How does Mr. Hunt, the constitutional law expert, think this issue was decided?

ROBERT L. RUSSELL

Falls Church, Va.

* * *

Of all the things I have read regarding this issue, the most intriguing is Mr. Hunt's sentence: "Several women very familiar with the former governor's sexual proclivities say in interviews that the Jones version of Mr. Clinton trying to force himself on an unwilling innocent doesn't ring true." Who are these "several women"? What did they say in these "interviews"? And how do they know of Clinton's proclivities and the fact that the situation does not "ring true"?

TIM LICKNESS

Danville, Calif.

*   *   *

The court's recent decision is hardly indicative of an inability "to understand the realities of high level politics." To the contrary, throughout the history of this nation the court has addressed many issues concerning the power of the president and has often bowed to political realities. The court has previously adopted several legal doctrines that limit its review of certain presidential policies and actions. These legal standards demonstrate the court's awareness of the political landscape and its need to tread lightly in certain circumstances. The Jones case simply does not warrant such deference.

The court has left the president with sufficient opportunity to control his own schedule. For example, it is hard to imagine a district court judge ordering the president to appear at a deposition on the day selected by opposing counsel after the president claims he must be in Europe. The fundamental flaw in the president's argument is that business at the White House continued as usual in the face of many instances of past presidential participation in the judicial system. Mr. Hunt's reference to the president's embarrassment or the effect the charges have on his credibility are irrelevant, especially in a case that Mr. Hunt concedes is not frivolous.

MICHAEL T. MATRAIA

Brighton, Mass.

*   *   *

Great bows and arrows! Al Hunt's myopic shot that the Supreme Court's decision to allow Clinton to face trial on Paula Jones's sexual harassment charges has weakened the presidency missed the target altogether. On the contrary, by reaffirming that the president of the United States is accountable under the same rules of conduct as the rest of us, the court's decision will probably aid in restoring the prestige the Oval Office has lost recently—a phenomenon wrought by Mr. Slick himself and and exacerbated by his pathetic supporters who have haughtily disparaged the character issue during the last five years.

JOSEPH A. WALSH

Chicago

REVIEW & OUTLOOK

Reno's Roll

If Hillary Clinton wins her appeal to apply attorney-client privilege to conversations with government lawyers, the precedent will impede public corruption investigations forever. With the Supreme Court de-

Janet Reno

ciding whether to hear the appeal, the Justice Department would normally file an amicus brief. So Attorney General Janet Reno has to decide whether to side with the Clinton White House, represent the institutional interests of her own prosecutors, or simply duck.

The potential Hillary precedent is spelled out in Independent Counsel Kenneth Starr's brief: "Under petitioner's theory, a government official (including a President) could tell a White House or other agency attorney that he shred-

ded subpoenaed documents or paid off a potential witness or erased a subpoenaed tape or concealed subpoenaed documents. An agency employee could tell an agency attorney that he had falsified his financial disclosure form or embezzled money from the agency. A prison guard might admit to a state attorney that he had beaten a prisoner. The possibilities are legion. Yet under petitioner's theory, such revelations of wrongdoing could be protected from disclosure to a federal grand jury."

Ms. Reno is in charge of the corps of prosecutors, in the Public Integrity Section and in U.S. Attorney offices around the nation, who are responsible for pressing such cases. No one contests that defendants can confide their wrongdoings to attorneys they've privately hired; that's a normal part of the advocacy system of justice. But government-paid attorneys have normally been expected to report wrongdoing and volunteer evidence to the Justice Department. Extending attorney-client privilege to government attorneys would dramatically tilt the law enforcement game against the prosecution. But to point out this reality, Justice would have to go to the High Court in opposition to Mrs. Clinton.

This hot potato has landed in Ms. Reno's "Home Alone" Justice Department. Normally, decisions on an amicus brief would be handled by the Solicitor General, but there is only an Acting Solicitor General. Acting status did not prevent Walter Dellinger from filing an amicus supporting President Clinton in the Paula Jones case, which of course lost 9-0. This time he's recused himself because of past White House connections; so the point man is Sam Waxman, who serves both as Deputy Solicitor General and Acting Deputy Attorney General pending action on Eric Holder's nomination to that post. Justice says a decision is expected "this week or next" on whether to file an amicus, and if so on which side.

Justice's attitude toward Mrs. Clinton's privileges will immediately tell a lot about the other tightrope Ms. Reno is walking, her contention that Justice can investigate the campaign finance scandal internally without recourse to an independent counsel. Of course, no independent counsel is required to investigate whether campaign finance laws were violated by John Huang or Charlie Trie or some Buddhist monks in California; what needs investigating is whether the President and his inner circle directed these violations in a conspiracy hatched in the Oval Office. The issue is whether Ms. Reno's investigators will follow the evidence up the food chain in the face of White House resistance.

Justice did get its first plea bargains in this investigation, for example, from Nora and Eugene Lum; they agreed to plead guilty to funneling $50,000 in illegal contributions to two candidates, including Senator Edward Kennedy. This is only a tiny corner of the Lums' activities, which included visits to the White House, friendships with Mr. Huang and the late Ron Brown. Their sudden and highly profitable entry into the Oklahoma gas business, under tutelage of a lawyer who also worked for President Clinton, also closed down a lawsuit threatening to revive publicity about illegal political contributions by a company headed by Presidential intimate "Mack" McLarty. Will Justice push this case as vigorously as an independent counsel would?

The Clinton White House has already invoked various privileges against several Justice Department investigations. Deputy Attorney General Philip Heymann resigned after the White House refused to let Justice attorneys examine documents in Vincent Foster's office. In the Travel Office investigation, the White House resisted subpoenas from the Public Integrity Section by claiming privilege on 120 different documents. Mr. Starr has steadily resisted such claims, and has now succeeded with an Eighth Circuit Court of Appeals ruling that no part of the government can "use its in-house attorneys as a shield against the production of information relevant to a federal criminal investigation."

Mrs. Clinton has appealed, and we now wait to see where Ms. Reno stands. If the Attorney General fails to support Mr. Starr's arguments she may as well fold up the Public Integrity Section outright; it will be a clear sign that Justice will roll over whenever the White House yells "privilege."

Review & Outlook

The Holder Hearing

We hope Friday's Senate confirmation hearing for Eric Holder Jr. to become Deputy Attorney General doesn't become a ritual formality. Given the many vacancies in top jobs at Justice, Mr. Holder is likely to wield substantial authority over policy decisions. Most specifically, we remain very concerned whether Mr. Holder is going to recuse himself from investigations touching on the affairs of the late Commerce Secretary Ron Brown. These will all be matters of judgment, and as such Mr. Holder's tenure as U.S. Attorney for the District of Columbia is relevant.

Eric Holder

Mr. Holder's confirmation hearing was delayed last month to give him time to respond to concerns about a request from his office that the IRS not investigate the tax returns of 600 District police officers involved in a tax fraud case. Then last week, the controversy escalated when U.S. District Judge Royce Lamberth declared a mistrial in the tax-fraud case citing "prosecutorial misconduct" on the part of lawyers from Mr. Holder's office. Judge Lamberth said that prosecutors had prepared a key witness contrary to his instructions.

We trust that some or all of this will be aired during Friday's confirmation hearing. We're less certain that there will be much discussion of Mr. Holder's increasingly curious role in a Freedom of Information Act (FOIA) lawsuit over Ron Brown's Commerce

Department records, where lawyers from Mr. Holder's office have been repeatedly rebuked by Judge Lamberth.

The FOIA lawsuit was filed in January 1995 by Larry Klayman, head of the conservative watchdog group Judicial Watch. Mr. Klayman believes that seats on Commerce Department trade missions were offered in exchange for campaign contributions by the office of Secretary Brown. Mr. Klayman so far has received 27,000 pages of documents from Commerce, but he continues to turn up evidence that the most crucial documents have been kept from him.

Last August, Judge Lamberth granted a motion for sanctions against Bruce Hegyi, a deputy to Mr. Holder who is representing Commerce in the Klayman lawsuit, "for discovery abuse" and for walking out of a deposition. In February, Judge Lamberth responded to Mr. Hegyi's arguments that Mr. Klayman's questions were too searching by saying: "Every time he turns up a rock, he finds something, so why are you telling me I can't let him turn up another rock?"

Royce Lamberth

Mr. Klayman has turned up some new rocks recently. For example, Graham Whatley, a Commerce deputy assistant secretary, revealed that Commerce kept a list of "minority donors" to the DNC, despite earlier denials such a list existed. The list of 139 names was broken into categories such as "DNC Friends" and "Chairman's Circle." Five of those on the list joined Mr. Brown on a single trade mission to South Africa in 1993.

When Mr. Klayman demanded a copy of the DNC donor list, it was finally turned over to him over two years after a court order by Judge Lamberth ordering a full FOIA search of all Commerce files. A department spokesman explained that the list was considered a "personal document, not a Commerce document." The list's discovery energized Mr. Holder, who wrote Judge Lamberth that the Whatley "testimony was a surprise" and that he was referring the matter to the Inspector General of the Commerce Department "for an appropriate investigation."

Mr. Klayman has asked Judge Lamberth to grant an immediate status conference on his case. Mr. Holder responded by writing

Judge Lamberth that an early hearing would be "problematic" because several of his lawyers with "an interest in attending the hearing" are on vacation during June. Separately, Mr. Holder has noted that Commerce employee Beth Bergere, who was responsible for searching a key office for FOIA documents, is unavailable for a deposition due to "a unique vacation opportunity." Mr. Holder asked that her deposition be rescheduled.

At a minimum, this temporizing sounds like a stretch. Or an attempt to push off any revelations from the status hearing to beyond Mr. Holder's confirmation hearing before the Hatch committee.

Against this backdrop, we think it is very important for the committee to raise the Brown recusal matter with Mr. Holder. Ron Brown was Mr. Holder's friend and mentor, and his activities are currently bound up in the campaign funding controversies. The Hatch committee needs to hear Mr. Holder's direct views on what we could expect to be his relationship to these matters as Deputy Attorney General.

REVIEW & OUTLOOK

Arkansas Justice

Once again a jury of ordinary Arkansans has weighed the evidence against a powerful state official and returned with guilty verdicts. While pundits in Washington and elsewhere yawn over anything connected to the swamp of corruption known as Whitewater, the people of Arkansas are busy draining the muck.

On Wednesday, the jury in Chief U.S. District Judge Stephen Reasoner's Little Rock courtroom convicted former county prosecuting attorney Dan Harmon of using his office as a criminal enterprise to extort narcotics and cash, handing in guilty verdicts on five counts of racketeering, extortion and drug distribution. Witnesses testified about drug deals and payoffs to a man perceived to have wide influence in the state. "I was afraid of Dan Harmon," one witness testified. "I thought Mr. Harmon controlled most of the counties of the state."

The wife of a drug dealer testified she brought Mr. Harmon $10,000 in his office for the release of her husband, but Mr. Harmon asked for more money and a night of sex. His former wife, Holly DuVall, testified she took cocaine and shot methamphetamine with him. U.S. Attorney Paula Casey, who brought the case against Mr. Harmon together with a reinvigorated Little Rock FBI office under Special Agent I.C. Smith, told the Arkansas Democrat-Gazette that she hoped the case would send a "signal" that federal authorities in Arkansas "take the administration of justice very seriously."

Mr. Harmon was twice elected on the Democratic ticket as prose-

REVIEW & OUTLOOK

Asides

Monkgate

People may never know exactly what was going on at the campaign fund-raiser inside the California Buddhist temple that Al Gore stumbled upon in some sort of unknowing daze last year. Senator Fred Thompson wanted to give some of the resident monks immunity to explain the money trail, but Democrats on his committee suddenly turned into unlikely hanging judges, almost literally screeching at Thursday's committee hearing that immunity would protect "criminals." But the best was yet to come. Attorney General Reno weighed in that immunity for the monks was "a matter of concern" for the Justice Department in light of "investigations to come." This really takes the cake. Amid a fund-raising scandal that stretches all the way to Asia, the Democrats are demanding that a bunch of Buddhist monks in California be the first to take the fall. Still the question remains: For whom?

REVIEW & OUTLOOK

Orrin Hatch's Matador D

Senator Orrin Hatch, chairman of the Judiciary Committee, was seen during the Chicago Bulls-Utah Jazz series, sitting on the Jazz bench itself, not three seats from Coach Jerry Sloan. What clout. Last Friday the Senator was seated at the head of his powerful and important committee, presiding over the confirmation hearing of U.S. Attorney Eric Holder for the No. 2 job at the Justice Department. Senator Hatch's performance was an astounding display of what Marv Albert would call "matador defense."

At issue in the Holder nomination was how the Clinton Justice Department, once turned over to crony Webster Hubbell, would keep politics and personal conflicts out of sensitive cases involving the late Commerce Secretary Ron Brown, whom Mr. Holder has cited as a friend and mentor.

Here, from the transcript, is the sound of Senator Hatch setting up as Eric Holder rolls toward him:

Sen. Hatch: "Some in the media urge that you recuse yourself from any matters involving former Commerce Secretary Ron Brown, who was a dear friend of mine by the way . . . . Would you be kind enough to explain why you have not recused yourself in this case in the past and whether you will do so as Deputy Attorney General?"

Mr. Holder: ". . . . The involvement of former Secretary Brown, who was a friend of mine, is really not apparent . . . . In an abundance of caution I have asked the appropriate people at the Justice Department to apply the appropriate regulations and statutes and ask them for an opinion. It is their opinion as well that there is not the need for me to recuse myself in that matter. I will however be extremely sensitive to matters involving former Secretary Brown or anybody else . . . ."

Sen. Hatch: "Well thank you and I think that is all we could ask of you."

Slam dunk. We wonder if one of the "appropriate people" at Justice might have included the Attorney General herself, who recently issued the opinion that if Senator Thompson's committee immunized Buddhist monks to find out who gave them money, it might interfere with her investigation of the monks. Mr. Holder, who finds distinctions between Secretary of Commerce Brown and the Commerce Department per se, should fit right in at Reno Justice.

In fact, Mr. Brown's controversial tenure at Commerce is at the center of a 30-month-old lawsuit in which attorneys from Mr. Holder's

Orrin Hatch

office appear to be stymieing requests for Commerce Department records sought under the Freedom of Information Act. Larry Klayman, head of the conservative watchdog group Judicial Watch, believes that seats on Commerce trade missions were offered in exchange for campaign contributions by Mr. Brown's office. Just in the last month, Mr. Klayman has deposed three Commerce officials who have testified it is likely key documents sought by Mr. Klayman weren't turned over to him. Among them is a list of 139 Democratic National Committee donors that has just been found in Commerce's files and given to Mr. Klayman with the explanation it was a "personal document, not a Commerce document."

Mr. Holder professed to have had almost nothing to do with this, perhaps the most politically sensitive case now being handled by the U.S. Attorney's office. Asked if he had personally reviewed and signed any pleadings in the case, Mr. Holder said he had not: "My name appears on the pleadings and there might be a signature there but my signature would be placed by the trial attorneys."

On the public evidence, this is a mind-boggling statement. Mr. Holder appears to have personally signed well over half a dozen pleadings in the case. Several others do indeed bear his signature next to someone's initials. Still others bear his name, but no signature. Perhaps Senator Hatch could bestir himself to seek a clarification of Mr. Holder's remarks before his committee formally approves the nomination.

When Mr. Holder takes his new job, he will inherit the ongoing investigation of Mr. Brown's affairs that was turned over to Justice by the Independent Counsel investigating Mr. Brown until his death. Just last month, Justice secured three guilty pleas in the case over illegal campaign contributions. Presumably, Mr. Brown's involvement is central to that probe.

At the moment, the Republicans don't look like they belong on the same floor with the Coach Clinton's legalistic slamma-jammas. Others, however, seem to be up to it. For starters, we commend the June 9 issue of the New Yorker magazine, wherein Peter Boyer describes the commercial/political world of Ron Brown and former business associate Nolanda Hill.

Finally, there is the judiciary. Yesterday, the D.C. Circuit Court of Appeals overturned a District Court decision that let the White House withhold documents from Donald Smaltz, independent counsel in the Mike Epsy case. Some issues remain and the District Judge will hold further hearings, but clearly this was a victory for Mr. Smaltz; the decision of the three-judge panel was written by Patricia Wald, leader of the D.C. Circuit's liberal bloc.

The laws of physics being what they are, it's reasonable to expect that further bones may tumble out of the Clinton scandal closet in the next few years and roll up to the steps of the Justice Department. Should that happen, we'll look back to this confirmation hearing, when the Judiciary Committee chairman told the nominee, "I'll do my best to be one of the best friends you have on Capitol Hill." That is Matador D.

Review & Outlook

A Loud No Comment

"We believe the strong public interest in honest government and in exposing wrongdoing by public officials would be ill-served by recognition of a governmental attorney-client privilege applicable in criminal proceedings inquiring into the actions of public officials. We also believe that to allow any part of the federal government to use its in-house attorneys as a shield against the production of information relevant to a federal criminal investigation would represent a gross misuse of public assets."

Those, of course, were not words attached to yesterday's Supreme Court decision rejecting a White House claim that Hillary Clinton's remarks to government lawyers are protected by attorney-client privilege. The Supreme Court issued what must be one of the loudest "no comments" in a long, long time. In doing so, it left the last word on this subject to Judge Pasco Bowman, quoted above for the Eighth Circuit Court of Appeals.

In April, the Eighth Circuit in St. Louis overturned a lower court order supporting Mrs. Clinton's refusal to provide to the office of Independent Counsel Kenneth Starr notes of her conversations with White House lawyers about Vincent Foster and Rose Law Firm billing records. The two sets of notes sought by Mr. Starr will now go before a Whitewater grand jury.

These columns through the years have defended the official capacities of the executive branch against unwarranted incursions. But the High Court's decision yesterday to deny certiorari, and last month's unanimous decision to allow the Paula Jones civil suit to proceed, is a clear message that the Justices understand the game at hand. The Clinton appeals are not at heart about issues of principle, such as privilege and immunity. They are about delay.

Indeed, if ultimately successful, the stonewall-and-delay strategy might prove to be Bill Clinton's lasting legacy to modern government. If you look back through the record, the pattern is clear. The upper-level course in delay began in 1993, when the Clintons stonewalled court actions to make public information about the secret health-care task force; ruling then against the Administration, Judge Royce Lamberth said it "submitted meritless relevancy objections in almost all instances."

Presidential-sleaze lawyer Bob Bennett won the day for his client by delaying a Paula Jones confrontation until after the 1996 election. White House stonewalls on documents and Democratic smears of Congressional witnesses ground down Whitewater investigatory committees. Susan McDougal, with the tacit approval of the President of the United States, refuses to talk to a Whitewater grand jury. A preposterous claim of executive privilege threw a wrench into Representative William Clinger's Travelgate probe.

More delay: Associates of the White House have refused to talk to Congressional panels about Filegate; and those linked to the campaign contributions scandal have fled the country in anticipation of public hearings. Stonewalls were built around inquiries into the matter of White House passes for past drug abusers, the Rose billing records, Vincent Foster's missing diary and finally the Asian campaign contributions.

Naturally, these lessons have been picked up by Clinton partisans in Congress and elsewhere. As new hearings into campaign-finance irregularities approach, Democrats are trying to delay Senator Fred Thompson's probe and demonize his House counterpart, Representative Dan Burton. In the lower courts, meanwhile, lawyers for two potentially critical Starr witnesses, former Arkansas Governor Jim Guy Tucker and Susan McDougal, are seeking more delays in efforts to bring Mr. Tucker and Ms. McDougal to new trials.

The ultimate tactic, of course, has been the attempt to thwart the credibility of Independent Counsel Kenneth Starr himself. The Supreme Court's decision not to take this case can only be read as a large boost to the legitimacy of the independent counsel's investigation.

Specifically at issue here is one set of notes taken at interview breaks in and after Mrs. Clinton's January 1996 grand jury testimony about the miraculous appearance of the Rose billing records in the private quarters of the White House. Also a second set of notes concerning a July 1995 meeting with Mrs. Clinton, her private attorney David Kendall, White House attorney Jane Sherburne and others about Mrs. Clinton's activities in the aftermath of the death of Deputy White House Counsel Vincent Foster. While it's not easy to imagine Mrs. Clinton revealing big secrets to her lawyers, the notes could prove important to what may be Mr. Starr's careful construction of a broad obstruction of justice case.

In the event, this White House's sweeping claims of privilege have, for once, been swept away.

Editorial Feature

Clinton Strikes Out Again At the Supreme Court

The Supreme Court has badly embarrassed the Clinton administration twice in under a month. Less than four weeks after unanimously rejecting the president's arguments in the Paula Jones case, the court refused on Monday to review a lower court order requiring the production of certain documents to Independent Counsel Kenneth Starr.

The documents are notes taken by two government attorneys of conversations with Mrs. Clinton about her activities in the hours after Vincent Foster's death and in connection with the mysterious reappearance in the White House living quarters of "lost" Whitewater billing records. Rather than comply with the order to produce the notes, Mr. Clinton asked the justices to review the case further, which would have delayed Mr. Starr's investigation for many months.

Rule of Law

By Douglas R. Cox

The justices gave no indication of their reasons for refusing to hear the appeal, and it is unwise to read too much into the court's decision not to review a lower-court opinion. But the decision in such a high-profile case, however cryptic, inevitably carries some significance. Three things are striking about the court's refusal even to entertain President Clinton's arguments.

First, it suggests that the Supreme Court gives less weight to the

Clinton administration's judgment that a case merits review than it has traditionally afforded the legal arguments of past administrations. Historically, the court has been inclined to place considerable weight on the president's belief that a case is worthy of the court's time and attention. For whatever reasons, legal briefs from this White House are apparently received with greater skepticism by the court.

The court's skepticism is all the more striking in this case because the Clinton administration had raised the stakes so dramatically. The White House treated the case as one of extraordinary importance to the daily functioning of the executive branch, even enlisting two different sets of attorneys to make two different arguments. Lawyers from the law firm where Clinton confidant and former Commerce Secretary Mickey Kantor is now a partner argued on the pres-

> *The justices may have been reluctant to lend themselves to the administration's strategy of delay.*

ident's behalf and at taxpayer expense for an absolute attorney-client privilege for government attorneys, a privilege so sweeping that it could be invoked in the most unlikely of circumstances to halt grand jury investigations into high-level wrongdoing by any administration.

In case that position struck the court as a little too reminiscent of the divine right of kings, the administration had another taxpayer-funded brief, submitted by its Justice Department, that advocated a less extreme version of the attorney-client privilege. The Justice Department's brief is of historic significance, because it takes a position in conflict with the department's law-enforcement function—a function that Mr. Starr championed.

Although restrained by the tradition of Supreme Court advocacy, which favors understatement over hyperbole, the president's rhetoric was designed to persuade the court that it was obligated to hear the case. For example, the independent counsel's arguments were "irresponsible," the lower court's decision was "extraordinary and unprecedented" and unless the court granted review, the president's ability to obtain sound legal advice would be "substantially impaired." A friend-of-the-court brief was even more apocalyptic, warning that the lower court's decision "will likely have an adverse effect on the current and future operation of not only the Office of the President of the United States, but also government at all levels."

Thus, the administration took unusual steps to persuade the justices that the case merited review. That the court nonetheless refused to hear the case only makes the administration's failure all the more remarkable. If the court's evident distrust continues, the Clinton administration will need to take that distrust into account in other cases in the years ahead. If the skepticism persists into the next administration, the relationship between the court and the executive branch will have changed profoundly.

Second, any skepticism about the administration's litigation position may have been underscored by the court's sensitivity to issues of delay. Both versions of the administration's argument shared one common element: They would have brought the independent counsel's investigation to a halt. Mr. Starr argued that Supreme Court review "would delay a highly sensitive criminal investigation; indeed several parts of the investigation could remain frozen for an additional three to twelve months."

The Supreme Court had seen this Clinton tactic before, in the Paula Jones case. There, the president's legal arguments were ultimately rejected unanimously, but only after the president enjoyed the political advantages of months of delay, extending through the 1996 election cycle. The justices may have been reluctant to lend themselves to what could be characterized as a similarly cynical strategy of delay, in the context of a grand jury investigation.

Third, President Clinton has now twice brought claims of privilege to the high court—a "temporary immunity" privilege in the Paula Jones case and attorney-client privilege in the notes case—and has lost both times. In his dealings with Congress, he routinely relies on another privilege, the "executive privilege" made notorious by Richard Nixon. Mr. Clinton has greatly expanded the scope of executive privilege, invoking it far more times than President Bush did and extending it into novel settings, in efforts to avoid complying with congressional subpoenas. The administration's failures before the Supreme Court may embolden congressional investigators to test the president's unprecedented use of executive privilege as well.

By advancing extreme legal arguments, in settings in which the president has an unusual personal stake in the outcome, the Clinton administration has invited its two recent rebuffs by the Supreme Court and has undermined the credibility of the White House and the Justice Department in the process. As with so many of the administration's problems, its legal wounds are largely self-inflicted.

Mr. Cox, a Washington attorney, served in the Office of Legal Counsel in the Reagan and Bush administrations.

Editorial Feature

Who Is Susan McDougal?

By Micah Morrison

SANTA MONICA, Calif.—From her jailhouse home at the Sybil Brand Institute for Women in Los Angeles, Whitewater felon Susan McDougal has waged an aggressive media campaign to convince the public she is a "political prisoner" of Independent Counsel Kenneth Starr.

Susan McDougal

To the Bunco-Forgery Division of the Los Angeles Police Department, however, Ms. McDougal is just a common thief. Indeed, the LAPD first swore out an arrest warrant for her in October 1993, months before there was an independent counsel for Whitewater. At this point charges by police and prosecutors are only allegations, to be sure, but Ms. McDougal will shortly go on trial here on 10 counts of grand theft, forgery, fraud, making false financial statements and income tax evasion, crimes she allegedly committed while a "trusted employee" of conductor Zubin Mehta and his wife, Nancy. While the case has encountered numerous delays, a pretrial hearing next week at the Los Angeles County courthouse in Santa Monica appears likely to set a trial date in August.

The trial will surely flesh out the character of one of the original Whitewater players—partner with her former husband, James McDougal, and Bill and Hillary Clinton in the original land development deal. The attention to Ms. McDougal will also cast a new light on the recent controversy over Mr. Starr questioning Arkansas state troopers and women who may have been romantically involved with Mr. Clinton when he was governor.

Contempt of Court

Ms. McDougal is currently in jail for contempt of court for refusing to answer grand jury questions from Mr. Starr's office. One question was whether Mr. Clinton was aware of the illegal loan to her that lies at the heart of the Whitewater felonies—a $300,000 advance from David Hale's Capital Management Services to Master Marketing, a front company Ms. McDougal ran as a subsidiary of her husband's Madison Guaranty Savings & Loan. The second question was whether President Clinton testified truthfully in the 1996 Arkansas trial, at which she was convicted of four felony counts related to the Master Marketing loan. Ms. McDougal could end her current jail term by answering either yes or no, but instead she refuses to answer and chooses jail.

Surely Mr. Starr has a legitimate prosecutorial interest in the motives behind Ms. McDougal's silence, a bizarre obstruction of the investigation into matters at the heart of his charter. And it's logical to suspect that some part of these motives revolves around the long-standing rumors that Mr. Clinton and Ms. McDougal were having an affair at the time of the loan and the Whitewater transactions. In the course of such a relationship, indeed, she might have confided in—or even conspired with—Mr. Clinton about the loan she refuses to discuss before the grand jury.

By now the Clinton-McDougal relationship is beyond the stage of idle rumor. Jim McDougal says that he discovered in 1982 that his wife was having an affair with Mr. Clinton, according to James Stewart's report in the Feb. 17 issue of The New Yorker. Mr. Stewart noted that in an early interview with Ms. McDougal, before her incarceration, she said that "she was on the phone with Clinton nearly every day, and that he was giving her much-needed emotional support at a time when she was separated from her husband and their financial world was collapsing." He also reports that Mr. Starr has obtained phone records showing "numerous calls" in 1986 and 1987 between Gov. Clinton's office and the Lowrance Heights housing site being developed by Ms. McDougal, a project under scrutiny by Mr. Starr.

In the Feb. 17 New Yorker, Ms. McDougal denied she had an affair with Gov. Clinton. But when ABC asked her about the subject last September, she replied, "It's too personal for me right now to even begin to talk about things like that." Here in Southern California, two of Ms. McDougal's former associates say she spoke of her intimate relationship with the governor. In particular, she confided many details of the relationship to Nancy Mehta, those familiar with Mrs. Mehta's account say. Mrs. Mehta has avoided press contact, although in a brief phone conversation with Mr. Stewart reported in The New Yorker, she said, "I could write a book on Susan McDougal and it would be a blockbuster, but I'm not going to."

Mrs. Mehta's book would relate how Ms. McDougal was hired in 1989 to help manage five luxury properties the Mehtas own in the Los Angeles area. For much of the following three years, court documents allege, Ms. McDougal milked the Mehtas for more than

---

Surely Mr. Starr has a legitimate prosecutorial interest in the motives behind Ms. McDougal's silence, a bizarre obstruction of the investigation into matters at the heart of his charter.

$150,000 by forging Nancy Mehta's signature on a credit-card application and checks, and by running up hundreds of credit-card charges ranging from the vaguely sinister to the criminally sublime: a post office drop-box and a rental storage unit, plane tickets to Arkansas and Texas and Michigan, computer equipment and car rentals, hotel flings with her boyfriend, a trip to Disneyland, and a steady stream of expensive purchases at restaurants, department stores and beauty salons.

The California prosecutors have amassed a significant paper trail. Among the strongest pieces of evidence is an application for a BankAmerica MasterCard with Mrs. Mehta as primary holder and Ms. McDougal as co-cardholder. At a pretrial hearing, LAPD investigators presented findings by a handwriting expert that Mrs. Mehta's signature was forged on the credit-card application and on checks drawn from a Mehta account handled by Ms. McDougal. An LAPD investigator also testified that the credit-card bills were sent to a mail drop registered to Ms. McDougal.

Mrs. Mehta's book would also likely include a substantial chapter on Pat Harris, the former Madison Guaranty employee who moved with Ms. McDougal to Los Angeles in 1988. Mr. Harris told Mr. Stewart that he found a job managing the Mehta properties through an employment agency, and in the fall of 1988 introduced Ms. McDougal to Mrs. Mehta. A year later, Mr. Harris quit to apply to law school. Ms. McDougal got the job as property manager, a post soon expanded to handling the Mehtas' bookkeeping as well.

Mr. Harris obtained a law degree and today is a member of Ms. McDougal's California defense team. Testifying at her August 1996 sentencing hearing in Arkansas on the Whitewater convictions, Mr. Harris foreshadowed Ms. McDougal's California defense, claiming that Mrs. Mehta was "well aware" of the credit-card use and had approved it as a means of payment for overtime work. Signaling another likely defense tactic, Mr. Harris attacked Mrs. Mehta as an "eccentric" who was "obsessed with Susan," charges he has repeated in radio and print interviews.

Bill Clinton

But Mr. Harris could turn out to be a poor witness for the defense. He appears to have himself been a recipient of Ms. McDougal's credit-card largesse, including a round-trip ticket to Michigan (where he was attending law school), dinners in Dallas, and a six-day rendezvous at the Ritz Carlton in Marina del Rey, Calif., where Ms. McDougal registered using her postal drop-box as an address. Mr. Harris attributes this frolic—at a cost of more than $1,500 and including hotel vouchers signed by him—to Mrs. Mehta's desire to keep Ms. McDougal happy.

Ms. McDougal's sentencing hearing in Arkansas provided an opportunity for Associate Independent Counsel Ray Jahn to cross-examine Mr. Harris, who conceded that he knew she had engaged in a fantastic series of lies on employment applications. "I was not going to sit there and lecture her on telling the truth," Mr. Harris said. Mr. Jahn replied: "Was this before or after you decided you wanted to become a lawyer, sir?" In Santa Monica, the prosecution will be handled by Deputy District Attorney Jeffery Semow, a seasoned prosecutor who can rely on a strong paper trail and the likelihood that Mrs. Mehta will make a sympathetic witness.

By the time Ms. McDougal arrived in Los Angeles in 1988, her spending patterns appear to have been well established. In 1985, according to FBI testimony at her Arkansas fraud trial, Ms. McDougal used some of the proceeds from the Master Marketing loan to feather her nest, buying clothes, renovating her house, paying dues at the tennis club and settling other personal debts. About $50,000 of the loan passed through the account of the Whitewater Development Co., jointly controlled by the McDougals and the Clintons, and $25,000 was used for a down payment on the Lowrance properties. After the independent counsel's net closed around them, both David Hale and Jim McDougal claimed Gov. Clinton played a pivotal role in inducing Mr. Hale to make the loan, though it did not comply with restrictions on his federally chartered investment company.

From her jail cell, meanwhile, Ms. McDougal has launched increasingly bizarre charges. She claims, for example, to have been left alone with a "contagious" prisoner, and on another occasion to have been chained to a toilet for "hours on end." In television and radio interviews, she continues to portray herself as a simple country girl and an innocent victim of cruel government prosecutors, led by Mr. Starr. "I dated ministers and I sang in choirs and I suppose I just thought I would end up a minister's wife," she told ABC's Diane Sawyer in September. But now Mr. Starr is "a million-dollar steam-roller," she told ABC. "Look what they have stolen from me for years. The very ability to live a normal life," she said. "I couldn't marry. I couldn't have children."

Complex Calendar

Ms. McDougal's incarceration calendar is a complex one. She has served 10 months on the civil contempt charge for refusing to testify to the grand jury. Yesterday in Little Rock, Judge Susan Webber Wright denied Ms. McDougal's motion to vacate the contempt order. If Ms. McDougal continues to refuse to testify, she'll likely serve out the contempt sentence. It runs for the life of the grand jury, which will expire in November unless Mr. Starr is granted another extension. After that, Ms. McDougal will begin serving her two-year sentence on the Whitewater convictions. Last December, Ms. McDougal was transferred to Los Angeles in anticipation of her Santa Monica fraud trial, which could result in a sentence of up to seven years. After the Santa Monica trial, she could face further sanctions for criminal contempt and federal tax evasion.

The Arkansas convictions are now before the Eighth U.S. Circuit Court of Appeals. If it upholds her convictions, Ms. McDougal may start to reconsider her silence. At that point, Mr. Starr could step in and offer her a reduction in her Whitewater sentence, possibly freeing her due to time served. Or Ms. McDougal may remain silent to the end, either out of calculating self-interest or perhaps in the self-deluding belief that she really is a "political prisoner," that none of all this is her fault, and perhaps that her old flame will come through with a pardon.

Mr. Morrison is a Journal editorial page writer.

Editorial Feature

What Did the President Know When?

By Micah Morrison

"Ugh," the president wrote.

That one-word response appeared next to a notation that the Democratic National Committee would be setting aside $1 million "for potential fines" relating to fund-raising, on the margins of an October 7, 1996, memorandum to the president from political aide Phil Caplan. The presidential "ugh," of course, can be interpreted in different ways. But along with the accompanying stamp "The President Has Seen," it does suggest that Mr. Clinton knew that some DNC fund-raising was presumptively illegal.

Presidential knowledge of illegal activities is just now a subject of some consequence, with hearings into illicit fund-raising in the 1996 election cycle opening tomorrow in Sen. Fred Thompson's Governmental Affairs Committee. The hearings are—or at least ought to be—about more than the mundane facts that campaigns cost money, that it has to be raised somehow, and that sometimes solicitors step over the line. By now the Democratic National Committee essentially has acknowledged rampant illegal solicitations, promising to return millions. What the country deserves to know is whether this pattern of violation was directed by a conspiracy hatched in the Oval Office.

Conspiracy Law

The law of conspiracy is instructive, perhaps the best way to frame the central issue amid the welter of revelations, including preemptive "document dumps" by the White House. Under conspiracy statutes, if Bill Clinton agreed with his top aides to raise money by means he recognized as illegal, and if actual criminal acts resulted, he would be a party to the conspiracy, as guilty of the crime as the actual perpetrators. The defining question is, in the lexicon of Watergate: What did the President know and when did he know it?

Conspiracy law is even more pertinent to Attorney General Janet Reno's defense of not appointing an independent counsel on campaign contributions. Her department is investigating underlings not covered by the independent counsel statute, and even refusing to approve Sen. Thompson's proposals to provide some of them with immunity from prosecution so they can tell their stories in public. But once the issue is framed as a possible criminal conspiracy involving the president and other covered officials, refusal to name an independent counsel is indefensible.

Investigators probing a White House conspiracy could even zero in on a suspected date of launch: Sept. 13, 1995.

Certainly Mr. Clinton's campaign operatives appear to have engaged in acts that routinely veered into impropriety and at times outright illegality. For starters:

• One of the central figures in the controversy, former Democratic National Committee vice-chairman John Huang, allegedly laundered millions in illegal funds into Democratic campaign coffers through the likes of poor monks at the now-famous Hsi Lai Buddhist Temple fund-raiser hosted by Vice President Al Gore, Indonesian gardeners, and a glorified former Arkansas burger-flipper named Charlie Trie. Mr. Huang has notified congressional investigators he'll plead the Fifth Amendment if called to testify.

• Bank records indicate that Mr. Trie funneled hundreds of thousands of dollars from foreign accounts at the Bank of China to the DNC. Mr. Trie also attempted to deliver more than $600,000 in suspicious checks to the Clintons' legal defense trust, and once showed up at a White House coffee with a Chinese arms dealer. Last Wednesday, the New York Times reported that Mr. Trie also appeared in Manhattan in August 1996 with $100,000 for the DNC as a presidential birthday party got underway at Radio City Music Hall. Mr. Trie has fled the country.

• According to news reports in the U.S. and Asia, Arkansan Mark Middleton, a former White House aide, attempted to solicit Taiwanese officials for $15 million in campaign donations at a time when China was conducting missile tests in the waters off Taiwan and President Clinton was deciding whether to dispatch the Seventh Fleet to the area; Mr. Middleton denies the charges and says he'll invoke the Fifth Amendment if called to testify.

• Hillary Clinton's top aide, Maggie Williams, received a $50,000 campaign check from California businessman Johnny Chung in the White House, although federal statutes bar government employees from accepting such contributions. Mr. Chung managed to contribute $360,000 overall to the Democrats, despite being labeled a "hustler" out to impress his Chinese business associates by a National Security Council official. Mr. Chung has not responded to congressional subpoenas.

Fred Thompson

• The NSC also objected to the presence in the White House of oil financier Roger Tamraz, wanted in Lebanon on a charge of embezzling $200 million. Mr. Tamraz, last spotted in the Georgian capital of Tbilisi, gave more than $170,000 to state and national Democratic organizations.

• With the help of Little Rock attorney Mark Grobmyer and Export-Import Bank director Maria Haley—both longtime Clinton associates—Thai lobbyist Pauline Kanchanalak pushed a $7 million deal at the Export-Import Bank for a Blockbuster video franchise in Bangkok, while channeling more than $500,000 to the Democratic Party. The deal fell apart and the Democrats have returned most of the money; Ms. Kanchanalak has decided to remain in Thailand for a while.

Democrats on the Governmental Affairs Committee, and apparently the attorney general, presumably regard these and other apparent offenses as merely random acts of excessive exuberance. Committee Democrats are expected to stress that fund-raising is messy and that everyone uses "soft money." They also likely will discover instances in which Republican fund-raisers have stepped over the line. But the hearings seem almost certain to develop a mass of evidence suggesting that the president knew a lot about what his agents were doing, and that he and his confidants must have understood that they were taking money from illegal sources.

Investigators probing a White House conspiracy could even zero in on a suspected date of launch: Sept. 13, 1995. On that day, the president and senior aide Bruce Lindsey met with Mr. Huang, Arkansas wheeler-dealer Joseph Giroir and James Riady, scion of Indonesia's Lippo Group.

White House accounts of the September 1995 meeting have been marked by stonewalls and half-truths since the final days of the 1996 presidential campaign, when New York Times reporters Jeff Gerth and Stephen Labaton revealed several White House meetings with James Riady. Before the election, the White House characterized the Riady meetings as "social" visits. After the election, the White House disclosed that the dispatch of Mr. Huang from Commerce to the DNC had been discussed at the September 1995 meeting; in the White House version of events, Mr. Huang had "volunteered" for the fund-raising post.

Yet a look at the players gathered in the White House that September day in 1995 continues to call into question the administration's version of events. The self-effacing Mr. Huang was the least important person in the room and seems the least likely to "volunteer" for anything. He had left the employ of Lippo Group in 1994 with a $700,000 bonus to join the Commerce Department with a top-secret clearance.

Mr. Riady, by contrast, was the former employer who provided the bonus, and presumably controlled other financial spigots. One week after Mr. Riady and his associates paid five visits to the White House in June 1994, for example, Lippo made a $100,000 payment to former Associate Attorney General Webster Hubbell, then under pressure to cooperate with the Whitewater probe. Independent Counsel Kenneth Starr is investigating that payment as possible "hush money." Mr. Riady's association with Mr. Clinton reaches back to the early 1980s, when his family owned an interest in Little Rock's Worthen Bank. At the same time he developed a relationship with Mr. Giroir, now involved in Lippo-related business ventures in Indonesia and China. Mr. Riady has now returned to Indonesia.

After the September meeting with the president, Mr. Huang was dispatched to the DNC, where his fund-raising career began. What were his orders? What understanding did he have with Mr. Riady, Mr. Giroir, the president, and Mr. Lindsey?

Following the September meeting, Mr. Lindsey delegated details of Mr. Huang's DNC transfer to White House Deputy Chief of Staff Harold Ickes. In two White House "document dumps," Mr. Ickes provided congressional investigators with thousands of pages of memoranda and notes on the 1996 campaign. In addition to providing several tantalizing clues about the origins of the violations of campaign laws, Mr. Ickes's dozens of memos to the president and vice president paint a detailed portrait of Mr. Clinton's obsessive control of seemingly every aspect of the campaign. The president tracks the weekly flow of money raised; he drafts campaign literature appeal-

---

If a president is willing to traduce the Lincoln Bedroom, can the Seventh Fleet be far behind?

---

ing for funds; he reviews the scheduling of White House coffees and directs the DNC apparatus to "start overnights right away" with big donors in the Lincoln Bedroom.

Included among the Ickes documents is an intriguing set of notes relating to Mr. Huang. On Oct. 10, 1995, following Mr. Lindsey's instructions, Mr. Ickes meets with Mr. Huang. "Willing to work out of DNC," Mr. Ickes writes in a tight, at times illegible hand. "But needs a reasonable title." At the top of the page, Mr. Ickes cryptically notes: "Overseas Chinese group" and "55 million overseas Chinese." The number vastly exceeds the number of Chinese-Americans who can legally donate to political campaigns, and appears to point directly at non-U.S. residents being targeted for illegal contributions.

Mr. Huang's starburst career as a fund-raiser was launched. He quickly began raising millions, working with Mr. Trie and others. Published accounts have raised questions about Mr. Huang's contacts with Indonesian and Chinese sources after receiving high-level intelligence briefings, adding a specter of espionage to the funding controversy.

Mr. Trie, meanwhile, was also trying to help out his old friend Bill Clinton with some substantial donations to the Clintons' legal trust fund. In March 1996, he delivered the first of two installments of more than $600,000 in suspicious money orders to the Clinton legal trust. This problem also ended up in Mr. Ickes's notes. The solution? "Don't report names if $ are returned," Mr. Ickes wrote, adding at the bottom of the page the name "Betsey Wright," a Clinton damage-control expert. The money was returned, and the incident did not become public knowledge until after the election.

The millions continued to pour in throughout 1996, financing Mr. Clinton's expensive media air war against the GOP. At a July 1996 fund-raiser in California, the president saluted his "longtime friend John Huang," adding that Mr. Huang had been "so effective I was amazed you were all cheering for him tonight." Yet only a year after the California salute to Mr. Huang, the bulk of his millions have been earmarked for return by the Democrats and are the subject of congressional and criminal probes. How much did the president and the vice president know about the questionable activities when glasses were raised to Mr. Huang in July 1996? The Ickes documents suggest they knew a great deal.

This degree of direct presidential control of fundraising, indeed, strikes many long-time political observers as extraordinary. "His direct, hands-on involvement was risky, certainly in violation of the spirit of the law and possibly illegal," Bob Woodward of Watergate fame wrote in "The Choice," his book on the 1996 campaign. By January 1996, he wrote, President Clinton "personally had been controlling tens of millions of dollars worth of DNC advertising. This enabled him to exceed the legal spending limits and effectively rendered the DNC an adjunct to his own re-election effort."

Fund-Raising Machines

All presidents are political, of course, but because of their official duties, nearly all have delegated political fundraising to keep some degree of insulation. The real question of the campaign finance probes is whether Messrs. Clinton and Gore obliterated these lines, turning their offices into fund-raising machines. The issue is not so much whether foreign contributors were trying to suborn the administration as whether the administration was shaking down foreign contributors.

Did the Lippo Group get policy preferences for its favors—perhaps, for example, Commerce Secretary Ron Brown's signing of a deal, brokered by Mr. Giroir, for Lippo and Louisiana's Entergy

Corp. to build a power plant in China. Were seats on Mr. Brown's trade missions for sale? Why precisely did the administration approve the transfer of high-technology aircraft manufacturing equipment from McDonnell Douglas to China despite the initial opposition of the Joint Chiefs of Staff? Was former White House aide Mark Middleton dispatched to a jittery Taiwan to raise funds with the promise of the imminent arrival of the Seventh Fleet? If a president is willing to traduce the Lincoln Bedroom, can the Seventh Fleet be far behind?

"We were fighting a battle not simply for re-election," the president told a news conference shortly after his victory, "but over the entire direction of the country for years to come." Mr. Clinton's view of the difference between himself and Bob Dole may strike many as preposterous, but it certainly suggests an anything-to-win attitude. What Sen. Thompson and his committee need to determine is whether this attitude led the president and his men to unleash John Huang, Charlie Trie and the rest knowing that laws would be broken. In criminal terms this is a conspiracy, and in Constitutional terms it is a breach of a president's duty to see that the law is faithfully executed.

Mr. Morrison is a Journal editorial page writer.

REVIEW & OUTLOOK

Everyone Does It?

We are on the eve of Senator Fred Thompson's hearings into the controversial campaign finance practices of last year's Presidential election, and the clear sense all over Washington is that no one out there much cares. If that is true, then we would have to conclude that Washington's most notable act at century's end was to discover just how much cynicism the system could bear.

We have felt for some time that the sophisticates who run things in Washington have pretty much gotten the country's politics down to the level of a video game, the whole enterprise presented to the public as little more than an exercise in maneuver and advantage.

In these terms, the state of play is that Senator Thompson will not be able to deliver the witnesses who've fled the country or proclaimed that they will take the Fifth amendment. Meanwhile Janet Reno's Justice Department and committee Democrats are approving immunity only for witnesses they've already determined know very little. So the hearings may not get very far tracing campaign-law violations up the line of command. Ms. Reno also declines to name an independent counsel to investigate possible conspiracy by high officials.

If you're a political sophisticate, you score this as: Thompson hearings lack drama; a box-office bust. The cover-up is succeeding; good show and congratulations. With this kind of leadership from political elites, little wonder the public has turned jaded and cynical toward its governors.

Since he arrived in Washington from Arkansas, Bill Clinton preyed on this mood, asking for a lot of tolerance from the people of this country. And they've given it, most importantly putting him back in the White House. But whatever other accomplishments he may claim before his term ends, President Clinton today sits atop a political class that largely disgusts the public.

For this, Bill Clinton bears some responsibility.

Travelgate, the trumped-up Billy Dale prosecution, the secret health-care task force, the 900 FBI files and bouncer/security chief Craig Livingstone, alerts to the White House from high Treasury officials on Resolution Trust Corp. investigations, the guy who told a Congressional committee he lied to his diary, the brightest minds in the Democratic Party suffering massive memory loss at Congressional hearings, the "lost" Rose Law Firm billing records, Webster Hubbell's passage from Justice to jail, Vincent Foster's torment, the Lincoln Bedroom rented out, Charlie Trie on the run, John Huang taking the Fifth, Jim and Susan McDougal convicted, the Buddhist monastery/money laundry, the drug dealers let in for White House photo-ops, the routinely cavalier treatment of legal and judicial procedures, and independent counsels appointed for three members of the Cabinet, one sitting American President and, for the first time in history, one First Lady.

Bill Clinton

Everyone does it? We don't think so. At least not up to now. If, however, there is no explanation, no clear accounting, no effort to discriminate between normal foibles and abnormal felonies, then yes, we would expect that in our future politics everyone will do it, or something like it.

It may be hoped that tomorrow's Thompson hearings on campaign finance will begin an altogether appropriate Congressional exercise in oversight and accountability. As these columns have noted repeatedly since the word "Whitewater" appeared early in Mr. Clinton's term, our interest is not in securing convictions, but *getting a credible explanation*. We would also submit that this goal, a full and timely accounting, is most likely what lay beneath the surface of the two most significant events in our recent politics: the Supreme Court's successive defeats of White House petitions on Paula Jones and attorney-client privilege.

Properly understood, the days ahead with the Thompson hearings and indeed the denouement of the Starr investigation will be a test for our political institutions. They will fail that test if as the political donations muck is exposed Senators of both parties try to insulate themselves from blame by grandiloquently blaming it all on "campaign finance," even as the media promise that campaign finance reform will make all these bad people go away. Put bluntly, the bad people who will be paraded before us in the days ahead won't go away until the public is able to vote better people into high office.

But the public won't do that—and our falling voter turnouts suggest a disinclination to try—unless they have some good reason to believe that better people can succeed or even survive inside the system we have now. It is perfectly obvious that the public today holds no such hope. Their confidence is low, their cynicism high and their instinct is to believe that the system's governing value is hypocrisy.

What the U.S. public most needs now is a reliable accounting of what exactly has been going on in Washington the past five years. That, theoretically, is what the Congressional oversight function empowers Senator Thompson to do and what three federal judges empowered Kenneth Starr to do. We are inclined to believe, amid all the partisan ranting and gamesmanship, that both men are capable of responsibly doing their duty—which is to get the facts out.

Yes, getting those facts before the public will probably have some effect on the mid-term and 2000 Presidential elections. The larger purpose at this juncture, however, is to restore public confidence that elections matter.

A Whitewater Chronology

Editor's note: *This updated Whitewater chronology includes matters related to Bank of Credit & Commerce International, the 1996 campaign finance scandal and other mysteries surrounding the Clinton administration. It supersedes the chronologies in Volumes I and II of* **A Journal Briefing: Whitewater.**

1976

Bill Clinton is elected Arkansas Attorney General.

Arkansas financier Jackson Stephens forms Stephens Finance with Indonesian banker Mochtar Riady to do business in Asia.

1977

Hillary Rodham Clinton joins the Rose Law Firm.

Stephens Inc. of Arkansas joins with a group of Arab investors to make an unsuccessful run at acquiring Financial General Bankshares in Washington, D.C.; the Arab investors would later be identified as principals and clients of Bank of Credit & Commerce

International. BCCI founder Agha Hasan Abedi hires Bert Lance, recently resigned as President Jimmy Carter's budget director, as an adviser to the group. Amid the legal maneuvers surrounding the Lance group takeover attempt, a brief is submitted by the Stephens-controlled bank data processing firm Systematics; two of the lawyers signing the brief are Hillary Rodham and Webster Hubbell.

1978

August: The Clintons purchase a 230-acre land tract along Arkansas's White River, in partnership with James and Susan McDougal.

October: Mrs. Clinton, now a partner at the Rose Firm, begins a series of commodities trades under the guidance of Tyson Foods executive Jim Blair, earning nearly $100,000. The trades are not revealed until March 1994.

November: Bill Clinton is elected governor of Arkansas. He makes James McDougal a top economic adviser.

1979

Feb. 16: The Federal Reserve rejects the bid by BCCI frontmen to take over Financial General Bankshares.

June: The Clintons and McDougals form Whitewater Development Co. to engage in the business of owning, selling, developing, managing and improving real property.

1980

November: Gov. Clinton is defeated by Republican Frank White. He joins the Little Rock law firm of Wright, Lindsey and Jennings.

1981

James McDougal purchases Madison Bank and Trust.

Aug. 25:   The Federal Reserve approves a new bid by largely the same Arab group of BCCI frontmen to acquire Financial General.

1982

Financial General changes its name to First American. Democratic Party icon Clark Clifford is appointed chairman. BCCI fronts begin acquiring controlling interest in banks and other American financial institutions.

In Arkansas, James McDougal purchases Madison Guaranty Savings & Loan. It begins a period of rapid expansion.

November: Bill Clinton defeats Frank White, winning back the governor's seat.

1983

Capital Management Services, a federally insured small business investment company owned by Judge David Hale, begins making loans to the Arkansas political elite.

Jackson Stephens forms United Pacific Trading with Mochtar Riady to do business in the U.S. and Asia.

1984

The Stephens family of Arkansas and Indonesia's Riady family join forces to buy First Arkansas Bankstock Corp., changing its name to Worthen Bank and installing 28-year-old James Riady as president.

Jan. 20:   The Federal Home Loan Bank Board issues a report on Madison Guaranty questioning its lending practices and financial stability. The Arkansas Securities Department begins to take steps to close down Madison.

| August: | According to Mr. McDougal, Gov. Clinton drops by his office during a morning jog and asks that Madison steer some business to Mrs. Clinton at the Rose Law Firm. |
| November: | Gov. Clinton wins re-election with 64% of the vote. |

1985

January:	Roger Clinton pleads guilty to cocaine distribution charges and is given immunity from further prosecution in exchange for cooperation. He testifies before a federal grand jury and serves a brief prison sentence.
Jan. 16:	Gov. Clinton appoints Beverly Bassett Schaffer, a long-time associate, to serve as Arkansas State Securities Commissioner.
March:	Mrs. Clinton receives from Madison Guaranty the first payment of a $2,000-per-month retainer. Madison's accounting firm, Frost & Co., issues a report declaring the savings and loan solvent.
March 4:	ESM Securities of Ft. Lauderdale collapses after fraudulent trading, causing $250 million in losses and triggering a bank crisis in Ohio.
April 4:	Mr. McDougal hosts a fundraiser to help Gov. Clinton repay campaign debts. Contributions at the fundraiser later draw the scrutiny of Whitewater investigators.
April 7:	Securities firm Bevill, Bresler & Schulman files for bankruptcy amid fraud charges and an estimated $240 million in losses; one of the biggest apparent losers is Stephens-dominated Worthen Bank, which holds with Bevill $52 million of Arkansas state funds in uncollateralized repurchase agreements.
April 30:	Hillary Clinton sends a recapitalization offer for the foundering Madison Guaranty to the Arkansas Securities Commission. Two weeks later, Ms. Schaffer informs Mrs. Clinton the plan is approved, but it is never implemented.
October:	Governor and Mrs. Clinton lead a trade delegation to Taiwan and Japan.

| October: | Mr. McDougal launches the Castle Grande land deal. |

1986

| Jan. 17: | Michael Fitzhugh, United States Attorney for the Western District of Arkansas, advises FBI he is dropping the money laundering and narcotics-conspiracy case against Arkansas associates of drug smuggler Barry Seal. Arkansas State Police Investigator Russell Welch and Internal Revenue Service Investigator Bill Duncan, the lead agents on the case, protest; later, both are driven from their jobs. |

| Feb. 19: | Barry Seal is gunned down by Colombian hitmen in Baton Rouge, La. Seal becomes the touchstone in murky allegations of cocaine trafficking, gun running, and intelligence-community activities swirling around his base at Mena in western Arkansas. |

| March 4: | The Federal Home Loan Bank Board issues a second, sharply critical report of Madison, accusing Mr. McDougal of diverting funds to insiders. |

| April: | Roger Clinton is paroled from prison. |
| | James Riady steps down as president of Worthen Bank. |

| April 3: | David Hale's Capital Management Services makes a $300,000 loan to Susan McDougal in the name of a front company, Master Marketing. Some of the funds wind up in a Whitewater Development Co. account. Indicted for fraud on an unrelated transaction in 1993, Mr. Hale claims that then-Gov. Clinton and Mr. McDougal pressured him into making the loan. |

| August: | Federal regulators remove Mr. McDougal from Madison's board of directors. |

| Oct. 5: | Deceased Mena drug smuggler Barry Seal's C-123K is shot down over Nicaragua with an Arkansas pilot at the controls and a load of weapons and Contra-supporter Eugene Hasenfus in the cargo bay. |

| Oct. 24: | Clinton friend and "bond daddy" Dan Lasater, and nine others, most of them from the Little Rock bond trading |

community, are indicted on cocaine charges. Roger Clinton, who has cooperated with the prosecution, is named an unindicted co-conspirator.

November: Gov. Clinton wins re-election. Gubernatorial terms are extended from two years to four.

1987

According to Susan McDougal, Whitewater records are taken to the Governor's Mansion and turned over to Mrs. Clinton sometime during the year.

Officials at investment giant Stephens Inc., including longtime Clinton friend David Edwards, take steps to rescue Harken Energy, a struggling Texas oil company with George W. Bush on its board. Over the next three years, Mr. Edwards brings BCCI-linked investors and advisers into Harken deals. One of them, Abdullah Bakhsh, purchases $10 million in shares of Stephens-dominated Worthen Bank.

Jan. 15: Dan Lasater begins serving a 30-month sentence for cocaine distribution. In July, he is paroled to a Little Rock halfway house.

Aug. 23: In a mysterious case later ruled a murder and linked to drug corruption, teenagers Kevin Ives and Don Henry are run over by a train in a remote locale a few miles southwest of Little Rock.

1988

October: A Florida grand jury indicts BCCI figures on charges of laundering drug money. It is the first sign of serious trouble at the international bank.

1989

Manhattan District Attorney Robert Morgenthau begins a wide-ranging probe of BCCI.

March: Federal regulators shut down Madison Guaranty

Savings & Loan, at a taxpayer loss of about $60 million. Mr. McDougal is indicted for bank fraud.

June 16: Mena investigator Bill Duncan resigns from the Internal Revenue Service following clashes with Washington supervisors over the probe.

1990

May: Mr. McDougal goes to trial on bank fraud and is acquitted.

November: Gov. Clinton is elected to a second four-year term, promising to serve it out and not seek the presidency in 1992.

Dec. 3: The Federal Deposit Insurance Corp. cites the Riady family's Los-Angeles-based Lippo Bank for poor loans and inadequate capital.

1991

Yah Lin "Charlie" Trie, operator of several Chinese restaurants in Little Rock and an acquaintance of Bill Clinton's, opens Daihatsu International Trading Co. in Little Rock. Mr. Trie later emerges as a central figure in the Indogate campaign-finance scandal in 1996.

January: The Federal Reserve orders an investigation of BCCI's alleged control of First American Bank.

July 5: Regulators world-wide shut down BCCI amid widespread charges of bank fraud and allegations of links to laundered drug money, terrorists and intelligence agencies.

Aug. 13: Chairman Clark Clifford and top aide Robert Altman resign from First American Bank.

Oct. 3: Bill Clinton announces his candidacy for president and attacks, among others, "S&L crooks and self-serving CEOs."

1992

March 8: New York Times reporter Jeff Gerth discloses the

Clintons' dealings with Madison and Whitewater.

March 20:   Washington Times reporter Jerry Seper discloses Hillary Clinton's $2,000-per-month retainer from Madison.

March 23:   In a hasty report arranged by the Clinton campaign, Denver lawyer James Lyons states the Clintons lost $68,000 on the Whitewater investment and clears them of improprieties. The issue fades from the campaign.

July 16:   Bill Clinton accepts the Democratic Party's presidential nomination in New York.

July 22:   A Manhattan grand jury hands up sealed indictments against BCCI principals, including Clark Clifford and Robert Altman. A week later, a grand jury in Washington and the Federal Reserve issue separate actions against Messrs. Clifford and Altman.

August: Clinton friend David Edwards arranges a $3.5 million lead gift from Saudi Arabian benefactors to the University of Arkansas for a Middle East studies center.

Aug. 31:   Resolution Trust Corporation field officers complete criminal referral #C0004 on Madison Guaranty and forward it to Charles Banks, U.S. Attorney for the Eastern District of Arkansas. The referral alleges an elaborate check-kiting scheme by Madison owners James and Susan McDougal, and names the Clintons and Jim Guy Tucker as possible beneficiaries. Later, Mr. Banks forwards the referral to Washington. In the heat of the campaign, the issue is sidelined.

Nov. 3:   Bill Clinton is elected President of the United States.

December: Vincent Foster, representing the Clintons, meets with James McDougal and arranges for him to buy the Clintons' remaining shares in Whitewater Development Co. for $1,000. Mr. McDougal is loaned the money for the purchase by Tyson Foods counsel Jim Blair, a longtime Clinton friend and commodities adviser. The loan is never repaid.

1993

Jan. 20:   Bill Clinton is sworn in as 42nd President of the

United States.

February: Arkansas Gov. Jim Guy Tucker announces a $20 million Saudi gift to the University of Arkansas for a Middle East studies center.

March 24: Year-old press clips about Whitewater are faxed from the office of Deputy Treasury Secretary Roger Altman to the office of White House Counsel Bernard Nussbaum. Mr. Altman also is serving as acting head of the Resolution Trust Corporation, an independent federal agency.

April 20: Arkansas businessman Joseph Giroir, former chairman of the Rose Law Firm, incorporates Arkansas International Development Corp. to bring Indonesia's Lippo Group together with American companies seeking to do business in Indonesia and China.

May 19: The White House fires seven employees of its Travel Office, following a review by Associate Counsel William Kennedy III, a former member of the Rose Law Firm. Mr. Kennedy's actions, which included attempts to involve the FBI and the Internal Revenue Service in a criminal investigation of the Travel Office, later are sharply criticized. Deputy White House Counsel Vincent Foster also is rebuked.

June 21: Whitewater corporate tax returns for 1989 through 1991, prepared by Mr. Foster, are delivered to Jim McDougal's attorney.

July 17: According to a White House chronology, Mr. Foster completes work on a blind trust for the Clintons. In Little Rock for a weekend visit, President Clinton has a four-hour dinner alone with old friend David Edwards, now in business for himself as an investment adviser and currency trader.

July 20: The Little Rock FBI obtains a warrant to search the office of David Hale as part of its investigation into Capital Management Services. In Washington, Deputy White House Counsel Vincent Foster drives to Ft. Marcy Park and commits suicide. That evening, Mr.

Nussbaum, White House aide Patsy Thomasson, and Mrs. Clinton's chief of staff Maggie Williams visit Mr. Foster's office. According to testimony by a uniformed Secret Service officer, Ms. Williams exits the counsel's suite with an armful of folders.

July 21: Early-morning calls are exchanged between Mrs. Clinton in Little Rock and White House operatives, including Maggie Williams and Susan Thomases. According to later Congressional testimony, Mrs. Clinton's concerns about investigators having "unfettered access" to the Foster office are conveyed to White House Counsel Bernard Nussbaum. Mr. Nussbaum meets with Park Police and Justice Department investigators and agrees to a search of the office the following day. A figure of later controversy, White House personnel security chief Craig Livingstone, also is spotted in the Foster office area with files.

July 22: Mr. Nussbaum again searches Mr. Foster's office, but denies access to Park Police and Justice Department investigators. In an angry phone call, Deputy Attorney General Philip Heymann asks, "Bernie, are you hiding something?" Documents, including Whitewater files, are removed. Details on the removal of Whitewater files do not emerge for months.

July 26: A torn-up note is found in Mr. Foster's briefcase.

Aug. 14: In New York, Robert Altman is acquitted of bank fraud in the BCCI case; Clark Clifford's trial is indefinitely postponed due to ill health.

Aug. 16: Paula Casey, a longtime associate of the Clintons, takes office in Little Rock as U.S. attorney.

September: Ms. Casey turns down plea bargain attempts from David Hale's lawyer, who had offered to share information on the "banking and borrowing practices of some individuals in the elite political circles of the State of Arkansas."

Sept. 23: Mr. Hale is indicted for fraud.

Sept. 29: Treasury Department General Counsel Jean Hanson

warns Mr. Nussbaum that the RTC plans to issue criminal referrals asking the Justice Department to investigate Madison. The referrals are said to name the Clintons as witnesses to, and possible beneficiaries of, illegal actions. The current governor of Arkansas, Jim Guy Tucker, also is said to be a target of the investigation. Mr. Nussbaum passes the information to Bruce Lindsey, a top White House aide and Arkansas damage-control specialist.

Oct. 4 or 5: Mr. Lindsey informs President Clinton about the confidential referrals. Mr. Lindsey later tells Congress he did not mention any specific target of the referrals.

Oct. 6: President Clinton meets with Arkansas Gov. Jim Guy Tucker at the White House.

Oct. 8: Nine new criminal referrals on Madison Guaranty are forwarded to U.S. Attorney Paula Casey in Little Rock.

Oct. 14: A meeting is held in Mr. Nussbaum's office with senior White House and Treasury personnel to discuss the RTC and Madison. Participants at the meeting later tell Congress that they discussed only how to handle press inquiries.

Oct. 27: The RTC's first criminal referral is rejected in Little Rock by U.S. Attorney Casey.

Nov. 3: Associate Attorney General Webster Hubbell recuses himself from the Whitewater case.

Nov. 9: In Little Rock, U.S. Attorney Casey recuses herself from the Madison case; in Kansas City, RTC investigator Jean Lewis is taken off the probe.

Nov. 18: President Clinton meets with Gov. Tucker in Seattle.

Dec. 19: Allegations by Arkansas state troopers of the president's sexual infidelities while governor surface in the American Spectator and the Los Angeles Times.

Dec. 20: Washington Times correspondent Jerry Seper reports that Whitewater flies were removed from Mr. Foster's office.

Dec. 30: At a New Year's retreat, President Clinton asks

Comptroller of the Currency Eugene Ludwig, an old friend, for "advice" about how to handle the growing Whitewater storm.

1994

Jan. 20: Amid mounting political pressure, Attorney General Janet Reno appoints Robert Fiske as special counsel to investigate Whitewater.

Jan. 27: Deputy Attorney General Philip Heymann resigns.

Feb. 2: Mr. Altman meets with Mr. Nussbaum and other senior White House staff to give them a "heads-up" about Madison. Washington RTC attorney April Breslaw flies to Kansas City and meets with investigator Jean Lewis; in a secretly taped conversation, Ms. Breslaw states that top RTC officials "would like to be able to say that Whitewater did not cause a loss to Madison."

Feb. 24: Mr. Altman gives incomplete testimony to the Senate Banking Committee about discussions between the White House and Treasury on the Madison referrals.

Feb. 25: Mr. Altman recuses himself from the Madison investigation and announces he will step down as acting head of the RTC.

March: Top Clinton aides Thomas McLarty, Erskine Bowles, Mickey Kantor and others begin a series of meetings and calls to arrange financial aid for Webster Hubbell, then facing charges of bilking his former Rose Law Firm partners and under growing pressure to cooperate with the Whitewater probe; the meetings are not revealed until April 1997.

March 5: White House Counsel Bernard Nussbaum resigns.

March 8: Lloyd Cutler is named White House Counsel.

March 14: Associate Attorney General Webster Hubbell resigns.

March 18: The New York Times reveals Mrs. Clinton's 1970s commodities trades.

March 23: The Association of American Physicians and Surgeons files suit against Mrs. Clinton's health reform task force for violating the Federal Advisory Committee Act by holding secret meetings.

May 6: Former Little Rock resident Paula Corbin Jones files suit against President Clinton, charging he sexually harassed her while governor.

June: Following five White House visits by Lippo Group scion James Riady, Lippo pays Webster Hubbell about $100,000 for undisclosed services, as pressure grows for Mr. Hubbell to cooperate with the Whitewater probe; reports of the payments and meetings do not emerge until 1996 and 1997.

June 30: Special Counsel Robert Fiske concludes that Mr. Foster's death was a suicide and clears the White House and Treasury Department of obstruction of justice on the RTC contacts, opening the way for Congressional hearings limited to the two subjects.

July: John Huang, president of U.S. operations for Indonesia's Lippo Group, joins the Commerce Department as a senior official with a top-secret clearance to oversee international trade.

July 26: Congressional Whitewater hearings open.

Aug. 1: The White House reveals that the Whitewater files removed from Mr. Foster's office were kept for five days in the Clintons' residence before being turned over to their personal lawyer.

Aug. 5: A three-judge panel removes Mr. Fiske and appoints Kenneth Starr as independent counsel. Mr. Starr continues to investigate all aspects of Whitewater, including Mr. Foster's death.

Aug. 12: The RTC informs Madison investigator Jean Lewis and two colleagues that they will be placed on "administrative leave" for two weeks.

Aug. 17: Deputy Treasury Secretary Roger Altman resigns.

Aug. 18: Treasury Department General Counsel Jean Hanson resigns.

Aug. 29: The RTC files suit in federal court to compel the Rose

Law Firm to turn over its client list in a conflict-of-interest probe.

Sept. 12: Donald Smaltz is named independent counsel to investigate activities of Agriculture Secretary Mike Espy.

Oct. 1: Abner Mikva replaces Lloyd Cutler as White House Counsel.

Oct. 3: Agriculture Secretary Mike Espy resigns.

Nov. 8: In a political earthquake, Republicans gain control of the House and the Senate.

Dec. 5: In Little Rock, Madison Guaranty real-estate appraiser Robert Palmer pleads guilty to one felony count of conspiracy and agrees to cooperate with the Starr probe.

Dec. 6: Former Associate Attorney General Webster Hubbell pleads guilty to two felonies in a scheme to defraud his former Rose Law Firm partners and says he will cooperate with the independent counsel.

Dec. 7: Former Travel Office director Billy Dale is indicted on charges of embezzling office funds.

Dec. 19: The FDIC sanctions the Riady family's Los Angeles-based Lippo Bank for failing to adhere to money-laundering regulations governing large cash transactions.

1995

Jan. 3: Republicans on the Senate Banking Committee, poised to move into the majority and renew the Whitewater hearings, issue a sharply critical report based on the summer hearings. It accuses Clinton administration officials of "serious misconduct and malfeasance" in the matters of the RTC criminal referrals and later congressional testimony.

Feb. 28: Arkansas banker Neal Ainley is indicted on five felony counts relating to Bill Clinton's 1990 gubernatorial campaign. He later pleads guilty to reduced charges and agrees to cooperate with the independent counsel.

March 21: Whitewater real-estate broker Chris Wade pleads guilty to two felonies.

March 27:	Legal Times reports that Independent Counsel Donald Smaltz's probe has been "significantly curtailed by the Justice Department." In recent months, Mr. Smaltz had been exploring Arkansas poultry giant Tyson Foods.
May 5:	Mena investigator Russell Welch fights off an attempt by the Arkansas State Police to discredit him, but is forced into early retirement.
May 24:	David Barrett is appointed independent counsel to probe charges that Housing Secretary Henry Cisneros made false statements to the FBI.
June 7:	An Arkansas grand jury hands up indictments against Gov. Jim Guy Tucker and two business associates in a complex scheme to buy and sell cable television systems.
June 8:	Stephen Smith, a former aide to Gov. Bill Clinton, pleads guilty to misusing a Capital Management loan and agrees to cooperate with the independent counsel.
June 23:	A report for the RTC by the law firm Pillsbury, Madison & Sutro says that funds flowed to the Whitewater account from other Madison accounts, but adds that the Clintons "had little direct involvement" in the investment before 1988.
July 6:	Daniel Pearson is named independent counsel to probe business dealings of Commerce Secretary Ron Brown.
July 18:	The special Senate Whitewater Committee opens a new round of hearings in Washington; they quickly become mired in partisan disputes.
Aug. 8:	In testimony before the House Banking Committee, RTC investigator Jean Lewis says there was a "concerted effort to obstruct, hamper and manipulate" the Madison investigation.
Aug. 17:	Independent Counsel Kenneth Starr indicts Arkansas Gov. Jim Guy Tucker and former Madison Guaranty owners James and Susan McDougal for bank fraud and conspiracy.
Sept. 5:	Federal District Judge Henry Woods dismisses the cable TV fraud case against Gov. Tucker and two asso-

ciates, saying Mr. Starr has exceeded his jurisdiction; the independent counsel appeals the decision to the Eighth Circuit court in St. Louis; the separate indictment against Gov. Tucker and the McDougals stands.

Sept. 13: At a White House meeting among President Clinton, Commerce official John Huang, Lippo Group scion James Riady, senior Clinton aide Bruce Lindsey and Arkansas businessman Joseph Giroir, a decision is reached to dispatch Mr. Huang to the Democratic National Committee as a senior fund-raiser.

Sept. 20: White House Counsel Abner Mikva announces his resignation. The president names Jack Quinn, Vice President Al Gore's chief of staff, as his fourth White House counsel.

November: House Banking Committee Chairman Jim Leach informs colleagues that he will investigate allegations of drug smuggling and money laundering at Mena airport.

Nov. 16: After deliberating less than two hours, a Washington jury acquits former White House Travel Office head Billy Dale of embezzlement charges.

Dec. 13: Drug suspect Jorge Cabrera attends a White House Christmas party after donating $20,000 to Democrats; three weeks later, he is arrested in Florida with 6,000 pounds of cocaine.

Dec. 29: A memo from former White House aide David Watkins placing responsibility for the Travel Office firings on Mrs. Clinton is discovered at the White House.

1996

Jan. 5: The White House announces that Mrs. Clinton's Rose Law Firm billing records, sought by the independent counsel and Congress for two years, have been discovered on a table in the "book room" of the personal residence.

Jan. 11: At a news conference, President Clinton says he is nearly broke and owes about $1.6 million in legal fees stemming from Whitewater and the Paula Jones sexual harassment suit.

Jan. 16 John Huang leaves the Commerce Department to join the Democratic National Committee as a senior fundraiser.

Jan. 22: The White House announces that Mrs. Clinton has been subpoenaed to testify before a Whitewater grand jury about the missing billing records.

Feb. 5: Federal District Judge George Howard Jr. rules that President Clinton must appear as a defense witness in the bank fraud case against Jim Guy Tucker and the McDougals.

Feb. 6: Charlie Trie escorts Chinese arms merchant Wang Jun to a White House reception for donors.

Feb. 8: The Wall Street Journal discloses that two of President Clinton's insurance policies have paid $900,000 into his legal defense fund.

Feb. 20: Arkansas bankers Herby Branscum Jr. and Robert Hill are indicted on bank fraud and conspiracy charges relating to Bill Clinton's 1990 gubernatorial campaign.

Feb. 29: The Whitewater Committee's mandate expires and Senate Democrats launch a filibuster to block an extension of the probe.

March 4: Gov. Tucker and the McDougals go on trial for bank fraud and conspiracy in Little Rock.

March 15: A three-judge panel of the Eighth Circuit Court of Appeals reinstates Independent Counsel Starr's indictment of Gov. Tucker and two associates in the cable television fraud scheme, and directs that Federal District Judge Henry Woods be removed from the case "to preserve the appearance of impartiality."

March 22: Independent Counsel Starr's jurisdiction is expanded to cover the Travel Office affair.

March 25: Arkansas insider David Hale is sentenced to 28 months in prison for defrauding the federal government.

April 1: BCCI-connected financier Roger Tamraz, the subject of a warrant for bank fraud in Lebanon, attends a White

House coffee klatch with nine other donors; Mr. Tamraz gave $177,000 to Democrats in 1995 and 1996.

April 3: Commerce Secretary Ron Brown and 32 others are killed in a plane crash in Croatia.

April 28: President Clinton gives four hours of videotaped testimony in the White House as a defense witness in the Arkansas trial of Gov. Tucker and the McDougals.

April 29: Vice President Al Gore attends a fundraiser at the Hsi Lai Buddhist Temple in California, raising at least $140,000. The donations, some of them apparently from monks who had taken a vow of poverty, later come under scrutiny.

May 28: An Arkansas jury convicts Gov. Tucker and the McDougals on 24 counts of bank fraud and conspiracy.

June 5: Documents obtained after a long struggle by the House Government Reform and Oversight Committee reveal that the White House has improperly obtained confidential FBI background files. "Filegate" mushrooms into another ethical crisis for the Clinton administration.

June 17: The trial of Arkansas bankers Branscum and Hill on charges of bank fraud relating to the 1990 Clinton gubernatorial campaign begins in Little Rock.

June 18: The Senate Whitewater Committee releases a 650-page final report detailing a "pattern of obstruction" by Clinton administration officials.

June 21: Independent Counsel Starr's jurisdiction is broadened to cover "Filegate."

June 25: The Supreme Court agrees to hear President Clinton's procedural appeal in the Paula Jones harassment suit, effectively delaying trial until after the November election.

June 26: In an appearance before a House oversight committee investigating the Filegate affair, White House personnel security chief Craig Livingstone announces his resignation.

July 7:	President Clinton gives videotaped testimony in the White House as a defense witness in the trial of Arkansas bankers Branscum and Hill.
July 15:	After a tumultuous day of political drama, Jim Guy Tucker steps down and Republican Mike Huckabee takes over as governor of Arkansas.
Aug. 1:	A federal jury in Little Rock acquits Arkansas bankers Branscum and Hill on four bank fraud charges relating to the 1990 Clinton gubernatorial campaign; a mistrial is declared on seven other counts on which the jury deadlocks.
Aug. 15:	After months of stonewalling, the White House releases 2,000 pages of documents to the House Government Reform and Oversight Committee; included is a long "task list" for dealing with the sprawling Whitewater probe.
Aug. 19:	Awaiting a liver transplant, former Arkansas Gov. Jim Guy Tucker is given a four-year suspended sentence in the Madison Guaranty bank fraud case.
Aug. 21:	Susan McDougal is sentenced to two years in prison for her part in the Master Marketing fraud scheme.
Sept. 4:	Susan McDougal refuses to answer questions about Bill Clinton before a Whitewater grand jury and is ordered jailed for contempt.
Sept. 23:	In a PBS interview, President Clinton says he has not ruled out pardons for Whitewater figures, touching off a campaign controversy.
Sept. 24:	In the probe conducted by Independent Counsel Donald Smaltz, a federal jury convicts agribusiness giant Sun-Diamond of giving illegal gifts to Agriculture Secretary Mike Espy.
Oct. 8	Following disclosures by Washington reporters of The Wall Street Journal of large illegal foreign donations, the campaign finance scandal emerges as a major national issue.
Oct. 18:	Democratic National Committee finance vice chairman John Huang is suspended after growing reports of

improper campaign solicitations.

Nov. 5: Bill Clinton re-elected President of the United States.

Nov. 8: In a declassified summary of a report to Rep. Jim Leach, the CIA for the first time admits it was present at remote Mena, Ark., but denies any association with drug trafficking or other illegal activities.

Nov. 29: Attorney General Janet Reno declines to name an independent counsel in the campaign finance affair, retaining the matter as a Justice Department probe.

Dec. 13: Jack Quinn, President Clinton's fourth White House counsel, announces his resignation.

Dec. 14: Susan McDougal is transferred to California to stand trial on charges of embezzling $150,000 from conductor Zubin Mehta and his wife; she remains jailed on civil contempt charges stemming from her refusal to testify before a Whitewater grand jury.

Dec. 16: President Clinton's legal defense fund announces it has returned $640,000 in suspect donations from Indogate figure Charlie Trie.

1997

Jan 7: Charles Ruff is named President Clinton's fifth White House counsel.

Jan. 13: Supreme Court hears oral arguments as to whether the Paula Jones sexual harassment case should be delayed until after Bill Clinton leaves office.

Jan. 20: Bill Clinton is sworn in for a second term as President of the United States.

Feb. 13: Webster Hubbell is released from federal custody after serving 15 months for mail fraud and tax evasion.

Feb. 17: Kenneth Starr unexpectedly announces he will step down as independent counsel to become dean of Pepperdine University Law School in California.

Feb. 21: After a storm of criticism, Kenneth Starr reverses his decision to leave the Whitewater probe, saying he will stay on until investigations and prosecutions are "substantially completed."

March 3:   Drawn deep into the campaign finance scandal, Vice President Al Gore defends himself at a press conference, declaring that "no controlling legal authority" indicates his actions were illegal.

March 19:   In a series of skirmishes over Congressional investigations into the campaign finance affair, House Democrats temporarily block funding for a probe by Rep. Dan Burton's Government Reform and Oversight Committee.

March 31:   For the third time in seven years, the FDIC sanctions Los Angeles-based Lippo Bank, imposing a stiff cease-and-desist order due to bad loans and financial losses.

April 1:   Facing imminent news reports, the White House discloses that in early 1994 top Clinton aides set out to funnel money to Arkansas insider Webster Hubbell, then under pressure to cooperate with the Whitewater probe.

April 14:   Following testimony by Independent Counsel Starr about significant cooperation, Jim McDougal is given a sharply reduced three-year prison sentence for his role in the Madison Guaranty bank fraud case.

April 15:   In a new public-corruption drive in Arkansas, former county prosecutor Dan Harmon is indicted on multiple drug and racketeering counts.

April 30:   For a second time, Attorney General Janet Reno turns down requests for an independent counsel in the campaign finance affair.

May 2:   The White House announces it will appeal to the Supreme Court a previously sealed Eighth Circuit ruling that government lawyers must turn over to Independent Counsel Starr notes taken of conversations with Hillary Clinton.

May 19:   Eight months into a contempt sentence for refusing to talk to a Whitewater grand jury, Susan McDougal petitions an Arkansas court for release, saying "there will never come a time" when she will testify. Her petition is denied.

May 27: The Supreme Court issues a unanimous decision ruling that Paula Jones's sexual harassment suit may proceed against Bill Clinton while he is in office.

June 11: An Arkansas jury convicts former county prosecutor Dan Harmon of running a drug-related criminal enterprise.

June 23: The Supreme Court declines to grant certiorari on Mrs. Clinton's notes, effectively compelling the White House to turn them over to Mr. Starr

July 8: Hearings into the campaign finance affair open before Sen. Fred Thompson's Governmental Affairs Committee.

Index

B

C

H

I

N

National Journal, 255, 335
National Review, 286
National Rife Association, 110, 254, 286
National Security Agency, 300
National Security Council (NSC)
  alleged Chinese influence in American politics and, 351-355, 385
  trade documents dispute and, 197-199
NationsBank, 115
Neill, Denis, 382
Nemetz, Miriam, 23, 428-4230
New Era Corporation, 265
New Republic Magazine, 219, 229, 247-248
Newsday, 286
News media
  alleged frenzy over Whitewater scandal, 246-252, 256-258
  coverage of campaign fund-raising scandal, 333-336, 361-362
  liberal bias seen in, 201-202, 208-212, 232-238
  public consensus and, 203-210
  public indifference to, 239-241
  Whitewater whitewash, claim of, 239-241
New York Daily News, 252
New Yorker Magazine, 250-251, 434, 469, 478-479
New York Times
  on Hubbell investigation, 422
  White House coverage by, 248-250, 257, 404
Nickles, Don (Senator), 285-288
Ning, Hashim, 23
Nixon, Richard M. (President), 62, 64, 132, 135, 143, 156-158, 313
  campaign finance reform and, 328-329
  Clinton compared with, 403-409, 438-439
  firing of Archibald Cox by, 230, 277
  impeachment inquiry against, 410-412
  manipulation of IRS, 253, 291
  possible indictment of, 337-339
  Watergate scandal and, 142-143, 158-159, 206, 312-314, 402-405, 475
Nixon vs. Fitzgerald, 261-262
Nofziger, Lyn, 120
Nolan, John, 3
Norquist, Grover, 288
North, Oliver, 119-120, 286

Q

R

Watergate compared with, 142-143, 158-159, 206, 312-314, 402-409

Whitman, Christine (Governor), 168-169

Williams, Jack L., 363, 372

Williams, Maggie, 178, 186, 485

Williams, Natalie, 14

Wilson, James, 411-412

Wiriandinata, Arief, 22-23, 95

Wolf, Frank (Representative), 33

Wollman, Roger, 421

Wood, Christopher, 207

Wood, James, 371-372

Woods, Henry (Judge), 116, 309

Woods, Rose Mary, 57, 83

Woodward, Bob, 172, 358, 488

Worthen Bank, 113-114, 117, 320, 486

Wright, Betsey, 116

Wright, Susan Webber, 43-45, 413-414, 420-423, 481
  contempt ruling on, 29-30

Y

Yee, Helen, 77

Yee, Melinda, 77, 129-131, 145, 149

Yoo, John C., 443-446

York, Byron, 201, 234-238

Yost, Peter, 309-310

Youck, David A., 454-455

Young, Andrew, 247

Young Americans for Freedom, 292

Yuanwang Group Corporation, 265

Z

Zeifman, Jerome M., 127, 141-143, 159-161

Zhou Beifang, 321-322

Zionist Organization of America, 294

Zogby, John, 174-175

Zuckerman, Mort, 252